THE CIVIL LAWYERS
IN ENGLAND
1603–1641

THE
CIVIL LAWYERS
IN ENGLAND

1603–1641

A Political Study

BRIAN P. LEVACK

OXFORD
AT THE CLARENDON PRESS
1973

Oxford University Press, Ely House, London W. 1

GLASGOW NEW YORK TORONTO MELBOURNE WELLINGTON
CAPE TOWN IBADAN NAIROBI DAR ES SALAAM LUSAKA ADDIS ABABA
DELHI BOMBAY CALCUTTA MADRAS KARACHI LAHORE DACCA
KUALA LUMPUR SINGAPORE HONG KONG TOKYO

*Printed in Great Britain
at the University Press, Oxford
by Vivian Ridler
Printer to the University*

PREFACE

THIS is a 'collective biography' of the civil lawyers in early seventeenth-century England, a professional élite which has not received the historical attention it deserves. In order to draw a more complete and accurate picture of this group, I have gathered as much information as possible about each one of the 200 civil lawyers who were in England between 1603 and 1641. This data, which is summarized in the biographical dictionary, forms the basis of both my statistical tabulations and my depiction of the civil lawyers' professional life. It also reveals the strength and consistency of the civilians' political support for the claims and policies of James I and Charles I. My main objective has been to explain this 'royalism'. I have used that word to connote a tendency to side with the King in different ways rather than to designate membership in a clearly defined political party.

I have used the academic criterion of receipt of the doctorate in civil law as the basis of my definition of this group of civil lawyers. The group, therefore, is somewhat larger than the full membership of Doctors' Commons, but considerably smaller than the entire profession of civil law, which included a wide variety of officials and lawyers. In referring to those who possessed the doctorate in law, I have used the terms 'Doctors of Civil Law' and 'Doctors of Laws' interchangeably, although technically the former designates recipients of the doctorate from Oxford, the latter from Cambridge.

In quoting manuscripts and seventeenth-century books, I have taken the liberty of modernizing spelling and punctuation. The titles of books, however, appear in their original form.

This book is a revision of my doctoral dissertation, 'The Politics of the English Civil Lawyers, 1603–1629', which I submitted to Yale University in 1970. Research for the dissertation was made possible by a travel grant from the Ford Foundation which was administered through the Council on Comparative and European

Studies at Yale. A generous fellowship from the American Bar Foundation and two grants from the University Research Institute of the University of Texas allowed me to undertake the work of revision.

Miss Norah Fuidge of the History of Parliament Trust, who was of assistance to me in countless ways, graciously permitted me to examine the biographies of those civilians who were M.P.s during the reign of Elizabeth. Dr. Robert Johnson of the Parliamentary Diaries Project at Yale University allowed me to use the transcripts of diaries for the Parliaments of 1624, 1626, and 1628. Dr. D. M. Barratt made available to me her notes on ecclesiastical officials in the diocese of Oxford, and Mr. C. M. Lloyd supplied me with information concerning the chancellors of Lincoln diocese. The City Librarian of Exeter provided me with data concerning a number of civil lawyers who came from Devon.

My greatest personal debt is to Professor J. H. Hexter, my mentor, for his guidance, criticism, and encouragement. I am also grateful to Professor William H. Dunham, Professor Lawrence Stone, and Professor H. R. Trevor-Roper for reading the manuscript and making many valuable suggestions. For advice and help of various kinds I am thankful to Professor Thomas Barnes, Professor Charles Gray, Professor John Gruenfelder, Professor Basil D. Henning, Professor Joel Hurstfield, Revd. A. J. Loomie, S.J., Professor W. J. Prichard, Mr. G. D. Squibb, Q.C., Mr. D. G. Vaisey, and Professor D. E. C. Yale. To my wife Nancy I am indebted not only for her patience but for her help in arranging the biographical dictionary. Finally, to my father, who is responsible for my original interest in history, I wish to dedicate this volume.

CONTENTS

LIST OF TABLES

ABBREVIATIONS

Al. Cant.	J. and J. A. Venn, *Alumni Cantabrigiensis*, Part I, Cambridge, 1922
Al. Oxon.	J. Foster, *Alumni Oxoniensis: The Members of the University of Oxford 1500–1714*, Oxford, 1891–2
APC	*Acts of the Privy Council of England*
BM	British Museum, London
Bodl.	Bodleian Library, Oxford
Borth. Inst.	Borthwick Institute of Historical Research, York
CJ	*The Journals of the House of Commons*
CPCC	*Calendar of the Proceedings of the Committee for Compounding*
CSPD	*Calendar of State Papers, Domestic*
CSP Ireland	*Calendar of State Papers, Ireland*
CUL	Cambridge University Library
DNB	*Dictionary of National Biography*
Doc. Com. Treas. Bk.	Public Record Office, Treasurer's Book of Doctors' Commons
DWB	*Dictionary of Welsh Biography*
EHR	*English Historical Review*
ERO	Essex Record Office, Chelmsford
Harl. Soc.	Publications of the Harleian Society
HMC	Historical Manuscripts Commission
HMCS	HMC, *Calendar of the Manuscripts of the . . . Marquis of Salisbury*
HRO	Hampshire Record Office, Winchester
ITL	Inner Temple Library, London
LJ	*The Journals of the House of Lords*
LPL	Lambeth Palace Library, London
NRS	Notestein, Relf, and Simpson, *Commons Debates 1621*, New Haven, Conn., 1935
Reg. Doc. Com.	LPL, Register of Doctors' Commons
VCH	*Victoria County History*
Walker Revised	A. G. Matthews, *Walker Revised, Being a Revision of John Walker's Sufferings of the Clergy During the Grand Rebellion 1642–1660*, Oxford, 1948

INTRODUCTION

BETWEEN the accession of James I in 1603 and the beginning of the Civil War in 1642, lawyers figured prominently in English politics. The larger and dominant branch of the legal profession, the common lawyers, actually earned a reputation as the heroes of the parliamentary cause. Led by the greatest jurist of the age, Sir Edward Coke, the common lawyers provided a 'defense of the law of the land in the face of Stuart absolutism'.[1] This they achieved by striving to place the King's prerogative under law, setting out to control, if not to destroy, the ecclesiastical courts, exhuming precedents from their law books to reconstruct the ancient Constitution of the Realm, and allying themselves with the parliamentary opposition to the King.[2] With the Puritans, the most persistent of the King's opponents, the common lawyers shared the same political and legal enemies, compatible parliamentary programmes, and in certain instances the same religious outlook.[3]

The common lawyers' reputation as the stalwart defenders of parliamentary freedom is not completely deserved. Royalists such as Sir Francis Bacon, Sir John Finch, and Sir John Davies belonged to the same profession and studied the same law as Sir Edward Coke, James Whitelocke, and John Selden.[4] Professional knowledge of the common law did not necessarily predispose one to oppose the policies of the first two Stuarts. The conclusion of one

---

[1] J. D. Eusden, *Puritans, Lawyers, and Politics in Early Seventeenth-Century England* (New Haven, Conn., 1958), p. 2.

[2] C. Ogilvie, *The King's Government and the Common Law, 1471–1641* (Oxford, 1958), pp. 134–43; G. M. Trevelyan, *England Under the Stuarts* (London, 1925), p. 122; I. D. Jones, *The English Revolution* (London, 1931), p. 22.

[3] M. F. Keeler, *The Long Parliament, 1640–1641: A Biographical Study of Its Members* (Philadelphia, Pa., 1954), p. 27; C. Hill, *Society and Puritanism in Pre-Revolutionary England* (London, 1964), p. 342; Eusden, *Puritans, Lawyers*, pp. 148–71; W. R. Prest, 'Some Aspects of the Inns of Courts, 1590–1640' (Oxford, D.Phil. thesis, 1965), pp. 348–83.

[4] For a discussion of the political theories of the royalist judges see M. A. Judson, *The Crisis of the Constitution* (New Brunswick, N.J., 1949), pp. 107–70.

legal historian that 'in the hands of Coke the common law forged the axe which beheaded Charles I'[1] should not obscure the knowledge that there was a common law case for the King as well as one against him.[2] In the three most important legal decisions in the common law courts during the first half of the seventeenth century—*Bate's Case* (1606), *Darnel's Case* (1627), and *Hampden's Case* (1637)—the majority of judges upheld the claims of the Crown. Admittedly support for the King was especially strong among judges and other common lawyers who held high office under the Crown. Two lawyers, William Noy and Dudley Digges, actually abandoned their opposition to royal policies once they had secured positions within the central government.[3] Yet royalism among common lawyers was not restricted to the bench. The Inns of Court, the four societies of common lawyers in London, had close links with the King's government during the 1630s.[4] Even within Parliament, where common lawyers inspired and directed opposition to the King, the members of the profession did not present a united front, especially after 1640. Of the seventy-five barristers who were returned to the Long Parliament, thirty-three eventually sided with the King.[5]

While the common lawyers were clearly divided in their political allegiances during the early years of the seventeenth century, the civil lawyers were not. This professional élite included all those scholars and practitioners who had earned the degree of Doctor of Civil Law (D.C.L.) at Oxford or Doctor of Laws (LL.D.) at Cambridge or who had been incorporated at either institution after earning an equivalent degree abroad. Their education and training was not in the common law of England

---

[1] A. K. Kiralfy, *Potter's Historical Introduction to English Law and Its Institutions* (4th edn., London, 1958), p. 43.

[2] J. G. A. Pocock, *The Ancient Constitution and the Feudal Law* (Cambridge, 1957), p. 55.

[3] J. P. Kenyon, *The Stuart Constitution 1603–1688* (Cambridge, 1966), p. 104. Conversely Coke did not inaugurate his parliamentary opposition to the Crown until after his last desperate effort to regain high office under the Crown had failed. See M. Prestwich, *Cranfield: Politics and Profits Under the Early Stuarts* (Oxford, 1966), pp. 143–4.   [4] Prest, 'Inns of Court', p. 373.

[5] D. Brunton and D. H. Pennington, *Members of the Long Parliament* (Cambridge, Mass., 1964), p. 5.

but in the civil law of Rome, a code that was believed at the time to support the autocratic power of the Crown.[1] The great majority of civilians, as these men were called, became members of Doctors' Commons, the society of civil lawyers in London who practised in the ecclesiastical courts of the Archbishop of Canterbury, the High Court of Admiralty, and the High Court of Chivalry. The primary service they performed in those courts was to argue or plead as advocates on behalf of their clients. Since pleading in the common law courts was performed by those lawyers who had been called to the Bar of one of the four Inns of Court, it is best to consider the civilians as the professional counterparts of barristers. Socially, however, the civil lawyers claimed a higher status than the barristers, ranking closest to the Serjeants-at-law, the élite corps of common lawyers who had exclusive rights of pleading in the Court of Common Pleas.

The civil lawyers were a rather small group, numbering only 200 during the period from 1603 to 1641.[2] By contrast there may have been as many as 2,000 common law barristers at the beginning of the seventeenth century.[3] It is true that a number of civilians, like barristers, chose not to engage in legal practice. Yet it is impossible to neglect the non-practitioners in a study of the civil lawyers' politics. Many of these lawyers were professors and authors residing at Oxford or Cambridge, and in some instances they had as much influence in national politics as the judges and advocates in London.

Almost invariably the civil lawyers supported the monarchy and the English Church in the political divisions of the early seventeenth century.[4] True to the reputation they had acquired

---

[1] C. H. McIlwain, 'The English Common Law, Barrier Against Absolutism', *The American Historical Review*, 49 (1943), 26; F. W. Maitland, *English Law and the Renaissance* (The Rede Lecture for 1901), pp. 14, 62 n.; *CJ* i. 430, statement of James Whitelocke. See also W. Howe, *Studies in the Civil Law* (Boston, Mass., 1896), p. 37.

[2] This number includes all those who were active in the profession at some time during this period. Those who received their degrees in 1641 are not included. For biographical sketches of all 200 see pp. 205–82 below.

[3] Thomas Wilson, *The State of England Anno Dom. 1600* (Camden Society, 3rd ser. lii, 1936), p. 25.

[4] Only five of the 200 civil lawyers can be considered even moderate opponents

during the reign of Elizabeth as 'Her Majesty's right trusty friends',[1] the civilians provided strong encouragement for James I and Charles I. Dr. John Cowell, the Regius Professor of Civil Law at Cambridge, made his political position clear by publishing a law dictionary in 1607 which defined the King of England as an absolute monarch.[2] Members of the House of Commons took such great offence that they actually initiated proceedings against Cowell, and it was rumoured that they 'would go very near to hang him'.[3] Even more prominent than Cowell was Sir Julius Caesar, Chancellor of the Exchequer, Master of the Rolls, and Privy Councillor who acted as a spokesman for King James in his parliaments.[4] No less enthusiastic in his support for the Stuart monarchy was William Juxon, Bishop of London, ally of Archbishop Laud, Lord Treasurer, and the chaplain who accompanied Charles I to the scaffold in 1649. One civilian, Alberico Gentili, the Regius Professor of Civil Law at Oxford, subscribed to the theory of royal absolutism with such conviction that he merited posthumous condemnation by an anonymous Parliamentarian pamphleteer in 1644.[5] Gentili's critic claimed that the Professor had encouraged both James I and Charles I to advance the royal

of James or Charles. See the biographies of Isaac Dorislaus, Calibute Downing, Henry Hawkins, Henry Marten, and Matthew Sutcliffe. Marten's and Sutcliffe's opposition was relatively moderate and developed late in their careers. For general assessments of the civilians' royalism see H. Malden, *Trinity Hall* (London, 1902), p. 105; *VCH Cambridge* iii. 365; L. W. Cowie, 'Doctors' Commons', *History Today*, 20 (1970), 422.

[1] W. Senior, *Doctors' Commons and the Old Court of Admiralty* (London, 1922), p. 91. This distinction was not completely deserved. See the biographies of John Hayward, Henry Hawkins, Thomas Legge, and Edward Stanhope. James Hussey, John Pope, Simon Smith, and Stanhope refused to contribute money to Her Majesty's Navy. See BM, Lansdowne MS. 81, ff. 80–1.

[2] John Cowell, *The Interpreter or Booke Containing the Signification of Words* (Cambridge, 1607).

[3] Sir Ralph Winwood, *Memorials of Affairs of State in the Reigns of Q. Elizabeth and K. James I* (London, 1725), iii. 125. James stole the thunder of the Commons by issuing, on his authority alone, a proclamation suppressing the work. 'This later age and times of the world wherein we are fallen' (1610).

[4] W. Notestein, *The House of Commons 1603–1610* (New Haven, Conn., 1971), pp. 339–44.

[5] Alberico Gentili, *De Potestate Regis Absoluta*, in *Regales Disputationes Tres* (London, 1605), pp. 5–38.

prerogative at the expense of the people's liberty and to lead the country into civil war. He argued that 'the greatest part of the unhappy heretical principles' of Gentili's book 'are at this day defended by force of arms by such as would be called Royalists'.[1]

Although many civil lawyers were not as prominent as Cowell, Caesar, Gentili, or Juxon, they did appear as a group to be 'more inclined to cherish arbitrary principles than to promote the cause of constitutional liberty'.[2] Many of the civilians formulated their political views in response to professional pressures. During these years the conflict between the common lawyers and the civil lawyers over the extent of their respective jurisdictions reached critical proportions, and the civilians found it necessary to appeal to King James to protect their professional interests. In attempting to justify his intervention in the dispute, the civilians defined their views on such constitutional questions as the nature and limits of royal authority and the place of the judiciary in the government. The result was a substantial number of treatises, letters, speeches, petitions, and collective legal opinions from the ranks of the profession. This literature exalted the authority of the King and minimized that of Parliament and of the common law judges.

The civilians also supported the position of the King in matters of ecclesiastical policy. As judges of the ecclesiastical courts the civil lawyers were entrusted with the legal enforcement of royal and episcopal standards of religious orthodoxy. This won them the implacable opposition of the Puritans, who refused to abide by those standards. So intense was the hatred of the Puritans for the civilians that a number of Puritan tracts which appeared in 1641 to celebrate the abolition of the Court of High Commission and the destruction of all criminal ecclesiastical jurisdiction used the term Doctors' Commons to epitomize the enemy which Parliament had just overcome.[3] This literature enhanced the reputation

---

[1] *Englands Monarch or a Conviction and Refutation by the Common Law of Those False Principles and Insinuating Flatteries of Albericus* (London, 1644), pp. 1–3.

[2] C. Coote, *Sketches of the Lives and the Characters of Eminent English Civilians* (London, 1804), p. 62.

[3] *The Last Will and Testament of Doctors Commons* (1641); *A Letter from Rhoan in France Written by Doctor Roane one of the Doctors of the Late Sicke Commons . . .* (London, 1641); *The Pimpes Prerogative . . . A Dialogue Between Pimp-Major Pig*

of the civilians as the opponents of political and religious liberty and as the allies of the Stuart kings.

The civil lawyers of the early seventeenth century, therefore, became associated with the cause of the English monarchy in many ways. In order to explain this political alignment, it is necessary to examine the various facets of these lawyers' careers. This study views the civilians as officials in the King's government, lawyers in financial difficulties, political theorists, critics of the common law, and defenders of the English Church. All five approaches, taken together, account for the exceptionally high incidence of royalism within the profession.

This study makes no attempt at offering one universal explanation of the civilians' politics. To claim that they all responded to the same stimuli would endorse an oversimplified view of political behaviour. Most of the civil lawyers' support for James I and Charles I arose from an interaction of ideas, economic necessity, and professional expediency. Indeed, even the civilians' most abstract statements about the powers of the English monarch cannot be completely divorced from the economic, social, and professional circumstances in which they formulated them. It is imperative, therefore, to establish exactly what these circumstances were before discussing the civil lawyers' political ideas.

and Ancient Whiskin . . . with Their Exultation at the Downfall of Doctors Commons (London, 1641); *The Proctor and the Parator Their Mourning Or the Lamentation of the Doctors Commons for Their Downfall* (London, 1641).

I

A PROFESSION OF CIVIL SERVANTS

THE growing conflict between the Court and the Country was one of the most distinctive features of early seventeenth-century English politics. These terms, which contemporaries used to identify the antagonists in the parliamentary debates of this period, have eluded precise definition.[1] Yet in their broadest sense they designated an important division within English society which cut across the traditional social categories of peers, knights, squires, and gentlemen. The Court comprised all those men, both in London and the shires, who held offices of profit under the Crown and who depended, therefore, upon the central government for at least a portion of their incomes. The Country, on the other hand, were those members of landed society who did not hold remunerative positions in the service of the King and who spent the greater part of their time managing their estates and participating in local government. These country gentry and peers displayed strong loyalties to their local communities, whose interests they defended, both in the shires and in Parliament, against the policies of an increasingly unpopular central government.

Common lawyers and civil lawyers stood in different relationships to this split between Court and Country. The common lawyers were clearly divided. Judges, Attorney-Generals, Masters in Chancery, and Masters of Requests were members of the Court

---

[1] H. R. Trevor-Roper, *The Gentry 1540–1640* (London, 1953), pp. 26–7; P. Zagorin, 'The Court and the Country: a note on political terminology in the earlier seventeenth century', *EHR* 87 (1962), 306–7; *The Court and the Country* (London, 1969), pp. 1–41; L. Stone, 'Revolution Then', *The New York Review of Books*, 14 (23 Apr. 1970), 41–3. The 'Country' is the more elusive of the two terms, since it connotes not only a social group but an ideal of simplicity, honesty, and frugality and a political programme of opposition to the monarchy. This study will use the word primarily in its broad social sense.

in no uncertain terms.[1] But barristers who restricted themselves
to pleading for clients, serving as recorders of towns, and acting
as stewards of manorial estates did not acquire official status.[2]
Many of these lawyers held estates of their own outside London
and resided there during the law-term vacations, thus establishing
a rapport and an identity with those families who comprised the
Country.[3] The civil lawyers, on the other hand, were almost all
members of the Court. Unlike the independent common law
barristers, they held offices of profit in the King's government or
in the Church, an institution linked to the central government
through the King's appointment of bishops.[4]

This alignment of the civil lawyers with the Court suggests one
possible explanation of the strong royalist consensus that prevailed within their branch of the legal profession. For although
there was no exact correlation between the Court–Country split
and the political divisions of the early seventeenth century,[5] the
Court was certainly more reluctant than the Country to oppose
the policies of the King. Those who ate bread off the King's table
doubtless thought twice before crossing their monarch. Christopher Hill has remarked of the civilians and other officers of
the Church courts that 'Such men were bound to be politically
prejudiced in favour of the régime whose maintenance was
necessary to their existence, like the party members and police
forces of a one-party state to-day.'[6]

[1] For the official activities of common lawyers see G. E. Aylmer, *The King's
Servants: The Civil Service of Charles I 1625–1642* (London, 1961), pp. 44–57, 94–5.

[2] The distinction between the practising barrister and the lawyer in office is
made clear in Aylmer, *King's Servants*, p. 251; Keeler, *Long Parliament*, p. 250;
A. Simpson, *The Wealth of the Gentry 1540–1640* (Chicago, Ill., 1961), p. 23. See
also W. Holdsworth, *A History of English Law* (London, 1931), vi. 438–9. For
the activities of barristers, see Prest, 'Inns of Court', p. 79.

[3] See the biographies of Henry Pelham and John Goodwin in Keeler, *Long
Parliament*, pp. 190, 299–300. A century earlier it was customary for common
lawyers to take an active part in the life of their counties. See E. W. Ives, 'The
Common Lawyers in Pre-Reformation England', *Transactions of the Royal
Historical Society*, 5th ser. xviii (1968), 149–50.

[4] Only certain Church officials, however, such as bishops and officers of the
Church courts, were clearly members of the Court. Clergy who received their
benefices through the patronage of laymen were not.

[5] See Zagorin, *The Court and the Country*, pp. 54–5.

[6] Hill, *Society and Puritanism*, p. 329.

The exact relationship between the civilians' royalist politics and their membership in the Court must stand close examination. The present concern, however, is to determine how these lawyers acquired their official status. What directed them to become members of the Court? How were they, unlike so many common law barristers, excluded from the Country? The answers lie in a wide variety of social, economic, and professional pressures that became operative early in their careers.

(a) *Social origins*

The common lawyers of early seventeenth-century England belonged to a genteel profession. Most of the young men who went down from the universities to attend one of the four Inns of Court came from families which boasted a social status of gentry or higher and which held sufficient land and property to sponsor the long process of university education and legal training.[1] At the end of the sixteenth century sons of yeomen and merchants had threatened to dilute the gentility of the profession,[2] but the King had commanded in 1604 that no student be accepted at any of the Inns unless he be 'a gentleman by descent'.[3] Although a number of complaints suggest that the four societies did not adhere closely to the policy established by this royal directive,[4] more than 90 per cent of their students continued to register as sons of gentlemen, esquires, knights, or peers.[5]

The figures for those students who stayed on at the Inns to complete their legal education and to be called to the Bar correspond closely to those for all admissions. The fathers of the barristers who were admitted to the Middle Temple after 1599

---

[1] L. Stone, 'The Educational Revolution in England, 1560–1640', *Past and Present*, 28 (1964), 58–9, calculated that an average of 81 per cent of Middle Temple students during this period were sons of gentlemen or above.

[2] See Wilson, *State of England*, p. 19.

[3] *The Pension Book of Gray's Inn 1569–1669* (London, 1901), i. 164; *The Records of the Honourable Society of Lincoln's Inn: The Black Books*, ii. 81.

[4] P. Lucas, 'Blackstone and the Reform of the Legal Profession', *EHR* 77 (1962), 473–4. See G. Buc, *The Third University of England*, appended to J. Stow, *The Annals or General Chronicles of England* (London, 1615), pp. 968–9.

[5] Prest, 'Inns of Court', pp. 46–7.

and were called to the Bar before 1642 can be divided into the
following broad social categories:[1]

Peers	0
Baronets	1
Knights	29
Esquires	115
Gentlemen	142
Urban 'gentry'[2]	26
Lawyers and members of professions	43
Commoners[3]	9
Unknown	7

Many residents of urban areas who styled themselves gentlemen,
and lawyers who held the rank of esquire by courtesy only did not
belong to landed society proper and hence should be distinguished
from other gentlemen and esquires. Yet even if one classifies all
urban gentry, lawyers, and members of professions as commoners,
the proportion of barristers who were born into landed society
still exceeds 77 per cent and could be as high as 79 per cent,
depending upon the status of the unknown cases. Moreover,
nearly two-thirds of these sons of knights, esquires, and
gentlemen, or 46 per cent of all barristers, were eldest sons and
therefore heirs to their fathers' estates.

The young scholars who received doctorates in civil law at the
universities comprised a considerably less genteel group than the
common law barristers. The fathers of the 200 civil lawyers who
form the basis of this study were distributed among the various
strata of English society in the following manner:[4]

[1] *Register of Admissions to the Honourable Society of the Middle Temple*, i (London,
1949). There was an incentive for students of humble origins to upgrade their
status, so the records cannot be considered completely accurate. See Prest, 'Inns
of Court', pp. 47–9.

[2] Residents from towns with a population of more than 1,000 who called
themselves gentlemen.

[3] Yeomen, merchants, and all those who clearly did not belong to landed
society.

[4] The individual entries in the biographical dictionary indicate all the sources
consulted. They include family pedigrees, county histories, parish registers, and
wills of civilians' fathers. University records are in many instances misleading and
were relied upon only in the absence of other information.

Peers	0
Baronets	3
Knights	14
Esquires	38
Gentlemen	44
Urban 'gentry'	10
Lawyers, Doctors, Civil Servants	9
Merchants	4
Yeomen	7
Lower clergy	8
Citizens and other Commoners	34
Foreigners	3
Unknown	26

If urban and professional gentry are once again grouped with the commoners, between 49·5 and 62·5 per cent of the civil lawyers came from the ranks of the landed classes. The exact figure depends upon the status of the unknown cases. Since a total lack of information concerning a seventeenth-century Englishman virtually assures us that he was not a peer, knight, or esquire, and makes it more likely that he was a commoner than a gentleman, the lower figure probably lies closer to the reality. It seems reasonable to conclude that the percentage of civil lawyers who were sons of commoners was roughly twice as high as the corresponding figure for common law barristers.

One reason for the wide discrepancy was the difference in the admissions policies of the universities and the Inns of Court. Even before the royal order of 1604 the Inns had become the preserve of the landed classes, despite their acceptance of some promising commoners.[1] This exclusiveness might very well have directed men of lower social calibre to stay on at the notably less restrictive universities[2] for an alternative form of legal education. The ready availability of fellowships for civil law students, especially at All Souls College and New College, Oxford, and at Trinity Hall,

---

[1] Lucas, 'Blackstone', 467–73; Stone, 'Educational Revolution', 58–9. There was a higher percentage of sons of gentry admitted before 1604 than after.

[2] Stone, 'Educational Revolution', 66–7.

Cambridge, also made the universities more attractive for commoners.[1] Sons of gentlemen, on the other hand, had good reason
to prefer the Inns to the universities. Since the law taught at the
Inns was fundamentally land law, knowledge of it was especially
useful to them as members of the landed classes. Moreover, since
most of the litigants in common law courts were landowners,
barristers who came from the ranks of the country gentry could
use their connections within landed society to build up their
practice. As civil lawyers, however, the same gentlemen would
have found little professional value in such connections. Civilians
catered mainly for merchants and mariners in the Admiralty
courts and for men of all classes in the ecclesiastical courts. Only
in the Court of Chivalry, which functioned for just a few years
during this period, did the civil lawyers regularly represent
members of landed society.[2]

Even more remarkable than the heavy concentration of sons of
commoners among the civil lawyers was the slight number of
first sons of gentlemen. Compared with the figure of 46 per cent
of Middle Temple barristers, only 9 per cent of all civil lawyers
are known to have been eldest sons of gentry and therefore heirs
to their fathers' estates.[3] This meant that the great majority of
civilians, even those who were born into gentry families, possessed
no guarantee of an independent income from land as they began
their legal education. Even if their father's assets were quite substantial, second or younger sons were usually excluded from all
but modest patrimonies. Herbert Pelham, for example, was the
fourth son of a knight who owned three manors and extensive
lands in Lincolnshire.[4] By his father's will, however, Pelham

[1] M. H. Curtis, *Oxford and Cambridge in Transition 1558–1642* (Oxford, 1959),
p. 152. There were five fellowships for civilians at Jesus College. See A. Gray
and F. Brittain, *A History of Jesus College, Cambridge* (London, 1960), pp. 47–8.

[2] The court's first seventeenth-century case was heard in 1623. Litigation concerned duelling, 'scandalous words' among gentlemen, and armorial disputes.
See G. D. Squibb, *The High Court of Chivalry* (Oxford, 1958), pp. 47–72.

[3] The contrast between civilians and common lawyers in this respect can often
be seen within the same family, where the eldest son became a common lawyer,
the younger son a civilian. See the biographies of Acred, Eden, Gwynn, Nicholas,
and Ferrand.

[4] *Lincolnshire Pedigrees*, iii (Harl. Soc. lii, 1904), 766.

received only an annuity of £50.[1] Similarly Nicholas Steward, despite his father's armigerous rank, received only £100 when his father died. As the sixth son in the family, Nicholas inherited no share in his father's manors of Stuntney and Thorney on the Isle of Ely, his estate at Lakenheath in Suffolk, or his other messuages, lands, and tenements in scattered parts of Cambridgeshire. In fact, to secure the money bequeathed to him, Steward was obliged to surrender all rights he had acquired to the manors of Stuntney and Thorney. These were to go entirely to the eldest son and heir, Robert.[2]

Likewise scantily endowed was Richard Clarke, the second son of John of Ardington in Berkshire, gentleman. Clarke received from his father an annuity of £6 in addition to a flat sum of £40. All of this was to be paid from the profits of the lands which Clarke's father bequeathed to William, the eldest son.[3] Richard received no land at all. Even less fortunate was Zachary Babington, the second son of Thomas of Cossington, Leicestershire, esquire. In Thomas's will only Humphrey, the first son, received any mention at all.[4] Like Pelham, Steward, and Clarke, Babington had to rely solely upon his legal talents if he wished to re-enter the landed society into which he had been born.

Of the seventy-three civil lawyers who were younger sons of gentry, only five appear to have begun their careers with lands of their own. The most richly endowed of these was Charles Tooker, who inherited the manor Caldecott in Berkshire.[5] Charles Twysden, Alexander Hyde, and James Masters, on the other hand, did not have Tooker's good fortune. They inherited much smaller parcels of land which could hardly have supported them as country gentlemen.[6] In similar fashion Matthew Sutcliffe, the

[1] Lincolnshire Archives Office, will of Sir William Pelham, Consistory Court Wills D. 70.

[2] PRO, will of Simeon Steward, PROB 11/50/10. See also PRO, C 142/150/188; *VCH Cambs.* iv. 40 n., 41; *The Visitations of Hertfordshire* (Harl. Soc. xxii, 1886), p. 94.

[3] PRO, will of John Clarke, PROB 11/93/54.

[4] PRO, will of Thomas Babington, PROB 11/50/1.

[5] PRO, will of Charles Tooker, PROB 11/151/6. *VCH Berkshire*, iv. 375.

[6] PRO, will of Roger Twisden, PROB 11/103/46; will of A. Hyde, PROB 11/325/161; will of J. Masters, PROB 11/313/18.

second son of a gentleman, inherited lands, buildings, and tenements which his father had purchased in Yorkshire.[1] But the
bequest was not substantial enough to lure Sutcliffe away from his
legal studies. One year after he received his degree Sutcliffe, then
a resident of London, sold all his Yorkshire property.[2]

Even first sons of gentry families did not always find their patrimonies in land attractive. Robert Newcomb stood in the direct
line of descent in a Lincolnshire family which had resided at
Ingoldmells since the fourteenth century. Moreover he was the
legatee of his grandfather's brother, so in effect he possessed control of the entire family estate.[3] Yet despite this endowment,
Newcomb had no interest in Ingoldmells and he surrendered his
lands in 1608.[4] In similar fashion Christopher Wyvell, endowed
by his father with lands in Middleton St. George in Durham, sold
his patrimony before finishing his degree, perhaps to help finance
his education.[5] Thus Newcomb and Wyvell joined the great
majority of civil lawyers who began their careers with no real
stake in landed society. Compared with so many common lawyers, only a handful of seventeen civil lawyers went down from
the university with one foot on the family estate and the other in
a court of law.[6]

Although so few young civilians claimed an inherited source
of independent income, most of them did begin their university
education with adequate financial backing. Even the lawyers of
non-landed origin often claimed assets which rivalled those of the
sons of knights, esquires, and gentlemen. This was because the

[1] PRO, will of John Sutcliffe, PROB 11/59/11, refers to him as a yeoman from
Lincolnshire. Elsewhere he is referred to as a gentleman. *Familiae Minorum
Gentium*, ii (Harl. Soc. xxxviii, 1895), 541. The first son stayed in Lincolnshire.

[2] *Notes and Queries*, iv. 152–3.   [3] *Lincolnshire Pedigrees*, iii. 713.

[4] Ibid. The Newcomb estate was not large. Robert's father, Thomas, was a
lesser gentleman and was referred to in his will as a yeoman. Lincolnshire
Archives Office, Wills, 1598, 144.

[5] R. Surtees, *The History and Antiquities of the County Palatinate of Durham*, iii
(London, 1823), 263. Durham University Library, will of Sampson Wyvill,
Durham Probate Records, Register iii, ff. 81ᵛ–85.

[6] Richard Stanes, for example, never relinquished the manor of Folyot's Hall
of High Ongar, Essex. P. Morant, *The History and Antiquities of the County of
Essex* (London, 1768), i, pt. 2, p. 130. PRO, C 142/266/87. ERO, D/ABW/36/227.

fathers of a good number of commoners were relatively successful yeomen, merchants, and citizens whose income matched or exceeded that of many members of landed society. Thomas Crompton, for example, was the second son of William, a citizen and mercer of London, who had prospered so well that he had been able to purchase lands in London, Staffordshire, and Kent. The annual income from his estate was, by his computation, just under £150. Thomas, though not as fortunate as his brother William, who inherited the bulk of these lands, none the less did receive an annuity of £20 by his father's will.[1] Although he had been excluded from a possible entrance into the lower ranks of the country gentry, Thomas was able to use his annuity to pay his way through his undergraduate years at Oxford. John Amye, a Cambridge civilian, profited in a similar way from his father's success as a yeoman. Even though he was the sixth son, and his family held only two closes in Little Abington in Cambridgeshire, Amye's father accumulated enough capital to send him to the university and to bequeath him £200 when he died.[2]

Like the gentry, therefore, commoners could often afford to support their sons during the early years of their university education, at least until their talented progeny could secure fellowships or ecclesiastical preferments. For this reason forty-six of the fifty-eight Cambridge civilians for whom information is available matriculated as pensioners, that is as students paying their way by independent means. Only one scholar, the son of a wealthy merchant who had risen into the ranks of the gentry,[3] could afford to join his college as a fellow-commoner, whereas at the other end of the economic scale thirteen had to work at the university as 'sizars' to earn their keep.[4]

The heavy preponderance of pensioners among the civilians underlines the marginal relationship that so many of them bore to

---

[1] PRO, will of William Crompton, PROB 11/50/7.

[2] PRO, will of John Amye, senior, PROB 11/73/61.

[3] William Spicer. See the biographical dictionary.

[4] Fellow-commoners dined with the fellows of the college. For a description of these three categories see Venn's preface to John Peile (ed.), *Biographical Register of Christ's College 1505–1905*, i (Cambridge, 1910), vii–viii. See also K. Charlton, *Education in Renaissance England* (London, 1965), pp. 131–2.

landed society. Most were endowed with sufficient wealth to finance at least part of their university education, but not with the land necessary to offer them a future as country gentlemen. Occasionally aspiring civilians barely missed this latter opportunity. Henry Marten's father, while technically a gentleman by virtue of the lands he held in Berkshire,[1] gained his livelihood as a London grocer. As the only son, Henry inherited all of his father's lands, which yielded a profit of about £40 per year.[2] In later life Marten was known to hypothesize that if his father had left him £80 instead of £40, he would never have gone to the university to become a civil lawyer, but would instead have lived on his lands. The poverty of his inherited estate had opened his way to wealth as the Judge of the Admiralty Court and as Dean of the Arches.[3]

Few civil lawyers, therefore, were able to anticipate joining the ranks of the country gentry immediately after completing their studies at the universities. Some may have hoped to join this social group after they became established in their legal practice. But this rarely happened. For the civil lawyers' legal education and professional training prepared them for careers as members of the Court, which in turn prevented them from participating in the life of the landed leisure class.

(b) Legal education

Although the purpose of the doctorate in civil law at Oxford and Cambridge was to qualify aspiring lawyers for careers in the ecclesiastical and Admiralty courts,[4] the instruction given to students in that faculty did not prepare them adequately for their future work. Unlike the education offered to common lawyers at the Inns of Court, the study of law at the universities was almost entirely theoretical and did not train the students in court proced-

---

[1] *The Four Visitations of Berkshire*, i (Harl. Soc. lvi, 1907), 43–4.

[2] PRO, will of Anthony Marten, PROB 11/62/3.

[3] Thomas Fuller, *The History of the Worthies of England* (London, 1840), ii. 370–1. See also David Lloyd, *Memoires of the Lives, Actions, Sufferings, Deaths . . . of Those . . . that suffered for the Protestant Religion* (London, 1668), p. 593.

[4] F. H. Lawson, *The Oxford Law School 1850–1965* (Oxford, 1968), p. 1; Charlton, *Education*, p. 46.

ures and techniques.[1] A few civil law students managed to practise in the courts of the universities, the Ely Consistory Court at Cambridge, or the Court of the Archdeacon of Berkshire near Oxford.[2] But the universities did not follow a policy of providing such opportunities for all civilians, and they did not have moot court. Most of the law that the civilians learned at the universities, moreover, differed markedly from the law that they eventually practised. The lectures of the Regius Professor, which constituted the hard core of the curriculum, like the lectures delivered at Continental universities, elaborated upon the traditional sources of the civil law, mainly the *Corpus Juris Civilis* of Justinian.[3] In the formal academic exercises that the doctoral candidate performed before receiving his degree, he himself was required to lecture 'solemnly' on the *Corpus*.[4] The scholar was expected, moreover, in the long course of his university career,[5] to familiarize himself with the wide variety of commentaries available on these legal codes. Two seventeenth-century guides to the study of the civil law recommend for the perusal of the dedicated scholar a host of respected authors including the great medievalists, like Baldus and Bartolus, and the humanists, such as Alciatus and Cujas.[6]

[1] W. Holdsworth, 'The Reception of Roman Law in the Sixteenth Century', pt. 3, *Law Quarterly Review*, 28 (1912), 141. Civil law education in France was no more practical. See B. Hall, 'John Calvin, the Jurisconsults and the *Ius Civile*', *Studies in Church History*, iii (Leiden, 1966), 204–5.

[2] Oxford University Archives, Registers of the Chancellor's Court 1594–1639, reveal that three civilians included in this study sat as judge at different times and two as proctors. R. A. Marchant, *The Church Under The Law: Justice, Administration and Discipline in the Diocese of York 1560–1640* (Cambridge, 1969), p. 11; Peile, *Christ's College*, i. 318; PRO, DEL 8/61, *passim*.

[3] For a summary of the entire curriculum see Curtis, *Oxford and Cambridge*, p. 155. Indirect evidence that the Professor's lectures focused almost entirely on the *Corpus* appears in a Cambridge student's outline of the civil law. See CUL, MS. Dd. II, 44.

[4] J. Griffiths (ed.), *The Statutes of the University of Oxford Codified in the Year 1636* (Oxford, 1888), p. 116.

[5] By university statutes nine to ten years of attendance was required to complete both the Bachelor of Laws degree and the doctorate. Sometimes, however, the process was spread over as many as thirty-three years. See the biographies of Lambe, Hawley, Stanes, and Babington in the Biographical Dictionary.

[6] William Fulbecke, *A Direction or Preparative to the Study of the Lawe* (London,

Both the lectures of the Regius Professor and the commentaries that a student happened to read offered him an understanding of numerous legal principles and rules, many of which were followed in the law courts of Continental countries.[1] But only a few sections of the *Corpus Juris Civilis* were applicable in the English courts where civil lawyers practised. What the students at Oxford and Cambridge most needed for their future work was a mastery of English ecclesiastical law and international maritime law, which were hardly conterminous with the Roman civil law.[2] Oxford and Cambridge offered instruction in neither. Ever since the Reformation the formal study of canon law had been banned, and a coherent system of English Church law to take its place had not yet been approved.[3] Maritime law, which consisted mainly of the Laws of Oleron and other sea codes of Continental origin,[4] was taught only at a superficial level to businessmen at Gresham College in London.[5]

Doctors of the Civil Law, therefore, irrespective of the quality of their legal education, came down from the universities virtually untrained to cope with the duties of the positions for which they had just become technically qualified. Some of the less talented or less ambitious among them elected to serve in minor ecclesiastical or legal positions in the dioceses, where they could easily acquire any necessary professional skills on the job. A few stayed on at the universities as fellows, masters, or professors. Those of course did not require any further legal training. But the great majority of civilians remedied the deficiencies in their formal education by joining Doctors' Commons, a college of Doctors of Laws who were practising advocates in London.

1600), p. 26ᵛ. See also Durham Cathedral Library, 'An Advertisement to one that would begin to study the Civil and Ecclesiastical Law here in England', Hunter MS. 12/1.

[1] See Squibb, *Court of Chivalry*, pp. 163–4; Hall, 'Calvin', 204.

[2] Robert Wiseman, *The Law of Lawes or the Excellency of the Civil Law Above All Other Humane Laws* (London, 1656), p. 29, admits that 'the civil law was originally made least of all for ecclesiastical matters'.

[3] For a complete discussion of this problem see H. B. Vaisey, *The Canon Law of the Church of England* (London, 1947), pp. 45–6.

[4] See Holdsworth, *History of Law*, i. 526–9.

[5] For the legal topics taught at this college see John Ward, *The Lives of the Professors of Gresham College* (London, 1740), pp. vi–vii.

As early as 1511, a number of civilians who were pleading in the provincial courts of the Archbishop of Canterbury formed a plan of association known as the College of Advocates. They agreed to live in contiguous houses and to dine together,[1] thereby contributing to a spirit of professional cohesion. In 1567 Henry Harvey, LL.D., the Master of Trinity Hall, Cambridge, procured for this college from the Dean and Chapter of St. Paul's a lease of Mountjoy House on Great Knight Rider Street in the parish of St. Benet, Paul's Wharf, in London.[2] This house, as well as the society of men who lived and dined in it, came to be known as Doctors' Commons.[3] In addition to fulfilling its original social purpose, Doctors' Commons looked after the further education of young civilians. One of the conditions of acceptance into the society was that the applicant should spend a 'silent year' in the Court of the Arches, the highest ecclesiastical court of the Archbishop.[4] During this year he became acquainted with the procedure of the court and he learned the art of pleading.

At Doctors' Commons civilians could acquire a knowledge of ecclesiastical and maritime law. The society's library contained all the published works on canon law, much of which was un-reformed and hence still in force, as well as copies of the Laws of Oleron and, after 1613, William Welwood's *Abridgement of All Sea Laws*.[5] Doctors' Commons, moreover, served as a clearing-house for the circulation of a number of practical guides to the forms and procedures a civilian would need to employ in his work. Widely used were two treatises on the practice of the ecclesiastical courts[6]

---

[1] Coote, *Eminent Civilians*, p. ii. Coote drew largely upon an eighteenth-century history of the society by A. C. Ducarel, 'A Summary Account of the Society of Doctors' Commons', LPL, MS. 958.

[2] Malden, *Trinity Hall*, pp. 103–4; R. W. Chandler, 'Doctors' Commons', *London Topographical Record*, 15 (1931), 6–7.

[3] E. J. Davis, 'Doctors' Commons, Its Title and Topography', *London Topographical Record*, 15 (1931), 36–7.

[4] Bodl., MS. Rawlinson Statutes 62, f. 12, 14, 16.

[5] For a complete listing of all the books in the library at the time of the dissolution of Doctors' Commons, see *A Catalogue of the Very Valuable and Extensive Library of the College of Advocates, Doctors' Commons, London* (London, 1861).

[6] Clerke's treatment of the ecclesiastical courts was not published until the Restoration, but BM, Harleian MS. 4117 appears to be a manuscript copy, entitled 'Praxis Curiarum Ecclesiasticarum sub Witgifto'.

and of the Admiralty Court[1] by Francis Clerke. There has also survived in the Bodleian Library a manuscript collection of judicial proceedings, known to have been at one time in the possession of John Cowell. Using cases from the Elizabethan period as examples, the compiler had illustrated the various types of libels, allegations, citations, and excommunications which the ecclesiastical judge used at different times.[2] All of these sources, which were made available at Doctors' Commons, as well as the everyday contact with experienced lawyers there, prepared the young civilian for service in the central ecclesiastical courts and the High Court of Admiralty.

Civil lawyers sought membership in Doctors' Commons not only for the legal training the society offered, but for the professional opportunity it controlled. Only those civilians who had successfully completed their silent year in the Arches and had been received into Doctors' Commons were entitled to practise law in any of the five provincial courts of the Archbishop of Canterbury,[3] the High Court of Admiralty, or the Court of Chivalry. Moreover, the judges of all these courts, as well as all the masters in the Court of Chancery who were civilians, were chosen exclusively from the membership of that society. The aspiring careerist found admission to Doctors' Commons an absolute prerequisite to professional advancement and success.[4]

Even some civil lawyers who established themselves at the universities as men of academic interests yielded to the lure of a legal practice in the London courts and joined Doctors' Commons. John Hayward, a Cambridge civilian who spent the first twenty-five years after receiving his degree as a historian and a

[1] Published in J. Hall, *The Practice and Jurisdiction of the Court of the Admiralty* (Baltimore, Md., 1809). See also W. Senior, 'Early Writers on Maritime Law,' *Law Quarterly Review*, 37 (1921), 328–9; Ward, *Gresham Professors*, p. 243.

[2] Bodl., Tanner MS. 427. For a similar formulary book, known to have been compiled by a Welsh civilian who was a member of Doctors' Commons, see LPL, MS. 1729, ff. 92–109.

[3] The five were the Court of the Arches, the Court of Audience, the Prerogative Court, the Court of Peculiars, and the Court of the Vicar-General. For a brief description of each see Holdsworth, *History of Law*, i. 601–2.

[4] Dr. D. Lewis instructed his young protégé, Julius Caesar, to make sure that he gain admittance to the society in 1579. BM, Add. MS. 11,406, f. 150ᵛ.

polemicist, was admitted to the society in 1616.[1] Shortly thereafter he became one of the Masters in Chancery.[2] Two Masters of Trinity Hall, John Cowell and Thomas Eden, entered Doctors' Commons and pursued active legal careers in London.[3] The division of their interests between Cambridge and London illustrates how much Doctors' Commons had become an extension of the universities.

Altogether, 148 or 74 per cent of the 200 civilians included in this study received warrants from the Archbishop of Canterbury to secure their admission to Doctors' Commons.[4] Of these 106 eventually become fellows or full members,[5] at which time they paid a fee of £13. 6s. 8d. and annual dues ranging from 10s. to 30s.[6] Fellows then had the option of choosing to be 'in commons', i.e. to take meals regularly at Doctors' Commons, or to be 'out of commons'. Thus while the total membership of Doctors' Commons in 1639 stood at fifty-two, the number of fellows was thirty-eight, of whom only thirty-two were in commons.[7]

(c) Occupational opportunities

Although all the members of Doctors' Commons were entitled to plead in the ecclesiastical, Admiralty, and Chivalry courts in London, few did so with any degree of regularity. Extant court records reveal that a small coterie or 'bar' of twelve to fifteen advocates at any one time and a total of forty-one during the entire period 1603–41 monopolized the practice of the London

[1] Reg. Doc. Com., f. 47ᵛ.   [2] PRO C 216/1. f. 60.

[3] Reg. Doc. Com., ff. 44, 47ᵛ. For their legal activities see the biographical dictionary.

[4] The warrants are recorded in the archiepiscopal registers in Lambeth Palace Library. MS. 1351 in that library provides a fairly accurate index. The warrants given between 1637 and 1640 are listed in PRO, SP 16/442/125. For the full procedure of admission see Bodl., Ashmole MS. 857, ff. 370–1; LPL, Bancroft Register, f. 138ᵛ.

[5] Reg. Doc. Com. Lists of all fellows are recorded in LPL, MS. 958; Coote, *Eminent Civilians*; E. Nys, *Le Droit romain, le droit de gens et le collège des docteurs en droit civil* (Brussels, 1910), p. 140.

[6] Doc. Com. Treas. Bk, *passim*.

[7] Borth. Inst., R. VII. PR 108. PRO, SP 16/474/108; Doc. Com. Treas. Bk., ff. 171–6.

civil law courts.[1] This suggests that the great majority of members of Doctors' Commons, as well as the civilians who never established any connection with that society, became engaged in other lines of professional activity. In fact even the active advocates in London rarely confined themselves to the art of pleading. They too became involved in a wide variety of professional services. Table 1 lists the most important posts that civilians staffed. Because of plural office-holding and frequent shifts from one position to another, it includes the number of civilians from the group of 200 who at one time during their careers are known to have held each office.

With the exception of the judgeships of the provincial courts of the Archbishop of Canterbury and the Regius professorships, Doctors of Laws did not hold a monopoly of the positions they customarily filled. Even offices of ecclesiastical jurisdiction in the dioceses and archdeaconries were not their exclusive preserve, since the men who staffed these posts were not required to possess doctorates in law. The Canons of 1604 insisted only that

No man shall hereafter be admitted a chancellor, commissary, or official, to exercise any ecclesiastical jurisdiction, except he be of the full age of six and twenty years at the least, and one that is learned in the civil and ecclesiastical laws, and is at the least a master of arts, or bachelor of law, and is reasonably well practised in the course thereof, likewise well affected, and zealously bent to religion. . . .[2]

Bachelors of Laws and Masters of Arts were, therefore, entitled to hold offices of this nature on an equal footing with Doctors of Laws. Yet in the competition for the better posts, civilians held an advantage because of their higher academic and social status. Thus

[1] The Admiralty records are the most complete. PRO, HCA 24/70–101, *passim*, supply the names of most of the active advocates. The records of the ecclesiastical courts were destroyed in the fire of 1666, but for the names of the advocates in the Court of the Arches at certain times see BM, Cotton/Cleo. MS. F II, f. 168ᵛ; Exeter Cathedral Library, MS. 7155/1, f. 26ᵛ; BM, Stowe MS. 558, f. 17ᵛ; Bodl., Tanner MS. 427; PRO, SP 16/421/108. Advocates on the High Commission receive occasional mention in the Act books, *CSPD 1634–1635*; *1635*; *1635–1636*; *1640*, *passim*. For advocates in the Chivalry Court see *Reports of Heraldic Cases in the Court of Chivalry 1623–1732* (Harl. Soc. cvii, 1956), *passim*.

[2] E. Cardwell (ed.), *Synodalia: A Collection of Articles of Religion, Canons, and Proceedings of Convocations* (Oxford, 1842), i. 318–19.

TABLE I

EMPLOYMENT OF CIVIL LAWYERS

Legal Positions in the Dioceses and Counties[1]

Chancellors of English and Welsh dioceses and of the Archdiocese of York   75

Commissaries for archdeaconries and officials of archdeacons
and deans   50

Deputies of vice-admirals and judges of local Admiralty courts   21

*Legal, Quasi-Legal and Administrative Positions in the Central Institutions
of Government*

Masters in Chancery   24

Masters of Requests   8

Judges of the Admiralty Court and of the provincial ecclesiastical courts of Canterbury   22

Diplomats   14

Privy Councillors   3

King's Advocates in the Admiralty, ecclesiastical and Chivalry
courts   8

Membership on Conciliar Courts and Commissions

Commissioners for Ecclesiastical Causes for Canterbury or York   44

Members of the High Court of Delegates   51

Members of the King's Council of the North   4

Academic Posts

Regius Professors of Law   10

Professors of Law at Gresham College   3

Masters, presidents, provosts, wardens, and principals of colleges and halls   16

Ecclesiastical Positions

Rectors   45

Vicars   10

Prebendaries of cathedrals   39

Archdeacons   9

Deans   12

Bishops   2

[1] This list contains only offices. Hence the occasional service of civilians as
advocates in diocesan consistory courts is not referred to.

in all but the most remote dioceses of England and Wales, the chancellors, who were the main legal representatives of the bishops, were usually civil lawyers.[1]

Civilians also held an advantage in competing for employment as officials of archdeacons, commissaries of bishops for archdeaconries, and commissaries of deans. Yet these positions were considerably less attractive than chancellorships, and civilians often regarded them merely as springboards to higher office. The net result was that only in the most populous dioceses of London and Norwich did civil lawyers regularly serve in such capacities.[2] In other dioceses archdeacons and deans relied upon men with less impressive academic credentials. The same was true for the twenty vice-admirals of England, who were expected to appoint deputies learned in the civil law to hold court for them, if they themselves were not capable.[3] Although civilians were pre-eminently suited to fill such positions, few actually did, and those usually held their offices in conjunction with chancellorships of the diocese in which the Vice-Admiral had jurisdiction.[4] By itself a judgeship of a vice-admiralty court was simply not lucrative enough to keep a civilian out of the main stream of national legal and political life.

For certain quasi-legal and administrative positions in the central government civilians were in many ways as qualified as they were for legal offices in the dioceses and counties. Early in the

[1] In the remote diocese of Carlisle, for example, no civilians were appointed as chancellors during this period. W. Hutchinson, *The History of the County of Cumberland* (1794), ii. 639. But in the dioceses of London, Norwich, Lichfield, Worcester, and even Chester, all the chancellors were civilians. Occasionally, as in Exeter, bishops would appoint unqualified friends and relatives. See I. Cassidy, 'The Episcopate of William Cotton, Bishop of Exeter 1598–1621' (Oxford, B. Litt. thesis, 1963), pp. 118–20.

[2] F. Blomefield, *An Essay Towards a Topographical History of Norfolk* (London, 1806), iii. 656–60. B. W. Quintrell, 'The Government of the County of Essex 1603–1642' (Univ. of London, Ph.D. thesis, 1964), p. 148, shows that eight of the eleven officials of archdeacons in the diocese of London during this period were civilians.

[3] BM, Lansdowne MS. 170, f. 275^v.

[4] In York the Judge of the Vice-Admiralty Court was always a judge in one of the Archbishop's courts as well. See J. S. Purvis, *The Records of the Admiralty Court of York* (York, 1962), p. 4.

sixteenth century Thomas More had decided that the State needed men learned in the civil law.[1] Thomas Smith, in his second lecture as Regius Professor of Civil Law at Cambridge in 1542, depicted the attractive opportunities open to a civilian who chose to enter the direct service of the King.[2] A nineteenth-century historian, looking back to this Tudor period as the golden age of the civil lawyers, observed that 'No bar can show more eminent men, or a greater number prominent in public capacities, than this college [of Advocates].'[3] With names such as Cuthbert Tunstall, Walter Haddon, Thomas Wilson, and Thomas Smith himself inscribed in the Register of Doctors' Commons, there is some merit in this view.[4] In the seventeenth century a good number of civilians, somewhat slighter in stature than these famous gentlemen, continued to devote their main efforts to the service of the State. In referring to the entire profession of civil lawyers in 1607, Thomas Ridley was still able to distinguish between ordinary careerists and those who 'attend about the Prince'.[5]

One reason for the employment of civilians in positions of political prominence was the belief that the study of the civil law helped to cultivate the art of statesmanship. Thomas Starkey wrote to Thomas Cromwell in 1532 that since he had decided to enter political life he had set himself 'these last years past to the knowledge of the civil law' in order that he might thereby make 'a more stable and sure judgment of the politic order and customs used among us here in our country'.[6] Early in the next century, Thomas Ridley was more specific in boasting that the real advantage of the civilian in public affairs was that he combined his own native intelligence with the skill of the civil laws themselves, 'which are a quintessence of wit above other human learning and

[1] L. B. Smith, *Tudor Prelates and Politics 1536–1558* (Princeton, N.J., 1953), p. 41.

[2] M. Dewar, *Sir Thomas Smith: A Tudor Intellectual in Office* (London, 1964), p. 22.

[3] 'The Civilians of Doctors' Commons', *The Law Magazine and Law Review*, n.s. 18 (1860), 266.

[4] Reg. Doc. Com., ff. 8ᵛ, 37, 38, 41ᵛ.

[5] Thomas Ridley, *A View of the Civile and Ecclesiastical Law* (2nd edn., Oxford, 1634), p. 106. See also Wilson, *State of England*, p. 25.

[6] Sidney J. Herrtage, *Starkey's Life and Letters*, pt. 1 of *England in the Reign of King Henry the Eighth* (Early English Text Society, Extra Series, xxxii, 1878), p. x.

were either wholly composed of the mature and deliberate resolutions of such Emperors as then swayed the whole world or were the dooms and judgments of such wise men as then managed the whole world'.[1] Calibute Downing argued in 1633 that an increase in the number of civilians would provide more 'commonwealthes men' for the State,[2] while as late as 1650 Henry Parker claimed that 'as politicians [i.e. statesmen] are generally the ablest servitors to all states, so no other study or breeding has more eminently accomplished learned politicians than this of the Civil Law'.[3]

More specific qualifications than a general aptitude for statesmanship contributed to the appointment of civilians to positions in the central government. The substantial number of doctors who joined diplomatic missions in the service of the King found their highly theoretical and otherwise impractical university education directly relevant to their tasks. Not only had it required them to become fluent in Latin, the language of international negotiation, but it had also acquainted them with the fundamental tenets of international law. The *Corpus Juris Civilis*, which treated such topics as the rights of princes, war, captivity, and treaties, constituted the main ingredient of what was then known as *jus gentium* or the law of nations.[4] Alberico Gentili, the Regius Professor of Law at Oxford, contributed greatly to the systematization of this body of legal knowledge.[5] Doctors of Laws, therefore, became valuable members of diplomatic teams. In organizing a mission to Denmark in 1600, Richard Bancroft demanded that a 'grounded civil lawyer' be joined with the group. He refused to accept a Doctor of Divinity as a substitute. 'I can say some part of St.

---

[1] Ridley, *A View*, p. 97. See also the statement of the civilians that they 'are men generally better furnished with liberal sciences as being instructed in the learned, both languages and arts, which are of best use and service in a state'. Bodl., Barlow MS. 9, f. 1, no. 4.

[2] C. Downing, *A Discourse of the State Ecclesiasticall of this Kingdom in Relation to the Civill* (Oxford, 1633), p. 31. See also BM, Add. MS. 12,505, f. 270^v.

[3] [H. Parker], *Reformation in Courts and Cases Testamentary* (London, 1650), p. 4.

[4] G. Mattingly, *Renaissance Diplomacy* (Boston, Mass., 1954), pp. 18–20. See also Wiseman, *Law of Lawes*, p. 161; Downing, *Discourse*, pp. 31–3.

[5] G. del Vecchio, 'The Posthumous Fate of Alberico Gentili', *The American Journal of International Law*, 50 (1966), 666.

Paul's Epistles by heart,' wrote Bancroft, 'but that will not serve to encounter in this case so much as with Bartolus.'[1]

Because of their knowledge and experience in dealing with questions of international law, civilians often served as consultants to the Privy Council concerning such matters. Groups of civil lawyers at various times were asked to submit to that body opinions on such wide-ranging topics as the legality of treaties,[2] the validity of assertions made in a treatise concerning the Hanseatic towns,[3] and the legal implications of granting political asylum to a prince of the Holy Roman Empire.[4]

If a civilian had become a member of Doctors' Commons and had demonstrated his competence as an advocate, he might rise higher in the central government to a position that offered more continuous employment than the diplomatic service. There were, of course, occasional openings in the judgeships of the courts of the Archbishop of Canterbury and of the High Court of Admiralty. There was also an opportunity to serve as the King's Advocate, or prosecutor, in the same courts.[5] In addition, usually half of the Masters in Chancery, who conducted hearings of cases and reported upon them to the Chancellor, were civilians.[6] The need for civil lawyers to serve in this capacity persisted in the seventeenth century despite a growing influence of the common law upon the court, especially in its forms of pleading.[7] One reason was that the decisions of the Chancellor appealed, at least in theory, to equitable principles which formed an integral part

---

[1] *HMCS* x. 96–7. See also BM, Lansdowne MS. 142, f. 455, for the argument that the civilians' profession should be protected to ensure a supply of diplomats. For the use of civil lawyers as diplomats in Europe see L. Martines, *Lawyers and Statecraft in Renaissance Florence* (Princeton, N.J., 1968), pp. 311–15.

[2] See, for example, *APC 1616–1617*, pp. 302–3.

[3] *APC 1597–1598*, p. 175.   [4] BM, Lansdowne MS. 160, ff. 73–5.

[5] *HMCS* xii. 492; xvi. 244–5; PRO, E 403/2455, f. 25; SP 14/154/74; SP 16/117/77.

[6] Prior to this period, a majority of masters had been civilians. George Carew, 'A Treatise of the Masters of the Chauncerie', *A Collection of Tracts Relative to the Law of England* (ed. F. Hargrave, London, 1788), p. 309. But see *NRS* vii. 587. For a list of masters, see PRO, index 16818, p. 45.

[7] W. J. Jones, *The Elizabethan Court of Chancery* (Oxford, 1967), p. 301; D. E. C. Yale (ed.), *Lord Nottingham's 'Manual of Chancery Practice' and 'Prolegomena of Chancery and Equity'* (Cambridge, 1965), p. 49.

of the civil law.[1] Civilians, therefore, could contribute to these decisions more competently than the common lawyers.[2] Moreover, the whole purpose of a trial in Chancery was the same as in a civil law court—to discover all the facts of a case, rather than to determine the validity of only one legal issue, as was the custom in the common law courts.[3]

Like the masterships in Chancery, the four masterships of the Court of Requests were divided between civilians and common lawyers. The civil lawyers were necessary for the smooth functioning of the court because its procedure was 'altogether according to the process of summary causes in the civil law',[4] and because its decisions, like those in Chancery, were based partially upon equity. Common lawyers, however, always sat with the civilians because the cases heard in this court were often similar to those litigated at the common law.[5]

Since the masterships of Requests and the other positions at the centre of government were so attractive, and since the civilians did not hold a monopoly over all of them, those seeking to secure such appointments could not simply rely upon their professional experience as civil lawyers.[6] They also had to call upon powerful patrons to represent their interests to the King. The higher one rose at Court, the more he needed such assistance. Julius Caesar, by far the most successful of the early seventeenth-century civil lawyers, utilized in the course of his long career the influence of Lord Burghley, Sir Francis Walsingham, Bishop Aylmer of London, Lord Admiral Howard, and David Lewis, the Judge

---

[1] Jones, *Chancery*, p. 301, claims that the appeal to equity was deceptive. See also Ogilvie, *King's Government*, pp. 92–3; Wiseman, *Law of Lawes*, pp. 161, 173.

[2] Ridley, *A View*, p. 275.   [3] Yale, *Nottingham*, p. 50.

[4] I. S. Leadam, *Select Cases in the Court of Requests* (Selden Society, xii, 1898), p. xxi.

[5] The masterships were usually divided evenly between the members of the two professions except during the latter years of James I's reign. T. Smith, *The Commonwealth of England* (London, 1589), p. 129; Ogilvie, *King's Government*, p. 88. For a complete list see Leadam, *Select Cases*, p. cvii.

[6] One applicant, for example, could not secure the post vacated by Daniel Dun even though he wrote: 'For my qualifications thereunto I have been these thirty five years a student of the civil law, languages, and other humane learnings requisite for such a place.' PRO, SP 14/93/131.

of the Admiralty Court.[1] Edward Stanhope, Thomas Ridley, and Thomas Crompton were all protégés of Archbishop Bancroft, while Christopher Parkins thanked the Cecils for every opportunity given to him.

A civilian did not require this type of patronage to obtain membership in certain conciliar courts which took the form of royal commissions. Either the prestige derived from the offices that they held or their legal expertise by itself placed a premium upon their services. Thus civilians were employed regularly on the High Court of Delegates, a commission of variable membership which passed final judgment on appeals from the ecclesiastical and Admiralty courts. While common lawyers were joined in equal numbers with the civilians for cases of major importance, the latter handled the bulk of the court's work by themselves.[2] The repertory books of the Delegates reveal that groups of five or six civilians, always members of Doctors' Commons and for the most part regular practitioners in the Court of the Arches, dominated the proceedings of the court.[3]

The commissions for ecclesiastical causes for both Canterbury and York, known collectively in each province as the Court of High Commission, developed almost as heavy a reliance upon civil lawyers. The commissions included all the high-ranking men of state, including the justices of the common law courts,[4] but the day-to-day hearings of these bodies devolved upon smaller groups of members known in each commission as the quorum. Since the main purpose of the commissions was to inquire into deviations from ecclesiastical conformity, the quorums almost invariably included civilians.[5] Indeed, the civil lawyers became as closely

---

[1] L. M. Hill, 'The Public Career of Sir Julius Caesar, 1584–1614' (Univ. of London, Ph.D. thesis, 1968), pp. 7, 8, 10, 17–18, 175.

[2] G. I. Duncan, 'The Court of Delegates' (Cambridge, Ph.D. thesis, 1964), pp. 312–13; PRO, SP 16/350/82, p. 5.

[3] PRO, DEL 8/70, passim; Duncan, 'Delegates', p. 312.

[4] R. G. Usher, The Rise and Fall of the High Commission (Oxford, 1913), pp. 307, 345–61.

[5] Civilians usually comprised more than one-third of the quorum. See S. R. Gardiner (ed.), Reports of Cases in the Courts of Star Chamber and High Commission (Camden Soc. n.s. xxxix), passim. P. Tyler, 'The Ecclesiastical Commission for the Province of York 1561–1641' (Oxford D.Phil. thesis, 1967), p. 163, describes the

identified with the commissions as with the courts which were properly their own. It is noteworthy that of the ten commissioners whom the House of Commons impeached in 1641 for their earlier proceedings against John Bastwick, seven were civilians.[1]

Civil lawyers held a much smaller share of the various academic and clerical posts which they staffed occasionally. They alone, of course, filled the professorships of law at the universities and at Gresham College. But civilians were distinctly in the minority as college masters, wardens, and presidents and as members of the ecclesiastical hierarchy. Since their legal education and training did not prepare them specifically for these offices, they were in no special demand. Their only qualification was their advanced academic standing or their professional distinction. Thus many civilians secured prebends and rectories merely by virtue of diocesan chancellorships they held as well.

(d) *Effects of office-holding*

With such a wide range of occupational opportunities, civil lawyers rarely restricted themselves to the sole occupation of advocacy, whether in the London courts of the Archbishop of Canterbury or in the diocesan consistory courts.[2] Not only did civilians usually accept at least one legal, academic, or ecclesiastical position to supplement their practice as advocates, but they also served as substitutes or surrogates to the judges of the courts in which they pleaded.[3] This is most important in assessing the character of the civilians' profession. For advocates, like counsellors in the common law courts, were not technically officers of the courts in which they practised, as were the judges, registrars,

usual membership of the quorum at York. W. Barlow, *The Summe and Substance of the Conference* (London, 1604), pp. 87–8, suggests that the reason for so many Doctors of Laws sitting 'at ordinary times' was that the Archbishop could command their attendance more easily than he could that of more prominent men.

[1] PRO, SP 16/477/62. The seven were Juxon, Marten, Lambe, C. Caesar, Brent, Eden, and Aylett. The three non-civilians were Archbishop Laud, William Bray, and John Wragg. See also Bodl., Tanner MS. 65, f. 82ᵛ.

[2] A number of civilians practised as advocates in the consistory courts at York and Norwich. See Marchant, *Church Under Law*, pp. 247–51; *The Registrum Vagum of Anthony Harison*, i (Norwich Record Society, xxxii, 1963), 28.

[3] See for example LPL, Laud Register, i, ff. 226ᵛ–228.

proctors, and attorneys.[1] At least theoretically, advocates were professionally independent and served only the clients whom they represented and from whom they received an 'honorarium', as opposed to a contracted salary or fee.[2] As advocates, therefore, civilians were not members of the Court, since they were not subject to an administrative or legal superior within the King's government. But by combining their primary function of pleading with the variety of offices discussed above, all but nine of the 200 civil lawyers did indeed become members of the Court. Like Francis James, they filled 'those poor, troublesome, and wearisome places . . . in the government of the Church or Commonwealth'[3] and thus became economically dependent upon and administratively subordinate to high-ranking members of the King's government or of the English Church.

The relationship between the civilians and their superiors first became apparent at the time of the lawyers' appointment to office. The Archbishop of Canterbury personally selected all the judges of his courts, while his direct subordinates, the bishops, appointed chancellors and commissaries for their respective jurisdictions. Bishops also confirmed the appointments of officials of archdeacons, which were made originally by the archdeacons themselves.[4] The Lord Chancellor named the masters in his court, while the Lord Admiral appointed the Judge of the High Court of the Admiralty. The Privy Council assigned all diplomats to their specific missions, and the King himself chose the Masters of Requests, university professors, and Privy Councillors. Indeed, only a few rectories in the hands of lay patrons and the offices in the university colleges and halls, which were filled by a vote of the fellows, lay outside the control of these great men of state or their immediate subordinates. As it was, the King or one of the bishops controlled the patronage to many of the benefices granted to the civilians; and a royal veto of the election of Gabriel Harvey

---

[1] Holdsworth, *History of Law*, vi. 434–5.

[2] See J. H. Baker, 'Counsellors and Barristers: an historical study', *Cambridge Law Journal*, 27 (1969), 225–9.

[3] PRO, will of James, PROB 11/127/43.

[4] See the appointments of Robert Mason as Commissary and Official of the Archdeaconry of Surrey. HRO, Register of Bishop Neile, ff. 19ᵛ, 198, 198ᵛ.

as Master of Trinty Hall suggests that royal influence was not lacking at the universities either.

Once they had received their appointments, civilians executed the duties of their offices as servants and as direct representatives of those who were responsible for their employment. Diplomats, for example, stood completely at the command of the Privy Council, which expected them to adhere to their instructions with 'diligence, discretion and zeal' to His Majesty's service.[1] The Judge of the Admiralty Court was considered above all a servant of the Lord Admiral,[2] and he often received instructions from the Privy Council.[3] Judges of local Admiralty courts also took direct orders from the Privy Council. Dr. George Newman, the Judge of the Admiralty Court of the Cinque Ports at Dover, received instructions in 1625 to discover the location of six chests of Spanish silver illegally taken from a ship and to deliver the money to the King.[4]

In similar fashion archbishops, bishops, and archdeacons directed the activities of their ecclesiastical judges. In 1627 the five civilian judges of the Archbishop of Canterbury's courts were reminded to be 'attendant and obedient' to archiepiscopal authority.[5] Sir Charles Caesar, Judge of the Court of Audience, later demonstrated his compliance with these instructions by revoking an inhibition that happened to meet with Archbishop Laud's disapproval.[6] The same obedience was expected of diocesan chancellors. A series of reports from Robert Redman, LL.D., the Chancellor of Norwich, to Bishop John Jegon of that diocese concerning the interrogation of a separatist, betrays a subservient compliance on the part of the civilian to the wishes of his episcopal superior.[7] Since a recommendation of an appropriate punishment

---

[1] *APC 1616–1617*, p. 268.

[2] K. Andrews, *Elizabethan Privateering* (Cambridge, 1964), p. 30.

[3] *APC 1613–1614*, pp. 12, 80–1; *1615–1616*, pp. 18–19; *1621–1623*, p. 203; R. G. Marsden, *Documents Relating to the Law and Custom of the Sea*, i (Naval Records Society, xlix), 281, 301–2; Andrews, *Privateering*, pp. 22–31.

[4] *APC 1625–1626*, p. 95.   [5] PRO, SP 16/80/72.

[6] *CSPD 1634–1635*, p. 410.

[7] CUL MS. Mm. VI. 58/7, ff. 5, 6, 10, 12, 14. For other examples of how civilians served their bishops see *CSPD 1631–1633*, p. 352; *1639*, p. 69.

for the accused from Archbishop Abbot is included among these reports, it is obvious that the line of command in which Redman stood originated at the very centre of government and at the head of the Church. The civilians who served as Commissioners for Ecclesiastical Causes found themselves in a similar position of subordination.[1] It is no wonder that Dr. Clement Corbett, a later Chancellor of Norwich and a member of the High Commission as well, should think that he and Bishop Matthew Wren of Norwich were 'but his Grace's [the Archbishop's] agents'.[2]

Regardless of where or in what capacities civilians performed the duties of their offices, they almost invariably served the interests and upheld the policies of those members of the central government upon whom they depended for their livelihood. When in the course of their work the civil lawyers confronted challenges to the authority of these superiors, their professional attachment and loyalty to them became even more manifest. Dr. John Burman, the Judge of the Vice-Admiralty Court in Norfolk, met such a test while holding court in the town of Lynn, where the inhabitants were trying to exclude the authority of the Lord Admiral completely from their precincts. In accordance with instructions from the Lord Admiral to the Vice-Admiral of that county, Burman had summoned jurors from Lynn and from parts of the neighbouring coast to appear at St. George's Hall to make presentments of all who had transported corn overseas during the previous eight months. As they were about to proceed, however, the Lord Mayor of the town, Mr. William Girlinge,

came in and directed the jurors there not to present any offence committed within their supposed liberties; whereby the people, being an hundred in number or more, were much amazed and many of them disordered, and the judge being somewhat affrighted with this tumult and uproar *acquainted the said Mayor that he was about Her Majesty's*

[1] Usher, *High Commission*, p. 307.

[2] Bodl., Tanner MS. 68, f. 7. Dr. Arthur Duck and Dr. John Lambe were also referred to by their opponents as 'Canterbury's agents'. See W. Senior, 'The Advocates of the Court of Arches', *Law Quarterly Review*, 39 (1923), 505. Archbishop Bancroft considered Dr. Francis James, the Chancellor of Bath and Wells, his main representative, in the diocese during the metropolitan visitation. LPL, Bancroft Register, f. 181ᵛ.

service and told him that he greatly wondered how he durst offer such a disturbance in the execution thereof.[1]

Burman could not override the authority of the Mayor, who quickly threatened to disfranchise any juror who made a presentment. Consequently the court failed to fulfil its prescribed function.

Burman's efforts to uphold the Lord Admiral's authority in the face of such local resistance helps to illustrate how firm a commitment service to the Crown one's membership in 'the Court' could foster. The civilians acquired a 'civil servant' mentality. Even when they held local office civilians became so involved in the effective representation of royal authority in its various forms that it became difficult for them to countenance any local or regional alternative to that authority. George Newman, who served as the judge of the most independent of all minor jurisdictions—the Admiralty Court of the Cinque Ports—could not accept the claims of autonomy raised in the court's favour. When some residents of the ports asserted that according to their chartered municipal liberties the Lord Admiral could not exercise any power within the jurisdiction of their towns, Newman argued convincingly that the claim was originated by 'a factious person at Romney' about 1611 and could not be upheld by ancient precedents.[2] Newman was still as much the servant of the Lord Admiral as he was the judge for the Warden of the Cinque Ports.

(e) *Isolation from the Country*

The civilians' attachment to the central government did more than place a few of their number, such as Burman and Newman, in conflict with men who were jealous of their local privileges. It isolated nearly all the members of the profession from the large and politically influential division of English society referred to as 'the Country'—those landed families who were not tied to the

---

[1] BM, Lansdowne MS. 142, ff. 137ᵛ–138. No date is given, but the incident occurred sometime between 1600 and 1603.

[2] PRO, SP 14/86/83. Two other civilians, Thomas Ryves and Richard Zouch, sought to restrict encroachments upon the Admiralty jurisdiction by towns and lords of manors on the sea. SP 16/238/38.

King by holding offices of profit in his government. This isolation was as much a social and physical segregation as it was an incompatibility of attitudes and priorities. For the civilians usually appeared to the country gentry as outsiders, men without local roots who did not share in their interests or style of life. Many civil lawyers did not even own land, and few of those who did actually resided on their property. The reasons for this isolation were that the civilians' occupations often pulled them away from their native counties and then made such great demands on their time that they could not lead the life of country gentlemen, a privilege that those who owned land were entitled to enjoy. Unlike practising barristers, who were able to become active in country society during the law-term vacations, civil lawyers stood at the continual call of their superiors.

Sir William Bird was one such busy civil lawyer and courtier. He spent most of his time proving wills as Judge of the Prerogative Court of the Archbishop of Canterbury and acting as a Master in Chancery, but he also served as an advocate in the Admiralty Court, a regular member of the Court of Delegates, and an occasional commissioner for piracy and Admiralty criminal causes in the home counties.[1] Moreover, as a Master in Chancery he was from time to time engaged in such administrative tasks as releasing prisoners from the Tower, discharging ships from arrest, and doing 'such other things which concern the King's own affairs'.[2] Although Bird was the son of an Essex gentleman[3] and maintained an estate of his own at Walthamstow in that county, he was 'driven to reside in London' with his family because his duties there required his presence 'almost all the year long'.[4] The only use he had for his country home was as a vacation retreat 'for some few weeks during the year'. The rest of the time it was more of a nuisance than an asset, since, by virtue of the land he held, Bird was required to appear periodically in the county muster to

[1] PRO, index 16818, p. 45, no. 91; HCA 24/70-6, *passim*; DEL 8/70, pt. 1, ff. 4-12ᵛ; C 181/1, ff. 122-3; 181/2, ff. 10-10ᵛ, 101-101ᵛ, 213, 219-20, 296-7; HCA 1/32/1, ff. 29, 38, 55, 90.

[2] Carew, 'A Treatise', p. 309.

[3] R. Braybrooke, *The History of Audley End* (London, 1836), p. 292.

[4] PRO, SP 14/152/71.

show his horse and armour. His request to be relieved of this cumbersome duty indicates the extent of his interested involvement in the landed society of Essex.[1]

For all those civilians who, like Sir William Bird, were actively employed in London, a residence there or in the vicinity was an absolute necessity. Unmarried advocates often found it convenient to lease chambers at Doctors' Commons for a period of twenty-one years. If rooms were still available, married civilians could also take up lodgings there, but not with their wives.[2] The married ones, therefore, usually kept a second London residence for their families. Sir Henry Marten had a house on Aldersgate Street, Sir Arthur Duck a mansion at Chiswick, and Thomas Edwards a residence in Fulham.[3] Those who did not lease chambers at Doctors' Commons very often lived in the immediate vicinity. This allowed them to be near the courts in which they practised and to join their fellow civilians for meals at Doctors' Commons. Nathaniel Brent, for example, lived on Aldersgate Street, while John Hone, who owned property in many parts of London, resided in the parish of St. Benet, Paul's Wharf.[4] Altogether, ninety-seven civil lawyers, or nearly half the profession, maintained their principal residence in London.

London, however, was not the only drawing card. Those who wished to pursue academic careers naturally stayed on at Oxford and Cambridge after completing their degrees, while aspiring clerics often accepted the best available benefices irrespective of location. The same was true of those civilians who became chancellors of dioceses and commissaries for archdeaconries, although some bishops and archdeacons did take care to appoint civilians who had some connection with the areas in which they exercised

[1] PRO, SP 14/152/71.

[2] Chandler, 'Doctors' Commons', pp. 8–9. Because their wives were not allowed, there arose the practice of dispensing a civilian to be 'out of Commons' when his wife was 'in town'. See Doc. Com. Treas. Bk., ff. 83ᵛ, 85ᵛ, 87ᵛ, *et passim*.

[3] *CSPD 1631–1633*, p. 118; W. Notestein (ed.), *The Journal of Sir Simonds D'Ewes* (New Haven, Conn., 1923), p. 173; PRO, will of Duck, PROB 11/208/103; will of Edwards, PROB 11/133/40.

[4] PRO, will of Brent, PROB 11/229/222; C 142/660/54; *CSPD 1635*, p. 588; PRO, will of Hone, PROB 11/128/122; *Al. Cant.* ii. 401.

jurisdiction. This was especially true for London, Norwich, and Bangor dioceses.[1]

The net result of this mobility was a considerable amount of physical dislocation and social adjustment for the civilians. Table 2 illustrates the extent of this dislocation. It indicates both the number of civil lawyers who are known to have come from the various counties of England and Wales and the number from each county who spent either all or a portion of their professional careers in their native counties.

TABLE 2

GEOGRAPHIC ORIGINS AND MOBILITY OF CIVIL LAWYERS

County	Civilians originating therein	Retained primary residence	Retained secondary residence
Bedfordshire	1	–	–
Berkshire	8	–	–
Buckinghamshire	2	–	–
Cambridgeshire	4	1	–
Cheshire	1	–	1
Cornwall	1	–	–
Cumberland	2	–	–
Derbyshire	–	–	–
Devon	6	1?	1
Dorset	6	–	3
Durham	1	–	–
Essex	17	3	4
Gloucestershire	3	–	1
Hampshire	5	1	–
Herefordshire	5	2	2
Hertfordshire	3	–	–
Huntingdon	–	–	–
Kent	7	2	–
Lancashire	2	–	–
Leicestershire	1	–	–
Lincolnshire	6	–	3

[1] See the biographies of Aylett and Stanes (London), C. Talbot and Corbett (Norwich), and Griffith, J. Lloyd, and W. Merrick (Bangor).

TABLE 2 *(cont.)*

County	Civilians originating therein	Retained primary residence	Retained secondary residence
Middlesex	19	15	2
Norfolk	9	3	4
Northamptonshire	6	–	2
Northumberland	1	–	–
Nottinghamshire	1	–	–
Oxfordshire	3	1	2
Rutland	–	–	–
Shropshire	3	–	–
Somerset	4	–	–
Staffordshire	4	–	1
Suffolk	4	1	–
Surrey	–	–	–
Sussex	2	–	1
Warwickshire	3	–	–
Westmoreland	–	–	–
Wiltshire	5	–	3
Worcestershire	4	–	1
Yorkshire	7	–	5
Anglesey	7	–	4
Brecknock	1	–	–
Cardiganshire	1	–	–
Carmarthenshire	2	–	1
Caernarvonshire	1	–	–
Denbighshire	2	–	–
Flintshire	1	–	1
Glamorgan	1	–	1
Merioneth	–	–	–
Monmouthshire	–	–	–
Montgomeryshire	3	–	–
Pembrokeshire	–	–	–
Radnorshire	–	–	–
Ireland	1		
Continent	3		
Unknown	21		

Only thirty civilians in all continued to maintain their principal residence in the counties of their origin, and half of these were from Middlesex. Another forty-three maintained a partial connection with the areas from which they came. This means that 106 of the 179 civilians for whom information is available became completely severed from the society they had known as youths. It is true that geographic mobility was hardly a rare phenomenon in England at this time.[1] But the high incidence of it among the civilians provides one illustration how difficult it was for members of the Court to establish a rapport with country families.

Once civil lawyers became situated in the areas of their employment, whether in London or in the provinces, they did of course have the opportunity to establish new connections with country gentry families. The more prosperous among them could do this most easily by purchasing land in the counties, as no fewer than seventy-two actually did. Yet all too often civilians regarded their acquisitions mainly as economic investments and not as places of residence. The purchase of land did nothing to change their style of life or to re-orient their interests. It did not make them any more a part of the Country or any less a part of the Court. The only social effect it had was to give real substance to the social status which they had acquired upon the completion of their doctorates. For all Doctors of Civil Law, like barristers at the common law, were officially entitled 'esquire'—a rank reserved otherwise for the heads of landed families that were permitted to display and wear coats of armour.[2] Among lawyers the title was strictly honorary, and it could not be passed on to the next generation. Only by buying enough land could civilians make permanent the status they had achieved professionally, and ensure that their heirs would remain in the same social class into which they themselves had risen.

Sir Thomas Crompton was one London civilian who did just this by purchasing land in Staffordshire. As mentioned above,

---

[1] E. E. Rich, 'The Population of Elizabethan England', *Economic History Review*, 2nd ser. 2 (1949), 260.

[2] Aylmer, *King's Servants*, p. 261. See also John Selden, *Titles of Honor* (3rd ii (Oxford, 1796), 281.

Crompton had failed to inherit his father's lands and was therefore not able, like his elder brother, to become an independent country gentleman. Instead he took a doctorate in civil law at Oxford, entered Doctors' Commons, and rose to become one of the most successful members of the profession. In the course of his career he served as both Elizabeth's and James I's Advocate for Foreign Causes in the Admiralty Court, Chancellor of the diocese of London, Master in Chancery, Judge of the Admiralty Court, and Member of Parliament. While these positions required his almost continual presence in London, Crompton invested his capital in lands and manors at Millwich and Creswell in Staffordshire. By virtue of his title to the Millwich estate, he was granted a coat of arms, which made him an esquire in the fullest sense of the word. Although Crompton himself was never able to spend much time on his lands, his investments made it possible for his sons John and Thomas to live on the two estates as integral members of landed society.[1]

Other London civilians who were able to accumulate sufficient capital from the profits of office used it in the same way as did Crompton. Thomas Ridley, a Master in Chancery and Vicar-General to the Archbishop of Canterbury, bought lands and manors in Hampshire and Worcestershire while he took leases to others in Berkshire and Middlesex.[2] Sir Julius Caesar invested his vast fortune in Lincolnshire, Middlesex, and Hertfordshire.[3] Arthur Duck purchased lands in Somerset and Dorset,[4] and Nicholas Steward established a family estate in Hampshire.[5] For all of these lawyers land was of tremendous economic and social value; but it did not define their way of life. Their energies and their interests still kept them in London, áway from their country estates.

Those civilians whose main residence was situated outside the London area often found themselves just as isolated as the

---

[1] *Grantees of Arms*, i (Harl. Soc. lxvi), 66; *The Heraldic Visitations of Stafford-shire . . . 1663 and 1664* (Collections for a History of Staffordshire, v, 1885), p. 104. PRO, will of Crompton, PROB 11/113/28.

[2] *VCH Hampshire*, iii. 334; *Worcestershire*, iii. 254; *Berkshire*, iii. 104; *Middlesex*, iii. 39.

[3] PRO, C 142/560/159.

[4] PRO, will of Duck, PROB 11/208/103.   [5] PRO, C 142/499/18.

Londoners from the country gentry. One reason was that economic success, the prerequisite for a lawyer's entrance into landed
society, was less common among the civil lawyers who were
employed mainly in the dioceses and counties. Moreover, because
of the nature of their professional duties, chancellors of dioceses
and civilians serving in academic capacities usually preferred to
reside in cathedral or university towns. Some chancellors even
managed to protest (i.e. petition) for residence in the cathedral
close—a great professional convenience as well as a mark of
ecclesiastical distinction.[1]

If non-London civilians could afford to purchase manors and
lands outside the towns, they still did not, as a rule, live on their
estates. Dr. Barnaby Gooch, for example, came into the possession
of a number of lands and manors in Lincolnshire, the county of his
origin, during the course of his career.[2] Gooch spent almost all of
his time, however, travelling back and forth between Cambridge,
where he served as Master of Magdalene College, and both Exeter
and Worcester, where he held chancellorships.[3] John Chippingdale, Commissary of the Bishop of Lincoln for Leicester and J.P.
for that county, lived in Leicester Castle, even though he owned
land in the country. 'His abode near them [the townsmen]', wrote
Sir Thomas Cave in 1604, 'greatly eases the country for the more
speedy dispatch of their occasions.'[4] William Ingram held extensive
lands throughout Yorkshire,[5] but he preferred to dwell in a house
in the cathedral city of York so that he could serve the Archbishop
more effectively.[6] Dr. Matthew Sutcliffe, Dean of Exeter, resided

[1] See W. D. Peckham (ed.), *The Acts of the Dean and Chapter of the Cathedral
Church of Chichester 1545–1642* (Sussex Record Society, lviii), no. 1083. Other
residentiaries include Corbett, Drury, Gibson, Twysden, J. Littleton, Parry, Hill,
and C. Talbot.

[2] PRO, C 142/422/47; PROB 11/149/71.

[3] In Exeter Gooch lived in the Archdeacon of Cornwall's house. Exeter
Cathedral Library, MS. 3553, f. 20. At Cambridge he was still considered a
resident. M. B. Rex, *University Representation in England 1604–1690* (New York,
1954), p. 65.

[4] *HMCS* xvi. 359.

[5] Borth. Inst., Wills 39/500ᵛ; PRO, C 142/674/77.

[6] He first lived with his brother in the ruins of the old Archbishop's palace.
A. Upton, *Sir Arthur Ingram c. 1565–1642* (London, 1961), p. 149. His will refers to
his later residence at Willskelse House.

almost all the time in the cathedral close despite his ownership of vast tracts of Devonshire real estate.[1]

Indeed, it appears that only a few of the less active or the less prominent non-London civilians ever managed regularly to live on their lands. Richard Stanes, whose sole position was Official to the Archdeacon of Middlesex, easily combined his legal duties with life on his father's estate in Essex.[2] Christopher Wyvell retired to Saffron Walden, Essex, after marrying into an established family from that locality, but at the same time he resigned his only position as Chancellor of Lincoln.[3] John Hunt spent fifteen years of retirement on his estate in Norfolk after a long career as Master in Chancery in London.[4] Sir William Vaughan lived a number of years in his native Carmarthenshire, but Vaughan was hardly a typical civilian, spending most of his time on colonial projects rather than in legal practice.

The physical isolation of so many civilians from the members of landed society who comprised the Country gave geographic expression to what was basically a division of interests and loyalties. The civilians as courtiers were spokesmen for the officers of state who were responsible for their employment. The country gentry represented the interests of the localities where they resided as well as those of the nation 'at large'. Yet despite these differences, civilians often joined these country gentry on the commissions of the peace for the English and Welsh counties, the main organs of local government. At least sixty-four of the civilians included in this study acted as J.P.s for some period of time during their careers.[5] Their inclusion within the commissions, however, does not alter their classification as courtiers. For in order to endow the

[1] Exeter Cathedral Library, MS. 3553, ff. 39, 45ᵛ, 49; PRO, will of Sutcliffe, PROB 11/156/94.

[2] Morant, *Essex*, i, pt. 2, p. 130; Quintrell, 'Government of Essex', pp. 150-1.

[3] See the biographical dictionary.

[4] PRO, will of Hunt, PROB 11/157/56.

[5] The names of all J.P.s during this period are not known. I have relied upon BM, Add. MS. 38,139; PRO, C 193/12/2; C 193/13/1-2; SP 16/212; and the lists included in J. H. Gleason, *The Justices of the Peace in England 1558 to 1640* (Oxford, 1969). Commissioners of the peace for boroughs and liberties are listed in PRO, C 181/2-3. Of the sixty-four civil lawyers, five were J.P.s only for boroughs or liberties.

commissions with maximum prestige and authority, the government appointed as members not only country gentlemen, but also
dignitaries, courtiers, churchmen, lawyers, and merchants.[1] Thus
some civilians were named to the commissions because they were
the chancellors of the dioceses wherein the counties lay; others
because they were prominent officials who owned land in those
counties. It seems, moreover, that a number of civil lawyers
became J.P.s during the reign of James in pursuance of a plan to
include on each commission at least one person who was familiar
with civil law procedure.[2]

A similar need for the civilians' professional knowledge explains
why seventy-two of the civilians under discussion were included
in various commissions of piracy, which resembled the commissions of the peace in composition.[3] The purpose of these commissions was to elicit from the inhabitants of the maritime
counties information concerning the activities of unlicensed ships,
the sale of illegal prizes, and the value of pirates' property.[4] Although numerous country gentlemen were placed on such commissions, civilians were chosen either because of their knowledge
of maritime law or by virtue of their positions as deputies to
vice-admirals. In no way did their designation as commissioners
deny their status as members of the Court.

(f) Court politics

Attachment to the Court characterized the civilians' political
standing as M.P.s. Thirty of the civil lawyers included in this study
were elected to seats in the House of Commons before the Civil
War, and all but one, William Awbrey, actually sat.[5] Even in this
parliamentary capacity the civilians retained a close association

---

[1] Gleason, *Justices*, p. 49.   [2] Ibid., p. 214.

[3] PRO, C. 181–5, *passim*. When such commissions were issued for London and
the home counties, all active members of Doctors' Commons were listed as
participants.

[4] For a set of instructions to these commissioners see BM, Lansdowne MS. 146,
ff. 13ᵛ–14. See also Lansdowne MS. 145, f. 325.

[5] Awbrey's election for Cardigan borough in 1601 was contested, and it
appears that he never took his place. W. R. J. Williams, *The Parliamentary History
of the Principality of Wales* (Brecknock, 1895), p. 37.

with those men who in professional life were their official superiors. These connections are indicated in Table 3, which lists the patrons or dominant influences in the election of each civil lawyer.[1] The fifty-four different seats for which the thirty civil lawyers were returned may be divided into the following broad categories of patronage:[2]

Episcopal nomination	9
Court influence	25
Families with some court connections	3
Non-Court influence	5
University elections	9
No apparent influence	3

Since university elections were controlled either by the King or by high university officials,[3] the preponderance of court influence in the placement of civilians in the House was overwhelming. It contributes to an understanding of the civilians' inclusion within the royal or court faction in Parliament[4] and their consistent support for the policies of the Crown and the Church during its sessions.

Nomination by a Privy Councillor or the Archbishop of Canterbury to sit for a certain borough did not by itself determine the civil lawyers' political behaviour. Parliamentary patronage simply reinforced political attitudes and goals which the civilians' professional attachment to their superiors had already helped to cultivate. Indeed, court patrons often selected civilians on the very assumption that a predisposition in favour of the interests of the

[1] In determining patronage for Elizabethan parliaments I have relied largely on the biographies of M.P.s in the possession of the History of Parliament Trust. Professor John Gruenfelder suggested a number of patrons of seventeenth-century elections.

[2] When more than one civilian sat for the same seat at different times, I have counted the seat once for each incumbent. Re-election to the same seat, however, does not figure in the tabulation.

[3] Rex, *University Representation*, p. 57.

[4] D. H. Willson, *Privy Councillors in the House of Commons 1604-29* (Minneapolis, 1940), pp. 106-9, and T. L. Moir, *The Addled Parliament of 1614* (Oxford, 1958), Appendix IV, include civil lawyers in their description of the composition of this faction or 'Official Group' in the Commons.

TABLE 3

ELECTION OF CIVIL LAWYERS TO PARLIAMENT

Name	Seat	Year	Patron or probable influence
Awbrey, W.	Cardigan	1601	No apparent influence
Bennet, J.	Ripon	1597, 1604	Archbishop of York
	York	1601	,, ,,
	Oxford Univ.	1614, 1621	
Bird, W.	Oxford Univ.	1608	
Caesar, C.	Weymouth and Melcombe Regis	1614	Thomas Howard, 3rd Viscount Bindon, Court
Caesar, J.	Reigate	1588	Charles Howard, Earl of Nottingham, Court
	Bletchingley	1593	,, ,,
	New Windsor	1597, 1601	,, ,,
	Westminster	1610	Court influence
	Middlesex	1614	,, ,,
	Malden	1621	Nominated himself
Chaworth, R.	Midhurst	1640 (Nov.)	Perhaps Francis Browne, 3rd Viscount Montague, Court
Chippingdale, J.	Leicester	1588	Earl of Huntingdon, Court
Crompton, T.	Shaftesbury	1589	Earl of Pembroke, Court
	Boroughbridge	1597	Robert Cecil, Court
	Whitchurch	1601	Episcopal influence
	Oxford Univ.	1604	
Duck, A.	Minehead	1624, 1640 (Apr.)	Prob. Bishop of Bath and Wells
Dun, D.	Taunton	1601	Archbishop of Canterbury
	Oxford Univ.	1604, 1614	
Eden, T.	Cambridge Univ.	1626, 1628, 1640 (Apr., Nov.)	
Farmery, J.	Lincoln	1640 (Apr.)	Perhaps Earl of Rutland
Fletcher, G.	Winchelsea	1584	Lord Warden Cobham and Privy Council
Gooch, B.	Cambridge Univ.	1621, 1625	
Hickman, H.	Northampton	1601	No apparent influence
Hussey, S.	Wareham	1601	Sampson and Strode families
Herbert, J.	Grampound	1586	Lady Warwick, Court family
	Gatton	1588	Court influence. Perhaps Charles Howard, Earl of Nottingham

TABLE 3 (cont.)

Name	Seat	Year	*Patron or probable influence
Herbert, J.	Christchurch	1593	Earl of Huntingdon, Court
	Bodmin	1597	Cecil
	Glamorganshire	1601	Herbert family influence
	Monmouthshire	1604	,, ,,
James, F.	Dorchester	1593	Episcopal influence
	Corfe Castle	1597	Cecil
	Minehead	1601	George Luttrell
	Wareham	1604	Prob. Thomas Howard, 3rd Viscount Bindon, Court
Jones, G.	Wareham	1640 (Apr.)	Perhaps Theophilus Howard, Earl of Suffolk, Court
Marten, H.	St. Germans	1625, 1626	Sir John Eliot, Court in 1625 only
	Oxford Univ.	1628	
	St. Ives	1640 (Apr.)	Court influence
Master, R.	Cricklade	1601	Cecil or Sir George Gifford, M.P.
Mountlowe, H.	Cambridge Univ.	1604	
Newman, G.	Dover	1601	No apparent influence
	Canterbury	1614, 1621	Archbishop of Canterbury
Parkins, C.	Ripon	1597, 1601	Cecil
	Morpeth	1604	,,
Parry, G.	St. Mawes	1640 (Apr., Nov.)	Bishop of Exeter
Ridley, T.	Chipping Wycombe	1586	Bishop Day of Winchester
	Lymington	1601	Earl of Nottingham, Court
Stanhope, E.	Marlborough	1584, 1586	Earl of Hertford
Steward, N.	Cambridge Univ.	1604	
Swale, R.	Higham Ferrers	1589	Sir Christopher Hatton, Court
Zouch, R.	Hythe	1621, 1624	Lord Zouch, Warden of Cinque Ports

King and the Church could be taken for granted. The government successfully engineered the election of Sir Julius Caesar for Westminster in 1610 and Middlesex in 1614 because Caesar was a Privy Councillor and hence would speak for the King and garner support for his cause in the House.[1] Caesar's extra-parliamentary service, like that of so many other civilian M.P.s, had already shaped his political allegiances before nomination and election.

As members of the House of Commons the civilians displayed remarkably consistent support for the Church and the Crown. They readily defended the ecclesiastical hierarchy by opposing bills against pluralities and non-residence, against the powers of ecclesiastical courts, and against abuses in Church government.[2] In questions of temporal concern, they kept the King's interests at heart. During the debate over monopolies in 1601, for example, John Bennet warned the House not to transgress upon the royal prerogative.[3] In 1607 Sir Daniel Dun defended the King's right to remand prisoners,[4] while three years later Sir Julius Caesar opposed the Great Contract on the grounds that it would have been detrimental to the King's financial as well as to his political position.[5] In 1621 Barnaby Gooch advocated the adjournment of Parliament in order to put an end to any further discussion of grievances against the government.[6] When Sir William Fleetwood reported a bill against wrongful imprisonment in 1624, Dr. Arthur Duck objected that it would restrain the power of the Lord Admiral, 'who imprisons by course of the civil law', the Lord Marshal, and the High Commission.[7]

The deep professional involvement of the civil lawyers in the official business of the Church and the Crown offers a coherent explanation why in these and in numerous other instances civilians

[1] Willson, *Privy Councillors*, pp. 69–72, 81. In November 1621 Caesar was instructed by the King to attend Parliament daily to represent his interest there. BM, Add. MS.34,324, f. 290.

[2] See below, pp. 172–5.

[3] G. W. Prothero, *Select Statutes and Other Documents Illustrative of the Reigns of Elizabeth and James I* (Oxford, 1898), pp. 112–13. Bennet none the less objected to the monopoly of salt. See J. E. Neale, *Queen Elizabeth and Her Parliaments, 1584–1601* (London, 1958), p. 378.

[4] D. H. Willson (ed.), *The Parliamentary Diary of Robert Bowyer 1606–1607* (Minneapolis, Minn., 1931), pp. 305–6.

[5] S. R. Gardiner, *Parliamentary Debates in 1610* (Camden Society, lxxxi, 1862), pp. 175–6. See also Caesar's reasons for the dissolution of that Parliament, BM Add. MS. 34,324, f. 61. For a complete discussion of Caesar and the Great Contract see Hill, 'Caesar', pp. 285–400.

[6] See Rex, *University Representation*, p. 103. [7] *CJ* i. 738

supported the interests of the King, the Court, and the Church on the floor of the House. Yet it was not only through their activities as M.P.s that civil lawyers became identified with the Court within the House of Commons. Proceedings by the country faction against certain civilians for extortion, bribery, and other abuses of their offices achieved the same effect. One example of a Court–Country conflict involving a civil lawyer occurred in the Parliament of 1621, where Sir John Bennet, Judge of the Prerogative Court of the Archbishop of Canterbury, faced thirty different charges of corruption.[1] In return for a substantial sum, for example, Bennet had granted the administration of the possessions of one Mr. Hill, valued at £8,000, to a person who was in no way related to the deceased or to his wife. He had also engaged in such shady dealings as suppressing true wills and ordering only the partial distribution of goods. In one instance he took money from both parties which were disputing the grant of an administration of goods, and he made £252 in the process.[2] The Commons sent sixteen of the thirty charges up to the Lords, who allowed Bennet to remain under house arrest at £20,000 bail until the next session of Parliament, where he was expected to defend himself.[3] Although final action was never taken and Bennet received a royal pardon, his guilt lies beyond all reasonable doubt. As Francis Bacon wrote in an appeal to the King for his own pardon, the difference between Bennet's case and his, according to general opinion, was 'not as between black and white but as between black and grey or ash-colored'.[4] Walter Yonge noted in his diary that Bennet was as corrupt as any judge in England.[5]

In addition to Bennet, another three civilians were accused in the same Parliament as having taken unwarranted fees as Masters in Chancery,[6] while John Lambe was charged with harassing the

---

[1] *NRS* iv. 245–7.

[2] *NRS* ii. 279–82; W. Cobbett, *The Parliamentary History of England* (London, 1806–9), i. 1270–1.   [3] *NRS* vi. 404.

[4] *Cabala Sive Scrinia Sacra: Mysteries of State and Government* (London, 1691), p. 62.

[5] G. Roberts (ed.), *Diary of Walter Yonge, Esq.* (Camden Society, xli, 1848), p. 37. Yonge claimed that Bennet had £200,000 in coin.

[6] *NRS* vi. 92. The three were: W. Bird, J. Hayward, and J. Hussey.

population of Northampton and of extorting money from them.[1] Proceedings against Lambe went as far as the House of Lords, but Lambe was saved by the adjournment of Parliament. In the Parliament of 1624 and in the Long Parliament complaints were again registered against Lambe, while John Farmery, William Roane, Edmund Peirce, and Clement Corbett also came under attack on similar charges in the Long Parliament.[2] Whether all these civilians were guilty of the alleged offences is impossible to determine. The important consideration, however, is not the validity of the charges but their effect on public opinion. The civilians, whether deservedly or not, acquired a collective reputation for corruption that not only brought their entire profession into disrepute[3] but also estranged them from country gentry, who regarded themselves as morally superior to members of the Court.[4]

The civilians' service as officials in government therefore had direct political ramifications. Their close professional ties with prominent statesmen and ecclesiastics made them almost natural exponents of royalist politics, while their alleged misdeeds as law officers of the Crown and the Church intensified their alienation and isolation from the country. Yet the connection between the civil lawyers' professional status and their position in national politics is even more complex. For the civilians of the early seventeenth century aligned themselves even more closely with the King to survive a professional crisis of the most serious proportions. To the nature and extent of that crisis we now turn.

[1] Ibid. 471–3; iv. 346–7.

[2] 'Diary of Edward Nicholas, 1624', PRO, SP 14/166/217ᵛ–218; *DCSP 1641–1643*, pp. 423–4; Notestein, *D'Ewes*, p. 414.

[3] In 1641 civilians were referred to popularly as 'civil villains'. *The Spiritual Courts Epitomized* (London, 1641).

[4] See Zagorin, 'The Court and the Country', 309–10.

II

THE CRISIS OF THE PROFESSION

As the reign of Queen Elizabeth drew to a close, the civil lawyers became increasingly aware that their profession was in a state of decline.[1] Numerically it had begun to shrink, as fewer students were taking advanced degrees in the faculty of civil law at the universities. For those who did complete their degrees the opportunities to succeed to important and lucrative offices were becoming scarcer, while all those civilians who depended upon legal fees for their income feared the financial repercussions of the common lawyers' attack upon the jurisdiction of their courts. All in all, the future looked bleak for the civilians, and appeals from Puritans for the abolition of the Church courts did not boost their morale.[2] As early as 1592, Dr. Matthew Sutcliffe recognized that the Puritans' programme, if implemented, would 'overthrow the most excellent study of the civil laws, yea civility itself'.[3] In 1603 there was 'a general rumour going about the nation that the Civil Law should be put down and quite exterminated the Kingdom'.[4]

(a) The crisis at the universities

The problems of the profession were most readily apparent at Oxford and Cambridge. As Table 4 indicates, the number of students receiving doctorates in civil law had increased steadily

[1] The most explicit collective opinions by the civilians themselves are contained in Bodl., Tanner MS. 280, f. 328, no. 13, and BM, Harl. MS. 358, ff. 184–5. See also Lawson, *Law School*, p. 2; Rex, *University Representation*, p. 40.

[2] One of the most explicit was William Stoughton, *An Assertion for True and Christian Church Policy* (London, 1604), pp. 78–90; C. Hill, *Society and Puritanism*, p. 321.

[3] M. Sutcliffe, *An Answere to a Certaine Libel Supplicatorie* (London, 1592), p. 94.

[4] Anthony Wood, *The History and Antiquities of the University of Oxford* ii, (Oxford, 1796) 281.

during the early years of Elizabeth's reign,[1] and in the 1580s a bumper crop of civilians finished their studies.[2] The rise was most dramatic at Cambridge, probably because Trinity Hall had achieved a primacy within the field of civil law by this time and had become institutionally affiliated with Doctors' Commons in 1567. After 1590, however, the number of doctorates at both

TABLE 4

DEGREES IN CIVIL LAW[3]

Years	Oxford	Cambridge	Total
1551–60	13	8	21
1561–70	12	15	27
1571–80	13	22	35
1581–90	18	22	40
1591–1600	14	15	29
1601–10	11	6	17
1611–20	11	12	23
1621–30	21	6	27
1631–40	27	15	42

universities began to drop until it hit a low point in the first decade of the seventeenth century. It rose slightly during the 1610s and 1620s but did not reach the level of the mid-Elizabethan years until the 1630s, when a record number of civilians completed their degrees. Nearly two-thirds of these civil lawyers took

[1] Enrolment had been at its lowest during the 1540s and 1550s. See Malden, *Trinity Hall*, pp. 82–4, and J. B. Mullinger, *The University of Cambridge from the Royal Injunctions of 1535 to the Accession of Charles I* (Cambridge, 1884), p. 127.

[2] Holdsworth, *History of Law*, iv. 234–5, attributes the success of the civil law faculties in the latter part of the sixteenth century to the welcoming of foreign civilians into England, the studying of English civilians abroad, and the rise of Doctors' Commons.

[3] A. Clark, *Register of the University of Oxford, 1571–1622*, iii (Oxford Historical Society, xii, 1888); A. Wood, *Fasti Oxonienses* (2nd edn., London, 1815); J. and J. A. Venn, *The Book of Matriculations and Degrees 1544–1659* (Cambridge, 1913); T. Fuller, *The History of the University of Cambridge since the Conquest* (London, 1655). The records of the degrees of some Cambridge civilians are missing. The warrants for their admission to Doctors' Commons and other documents which indicate their academic status at a particular time have been used to establish the approximate dates of their doctorates.

their degrees at Oxford, perhaps because their discipline was less vulnerable to Puritan criticism there than at Cambridge.

University records, therefore, suggest that the crisis in the profession of the civil law lasted from about 1590 until approximately 1630 and reached its most critical stage during the first decade of the seventeenth century. University officials first became fully aware of the crisis shortly after James I acceded to the throne. They expressed concern that the civil law faculties 'had of late been barren of such children as they were wont to bring forth',[1] and they feared that if the decline in enrolment continued, they might have to drop the study of civil law from the curriculum and thereby undermine the traditional structure of university education.[2] There was little, however, that they could do to remedy the situation. For the cause of the decline did not lie in the quality of the civil law faculty at either university. On the contrary, Alberico Gentili, the Regius Professor of Law at Oxford since 1587, had 'quickened the dead body of the civil law written by ancient civilians' and had thereby given new life to the discipline.[3] At Cambridge, John Cowell (1594–1611) devoted his energies as Regius Professor to the reinvigoration of the civil law in order to restore it to the importance it had held in ancient Rome and medieval Europe.[4] There was little more that these men could have done to lure more students into their lecture halls.

Even if there had been room for improvement in the curriculum, it would not have affected the enrolment. For the whole purpose of taking a degree in the civil law was to become qualified for careers in the ecclesiastical and Admiralty courts or in the direct service of the King. '[I]f when they [the Doctors of Laws] have completed their studies', asked the Vice-Chancellor and Senate of Cambridge in 1603, 'there is no room in the state for the exercise

[1] BM, Harleian MS. 358, f. 184.

[2] Wood, *Antiquities*, ii. 281; BM, Cotton MS. Cleo. F II, f. 230 expresses the civilians' fear that 'that whole faculty must needs withall fall to the ground *honos ali artes*'.

[3] Mullinger, *Cambridge*, p. 425; C. E. Mallet, *A History of the University of Oxford* (London, 1924), ii. 147.

[4] S. B. Chrimes, 'The Constitutional Ideas of Dr John Cowell', *EHR* 64 (1949), 462; Holdsworth, *History of Law*, v. 20–3; Mullinger, *Cambridge*, p. 425. Mullinger's statistics concerning enrolment are erroneous.

of their profession, of what avail all their labours?'[1] Students
pursued doctorates in the civil law not to quench their thirst for
academic learning but to set themselves on 'the high road to
rewards and preferments'.[2] The more plentiful those rewards
promised to be, the more likely would students be to embark upon
the study of the civil law. The fate of the civil law as an academic
study depended almost completely upon the availability and value
of the offices for which the students were preparing themselves.[3]

The number of degrees conferred during a span of years,
therefore, serves as a fairly reliable barometer of the attraction of
the profession at that particular time. The relatively low number
of doctorates between 1591 and 1630 suggests that there were
fewer incentives for young students to become civil lawyers
during that period than immediately before or after. Indeed, at
the beginning of the seventeenth century there was general agreement that the jobs which civilians customarily filled were neither
plentiful nor profitable. A petition to the King in 1607 requested
that

some provision may be made for the better encouragement of students
of the civil laws, whose discouragements have been so many and their
hopes of late years of competent means to live by so small, that the
profession is like to be wholly mined and neglected and the church
and commonwealth in short time deprived utterly of the service of
such men.[4]

About the same time the civil lawyer Sir Thomas Ridley grimly
reflected that his profession 'doth scarce keep beggary from the
gate'.[5]

(b) *The wealth of the civilians*

What was the exact meaning of contemporaries when they referred to the poverty of the civil lawyers? What was a 'competent

---

[1] *HMCS* xvi. 39.

[2] A. Duck, *De Usu et Authoritate Juris Civilis Romanorum Per Dominia Principum
Christianorum* (London, 1679), p. 311. A translation of the section on England is
appended to C. J. Ferriere, *The History of the Roman Civil Law* (London, 1724),
p. xx. The first edition of Duck's work was 1653.

[3] Mullinger, *Cambridge*, p. 425.   [4] *HMCS* xix. 477–8.

[5] Ridley, *A View*, p. 274.

means to live by', and how many civilians found themselves in dire financial straits? There is evidence that a number of civil lawyers lived above their means and that others mismanaged their financial affairs. Sir Daniel Dun, the Dean of the Arches and Judge of the Admiralty Court, 'did not die a rich man, although he held three offices',[1] while Richard Trevor, who assisted Dun on the Admiralty Bench, reputedly 'died a very beggar'.[2] But it is doubtful whether these prominent civilians were the object of Ridley's concern. For many civil lawyers, including Dun, profited quite handsomely from their employment, even during the period of their profession's decline. Although it is impossible to calculate each civil lawyer's annual earnings, which usually included unspecified legal fees, one can gain a general impression of how much capital he was able to accumulate over an extended period of time. Since civilians tended to invest the profits they realized from their employment in land,[3] the amount of property owned by each civil lawyer provides one fairly reliable indication of his economic status. Table 5 lists all those civilians who are known to have purchased at least one manor or substantial amounts of land between 1590 and 1630, as evidenced by records of land sales, *inquisitiones post mortem*, and personal wills. When the value of a civilian's property is known it is also included. A second reliable indication of a civil lawyer's wealth is the amount of money he dispensed with in his will. Dr. J. H. Gleason has calculated that commissioners of the peace, who usually were numbered among the most prosperous members of their communities, bequeathed an average of £1,777 to their unmarried daughters during the early seventeenth century.[4] It is safe to assume that those civilians who left

[1] PRO, SP 14/93/124.

[2] N. E. McClure (ed.), *The Letters of John Chamberlain* (Philadelphia, Pa., 1939), i. 544–5. Trevor was assessed for the subsidy in 1600 at a lower figure than any other member of Doctors' Commons. PRO, E 179/146/399.

[3] Seventeen civilians invested in commerce and colonization as well as in land. See T. Rabb, *Enterprise and Empire* (Cambridge, Mass., 1967), pp. 233–410. The amounts invested are not known, although Christopher Parkins did invest more than £2,000 in the Merchant Adventurers. All but two of the seventeen civilians are included in Table 5. For full details see the biographical dictionary.

[4] Gleason, *Justices*, pp. 263–4. Wilson, *State of England*, p. 23, claimed that commissioners of the peace usually received £500 to £1,000 per annum in rents.

TABLE 5

WEALTH OF CIVIL LAWYERS 1590-1630

Name	Indication of wealth	Main positions held before 1630[1]
Alexander, F.	£1,900 in bequests	Preb.; Rector; Surrogate to Diocs. Chanc.
Belley, J.	One manor	Diocs. Chanc.; M. Chancery?
Bennet, J.	Two manors	M. Chancery; Judge of PCC; Diocs. Chanc.
Bennet, T.	One manor	Advocate
Caesar, C.	At least two manors	M. Chancery; Judge of Audience Court
Caesar, J.	Eight manors; Income of £2,000 p.a. in 1595	Judge of HCA; Master of Requests; Chancellor of Exchequer; Master of the Rolls
Carew, M.	Estate valued at more than £9,600	M. Chancery; Archdeacon
Chippingdale, J.	Two manors	Preb.; Official of Archdeacon; Advocate
Colmore, C.	Extensive lands	Diocs. Chanc.; Preb.
Corbett, C.	Two manors	Diocs. Chanc.
Cowell, J.	One manor	Regius Professor; Vicar-General of Archbishop; Official of Archdeacon
Crompton, T.	At least one manor	Judge of HCA; Diocs. Chanc.; Vicar-General of Archbishop
Drury, J.	£4,200 in bequests	Diocs. Chanc.
Duck, A.	Estate late valued at £20,000	Diocs. Chanc.; King's Advocate
Dun, D.	One manor	Judge of HCA and of Audience Court; Dean of the Arches
Eden, T.	£8,000 in bequests	M. Chancery; Diocs. Chanc.
Edwards, T.	£4,600 in bequests	Diocs. Chanc.
Gibson, J.	Two manors; £390 p.a. from lands	Diocs. Chanc.; Judge of PCC; M. Chancery
Hawley, J.	One manor	Principal; Judge of Vice-Chancellor's Court
Helme, C.	One manor	Diocs. Chanc.
Herbert, J.	At least one manor and extensive lands	Secretary of State; diplomat
Hickman, H.	One manor	Diocs. Chanc.; M. Chancery
Hunt, J.	Three manors	M. Chancery; Commissary for archdeaconry

[1] Abbreviations used in this table are as follows: Diocs. Chanc.—Chancellor of a diocese; PCC—Prerogative Court of Canterbury; HCA—High Court of Admiralty; M. Chancery—Master in Chancery; Preb.—Prebendary.

TABLE 5 *(cont.)*

Name	*Indication of wealth*	*Main positions held before 1630*
Hussey, J.	One manor	M. Chancery; Diocs. Chanc.; Commissary of Archbishop of Canterbury
James, F.	Four manors; £2,000 to daus.	M. Chancery; Diocs. Chanc.; Judge of Audience Court
Marten, H.	Ten manors	Judge of HCA and of PCC; Dean of Arches
Mason, R.	One manor	Diocs. Chanc.; Commissary for Archdeacon
Newcomb, R.	£2,300 in bequests	Commissary of two bishops
Parkins, C.	Two manors; at least £450 p.a. from land and office	Dean; Master of Requests; Diplomat
Ridley, T.	Two manors	Diocs. Chanc.; M. Chancery; Vicar General of Archbishop of Canterbury
Stanhope, E.	Six manors; estate valued at £40,000	Diocs. Chanc.; M. Chancery; Vicar-General of Archbishop of Canterbury
Steward, N.	One manor	Advocate
Sutcliffe, M.	One manor; purchased lands for £3,000	Dean; Preb.; Rector
Swale, R.	Three manors	Diocs. Chanc.; Diplomat; Auditor of Audience Court
Talbot, T.	One manor	Advocate; Judge of Vice-Admiralty Court; Official of Archdeacon

equivalent or higher amounts of capital to their daughters, or even to other relatives and friends, encountered few financial problems in their careers. Hence these civilians are included in the Table with the owners of extensive lands.

Some of the civilians acquired truly outstanding wealth. Sir Julius Caesar was probably the most prosperous. Even before he became Master of Requests and Chancellor of the Exchequer he evoked from one contemporary the observation that 'His estate of living I dare make it good to be at the least twenty hundred lib. a year; his estate otherwise in purse and goods as well as most barons I know in this land.'[1] That estate grew to enormous proportions

---

[1] BM, Add. MS. 11,406, f. 290. This was in 1595.

during his long career, and his son Charles, also a civilian, inherited the bulk of it,[1] preserved it, and added to it.[2] Charles was so well off in 1638 that he was able to pay the high sum of £15,000 for the office of Master of the Rolls, £5,000 of it in ready cash.[3] Edward Stanhope, Chancellor of London, Master in Chancery, and Vicar-General to the Archbishop of Canterbury, almost matched the Caesar fortune. Valued at £40,000,[4] the Stanhope estate included at least six manors as well as £3,300 of uninvested capital, all of which this civilian distributed meticulously in a twenty-three-page will.[5] In the same category was Sir Henry Marten, who used the profits from three judgeships to purchase ten manors in Berkshire and to establish his family at Hinton-Waldrist in that county.[6]

It is true that only a few civilians, such as the Caesars, Stanhope, and Marten, rivalled the great fortunes of the more prominent seventeenth-century common lawyers. Although no one has attempted a systematic study of the common lawyers' wealth, one H. Phillips in the late seventeenth century did compile a list of families whose fortunes had been augmented considerably through the practice of the law.[7] Among the hundreds of lawyers who received notice only two, Julius and Charles Caesar, were civil lawyers. But even if civil lawyers rarely matched the spectacular wealth of some common lawyers,[8] they do seem to have done

[1] PRO, will of Julius Caesar, PROB 11/170/34.   [2] PRO, C 142/774/20.

[3] *DNB* iii. 655. In the same year he was reported to have £2,000 on hand, which he refused to lend to the King for the campaign against the Scots. PRO, SP 16/415/4.

[4] Trevor-Roper, *The Gentry*, p. 11.

[5] PRO, C 142/300/173; C 142/310/53; PROB 11/111/22.

[6] *VCH Berks.* iii. 107, 175; iv. 457, 464, 467, 530, 533, 535, 538. Brotherton Library, Leeds, Loder-Symonds Papers, 88, ff. 1, 42; 92, f. 8. Marten was the wealthiest member of Doctors' Commons in 1639. LPL, MS. 943, p. 651.

[7] H. Phillips, *The Grandeur of the Law: or an exact Collection of the nobility and gentry of this kingdom whose honors and estates have by some of their ancestors been acquired or considerably augmented by the practice of the law or offices and dignities relating thereunto* (London, 1684).

[8] *A Looking Glass for all proud, Ambitious, Covetous and Corrupt Lawyers* (London, 1646) mentioned that it was not unusual for lawyers to make £5,000 to £10,000 p.a. Simpson, *Wealth of the Gentry*, p. 114, estimated that a very successful lawyer, Sir Nicholas Bacon, received £3,882 from his lands, office, fees, and

fairly well for themselves, especially since so few of them began their careers with large patrimonies.

Should we then discount the complaints of the civilians? Not completely, since the Table includes only thirty-five of the 140 civilians who were active professionally between 1603 and 1630. These men occupied the choicest positions open to members of their profession. As the Table indicates, nearly all of them held one or more posts in the central institutions of government or belonged to the 'bar' of active advocates in London. The remaining few were distinguished clerics or chancellors of dioceses. In effect these men comprised an élite among the Doctors of Civil Law, and some contemporaries took care to distinguish between them and their less fortunate colleagues. 'There have been and are few wealthy civilians in the land', wrote one observer in 1597, 'except such as were otherwise advanced by the Prince's service.'[1] In 1600 Thomas Wilson, a frustrated civilian who never managed to complete his doctorate, made an even more precise distinction between those civilians who secured choice positions and those who did not. In describing the entire profession Wilson remarked:

This state of all others is the weakest, they having no means but by practice in the Arches and other the Bishops of Canterbury's courts, and some small practice in some other consistories. There are of them 24 belonging to the Arches which gain well, and every Bishop hath a chancellor that liveth in some good credit, the rest, god wot, are fain to become poor Commissaries and Officials of deans and archdeacons, which ride up and down the country to keep courts for correcting of bawdy matters etc. and take great pains for small gains. Unless he chance to prove so rare man of conceit in State matters and that hath good friends in the court, and then perhaps he may be called to be a Master of the Requests or Secretary of State.[2]

Wilson might have included those civilians who pursued exclusively academic careers and those who settled for minor

annuities in 1575. A puisne judge of the Common Pleas received a minimum of £2,000 p.a. during the reign of Charles I. Aylmer, *King's Servants*, p. 210. William Lenthall made £2,500 from private practice. Keeler, *Long Parliament*, pp. 25, 250.

   [1] Bodl., Tanner MS. 280, f. 326ᵛ.   [2] Wilson, *State of England*, pp. 25–6.

ecclesiastical benefices together with the officials of archdeacons and deans. Although it is impossible to gather complete statistics concerning the wealth of all the civilians who occupied the lower ranks of the profession, few appear to have lived prosperously. Henry Mountlowe, who was appointed the first Professor of Civil Law at Gresham College and who won public recognition as M.P. for Cambridge University in James's first Parliament, was in debt in 1611 and left only one legacy of £50 at his death.[1] Even the Regius Professors of Civil Law did not receive an attractive income. Their stipend was £40 per annum.[2] Some of these academics managed to supplement their incomes by engaging in legal practice when they were not occupied at the universities. Alberico Gentili spent the last three years of his life serving as advocate in the Admiralty Court on behalf of the Spanish embassy.[3] But professors who, like Dr. George Porter, acted in no additional capacity outside the university, did not find money plentiful. Porter died £20 in debt.[4] As one contemporary observed, 'some civilians there are and have been lately of very good gifts, and otherwise furnished with all kind of good learning, that have died in poverty or yet live in poor estates'.[5]

Commissaries for archdeaconries and officials of archdeacons and deans were not much more successful than the full-time academics. The income for such officials varied from place to place. Walter Walker claimed that his two positions as Official to the Archdeacon of Leicester and Commissary for Leicester were worth £150 per annum, but this figure was cited in a lawsuit and could well have been inflated.[6] The Official of the Archdeacon of Nottingham probably did not receive more than £23

---

[1] Cambridge University Archives, will of Mountlowe, Vice-Chancellor's Court 3/209. PRO, will of John Cowell, PROB 11/118/86, which refers to Mountlowe's debt.

[2] C. H. Cooper, *The Annals of Cambridge* (Cambridge, 1842–52), i. 397; Duck, *De Usu*, p. 318, claimed that James I attached a prebend to the professorship, which Phillimore, *Ecclesiastical Law*, i. 311, identifies as Shipton.

[3] See K. R. Simmonds, 'Alberico Gentili at the Admiralty Bar 1605–1608', *Archiv des Völkerrechts* (1958), 3–23.

[4] Cambridge University Archives, will of Porter, Vice-Chancellor's Court 3/219.

[5] Bodl., Tanner MS. 280, f. 326ᵛ.   [6] *LJ* iv. 183.

per annum.[1] Such positions may have been worthwhile keeping, but by themselves they did not bring prosperity to civilians. They did not even place the incumbents within the same economic bracket as many poor country gentlemen.[2] The same could be said of the office of deputy to a vice-admiral. Deputies received slightly higher fees than officials of archdeacons, but they had to share the profits of their office with the vice-admirals themselves.[3] The office at Bristol, accordingly, was regarded as being of little value in 1635.[4] Nevertheless civilians could use the profits from such positions to supplement their other sources of income, and for this reason alone they accepted and occasionally competed for such employment.[5]

(c) *The shortage of jobs*

While it may be safe to conclude that the civilians who occupied the lower rungs of the professional ladder did not profit greatly from their work, it would be a mistake to construe the crisis that the lawyers faced as strictly financial in origin. Thomas Wilson and the civilians complained not so much that commissaries and the like were paid so poorly but that civil lawyers had to settle for such low and unremunerative positions. In the final analysis the crisis was numerical, caused by too many civilians competing for a limited supply of attractive offices. The high number of doctorates awarded in the 1570s and 1580s had swollen the ranks of the profession and made it more difficult for civil lawyers to find satisfactory employment. As early as 1576 Dr. William Awbrey, the Dean of the Arches, complained that nearly half the advocates at Doctors' Commons lacked a competent living.[6] Awbrey proposed that Archbishop Grindal alleviate the problem by restricting the membership of Doctors' Commons, and three years later Grindal issued an order that was intended to reduce the number of advocates to twenty.[7] Yet

---

[1] Marchant, *Church Under Law*, p. 160.

[2] See for example, the will of John Tuer, Official of the Archdeacon of Colchester. Greater London Record Office, DL/c/361.

[3] Marchant, *Church Under Law*, pp. 190–1.   [4] *CSPD 1635–1636*, p. 374.

[5] PRO, SP 16/326/80.   [6] Bodl.,Tanner MS. 280, f. 322ᵛ.

[7] LPL, MS. 958, pp. ix–x. See also, BM, Cotton MS. Cleo. F II, f. 166.

young civil lawyers continued to seek and to gain admission to the society. By 1587 Doctors' Commons had fifty-four fellows, fourteen more than in 1570.[1]

If the number of attractive positions open to civilians had remained fixed, the sharp reduction in the number of degrees in civil law after 1590 would have mitigated the severity of the job shortage. By 1605 the membership of Doctors' Commons had dwindled to forty-nine.[2] Yet at the very time the profession experienced a reduction in size, non-civilians began to replace civil lawyers in some of their most lucrative employments, thereby prolonging the crisis. The civilians felt the pressure most heavily in the central institutions of government. The masterships of the Court of Requests were traditionally divided evenly between common lawyers and civilians.[3] After Queen Elizabeth raised the number of masters from two to four, however, she began to appoint a majority of civil lawyers to the court.[4] The balance was clearly tipped in 1596 when Julius Caesar replaced Robert Rokeby in one of the masterships which had been earmarked for a common lawyer.[5] When the Queen died in 1603, three of the four masters were civilians.[6] James I, however, assigned no civil lawyers to the court, so that by the end of his reign common lawyers were in complete control.[7] The reason for James's policy is not certain. Charles Ogilvie suggests that it was intended to appease the common lawyers, who by the turn of the century had begun to attack the jurisdiction of the Court of Requests.[8] Whatever the reason, the effect upon the civilians was crucial. One of the choicest plums of their profession had been snatched by their rivals.

---

[1] Doc. Com. Treas. Bk., ff. 14, 42. I have counted only Doctors of Laws, not honorary members. Doctors' Commons, of course, did not include all civil lawyers, and therefore the Treasurer's Book provides only a relative rather than absolute indication of the size of the profession at a particular time.

[2] Ibid., ff. 85–85ᵛ.   [3] Smith, *Commonwealth of England*, p. 129.

[4] Leadam, *Select Cases*, p. xix. In 1631 there were five masters. See PRO, REQ 1/34, f. 3.   [5] *HMCS* vi. 215.

[6] PRO, REQ 1/21–2. These order books reveal that Caesar, Dun, Parkins, and the one common lawyer, Wilbraham, were sitting on the court at that time.

[7] For the list of James's appointments see Leadam, *Select Cases*, p. cvii; also BM, Add. MS. 25,248, ff. 8–9ᵛ.

[8] Ogilvie, *King's Government*, p. 88.

The civilians were not much more successful in retaining the
masterships in Chancery, which in the Tudor period had been
distributed almost exclusively among the members of their
profession. During the first forty years of Elizabeth's reign all but
two of the twenty-two lawyers appointed to masterships were
civil lawyers.[1] Towards the end of the sixteenth century, however,
the civilians witnessed a gradual reduction in their strength on
the Chancery bench. Of the twenty-four masters who received
appointments to the court between 1598 and 1629, sixteen were
common lawyers.[2] The growing influence of the common law
upon the forms of pleading and the decisions of the court had
called for more of a balanced representation from the two sides
of the legal profession. For the civilians this meant added dis-
couragement. The masterships in Chancery were the highest
positions to which the ordinary civilian careerists usually aspired,
and they were the expected reward of those who had become
members of the 'bar' of advocates in London. The appointment
of their rivals to the positions which had traditionally been
guaranteed to members of Doctors' Commons contributed to
their sagging fortunes.

The Privy Council recognized somewhat belatedly how serious
a blow the loss of so many masterships was to the civil lawyers. In
a meeting called in 1633 to implement all possible means 'for the
breeding up of able and sufficient professors of the Civil and Canon
Laws' and to provide them with 'reasonable comfort and encouragement' the Councillors declared

That His Majesty findeth by experience that the places in the ecclesiastical courts are not many, neither of such value as the hope thereof may
reasonably incite a sufficient number of men of eminent parts and
abilities to apply their industry to the said studies and professions; that
therefore his Majesty according to the intention of his father of ever

---

[1] A list of Elizabethan masters is in J. Haydn, *The Book of Dignities* (London,
1894), p. 395. See also Jones, *Chancery*, p. 111; Carew, 'A Treatise', p. 309.

[2] PRO, index 16818, lists the appointments enrolled on PRO C 216/1. I have
not included masters extraordinary in the computation, but there is some uncertainty as to which civilians fell into this latter group. See Jones, *Chancery*,
pp. 117–19. For one list of masters extraordinary see BM, Add. MS. 38,170,
f. 358.

blessed memory to the end the same may take effect hath resolved hereafter, he will have all places that shall become vacant of Masters of Requests to his Majesty and likewise eight of the eleven places of the Masters of the Chancery shall be supplied with men of those professions of the civil and canon laws only.[1]

The Council's directions were followed closely. Between 1633 and 1641 the Lord Chancellor named seven new Masters in Chancery, all of them civilians,[2] while the King appointed Robert Mason, a civil lawyer, to fill the one vacancy created on the Court of Requests.[3]

The Privy Council was also asked to give assistance to the civilians in the dioceses, where unqualified friends and relatives of the bishops were usurping their positions as chancellors. The root of the problem was the nepotism of a few bishops, like Francis Godwin of Llandaff, later of Hereford. Godwin proved to be the most obstinate of the civilians' enemies. Early in his episcopate at Llandaff he had, according to accepted practice, appointed a qualified civilian, Dr. Richard Trevor, to be the chancellor of his diocese, along with a Bachelor of Civil Law, one Griffins. Trevor, who was involved in other legal work in London at the time, sold the full right of his office to Griffins for £350. When Griffins died, Godwin appointed to the office his own son-in-law Robert Robotham, a divine who had a Master of Arts degree and who made a false pretence of having been a practitioner of the civil law for most of his life. After an unsuccessful attempt by Trevor to recover the office by legal action,[4] the members of Doctors' Commons petitioned James I to have Robotham removed because of his lack of legal training. James signified his displeasure to the Archbishop of Canterbury concerning this irregularity, and Godwin was forced to relieve Robotham of his duties.[5]

---

[1] BM, Add. MS. 34,324, f. 282–282ᵛ.   [2] PRO, index 16818, pp. 45–6.
[3] Leadam, *Select Cases*, p. cvii.
[4] Richard Brownlow and John Goldesborough, *Reports of Diverse Choice Cases in Law* (London, 1651), ii. 11–12; George Croke, *The Second Part of the Reports of Sir George Croke . . . during the Whole Reign of the Late King James* (2nd edn., London, 1669), p. 269; Sir Edward Coke, *Reports*, xii. 78–9.
[5] LPL, MS. 958, pp. xiv–xv.

The civilians' troubles with Godwin, however, were far from over. Ten years after Robotham's removal Godwin appointed his own son Thomas, a Bachelor of Divinity, to the chancellorship of the diocese of Hereford, the see to which Godwin had just been translated from Llandaff. The irritated civilians immediately made their complaint known to the new King, Charles I:

the said now Lord Bishop of Hereford, notwithstanding the promises, hath a second time of late preferred his own son, furnished with sundry Ecclesiastical benefices, preferments, and dignities, and altogether ignorant in the said Laws, to be Honourable Chancellor of Hereford, *being one of the best of that kind in England*.[1]

The reason for the collective concern of the civilians was the same as it was for their loss of the masterships of Requests and of Chancery. Outsiders were usurping the few lucrative positions traditionally reserved to them alone.

The King directed the Archbishop of Canterbury to install a new chancellor after he examined the case completely. He also directed him to confer with some other members of the Privy Council to decide upon some method of ensuring in the future that all offices of ecclesiastical jurisdiction be conferred upon the 'professors of the Civil Law'.[2] For the problem was more widespread than within the dioceses of Llandaff and Hereford. Bishop Cotton of Exeter had twice appointed relatives to the chancellorship of his diocese during the reign of James.[3] In Hereford Bishop Robert Bennet deprived Oliver Lloyd of his chancellorship in 1608,[4] while both Hugh Barker of Chichester[5] and John Farmery of Lincoln[6] almost suffered the same fate at the hands of their episcopal superiors. In 1624 Bishop Goodman of Gloucester appointed a divine, William Sutton, to succeed a civilian, John Seaman, as the chancellor of that diocese.

[1] Reg. Doc. Com., f. 78ᵛ.
[2] Ibid. The entry was dated 5 Dec. 1625. LPL, MS. 958, p. xv. Dr. Ryves was suggested as T. Godwin's replacement, but it is unlikely that he took the position. PRO, SP 14/214, p. 240. Dr. William Skinner, a civilian, became the chancellor of the diocese shortly thereafter.
[3] See above, p. 24, n. 1.   [4] Hatfield House, Salisbury MS. 195/22ᵛ.
[5] Richard Burn, *Ecclesiastical Law* (6th edn., London, 1797), i. 294.
[6] PRO, SP 14/124/97.

The case of Dr. Sutton called for a petition similar to that presented against Bishop Godwin, and the King's answer was identical to his previous reply.[1] The Privy Councillors, however, were lax in issuing directives concerning the appointment of future chancellors, and in 1627 the civilians again asked the King to direct the Council to take some action.[2] This time Charles made certain that the Privy Council carried out his instructions. Within the year a young civilian, Dr. Francis Baber, was appointed chancellor jointly and severally with Dr. Sutton.[3] At the same time the High Commission, which was heavily staffed by civilians, brought suit against Sutton. The defendant appealed for a prohibition, but the common law judges denied his request. In 1631 Sutton was deprived and Baber became sole chancellor.[4]

Royal intervention on behalf of the civilians naturally reinforced the political ties that existed between the civil lawyers and the monarchy. Through the action of his Privy Council, Charles I ensured that this professional group would not be driven by disappointment in the pursuit of office to consider opposition to the established government. Professor Curtis had shown how a number of ministers who, like the civil lawyers, were faced with a shortage of jobs became alienated from the established political and religious order and sought employment outside the limits of ecclesiastical control.[5] It is doubtful whether the civil lawyers could have been driven to this point of despair. At least civilians had an abundance of lowly positions which they could fall back upon when more lucrative offices eluded them. Most civilians, moreover, had the option of staying on at either Oxford or Cambridge as fellows of their colleges until they could find suitable employment in the Church or in the King's service. But even if the civilians' situation had not reached a point of desperation, the Privy Council did forestall the development of any potential

---

[1] PRO, SP 16/56/27. [2] PRO, SP 16/70/55.

[3] S. Rudder, *A New History of Gloucestershire* (Cirencester, 1779), p. 164.

[4] Sir George Croke, *Reports . . . Charles I* (London, 1657), p. 65; Burn, *Ecclesiastical Law*, i. 291.

[5] M. Curtis, 'The Alienated Intellectuals of Early Stuart England', *Past and Present*, 23 (1962), 25–43.

disaffection among the civilians and ensured their continuing loyalty to the established government.

Irrespective of its political consequences, royal intervention on behalf of the civilians contributed to a revival of their professional fortunes during the 1630s. It is doubtful whether the improved employment prospects alone prompted more students to enter the faculties of civil law at the universities, but the success of the civilians in securing a virtual monopoly of so many posts at a time when the size of their profession reached its lowest point since 1590[1] put an end to the gloomy forecasts of men like Thomas Wilson. Indeed, Sir Robert Wiseman later boasted that during the 1630s civil lawyers were active in the administration of every English county.[2] The civilians appeared to have been better off than at any time since the previous century, even though the virtual destruction of their profession was less than a decade away.

(d) *Reduction of legal fees*

A shortage of jobs was not the only crisis the civilians faced during the early seventeenth century. For even those civil lawyers who had been fortunate to secure the better positions open to members of their profession registered complaints between 1590 and 1630 concerning their reduced income from legal fees. Referring specifically to their positions as chancellors of dioceses, civilians bemoaned 'how poor maintenance and small encourage-ments they had therein'.[3] Those who were Masters in Chancery protested a shrinkage in their judicial revenues,[4] while those who were judges in ecclesiastical courts laboured under a strict regula-tion of the fees they were entitled to receive for their services.

Civilians who served as chancellors of dioceses generally com-manded greater opportunities for income than officials to arch-deacons. At York they were able to earn £100 per annum, which was in itself not a very attractive income.[5] But the chancellors

---

[1] Doc. Com. Treas. Bk., ff. 141–2. The membership in 1630 was thirty-five.
[2] Wiseman, *Law of Lawes*, p. 180.   [3] Bodl., Tanner MS. 280, f. 328ᵛ.
[4] Carew, 'A Treatise'; PRO SP 14/26/19; SP 14/147/8; *NRS* iv. 196.
[5] Marchant, *Church Under Law*, p. 246. Richard Trevor sold his share of the chancellorship of Llandaff for £350. If the value of the office was equivalent to seven years' profits, the annual value would be the same as at York.

usually proved to be most adept at combining the profits of two or more offices. Anthony Blincow held the chancellorships of Oxford and Chichester jointly while also serving as the Provost of Oriel College in Oxford. John Amye kept himself busy as Chancellor of Worcester, Master in Chancery, and one of the most active advocates in London. Other civilians supplemented their incomes as chancellors with lucrative ecclesiastical preferments. Dr. David Yale, Chancellor of Chester diocese, drew an additional income of £133. 6s. 8d. from the Vainoll prebend of the Cathedral Church of St. Asaph as well as the profits from another prebend in Chester Cathedral.[1] In this way he was able to invest £500 in land in Derbyshire and Denbighshire and acquire other goods and cash that were valued at £692 when he died.[2] Clement Colmore, the Chancellor of Durham, did even better than Yale. He was well graced with the tithes of three rectories in Durham, half the tithes of another rectory bequeathed to him by a friend, and the profits attached to prebends in both Durham and Lichfield Cathedrals.[3] In Durham, where Colmore held the eleventh stall, he received not only the customary tithes but an annual sum of £23. 6s. 8d. from the common fund of the Dean and Chapter.[4] All of these additional sources of income helped to supplement what he made as Chancellor. During his tenure of office Colmore purchased land in four different parts of Durham and Yorkshire, and, judged by a list of contributions to a benevolence for the King in 1614, he became the fourth-wealthiest clergyman of the entire diocese.[5]

Pluralism may have made it possible for chancellors to live 'in some good credit', but a number of them none the less experienced severe restrictions of their incomes during the early seventeenth century. The main problem was that some chancellors were not allowed to realize the full economic potential of their offices. For

[1] He held this from 1583 to 1608. J. LeNeve, *Fasti Ecclesiae Anglicanae* (London, 1854), iii. 269–70.

[2] Cheshire County Record Office, will and inventory of Yale, WS 1626.

[3] *Al. Oxon.*, i. 311; Borth. Inst., will of Colmore, Wills 35/435.

[4] Durham Cathedral Library, Dean and Chapter Treasurer's Book, 1609–10, f. 3. See also the books for 1612–13; 1614–15; 1616–17.

[5] Durham Cathedral Library, Hunter MS. 11/12. Colmore's contribution was £8. 7s. 9d. The highest donation was £12, while the majority were noted in shillings.

a chancellor not only staffed the bishop's consistory court, the highest ecclesiastical tribunal in the diocese, but also performed a number of supplementary administrative and judicial tasks which netted him additional income. These included proving wills, granting marriage licences, installing ministers in their cures, certifying teachers and preachers, and conducting visitations of the diocese. Such activities, which comprised the chancellor's 'voluntary' as opposed to his 'contentious' jurisdiction, could be quite extensive and bring the chancellor considerable profit.[1] But this voluntary jurisdiction technically belonged to the Bishop,[2] who was under no statutory obligation to delegate it to his chancellor. Even when he did, he had the right to determine what percentage of the fees for such services his chancellor would receive. Between 1590 and 1630 a number of civilians who held chancellorships were deliberately deprived of at least a portion of their voluntary jurisdiction. The bishops under whom they held office had taken Queen Elizabeth at her word when, under pressure from the Puritans, she had recommended that bishops take a personal care in the granting of marriage licences and refuse to delegate that work to subordinates.[3] Thus Bishop Henry Cotton of Salisbury had specifically excluded William Wilkinson in his patent from a number of licensing services traditionally reserved for the chancellor. The Bishop's defence of this policy was that he wished to take a more personal interest in his jurisdiction and to issue the licences himself. He hoped in this way to reduce or to eliminate the fees that chancellors were known to exact, especially from poor ministers for installation in their cures.[4]

In Lincoln John Farmery encountered a similar problem when the bishop of that diocese did not allow him any fees whatsoever

[1] In the course of his six-year tenure as Chancellor of London Thomas Edwards and his deputies proved more than 400 wills and issued 686 marriage licences (for marrying without banns or during Lent and Advent) as well as a host of licences to clergy, midwives, surgeons, parish clerks, and school teachers. Greater London Record Office, Vicar-General's Book 11, *passim*.

[2] K. Oughton, *Forms of Ecclesiastical Law* (London, 1844), p. 216. Burn, *Ecclesiastical Law*, i. 289.

[3] 'Reasons why the Chancellors and Vicars General ought to grant marriage licences', no. 13. Bodl., Tanner MS. 280, f. 328–328^v.

[4] *HMCS* x. 160–1.

for his collection of money from all the clergy of the diocese to assist the Protestants of the German Palatinate. Farmery pointed out that in Exeter, where civilians seemed to fare better than in Lincoln, Dr. Gooch received 2½ per cent of all the proceeds as remuneration for the same service.[1] Farmery's troubles did not stop there. The triennial visitation of the diocese, which he claimed was 'the chief cause of profit to the chancellorship', did not bring him any financial gain, even though he was the main judge of the entire proceedings. Farmery felt particularly aggrieved at this misfortune because his subordinates, the registrar and the apparitor, made £300 and £100 respectively at the occasion.[2]

Bishops were not always the main cause of chancellors' troubles. Robert Redman, the Chancellor of Norwich, lost a great deal of judicial business not only to his episcopal superior, with whom he was on bad terms, but to competing subordinate officials, such as commissaries for archdeaconries.[3] Since these officials, many of them civil lawyers, were not earning very much money themselves, it is understandable why a conflict could occur. The commissaries were issuing licences, proving wills, and even judging cases which technically belonged at the diocesan level but which these officials never allowed to leave the archdeaconries.[4] Redman protested against these encroachments upon his jurisdiction, and if the noticeable increase in his assessed income is any indication of a larger volume of legal business, he was probably able to keep his subordinates in line.[5]

[1] *CSPD 1623–1625*, p. 150.

[2] PRO, SP 14/176/69. Another civilian, Nathaniel Brent, allegedly received £50 from one parish alone during a visitation a few years later. Notestein, *D'Ewes*, p. 386. [3] *Registrum Vagum*, i. 33–4.

[4] In the diocese of London the Archdeacon of St. Albans was posing the same threat to the chancellor. See R. Peters, 'The Administration of the Archdeaconry of St. Albans 1580–1625', *Journal of Ecclesiastical History*, 13 (1962), 66–7. In the diocese of Durham the Archdeacon of Northumberland was issuing licences as well. See Durham Cathedral Library, Hunter MS. 12/188. In Norwich during the 1630s apparitors were issuing licences to marry and were also proving wills. Bodl., Tanner MS. 68, f. 220ᵛ. See also Cardwell, *Synodalia*, ii. 582.

[5] BM, Harl. MS. 6822, f. 293, lists Redman as one of the six commissioners of the peace of Norfolk with an assessment for the subsidy at less than £20. His figure was £8. Later it rose to £10. See PRO, E. 179/153/583, mem. 2d. In 1609 his assessment finally reached £20. See Gleason, *Justices*, p. 151.

Because of problems such as those that Wilkinson, Farmery, and Redman faced, the civilians of the early seventeenth century were confronted with a challenge to one of the mainstays of their profession. But the chancellors were not alone. Civilians who were Masters in Chancery complained even more bitterly about their diminishing legal revenue. In real terms the plight of the masters could awake few pangs of sympathy. Matthew Carew, the one civil lawyer who took individual initiative to remedy the problems of the masters, commanded substantial financial assets amounting to at least £9,600 until he lost most of it by fraud in later life.[1] Another twelve masters profited sufficiently from their work, which usually involved more than service on the Chancery bench, to invest substantial sums of money into land. But the masters did have some cause for complaint. A change in their status and income had indeed taken place during the Elizabethan period, as an increasing load of judicial work had taken them from their lucrative administrative duties, such as assisting the Chancellor with the issuing of writs and letters patent.[2] The shift had made them more and more dependent upon judicial fees, which in theory were supposed to be strictly voluntary and hence were never established by statute. The masters protested that this had resulted in a serious diminution of revenue.

It is certainly possible that the masters exaggerated the extent of their financial crisis. The large volume of judicial work that passed through their hands brought them profits, which, in an accurate appraisal of their situation, must be balanced against their losses from administrative work. Indeed, the masters were suffering more of a comparative than a real monetary loss. The value of their office had not expanded on the same scale as other Chancery posts, such as that of the Six Clerks.[3] Since at this time the institutional importance of the masters was rising in relation to that of the other officials of the court, the masters regarded their lower monetary reward to be a grating injustice. The masters were not

---

[1] *DNB* iii. 965. PRO, SP 14/88/135 sets his losses at £12,000. He sought financial assistance at this time, but he still had a house valued at £1,600 plus other assets, SP 14/88/9; 14/86/95.

[2] Jones, *Chancery*, pp. 104–6.   [3] Ibid., p. 110.

doing as well as they should have been, and those were legitimate grounds for complaint.

In addition to the specific difficulties of chancellors and Masters in Chancery, civilians involved in all forms of ecclesiastical jurisdiction suffered from a strict regulation of their legal revenue after 1590. Until that time fees in Church courts had been rising, mainly to offset the effects of inflation. Consequently the Puritan faction in the Parliaments of 1584 and 1587 spearheaded attempts to regulate the excessive fees that the officials of the ecclesiastical courts were exacting.[1] These efforts constituted a real threat to the civilians. One contemporary predicted that if the bills passed, civilians would receive ten times less than they were accustomed;[2] another that chancellors of dioceses would earn no more than £20 a year and hence would live in a 'base and beggarly estate'.[3] Both attempts met with failure, but to stem the rising tide of popular criticism Archbishop Whitgift formulated in 1597 a standard table of fees, which was included among the Canons of 1604.[4] The table, which set the maximum allowable fees for judges, registrars, and proctors, had the effect of stabilizing fees for the next four decades at a rather modest level. During an inflationary period such a restriction amounted to a reduction of the civilians' earning power.

The question remains, however, whether the civilians actually adhered to the official scale of fees. Circumstantial evidence suggests that they did not. Thirteen years after the publication of Whitgift's table, James I established a commission to inquire into excessive fees taken in spiritual as well as temporal courts.[5] In 1621 Parliament was still seeking ways to enforce the rates set down by the table.[6] Throughout the late sixteenth and early seventeenth

[1] Hill, *Society and Puritanism*, pp. 307–8. See also BM, Cotton MS. Cleo. F II, f. 218. Some fees had allegedly risen from 15*d.* to 20*s.*

[2] BM, Cotton MS. Cleo. F II, f. 231.

[3] Bodl., Tanner MS. 280, f. 326ᵛ.

[4] Cardwell, *Synodalia*, i. 324. The first instructions for the table to be drawn up are in Bodl. Tanner MS. 77, f. 62. The actual table is in J. Ayliffe, *Parergon Juris Canonici Anglicani* (London, 1734), pp. 551–2. Whitgift also ordered an inquiry into the venality of chancellors. See P. Collinson, *The Elizabethan Puritan Movement* (London, 1967), pp. 450–1.

[5] BM, Add. MS. 34,324, ff. 45ᵛ–60; Aylmer, *King's Servants*, pp. 186–7.

[6] *NRS* ii. 388, 442; iv. 434.

century there persisted frequent and bitter condemnation of all the officers of the Church courts, including civilians, for their extortion, bribery, and preoccupation with the accumulation of legal revenue instead of with the establishment of a godly discipline.[1] Occasionally individual civilians, such as Sir John Lambe, George Parry, and Robert Mitchell, were singled out by name.[2] Yet even if these civil lawyers were guilty as charged, their malfeasance should not impugn the integrity of the entire profession. Dr. B. W. Quintrell has concluded that in Essex the personnel of the Church courts did adhere closely to the rates set down in 1597 and that specific complaints of corruption were rare.[3] Unless one wishes to accept all the allegations of Puritans at face value, he would have to admit that a good number of civil lawyers took only what was allowed and therefore suffered when fees were frozen in an inflationary period. The civilians' situation did not improve until the 1630s, when the increased activity of the Church courts brought them larger incomes from legal fees.[4]

(e) *Prohibitions*

While the shortage of well-paid jobs and the reduction of legal fees certainly contributed to the civilians' professional crisis, the civil lawyers themselves more frequently attributed their difficulties to the vigorous competition they were receiving from the courts of common law. In a petition to the Archbishop of Canterbury during the early years of James I's reign, the advocates, along with a number of concerned judges and professors of the civil law, mentioned that they detected

the sensible feeling of the apparent decline of our profession ensuing for want of maintenance, and that this decline hath arisen of late years from a power that the temporal judges have assumed to send prohibitions in cases of mere ecclesiastical and civil cognizance in such multitude as (if the records be searched) all the prohibitions since the

[1] See Hill, *Society and Puritanism*, p. 308; W. Pierce (ed.), *The Marprelate Tracts* (London, 1911), pp. 148–9; Stoughton, *Assertion*, pp. 73–4; *NRS* ii. 370.
[2] PRO, SP 16/530/131.
[3] Quintrell, 'Government of Essex', p. 185.
[4] See Marchant, *Church Under Law*, p. 194, for the increase of legal business in the archdeaconry of Nottingham.

Conquest until our late Queen's time are not half so many as have swarmed within these last twenty years . . .[1]

University officials agreed with this interpretation of the decline of the civilians' profession. The Vice-Chancellor and Senate of Cambridge, recognizing that the civil lawyers' problems threatened the entire faculty of civil law at their institutions, complained that the civilians could not find jobs in the government because 'the common law was too potent for them.'[2] William Fleetwood feared that the common lawyers' attack on the Admiralty jurisdiction would dissuade so many civilians from pursuing a career that 'in a small time this kingdom shall be utterly bereaved of the professors of that study'.[3]

Prohibitions were orders from the judges of the common law courts at Westminster to the judges of the civil law or prerogative courts to desist in the hearing of certain cases which did not fall within their jurisdiction. To test the validity of these orders the judges from both sides met in conference after the prohibition had temporarily halted the legal proceedings in question. If the judges of the civil law courts could show adequate justification why a particular case should remain within their jursidiction, the common law judges would award a 'consultation', and the interrupted proceedings could continue. If, however, the judges of the Westminster courts decided upon closer examination that the original order would remain in force, the plaintiff who had filed the original suit would have to bring action against the defendant in a common law court if he wished a final decision to be reached.

In the 1590s the common law judges inaugurated a full-scale attack upon the jurisdictions of inferior courts by issuing prohibitions against suits pending therein with much greater frequency than they ever had before. None of the courts in which civilians

[1] BM, Harl. MS. 358, f. 184. See also BM, Lansdowne MS. 142, f. 455, which requested that civilians be freed from the curse of prohibitions so 'that an handful of civilians, now less, may be suffered to live amongst the many thousands of common lawyers.'

[2] *HMCS* xvi. 39.

[3] PRO, SP, 16/208, p. 301. Sir Thomas Ridley considered the threat from the common law so severe that he predicted it would render the civil and ecclesiastical law 'idle' and 'unfit for the State', *A View*, dedication.

practised was exempted from this attack. Archiepiscopal as well as diocesan ecclesiastical courts, the Admiralty Court, the Courts of Chancery, Requests, and Delegates, the High Commission, and even the Council of the North all lost cases which the common law judges claimed did not belong there.[1] In their zeal to keep the inferior courts within the bounds of their jurisdiction, to have litigation transferred to their own courts and to make money from the actual writs of prohibition themselves (the price rose from 7s. 6d. to £14 during this period), the common law judges often exceeded the bounds of impartiality.[2] Although they did issue some writs on just causes, they were also known to grant prohibitions on frivolous and ostensibly fabricated grounds, and then to allow years to lapse before consenting to consultations. They acted rashly in issuing some prohibitions before the libels in question were even presented to the judges of the civil law courts, while in other cases they granted writs after sentence had been passed.[3] Instead of more clearly delimiting the various jurisdictions of England, the judges were subjecting the personnel of the inferior courts to a policy of calculated harassment.

Although no complete records of prohibitions have survived, various reports and estimates of their numbers have been made. They indicate that the attack of the common lawyers was determined but not overwhelming.[4] In the Court of the Arches the civilians counted a total of 488 prohibitions during the Elizabethan period and 82 in the first three years of James I's reign. In pursuance of all of these, only 113 consultations had been granted.[5]

[1] Ogilvie, *King's Government*, *passim*; Strype, *Whitgift*, ii. 434. Usher, *High Commission*, p. 188, claims that the High Commission suffered the most. For prohibitions to the Court of Delegates see BM, Lansdowne MS. 142, f. 449, no. 1.

[2] James I referred to the efforts of each court 'to bring in most moulture to their own mill'. *The Works of the Most High and Mightie Prince James* (London, 1616), p. 534. For the cost of prohibitions see Carew, 'A treatise', p. 313.

[3] For summaries of the alleged abuses see BM, Lansdowne MSS. 142, ff. 453–5 and 161, f. 223; Cotton MSS. Cleo. F I, ff. 109–11, 114 and F II, ff. 312–319ᵛ; Cardwell, *Documentary Annals of the Reformed Church of England* (London, 1844), ii. 116–39. *The Journal of Sir Roger Wilbraham . . . 1593–1616* (Camden Soc. Miscellany x, 1902), pp. 95–6; *NRS* iv. 351.

[4] Usher, *High Commission*, p. 181, claims that at least for the High Commission the number was 'infinite', but he presents no statistics to support this.

[5] Cardwell, *Annals*, ii. 119.

Although the common lawyers disputed the validity of these figures on the grounds that the civilians were prone to exaggerate,[1] a fully detailed abstract of prohibitions sent to that court between 1558 and 1609 reported a total of 258. Of these sixty-seven eventually resulted in consultations. Since the large bulk of the prohibitions were issued after 1594, this meant that a rough average of about thirteen prohibitions per year succeeded in stopping cases pending in that court.[2] The Norwich Consistory Court, whose work load was not as heavy as that of the Arches, received seventy-seven prohibitions between 1575 and 1603, and fifty-two between 1603 and 1608.[3] The Admiralty Court suffered even less. During the first eight years of James I's reign the common law judges directed forty-five prohibitions or about six per year to that court;[4] and if the judges of the Admiralty defended the jurisdiction of their court as successfully as they had in the sixteenth century,[5] a good number of those forty-five should have ended in consultations.

Measured in relation to the large volume of case work that these courts handled, the number of actions against which prohibitions were awarded is surprisingly low. The Court of the Arches heard as many as 117 cases in one day, although many of these were only partial proceedings.[6] More modestly, the Admiralty Court took on about 400 suits per year,[7] and diocesan consistory courts between fifteen and fifty per day. The comparatively small number of prohibitions could hardly have accounted

[1] Usher, *Reconstruction of the English Church* (New York, 1910), ii. 82. Instead they claimed that only 251 had been granted to all ecclesiastical courts since the accession of James I.

[2] BM, Cotton MS. Cleo, F II, ff. 353–7.

[3] CUL, MS. Mm 6.57, ff. 13–15.

[4] C. Hill, *The Intellectual Origins of the English Revolution* (Oxford, 1965), p. 239.

[5] PRO, HCA 30/542. All except three of the entries pertain to sixteenth-century cases. L. Hill, 'Caesar', p. 108, has computed that of the nineteen prohibitions included therein that arose during the judgeship of Caesar, all but four resulted in consultations.

[6] PRO, SP 16/421/108. See Hill, *Society and Puritanism*, p. 307; Marchant, *Church Under Law*, pp. 243–4.

[7] L. Hill, 'Caesar', p. 149, calculates that the case load of the Admiralty Court was 7·87 cases per week in 1604.

therefore for a large enough reduction of court business to send the members of Doctors' Commons into a spiralling economic decline. If prohibitions did lie at the root of the civilians' difficulties, their impact must have been felt elsewhere than in the volume of legal business that they were adjudicating.

Actually, the real damage that prohibitions were causing was potential. It was the predictable effect of the legal precedents such orders were establishing. If left uncontested, the type of prohibitions that the judges were issuing could have removed from the civilians' cognizance whole areas of jurisdiction which had traditionally been their preserve. This indeed would have placed the civil lawyers in a severe financial crisis. It was the nature of the common lawyers' attack upon their courts and the threat it held for the future, much more than its immediate economic consequences, that led the civil lawyers to attribute to it the erosion of their entire profession.

Consider, for example, the grounds upon which prohibitions were being granted to the ecclesiastical courts. More than 75 per cent of them referred to cases dealing with the payment of tithes. The reasons the common lawyers suggested for such prohibitions varied: that those being sued for tithes possessed a previous immunity to the exaction and that this was recognized by the common law; that they had a customary right to submit alternative forms of payment or composition of tithes in kind; that the recipient had no just title to the proceeds he claimed.[1] In each of these cases the point in question had to be argued on its own merits. Yet two prohibitions during the first decade of James's reign appealed only to the justification that all cases of tithes were to be tried at the common law.[2] Consultations were granted in both instances, but the writing was on the wall. If most prohibitions in cases of tithes continued to be upheld, this would be the final result. The civilians would suffer a serious financial blow. Taking all litigation concerned

---

[1] BM, Cotton MS. Cleo, F II, f. 353. The breakdown in cases under each reason was forty-seven for immunity, seventy-three for customary rights, and twenty-seven on lack of title. For a general discussion of the problem of tithes see C. Hill, *Economic Problems of the Church* (Oxford, 1956), pp. 77–131; *Society and Puritanism*, pp. 331–2.

[2] BM, Cotton MS. Cleo, F II, f. 354.

with the payment of tithes out of the Church courts would deprive the civilians of many legal fees and transfer their lost business to the common lawyers.

A second type of prohibition first served upon the Court of the Arches in 1609 threatened the civilians' employment even further. On the basis of their interpretation of an Henrician statute[1] the judges of Common Pleas prohibited cases in which the Dean of the Arches cited before his court, which was situated in the church of St. Mary-le-Bow in London, any inhabitants of London diocese.[2] Since London was the largest and most judicially active diocese, the threat to all the civilians employed in the Arches was a substantial one. They complained that if the prohibition were sustained it would 'cut off all the chief maintenance of civilians' and result eventually in the 'overthrow of the civil law, ourselves and other ministers of these courts'.[3]

Prohibitions to the Admiralty Court threatened to do almost as much harm. Throughout the fifteenth century the court of the Lord Admiral was entitled to hear cases concerning contracts made and things done upon the high seas. If any of these actions arose on land, within the body of an English county, the common law courts were to have jurisdiction over them.[4] Henry VIII, seeking to revitalize the Admiralty Court, dispensed his Admiral from statutory impediments and allowed him to judge pleas concerning contracts *concluded in England* for the performance of anything to be done on the seas or 'beyond the seas' in foreign countries.[5] The first prohibitions sent to the Admiralty Court disputed the court's cognizance of such causes.[6] The common law judges did not restrict themselves, however, to challenging just this one type of case. They also tried to gain unquestioned cognizance of all contracts made and acts committed *beyond the seas*, an area of

---

[1] 23 Hen. VIII, c. 9. See also PRO, SP 16/350/82, p. 1.

[2] 6 Jac. Mich. 1 Common Pleas, BM Cotton MS. Cleo. F II, f. 431.

[3] BM, Harl. MS. 358, ff. 184–5.

[4] 13 Richard II, c. 5; 15 Richard II, c. 3.

[5] Patent of Henry Duke of Richmond as Lord Admiral, 1525, in T. Rymer, *Foedera* (London, 1705), xiv. 42.

[6] *Kyrkby* v. *Barfoote* (1527) and *Porter* v. *Bremer* (1536) in R. G. Marsden, *Select Pleas in the Court of the Admiralty*, i (Selden Soc. vi, 1892), 172–3, 194.

highly disputed jurisdiction since the middle of the sixteenth century.[1] To bring such cases within the jurisdiction of the common
law, defendants about to lose their cases in the Admiralty Court
resorted to a legal device called a Fiction—an assumption of the
law upon an untruth.[2] Since the place at which a contract is
concluded was of no legal importance at the common law, they
argued that they might have been made anywhere.[3] They 'supposed' as fiction that the contracts in dispute were negotiated
within an English county, instead of overseas[4] and then sued
for a prohibition.

The common law judges obliged. In 1611 they prohibited
further action against a suit arising from a contract concluded at
Marseilles but alleged by the defendant to have originated at
'Marseilles in Kent'.[5] In fact the judges were so successful in this
endeavour that Sir Edward Coke began to extend the use of the
fiction to acts performed upon the high seas, the previously
undisputed territory of the Admiralty. The Lord Admiral was so
irritated at this usurpation of his jurisdiction that he headed a list
of grievances submitted to the King in 1611 with the complaint
that contracts concluded upon the high seas were being tried at
the common law 'by supposing that the same to be done in Cheap-
side and such places'.[6] The common lawyers had within some
twenty years begun to challenge just about every aspect of
Admiralty jurisdiction. They even prohibited prize and reprisal
cases,[7] which were of an exclusively maritime character. There is

[1] The common lawyers started making encroachments in this area as early as
1543. For specific cases see Coke, *Institutes*, iv. 139–40; id., *Reports*, xii. 104; BM.
Lansdowne MS. 161, f. 227, for the cases of *Primounte* v. *Bucknan* and *Fenne* v.
White.

[2] Ridley, *A View*, p. 171.

[3] Coke was able to do this because the contracts in question were transitory,
i.e. causes which do not necessarily refer to or arise in any particular locality.
Mercantile causes were transitory, whereas criminal cases were not.

[4] John Godolphin, *A View of the Admiralty Jurisdiction* (London, 1661), p. 107.

[5] Brownlow, *Reports*, ii. 110–11.

[6] Coke, *Institutes*, iv. 134. For Dun's reply to Coke's answer see BM, Lansdowne
MS. 142, ff. 431ᵛ–432; PRO, SP 16/208, pp. 580–1.

[7] R. Marsden, *Documents Relating to Law and Custom of the Sea*, i (Navy Records
Society, xlix, 1915), 359. Consultations were awarded in all such cases until 1606,
when Coke became Judge of Common Pleas.

good reason to suspect that Coke, if given the necessary freedom of action, would have destroyed the entire Admiralty jurisdiction.[1]

The same danger confronted the High Commission. Gradually the common lawyers had nibbled away at the jurisdiction of this court, so that by 1610 it could adjudicate freely only cases between parties concerning heresy and schism. Then in February 1611 Coke issued a prohibition against a case in which the minister and churchwardens of St. Botolphe in London had brought action against one Cheekitt on precisely these grounds. The reason alleged for the prohibition was hardly novel. Cheekitt had refused to take the oath *ex officio* until he saw a copy of the articles presented against him and consequently had been imprisoned.[2] But Coke's action had broken new ground and had rendered vulnerable the last remaining preserve of the Commission's jurisdiction. As R. G. Usher has remarked, 'if Cheekitt's prohibition could be upheld, the High Commission would have in practice no jurisdiction left at all.'[3]

As prohibitions made inroads upon so many aspects of both ecclesiastical and Admiralty jurisdictions, the full extent of the danger to the civilians was apparent. If too much litigation passed from the civil law courts to the common law courts, the civil lawyers would be faced with the loss of their livelihood. It is not certain whether the common lawyers wanted to destroy all civil law jurisdiction, but they made enough preliminary encroachments upon every facet of it to lead the civilians to believe that they would. And to confirm their suspicions the Puritans, who supported the common lawyers on this question, were calling for the abolition of all ecclesiastical jurisdiction.[4] The magnitude of

---

[1] Justice Bruce *et al.*, *A Treatise on the Jurisdiction and Practice of the English Courts in Admiralty Actions and Appeals* (London, 1902), p. 7. Coke denied this. See *Institutes*, iv. 135.

[2] For a discussion of this oath see below, pp. 150–1.

[3] Usher, *High Commission*, p. 209.

[4] Stoughton, *Assertion*, pp. 78–90; Usher, *High Commission*, p. 189; C. Ritchie, *The Ecclesiastical Courts of York* (Arbroath, 1956), p. 215, n. 52. For the statement of Sir Robert Phelips in 1628 see ITL, Petyt MS. 537/23, f. 235. For an earlier threat see *The Marprelate Tracts*, pp. 248–51. Neither Stoughton nor the author of the *Marprelate Tracts* believed that the abolition would hurt the civilians since they could do better financially in non-ecclesiastical positions.

the threat to the civil law courts explains why the judges of these courts, who were doing quite well financially, joined in the protests about prohibitions just as vociferously as did the poorer advocates.[1] If the entire system were to crumble, they too would be included among the victims of the disaster.

With so much at stake for the civilians, it is even more understandable why the number of students taking doctorates in civil law at the universities declined during those years when prohibitions were most frequent. It was not merely because the shortage of jobs and the reduction of civilian's income from legal fees made the profession less appealing than it had been in previous years, but because there was no sure future to the entire profession. Men are rarely attracted to a lost cause, which is what the civil law profession appeared to be at the beginning of the seventeenth century.

The civilians' cause, however, did not remain lost. During the decade preceding the Civil War the fortunes of the civil lawyers improved. Their earlier protests had won them some consideration, and the fury of the common lawyers gradually abated after 1611. In the 1630s specific steps were taken to protect the members of the profession from further harassment. In February 1633 the Privy Council promulgated five articles settling the jurisdiction of the Admiralty Court. These directed that no prohibitions were to be issued against cases commenced in the Admiralty Court concerning contracts made and things done beyond or upon the High Seas.[2] With respect to ecclesiastical jurisdiction, both Archbishop Laud and the Privy Council took action to reduce the number of prohibitions during the years of that prelate's supremacy.[3] Although the common lawyers continued to issue enough prohibitions for John Lambe to complain in 1639 that they were ruining the profession little by little,[4] the situation was by no

[1] Dun, Bennet, and Marten were the three most articulate critics of prohibitions.

[2] PRO, PC 2/42, ff. 456–7. For a printed text of the articles see Godolphin, *A View*, pp. 157–60.

[3] PRO, PC 2/42, p. 458; W. Prynne, *Canterburies Doome* (London, 1644), p. 369; C. Hill, *Society and Puritanism*, p. 333; *CSPD 1629–1631*, p. 81.

[4] PRO, SP 16/442/37. In this year Robert Aylett also still felt the bite of prohibitions, praying 'that we may be preserved from the jurisdiction of temporal lawyers, else *Domine miserere nostri* . . .'. J. H. Round, 'Dr. Robert Aylett', *Transactions of the Essex Archaeological Society*, n.s. 10 (1909), p. 32.

means as critical as it had been earlier in the century. And as the Church courts became more active during this period of rigid enforcement of ecclesiastical law, the demise of the civilians' profession did not appear to be as imminent as in fact it really was. Once again, although one civilian saw 'a cloud arising which threatens a foul storm',[1] the profession as a whole anticipated a better future. As mentioned before, the Privy Council gave added encouragement by reserving for them all the masterships of Requests, eight of the masterships of Chancery and most of the diocesan chancellorships. With a more promising future in store for civilians, the number of students receiving doctorates from the universities reached the highest point since the Reformation.

(f) *The appeal to the King*

In the face of the common lawyers' challenge, the civilians found themselves with few allies. Confronted with opposition from judges who commanded almost limitless legal power, they had two higher authorities to whom they could appeal. The first was Parliament. But there they found little sympathy for their plight. Common law influence was overwhelmingly dominant in that assembly, and the claims of Cowell in *The Interpreter* did little to ingratiate M.P.s to the cause of the civil law. Already the Lower House had twice tried to regulate the fees of the officers of the ecclesiastical courts, and it had actually passed a bill awarding legal costs to the party that obtained a prohibition from the common law judges.[2] With opposition growing to the entire ecclesiastical establishment as well as to all the members of 'the Court', the civil lawyers could expect nothing but resistance from Parliament.

This left the King as their only resort. If there was any hope for an amelioration of the civilians' troubles, it lay with James. The university officials at Cambridge recognized this in 1603 when they concluded that 'all their hope is in the justice of a most wise King';[3] and when the civilians drafted their first petition to draw attention to the problems of their profession, they submitted it to

---

[1] PRO, SP 16/223/4.
[2] BM, Cotton MS. Cleo. F II, f. 236ᵛ. A more equitable bill was proposed in 1621. *NRS* vii. 211.   [3] *HMCS* xvi. 39.

the monarch.[1] The Archbishop of Canterbury later responded to a similar appeal by suggesting that it would have been better for them to have directed it to His Majesty.[2] Thomas Ridley dedicated his apology for the civil law to James, hoping that he would 'take knowledge of some differences that are in judicature between your ecclesiastical and civil law and the temporal law of this land'.[3]

From King James in particular, the civilians could expect an honest deal. Having lived most of his life in a country whose law was based upon Roman law,[4] James was predisposed toward preserving a place for that same legal tradition in England. He proclaimed a love for the civil law, and as a token of his affection he once took his place, symbolically, on the Admiralty bench.[5] Although he professed an equally high regard for the common law, as did his son when he succeeded to the throne,[6] and played the role of an impartial mediator trying to keep each jurisdiction within its own bounds,[7] there was little question whose cause he was defending. In a king who could say of Sir Thomas Crompton that he was as good a man as Sir Edward Coke, the civilians had a strong ally.[8]

Thus in their search for assistance to reverse the declining fortunes of their profession, the civilians became even more dependent upon the monarch than they already were by the very nature of their occupations. Their recourse to the King in this crisis reinforced the relationship they already bore to him as members of the Court. Not only did they strengthen this political alliance, but they also articulated constitutional theories which exaggerated

---

[1] Usher, *High Commission*, p. 211. Probably the same one referred to in BM, Harl. MS. 358, f. 184.

[2] BM, Cotton MS. Cleo. F II, f. 121.   [3] Ridley, *A View*, dedication.

[4] Wiseman, *Law of Lawes*, p. 140; Pocock, *Ancient Constitution*, p. 89. None the less, Scottish law was still largely customary. See Willson, *Diary of Bowyer*, pp. 147–8.

[5] C. H. McIlwain (ed.), *The Political Works of James I* (Cambridge, Mass., 1918), p. 310; *Calendar of State Papers, Venetian*, xi. 312; Senior, *Doctors' Commons*, p. 88.

[6] *Political Works of James I*, p. 310; S. R. Gardiner (ed.), *Commons Debates 1625* (Camden Society, n.s. vi, 1873), pp. 4–5.

[7] E. Foster (ed.), *Proceedings in Parliament 1610* (New Haven, Conn., 1966), ii. 61.

[8] R. Usher, 'James I and Sir Edward Coke', *EHR* 18 (1903), 669.

the power of the Crown and minimized that of Parliament and
of the common law judges. For in appealing to James they set out
to convince him that he possessed the constitutional authority to
arbitrate the dispute and to implement whatever reforms he
deemed necessary.[1] They asserted that since the King was the
fountain of justice who had delegated his personal jurisdiction to
the judges of his various courts, he was empowered to continue
to regulate that distribution of legal authority. If a dispute should
arise as to where the exact boundary between two jurisdictions
lay, the monarch alone was entitled to solve the problem. Referring specifically to conflicts between the Admiralty and the
common law courts, Julius Caesar argued at the very beginning
of the crisis that

the magistrates both of sea and land are equally authorized in their
several offices to govern by several laws in like immediate degree from
the Prince; and therefore if it falls out that a question doth arise
concerning the limits of either their jurisdictions, it seemeth that this
question is not fit to be decided by either of themselves; but rather by
the Prince herself in her own person or by such special commissioners
or delegates as Her Majesty shall appoint superior and indifferent to
the both.[2]

Since the theory of equality between the various jurisdictions of
the King applied with even more aptness to the judicial division
between ecclesiastical and temporal affairs,[3] the civilians appealed
to it repeatedly throughout the debates over prohibitions in the
early seventeenth century. Once the theory of parallel and equal
jurisdictions was conceded, the position of the King as sole arbiter
could not be denied. Yet as added justification for James to intervene in this dispute, the civilians and their spokesman, Archbishop
Bancroft, extended the King's right of personal involvement in the
judicial process even further than settling disagreements over juris-
dictional boundaries. In one of their more famous utterances they
allowed the monarch the right 'to hear in his own person any case

---

[1] BM, Cotton MS. Cleo. F II, f. 282; Cardwell, *Annals*, ii. 116–17. The latter
appeared in Bancroft's name but represented the views of the entire profession
of civilians and was reputedly composed by Cowell and other civil lawyers,
probably Ridley and Stanhope. See Chrimes, 'Cowell', 478.

[2] BM, Lansdowne MS. 129, f. 81ᵛ.   [3] Usher, *Reconstruction*, ii. 211.

whatsoever'.[1] This did indeed seem to place the King above the law categorically and to give him the opportunity to circumvent regular judicial processes even when 'affairs of state' were in no way involved. The civilians and Bancroft were devising 'to make the King believe that he is one absolute monarch and may *jure regio* do what he list'.[2]

None of this sat very well with the common lawyers, irrespective of how 'royalist' some of them may have been. Not only did they believe that the common law was superior to all other jurisdictions, but they claimed that it enjoyed an autonomous status which exempted it and the judges who professed it from any interference on the part of the King. While still admitting that the King was the source of all justice and that legal authority was still technically his,[3] the common lawyers claimed that none the less the law possessed an independent existence and that only those trained in the law could attempt the proper application of its 'artificial reason'.[4] Thus the King had no right to interfere with the judges' granting of prohibitions, since in so doing the judges were merely following the law, and 'what the law doth warrant in cases of prohibitions to keep every jurisdiction in his true limits is not to be said an abuse, nor can be altered but by parliament'.[5]

The civilians' defence of the royal prerogative and the common lawyers' insistence that the prerogative be restricted by law became even more determined as the debate concerning prohibitions descended to particulars, especially those pertaining to the authority of the High Commission. Each individual Commission for Ecclesiastical Causes was empowered by royal Letters Patent, but the Elizabethan Act of Supremacy (1559) had supplied the general sanction that the monarch should appoint the members of such bodies and authorize them to perform specific functions.[6] Since the commissioners were engaging in activities not designated by

[1] Bodl., Barlow MS. 9, pp. 68–9; ITL, Petyt MS. 518, ff. 551–2; BM, Cotton MS. Cleo. F II, ff. 280–1.   [2] Bodl., Barlow MS. 9, p. 68.
[3] BM, Cotton MS. Cleo. F I, f. 116ᵛ; ITL, Petyt MS. 518, f. 23ᵛ.
[4] J. R. Tanner, *Constitutional Documents of the Reign of James I* (Cambridge, 1930), p. 187.
[5] T. B. Howell, *State Trials* (London, 1816), ii. 134.
[6] 1 Eliz., c. 1. viii. Quoted in Usher, *High Commission*, p. 336.

the act of 1559, and since the common law judges were prohibiting cases in which the Commissioners performed such functions, it was imperative to decide whether or not the letters patent held greater authority than the parliamentary statute. Once again the civilians came down on the side of the royal prerogative, which through letters patent was allowing the commissioners to exercise the functions in dispute. The common lawyers, however, desiring to restrict the activities of the commissioners, regarded the parliamentary statute as the highest source of the commissioners' authority and as the definition of the full scope of their powers. Beyond the terms of this authorization the King could not go. He could not act outside the framework of existing laws.[1]

In claiming for the King the power both to regulate the jurisdiction and proceedings of his courts and to authorize ecclesiastical commissioners to exceed their statutory authority, the civilians freed the royal prerogative from the restraints of both customary and statutory law. The common lawyers, on the other hand, while never denying that the royal prerogative was part of the law, still insisted that it was controlled and limited by that law. The disagreement between the two groups of lawyers over such constitutional essentials helped to clarify the main lines of political debate in the early seventeenth century. Their arguments 'foreshadow, in relation to this smaller question, the Royalist and Parliamentarian positions in the greater controversy which was soon to arise'.[2]

As the debate between the common lawyers and the civil lawyers clearly suggests, a thorough analysis of the civilians' royalism cannot ignore the professional context within which they developed their political views. Yet the question remains whether their royalist theories received reinforcement from other sources. Historians and contemporaries have attributed the civil lawyers' defence of the royal prerogative to their academic assimilation of a distinct body of legal doctrine. The next chapter will discuss the political implications of their education in the civil law of Rome.

---

[1] Usher, *High Commission*, p. 223; Bodl., Tanner MS. 280, ff. 119–122ᵛ.

[2] J. R. Tanner, *English Constitutional Conflicts in the Seventeenth Century* (Cambridge, 1928), p. 35.

III

POLITICAL THEORY

INDEPENDENT of the crisis over prohibitions, the English civil lawyers allegedly acquired from their study of the civil law a concept of an absolute sovereign which they applied to their own monarch.[1] The *Corpus Juris Civilis* could easily have suggested this depiction of royalty, for it included a large amount of public law that touched upon such vital political questions as the authority of the Prince and his relationship to the law.[2] Two sections of the *Corpus* supply the most explicit support for the theory of absolutism. The first is a maxim from the first book of the *Institutes* which is attributed to Ulpian[3] and is paralleled by an almost identical repetition in the *Digest*: 'Quod principi placuit legis habet vigorem, cum lege regia quae de imperio eius lata est, populus ei et in eum omne suum imperium et potestatem concessit.'[4] The second is the terse but powerful excerpt from the Digest, 'Princeps legibus solutus est', i.e. the Prince is not tied to the laws.[5] Taken together, the two statements appear to sanction a legally unrestricted monarchy and almost to invite arbitrary and despotic rule. If understood literally, they 'import as if property, life, liberty, and all were subject, and did hold of, the Prince's will'.[6]

To members of the English Parliament in the seventeenth century such theories were the 'dangers drawn from imperial Rome' which 'lurked in the study of the civil law'.[7] The civilians were 'being trained in a law which regarded the will of the prince

---

[1] F. Wormuth, *The Royal Prerogative 1603–1649* (Ithaca, N.Y., 1939), p. 53.

[2] See B. Tierney, 'Bracton on Government', *Speculum*, 38 (1963), 312.

[3] Roman jurist who died in A.D. 228.

[4] *Institutes*, i. 2. 6; *Digest*, i. 4. 1. 'Whatsoever has pleased the Prince has the force of law, because by the regal law which has been laid down concerning his authority the people yielded to him and bestowed upon him all their authority and power.'

[5] *Digest*, i. 3. 31.   [6] Wiseman, *Law of Lawes*, p. 19.

[7] T. L. Humberstone, *University Representation* (London, 1951), p. 24.

as ultimately supreme',[1] a law which Maitland claimed could provide 'pleasant reading' for a king who wished to be monarch in Church and State,[2] and which C. H. McIlwain believed supplied James I with one of the intellectual foundations of his writings on the nature of kingship.[3] Indeed, one jurist has argued that the public law which the civilians studied at the universities accounts even more for the political division between them and their common law rivals than did their bitter disagreement over the important question of prohibitions:

But an even deeper ideological issue emerged from the study by civilians and common lawyers of their respective literary sources. In the *Corpus Juris* it was written 'What pleases the Prince is law.' To which Coke replied by quoting the famous words of Bracton, 'The King is subject not to men, but to God and the Law, because the Law makes the King'. There you have the confrontation. On the one hand, law is what pleases the prince: on the other, the King is subject to the law. These proved fighting words. They put the civil lawyers in the royalist camp and ranged the common lawyers against the royal pretensions.[4]

Generalizations such as these concerning the influence of the *Corpus Juris Civilis* on the civilians' political ideas must be viewed with considerable caution. The civil law was vague with respect to many political questions and in some instances it clearly suggested limitations to royal authority.[5] Indeed, the twelfth-century jurist Bracton used the precepts of the civil law to support his main contention that the King was under the law.[6] It does not follow, moreover, that just because the civil lawyers were exposed to the civil law, they automatically subscribed to the political theories

[1] R. A. Marchant, *The Puritans and the Church Courts in the Diocese of York 1560–1642* (London, 1960), p. 2. See also G. Williams, *The Welsh Church from Conquest to Reformation* (Cardiff, 1962), p. 312.

[2] Maitland, *English Law and the Renaissance*, pp. 14, 62 n.

[3] McIlwain, *Political Works of James*, p. xlii. D. H. Willson, *James VI and I* (London, 1956), p. 257; S. Prall, *The Agitation for Law Reform During the Puritan Revolution* (The Hague, 1966), p. 21, warns not to exaggerate the Roman influence.

[4] J. Simon, 'Dr. Cowell', *Cambridge Law Journal*, 26 (1968), 267.

[5] M. P. Gilmore, *Argument from Roman Law in Political Thought 1200–1600* (Cambridge, Mass., 1941), pp. 131–2.

[6] Tierney, 'Bracton', 297–8, 305. See also A. J. Carlyle, *A History of Medieval Political Theory in the West*, ii (Edinburgh, 1909), p. 69; E. Lewis, 'King Above the Law? "Quod Principi Placuit" in Bracton', *Speculum*, 39 (1964), 261.

thereby suggested. Only a small number of them composed formal political treatises, and of these an even smaller number cited the *Corpus Juris* frequently enough to indicate a causal connection between their legal education and their political views. Even when the connection is apparent, it is often difficult, if not impossible, to establish whether the civilians used the texts of the civil law to reinforce political positions already arrived at, or whether the law itself helped them to formulate a political ideology independent of external political and professional pressures.

The fact remains, however, that a number of civilians did grapple with fundamental political questions, such as the nature and extent of royal authority, in a wide variety of published and unpublished tracts, treatises, lectures, sermons, and parliamentary debates. These merit close scrutiny, since they shed considerable light on the nature of the civilians' royalist politics. They also provide a basis for comparing the theories of civil lawyers with those of royalist common lawyers, who in a number of judicial decisions upheld the King's right to exercise an absolute power when dealing with affairs of state or acting for the benefit of the commonwealth.[1] Finally, the theoretical statements of the civil lawyers allow an examination of the small but outspoken minority of civilians who dissented from the royalist consensus of their colleagues and have not yet received the attention they deserve.

(a) *The legitimacy of royal authority*

A number of civil lawyers gave formal expression to their political views in response to the statements of those Catholics who asserted that James I's claim to the throne was invalid, that the Pope had the right to depose him, that his subjects had no obligation to obey him, and that he had no authority in matters of religion.[2] Because of their hatred of Catholicism, or perhaps because of their desire to please the monarch upon whom they depended for their livelihood, the civil lawyers provided James

---

[1] See Judson, *Crisis*, pp. 107–70.

[2] For the arguments and political theories of the Catholics see T. H. Clancy, *Papist Pamphleteers: the Allen–Persons Party and the Political Thought of the Counter-Reformation in England, 1572–1615* (Chicago, Ill., 1964).

with considerable intellectual assistance in his attempt to counter these claims. John Hayward published three tracts, one as a direct reply to the English Jesuits,[1] and two in defence of the royal supremacy in religion.[2] Three treatises by Matthew Sutcliffe, the Dean of Exeter, served the same purposes equally well,[3] while Thomas Crompton composed a short piece on the excommunication of princes.[4] James Cooke, a relatively obscure Oxford civilian, inquired into the royal supremacy and the inviolability of the royal person in a study entitled *Juridica Trium Quaestionum ad Majestatem Pertinentium Determinatio*.[5]

Since some Catholics had challenged the very legitimacy of the English monarchy, these civilians found it necessary in their work to establish a certain foundation of James's position. The theory that they most consistently used for this purpose was that of divine right, according to which the King received his authority directly from God. Yet in addition to this standard religious justification of royal authority, the civilians had at their disposal a more secular, juristic rationale which was suggested by the *Corpus Juris Civilis*. For the Justinianic code stated unequivocally that the Roman people had transferred their authority and power to the emperor.[6] John Hayward demonstrated that this justification of Roman imperial authority could be applied with equal validity to England. In discussing the ways in which people abdicate their right to change the form of government under which they live, he wrote:

The first is by cession or grant; for so the Romans by the law of royalty yielded all their authority in government to the Prince. Of this law[7]

---

[1] J. Hayward, *An Answer to the First Part of a Certaine Conference Concerning Succession* (London, 1603).

[2] Id., *A Reporte of a Discourse Concerning Supreme Power in Affairs of Religion* (London, 1606). A later edition of this, dedicated to Prince Charles, entitled *Of Supremacie in Affairs of Religion*, appeared in 1624.

[3] M. Sutcliffe, *An Answere to a Certaine Libel* (London, 1592); *The Examination and Confutation of a Certain Scurrilous Treatise Entitled 'The Survey of the New Religion'* (London, 1606); *A Ful and Round Answer to N.D. alias Robert Parsons* (London, 1604).

[4] 'Dr. Crompton's Notes About Excommunication of Princes', ITL, Petyt MS. 538/38, ff. 47–8ᵛ.

[5] Oxford, 1608. This was intended as a reply to Robert Parsons's *Answer to the Fifth Part of Reports Lately Set Forth By Sir E. Coke* (1606).

[6] *Digest*, preface, 7. 1; i. 4. 1.   [7] i.e. *lex regia*, or regal law.

Ulpian maketh mention; and Bodin reporteth that it is yet extant in Rome graven in stone. So the people of Cyrene, of Pergame and of Bithynia, did submit themselves to the Empire of the Romans. So the Tartarians commit absolute power both over their lives and their livings to every one of their Emperors: & *so have our people many times committed to their king the authority of the Parliament either generally or else for some particular cause.* For it is held as a rule that any man may relinquish the authority which he hath to his own benefit and favour. Neither is he again at pleasure to be admitted to that which once he did think fit to renounce.[1]

This illustrates in striking fashion how the civil lawyers could use the text of the civil law to support their political views. But oddly enough the civilians who were engaged in the Catholic controversy did not rely heavily upon the prescriptions of that law. Even Hayward placed relatively slight emphasis on his analogy between Roman and English government. The other civilians made no allusion whatsoever to the theory of translated legislative sovereignty. One reason for their reluctance was probably the relative weakness of the argument, which can easily evoke its antithesis. For if the people originally possessed all legislative authority, could they not reclaim it from the emperor if they deemed it necessary? Indeed, when Roman lawyers of the eleventh century first used the text of *Corpus Juris Civilis* to justify the absolute authority of the Holy Roman Emperor against claims of papal superiority, the German monk Manegold of Lautenbach answered these jurists by arguing that even after surrendering their power the people remained the source of all political authority.[2] Throughout the later Middle Ages jurists such as Azo, Hugolinius, and William of Cuneo argued that the people never parted with their power in such a way that they could not reclaim it if necessary.[3] One French lawyer, Johannes Faber, actually went so far as to justify deposition of a monarch on the basis of this sanction contained in the *Corpus Juris Civilis*.[4] Even in the sixteenth

[1] Hayward, *Succession*, pp. 21–2. My italics.
[2] F. Kern, *Kingship and Law in the Middle Ages* (trans. and ed. S. B. Chrimes, New York, 1956), pp. 118–20.
[3] Carlyle, *History of Political Thought*, ii. 66; vi. 16–18.
[4] Ibid. vi. 22.

century, when most civil lawyers were developing the theory of unrestricted royal absolutism,[1] others took the opposite tack. In his study of sixteenth-century political thought J. W. Allen has explained that

Two conceptions were found in the *Corpus Juris*: the conception of a sovereign law-making *princeps* and the conception of the *princeps* as delegate of a sovereign people. The stress might be laid on one or the other, or even alternately on both. The study of the *Corpus Juris* did not necessarily turn men into royal absolutists. . . . The opponents of absolutism could have found texts on their side in the writings of these jurists had they looked for them: as in fact some did.[2]

Allen singles out Salamonius as one theorist who drew directly from the text of the civil law to establish legal limitations on the use of royal power.[3] Another civilian, François Hotman, rejected the theory of royal absolutism even more unequivocally than Salamonius.[4] Indeed, not only French Huguenots like Hotman, but Scots who wished to depose Mary Stuart[5] and Dutchmen who defended their revolt against their Spanish sovereign all used the prescriptions of the civil law to justify their acts of rebellion.

The Dutchman who made the most explicit use of the *Corpus Juris Civilis* to support the cause of popular sovereignty was Isaac Dorislaus, who emigrated to England and became one of the civilians who form the basis of this study. As a Dutchman, a republican, and eventually one of the regicides, Dorislaus could hardly be classified as a typical English civil lawyer. But although his views cannot be considered representative of those of his colleagues, they do illustrate that even in England the civil law was not always associated with the cause of absolute monarchy.

Dorislaus received his doctorate in civil law from the University of Leyden, but it was mainly through his interest in historical and antiquarian studies that he befriended such English notables as

[1] W. F. Church, *Constitutional Thought in Sixteenth Century France* (Harvard Historical Series, xlvii, 1941), pp. 43–73.

[2] J. W. Allen, *A History of Political Thought in the Sixteenth Century* (London, 1928), p. 281.   [3] Ibid., p. 333.

[4] Ibid., pp. 308–12; Pocock, *Ancient Constitution*, pp. 26–7.

[5] For arguments of Englishmen against Mary see J. E. Neale, *Queen Elizabeth and Her Parliaments, 1559–1581* (London, 1958), pp. 272–3.

John Selden, Lord Wharton, and Fulk Greville, Lord Brooke.[1] In 1627 Brooke nominated Dorislaus to hold a lectureship in history which he established at Cambridge that year.[2] Dorislaus delivered only two lectures as a Cambridge professor.[3] Both concerned the *Annals* of Tacitus, a historian who was highly critical of the rulers of early Rome. The lectures, therefore, gave the Dutchman an opportunity to expound upon his own theories of government. In doing so he made sufficient reference to the *lex regia* and the translation of power from the people to the emperor to confirm that he was concerned with the correct interpretation of the famous text of Justinian. In his inaugural lecture he addressed himself to the problem of tyranny and rebellion by posing the introductory question why 'some Kings rule their subjects as masters do their slaves, by the power of life and death', whereas others 'rely upon legitimate authority and are prevented from gaining absolute power by the restrictions of the laws'. The reason, he explained, was that the people often became so dependent upon one person that they 'transfer the highest power of ruling unto him, retaining no part to themselves'.[4] Alternatively, the people in 'electing a King' often reserve some functions to themselves, while conferring others upon the King in the fullness of the law.[5]

This first lecture, being largely descriptive, provoked little comment, although Matthew Wren, Master of Peterhouse, took offence that Dorislaus 'seemed to acknowledge no right of kingdoms but whereof the people's voluntary submission had been the *Principium Constitutum*'.[6] In his second lecture, however, the Cambridge professor gave much greater irritation to his conservative audience. In discussing the Roman form of government, he emphasized the people's continuing share in the political authority of the state:

The Populus Romanus, from whom the Kings claim to have acquired all their authority, was more powerful than the kings, and the people

---

[1] Hill, *Intellectual Origins*, p. 176.

[2] For full details of the appointment see R. A. Rebholz, *The Life of Fulke Greville, First Lord Brooke* (Oxford, 1971), pp. 293–4.

[3] The only extant record of the lectures are Matthew Wren's notes. PRO, SP 16/86/87 I.

[4] Ibid., f. 1.   [5] Ibid., f. 2.   [6] PRO, SP 16/86/87.

controlled that authority in the kings, because each successive king acquired it from the people. . . . The highest power of Rome remained in the people.[1]

Dorislaus admitted that some peoples, such as the Hebrews and early Christians, did transfer all authority to the King and his successors unconditionally. But others, like the Romans, kept it divided between Prince and people. The major problem in such an arrangement was the prevention of one party's taking possession of the other by force. And since each party naturally sought to defend its share in the sovereignty of the State, conflict could result, as it had in the Netherlands between the Dutch people and their Spanish King.[1]

The reference to Holland led Dorislaus into a short digression on the legality of rebellion against a Prince. He inquired what the duty of the good citizen was when some 'hostile spirit' arouses the King to the destruction of his entire nation, as it had in the reign of the Emperor Caligula. Dorislaus admonished private citizens to exercise caution in deciding what action they should take, but his refusal to condemn an entire people's rebellion against an unjust Prince betrayed his Calvinist and Dutch nationalist sympathies.[2] Then, in order to destroy any formal legal argument against the ideas that he had put forth, Dorislaus concluded his lecture with a historical critique of the famous Justinianic text:

In the time of those princes who usurped the regium imperium in the free Republic of Rome, I find no instance of popular sovereignty abolished by authority or by law. For as far as the *lex regia* is concerned, by which it is said that the Populus bestowed all its authority upon the Prince *and also upon itself*, that law was of such a kind, acquired at what time, by whom [and] in what words that no one skilled in the law could explain it, nor can the truth be ignored that the most nefarious Tribonianus presented this fabrication to the Emperor Justinian.[3]

Tribonianus was the principal jurist who had compiled the *Corpus Juris Civilis* for Justinian.[4] Dorislaus claimed that the transfer of

---

[1] SP 16/86/87 I, f. 2.

[2] Ibid., f. 3. For the Calvinist theories of resistance see Allen, *Political Thought*, pp. 302–42, *passim*.   [3] SP 16/86/87 I, f. 3.

[4] W. Kunkel, *An Introduction to Roman Legal and Constitutional History* (Oxford, 1966), pp. 155–6.

authority from the people to the emperor, in the way that Tribonianus had described it, had never actually occurred. There is some merit in this view. The source that the *Corpus* cited was Ulpian, who the historian Fritz Schulz has proved could not possibly have written the exact words of the *Digest*. Apart from literary inconsistencies, the emperors of Ulpian's time ruled by the classical *lex de imperio Vespasiani*, which gave them only limited power, although this power did include the right to make law.[1] According to Schulz, therefore, the compilers of the *Digest* had actually remodelled Ulpian's dictum (which is now unknown) and had adapted it to the constitutional law of their own times.[2] Dorislaus appears to have been absolutely correct.

Irrespective of its historical accuracy, Dorislaus's lecture was not well received. He had avoided any mention of England in the course of his lecture, but his words, 'being bred in a popular air . . . were interpreted by high monarchical ears, as overpraising a state in disgrace of a kingdom'.[3] Wren sent notes of both lectures to William Laud, who brought pressure upon the Duke of Buckingham, then Chancellor of Cambridge, to ask Dorislaus to resign.[4] The civilian expressed surprise that his comments had caused such alarm, and he claimed that he did not understand why what was heard abroad with such applause could not be spoken of freely elsewhere.[5] Brooke hoped that Dorislaus would resume his lectures at some later date under happier auspices,[6] but his hopes were never realized.

Dorislaus's brief lectures reveal how effectively the precepts of the civil law could be marshalled in favour of republican political

[1] F. Schulz, 'Bracton on Kingship', *EHR* 60 (1945), 154.

[2] More recent scholarship, however, has placed responsibility for the falsification on jurists of the third century. Kunkel, *Legal and Constitutional History*, pp. 119, 137, 160–2.

[3] Fuller, *Cambridge*, p. 165.

[4] V. H. H. Green, *Religion at Oxford and Cambridge* (London, 1964), p. 131.

[5] PRO, SP 16/86/87.

[6] N. Farmer, Jr., 'Fulke Greville and Sir John Coke: An Exchange of Letters on a History Lecture and Certain Latin Verses on Sir Philip Sidney', *Huntington Library Quarterly*, 33 (1970), 234. Dorislaus seems to have nursed a strong dislike of Cambridge. See his letter to Grotius, 10 Feb. 1631, *Briefwisselung van Hugo Grotius*, iv. (Riks Geshiedkundige Publicatien Grote Serie cxiii), p. 325.

views. Those civilians who endeavoured to set forth the most certain rationale of royal authority were doubtless aware of this, and hence they chose a theological rather than a juristic argument to support their case. Certainly appointment by God was a far less disputable foundation of James's authority than a legal precept which claimed that all his power came originally from the people. Later in the seventeenth century a Scottish civilian epitomized the preference of his English predecessors by declaring that 'The King is the author and fountain of all power, and is an absolute Prince, . . . deriving his power from God Almighty alone and so not from the people.'[1]

(b) *The nature and attributes of sovereignty*

While the civilians who were involved in the pamphlet war against the Catholics were concerned with the foundation of the English King's authority, some of their colleagues inquired into the nature of that authority, often concluding that is was 'sovereign' or 'absolute'. One sense in which the civilians used these terms with respect to the English monarch was not as politically controversial as one might suspect. Since the Reformation the concept of England as an empire in the Roman fashion, as one free from all external control, had become a commonplace.[2] To say that the King was the emperor, sovereign, or absolute monarch of this political entity could hardly be denied, except by Papists.[3] These titles simply designated the King as the ruler of an autonomous state and did not define a precise constitutional relationship between him and his domestic subjects. They declared him to be free from the laws of all foreign powers, especially the Papacy, but not from the laws of his own kingdom. Sir Edward Coke, a lawyer most insistent upon the King's subjection to the common law of the realm, found no difficulty in stating his belief 'that the

---

[1] Sir George MacKenzie, *The Institutions of the Laws of Scotland* (Edinburgh, 1684), pp. 17–18.

[2] 24 Henry VIII, c. 12; Curtis, *Oxford and Cambridge*, p. 156.

[3] Ridley, *A View*, p. 103. 'By the Empire I understand not only the Empire of Rome . . . but also every several Kingdom, which acknowledgeth no other Emperor than his own sovereign.'

kingdom of England is an absolute monarchy, and that the King
is the only supreme governor as well over ecclesiastical persons
and in ecclesiastical causes as temporal within the realm'.[1] When
civilians described the legal status of their King, they often asserted
nothing more than had Coke. Thus Arthur Duck wrote that 'our
kings acknowledge the [Holy Roman] Emperor neither in law
nor fact, have no superior in their dominions but God alone,
exercise all rights of sovereignty; are monarchs, and as sovereign
princes no appeal can lie from them'.[2] Duck's frame of reference
was international, not domestic law. Even his allusion to the
King's superiority within the realm was intended more as a denial
of the authority of foreign rulers over him than as a confirmation
of his universally acknowledged superiority at English law over
all other persons in the kingdom.

Perhaps on account of their professional involvement with
problems of international law, the English civilians devoted considerable attention to the question of which rulers qualified as
sovereign princes or absolute monarchs.[3] Dr. Calibute Downing,
in order to accommodate the Protestant German princes who
were at war with the Holy Roman Emperor within that category,
applied fairly liberal criteria to this problem.[4] Other civilians were
much stricter. Gentili doubted whether even the kings of France
and Spain qualified as truly absolute rulers, since those monarchs
still recognized the jurisdiction of the Pope in spiritual affairs. He
insisted that

Genuine and happy princes are those who acknowledge foreign jurisdiction in not even the smallest matter and who do not have any
citizens who pay respect to a foreign jurisdiction, either temporal or
spiritual, in any concern, however minor. The others are not supreme
princes; on the contrary they are not even princes if others assume the
first place before them.[5]

---

[1] Coke, *Reports*, v. 40.   [2] Duck, *De Usu*, pp. 320–1.
[3] BM, Lansdowne MS. 152, ff. 352–3. Bird, in defending the Jew Pallachia
against the Spanish Ambassador in the Admiralty Court, referred to his client as
the minister of an 'absolute Prince'—the King of Morocco.
[4] Calibute Downing, *A Discourse Upon the Interest of England* (London, 1641),
pp. 10–11.
[5] Gentili, *De Potestate*, p. 8.

Gentili and his colleagues never even disputed the classification of the King of England as one of the absolute rulers of the world. To Thomas Crompton the English monarch was 'more absolute in his dominions than the Emperor',[1] while in John Cowell's estimation there was not one point of regality 'that belonged to the most absolute Prince in the world which doth not also belong to our King'.[2]

While the civilians often prefaced their arguments concerning royal power with references to the imperial status of England and of its monarch, their presentations rarely remained, as had Arthur Duck's, at the level of international law. Once they established the King's sovereignty and freedom from external control, they proceeded to demonstrate how it was similarly exempt from all internal restrictions. Verbally they made the transition in the meaning of 'absolute' or 'sovereign' from 'autonomous' to 'legally unrestricted'.[3] Gentili accomplished this without even breaking the continuity of his thought. In the context of his discussion about which princes qualified as absolute rulers he claimed that 'supreme princes are those who are above all men in all things'—a phrase that encompassed both interpretations of the term absolutism.[4] He then proceeded to quote Jean Bodin's description of sovereign power within the State, defining it as that 'absolute and perpetual power which the Latins called *majestas*'.[5] Gentili's reliance upon and imitation of Bodin was strong, and one historian has drawn the comparison that 'just as Bodin in France, he was the theoretical founder of absolutism in England'.[6]

Other English civilians, most notably Hayward, Zouch, Cooke, and Fletcher, similarly tapped the ideas of their famed French colleague, some quoting him directly.[7] But the important question

[1] BM, Cotton MS. Titus F. IV, f. 242ᵛ.

[2] Cowell, *Interpreter*, sub 'Prerogative of the King'.

[3] Chrimes, 'Cowell', 481, n. 1.

[4] Gentili, *De Potestate*, p. 8; for Crompton's transition see Judson, *Crisis*, pp. 138–9.

[5] Gentili, *De Potestate*, p. 9. See J. Bodin, *Les Six Livres de La République* (Paris, 1576), p. 125.

[6] G. van der Molen, *Alberico Gentili and the Development of International Law* (Amsterdam, 1938), p. 239.

[7] Hayward, *Of Supremacie*, pp. 9–10; L. Berry (ed.), *The English Works of Giles*

for all of these English civilians, as it was for Bodin, was not whether sovereign power existed or even where it was located, but in what it consisted. It was one thing to claim that the Prince possessed absolute power, but quite another to spell out exactly in what ways that power found expression. Bodin himself, while stressing the breadth and unlimited nature of the sovereign's power, nevertheless identified that power with a constellation of specific prerogatives, such as the right to make law.[1]

Most English thought upon this subject, even among those royalist common law judges who admitted that the King possessed an absolute power, was vague. The royalists did specify that the King's absolute power was applicable only when he was dealing with 'affairs of state', and among these they occasionally mentioned such matters as the making of war and peace, the use of martial law, and the regulation of trade.[2] Yet they referred to these individual areas of activity within the context of judicial decisions concerning cases in which the King's right to act absolutely in one such capacity was the point at issue. They did not set down, independent of judicial action, the sum total of the King's prerogatives. One reason was that the royal prerogative was of such a sacred and mysterious quality that unnecessary discussion of it was to be avoided. Queen Elizabeth had repeatedly reminded her parliaments of this,[3] and James I objected to Cowell's *Interpreter* on the same grounds.[4] The very strength of the prerogative lay in its vagueness, for to define was to limit.

A further reason why the common lawyers did not submit the royal prerogative to definition was that the common law itself failed to do so. That law did, of course, distinguish a number of

Fletcher the Elder (Madison, Wisc., 1964), pp. 194–5; Cooke, *De Juridica*, p. 30. It is noteworthy that an English edition of Bodin (trans. Richard Knolles), *Of the Lawes and Customs of a Commonwealth* or *The Six Bookes of a Commonweale* appeared in 1606. Sir Anthony Cope may have been referring to Bodin when in 1610 he inquired if Cowell had 'confederates . . . from beyond the sea'. *CJ* i. 400.

[1] Bodin, *Six Livres*, pp. 190–218.

[2] For Sir Thomas Fleming's and Sir William Berkeley's statement see *State Trials*, ii. 389; iii. 1099. Sir Francis Crawley provided the most complete treatment of the question. See Judson, *Crisis*, p. 140.

[3] Neale, *Parliaments 1584–1601*, pp. 211–12, 357, 378.

[4] James I, 'This Later Age'; Chrimes, 'Cowell', 473.

special feudal and legal rights and privileges that belonged to the King,[1] but these components of his prerogative were of a different nature from the absolute or discretionary power that freed the King from the rules of the law.[2] If a common lawyer wished to justify the exercise of that absolute power, he had to rely upon either historical evidence of its customary use in the past[3] or the prescriptions of such other legal codes as the law merchant or the law of nations. Sir John Davies actually suggested that the King had acquired the sum total of his absolute power from the law of nations, which held sway in England before the common law came and imposed restrictions upon it.[4] The common law exerted only a negative influence in the definition of absolute royal power. Its purpose was to define the rights of the subject, not the prerogatives of the monarch.

The civil law, however, comprising large portions of public as well as private law, contained explicit statements of what activities were proper to an absolute prince. The civilians, having mastered this law, were more inclined than their professional rivals to summarize the points in which sovereignty consisted.[5] Because of their individual prejudices, their failure to adhere to the actual words of the civil law, and the variety of purposes for which they wrote, they did not even approach unanimity of opinion. Yet each civilian's formulations do contribute to a general indication of how much freedom of action the members of the profession were willing to concede to their King.

In general terms the civilians claimed that the absolute power that they ascribed to the King was no wider than the absolute royal prerogative which the royalist common lawyers defined so imprecisely. Gentili said of *majestas* that

it is an extraordinary and free power; it is that which in England we signify by the name (at least as far as I understand it) the *royal*

[1] Many of these are included in Staunford, *An Exposition of the Kinges Prerogative, Collected out of the Great Abridgement of Justice Fitzherbert* (London, 1577). See Judson, *Crisis*, pp. 23–4.
[2] Ibid., pp. 23–43; see also Wormuth, *Prerogative*, p. 53.
[3] As Fleming did, *State Trials*, ii. 392–4.
[4] J. Davies, *The Question Concerning Impositions* (London, 1656), pp. 29–30.
[5] Wormuth, *Prerogative*, pp. 5–6, 53.

prerogative. And so the interpreters of that law commonly write, there is a double power in the king, an ordinary one bound to the laws and another extraordinary one, free from the laws.[1]

John Cowell, in working out a definition of the royal prerogative, arrived at the same equation:

Prerogative of the King (*Prerogativa Regis*) is that especial power, pre-eminence, or privilege that the King hath in any kind, over and above other persons and above the ordinary course of the common law, in the right of his crown. And this word (*Prerogativa*) is used by the civilians in the same sense . . . so our lawyers *sub prerogativis regis* do comprise also, all that absolute height of power that the civilians call *majestatem vel potestatem vel juris imperii.*[2]

John Hayward supplied the rest of the common law theory by restricting the use of the absolute power to 'those affairs of state which are of greatest importance and weight'—those that 'are of so high nature that upon the ordering of them dependeth not only the honour and dignity but the safety also and liberty of the people'.[3]

When the civilians descended to particulars and explained exactly what those important affairs of state were, they revealed the true breadth of their conception of sovereignty. Richard Zouch, of all the civilians, furnished the most orderly summary of the attributes of the supreme prince. He distinguished, in addition to a number of 'personal prerogatives', five 'prerogatives of justice' which he culled from the texts of the *Corpus Juris Civilis:*

1. The power of determining weights and measures;
2. The power of coining money;
3. The power of constituting magistrates for the dispensation of justice;
4. The authorship and interpretation of the laws, as well as independence from those laws;
5. The power of life and death; hence of reducing punishments and of pardon.[4]

---

[1] Gentili, *De Potestate*, p. 10.
[2] Cowell, *Interpreter*, sub 'Prerogative of the King'.
[3] Hayward, *Reporte*, pp. 7–8.   [4] Zouch, *Elementa*, pp. 60–1.

This list was less comprehensive than the catalogue of prerogatives compiled by Bodin,[1] but Giles Fletcher and Thomas Crompton, in less formal statements, mentioned the two glaring omissions in Zouch's work: the power of making war and peace and the power to levy taxes.[2] John Cowell in his *Interpreter* extended the power of life and death to include the administration of martial law, according to which the King in time of war 'useth absolute power, in that his word goeth for law'.[3]

Those civilians who were concerned almost exclusively with the Catholic threat referred to the supreme control of ecclesiastical affairs as one of the most essential attributes of sovereignty. Hayward, Sutcliffe, and Cooke were so preoccupied with the establishment of this point that they forewent any further elaboration upon how the supreme power of the Prince found expression. It was enough for Hayward to assert that 'the political government in ecclesiastical affairs should be a point of regality',[4] and for Cooke to spell out in the most precise terms what parts of the spirituality were properly 'imperial'.[5]

(c) *The relationship of the King to the law and to Parliament*

There was nothing novel in the assignment of most of these powers to the King. Few Englishmen of the early seventeenth century would have objected to the King's right to coin money or pardon the accused, and only a distinct minority contested his supremacy in religion. Yet the assertion by Zouch and some other civil lawyers that the King possessed the sole power of making and interpreting the laws was bold, innovative, and dangerous. Certainly it was the most comprehensive of all the King's prerogatives. For Bodin it had been the first and chief mark of sovereignty,

---

[1] The nine were making laws, war and peace, creating and appointing magistrates, last appeal, grace and pardon, liege fealty and homage, coining money, determining weights and measures, and imposing taxes, Bodin, *Six Livres*, pp. 190–218.

[2] *Works of Fletcher*, p. 194. Crompton, like Davies, only allowed a tax on trade for its regulation, BM, Cotton MS. Titus F IV, f. 242. No civilian explicitly included a general right of taxation among the King's powers.

[3] Cowell, *Interpreter*, sub 'Martial Law'. See also Smith, *Commonwealth*, pp. 7–8.
[4] Hayward, *Reporte*, p. 4.   [5] Cooke, *Juridica*, pp. 4–30.

the *sine qua non* of true absolutism.¹ Yet the public endorsement of Bodin's views in England was the height of constitutional heresy. During the Tudor period legislative sovereignty was generally considered to have been located in Parliament. According to Sir Thomas Smith, a civilian, Parliament was the 'most high and absolute power of the realm of England'.² The legislative power of the government was shared, therefore, by the participants in the parliamentary process—King, Lords, and Commons. This constitutional arrangement did not detract from the authority of the King, since the monarch was indispensable to the proper functioning of Parliament and since the Lords and Commons reinforced rather than restricted his own power therein. Parliament served the purposes of the King by passing legislation which he and his ministers devised, including a number of statutes whose desired effect was to exalt the authority of the Crown.³ As long as this convenient harmony persisted, there was no need to attempt a more precise distinction between the legislative power of the King and that of Parliament.

During the reign of Elizabeth, however, dissension between the monarch and members of the House of Commons, especially a number of Puritan M.P.s, began to mount. The Queen used her veto power against parliamentary legislation more frequently, with the result that fewer parliamentary bills passed into law.⁴ Consequently she became increasingly dependent upon other legal powers that the monarch possessed by virtue of the royal prerogative, all of which were subsumed under the generic name *lex coronae*.⁵ This *lex*, as distinct from the *lex parliamenti* or statute law, sanctioned the monarch's use of royal proclamations (a law of sorts) and her administration of justice through royal commissions. In *Cawdrey's Case* (1591) the judges determined that with respect to

¹ Bodin, *Six Livres*, p. 197; Bodin explains that in one sense this was the only mark of sovereignty, since it embodied all the others.

² Smith, *Commonwealth*, pp. 45–6.

³ See W. H. Dunham, 'Regal Power and the Rule of Law: A Tudor Paradox', *Journal of British Studies*, 3 (1964), 30–2.

⁴ R. W. K. Hinton, 'The Decline of Parliamentary Government Under Elizabeth I and the Early Stuarts', *Cambridge Historical Journal*, 13 (1957), 116–32.

⁵ Dunham, 'Regal Power', 25, 51–6.

the establishment of ecclesiastical commissions 'the ancient law of the Crown' (the power to render justice) and the laws of Parliament were of equal validity and force,[1] thereby discrediting the notion that in such matters the Lords and Commons were indispensable. Shortly thereafter King James declared that even when the monarch did decide to legislate in a parliamentary way, the 'laws are but craved by his subjects and only made by him at their rogation and with their advice'.[2] Members of the House of Commons, however, would not stand for such a belittlement of their importance within the legislative process, and they brought the issue to a head in the early seventeenth century.

Most civilians were reluctant to become involved in this thorny constitutional dispute. Hayward emphasized the King's original establishment of Parliament and his continuing role as a legislator, but he did not press the issue any further.[3] Sutcliffe and Cooke confined themselves to a discussion of the King's authority in spiritual affairs and thereby avoided the problem completely. But Cowell, Gentili, and Zouch took a definite stand and placed legislative sovereignty with the King alone. Zouch did so in passing, without making specific reference to Parliament.[4] Gentili was not much more explicit in arguing that the King was under no obligation to legislate in conjunction with 'conciliar bodies'.[5] Cowell, however, made specific reference to the English Parliament in treating this constitional issue. Under the titles of 'King', 'Parliament', 'Prerogative of the King', and 'Subsidy' in *The Interpreter*, Cowell set forth his views. In effect he made four claims: that the 'Prince of his absolute power might make law of himself'; that when the King made laws in Parliament he admitted the Lords and Commons 'not of constraint but of his own benignity' and received their consent only for the better justice and effectiveness of the laws; that he could quash any law passed by the Lords and Commons; and that he was above the positive laws of Parliament and therefore could dispense with statutes by his own will.

---

[1] Coke, *Reports*, v. 8–9; Dunham, 'Regal Power', 52.
[2] McIlwain, *Political Works of James I*, p. 62.
[3] Hayward, *Succession*, p. 34; Allen, *Political Thought*, p. 259.
[4] Zouch, *Elementa*, p. 60.   [5] Gentili, *De Potestate*, pp. 23–4.

Why these suggestions infuriated the members of the House of Commons needs little explanation.[1] Cowell was ascribing to James I by law everything that monarch had arrogated to himself by divine right. He was claiming that among the participants in the parliamentary process the King was the dominant, controlling, and in the final analysis superior partner, who possessed the right not only to veto any bill he wished but to dispense with the application of statutes which had already passed into law. By themselves the Lords and Commons had no legislative power whatsoever. Conversely, the King had no need of the Lords and Commons and could, if he so wished, legislate of his own independent authority.

If one recognizes that Cowell compiled his dictionary well before the disagreements between King and Parliament erupted into civil war, and that his purpose in defining these legal terms was not to advocate any particular course of political action but simply to clarify the nature of a complex constitutional arrangement, the author does not appear to have been the irresponsible political rascal that historians such as Gardiner have made him out to be.[2] Cowell never suggested that James dispense with Parliament altogether. Indeed, the professor made it quite clear that the King's 'merciful policy' to make law by the consent of the whole realm was 'not alterable without great peril'.[3] He merely set out to clear up centuries of constitutional and legal ambiguity, and actually came up with a tenable solution to the problem. Few Englishmen of his day would have denied that the King could legislate by himself through proclamations, that he could dispense with at least certain types of statutes,[4] that he could veto parlia-

[1] See above, p. 4. A second, unauthorized printing of Cowell's dictionary by J. Hodgkinson in 1638 at Doctors' Commons also gave rise to angry protests. Bodl., Tanner MS. 67, f. 25; *CSPD 1638–1639*, p. 55; *1641–1643*, pp. 551–2; W. Laud, *The History of the Troubles and Tryal of . . . William Laud* (London, 1695), p. 235.

[2] S. Gardiner, *History of England from the Accession of James I to the Outbreak of the Civil War 1603–1642* (London, 1884), ii. 66–7.

[3] Cowell, *Interpreter*, sub 'Parliament'.

[4] See P. Birdsall, ' "Non Obstante": A Study of the Dispensing Power of English Kings', *Essays in History and Political Theory* (Cambridge, Mass., 1936), pp. 37–76.

mentary legislation, and that without his approval decisions of Parliament had no validity at law. If forced to distinguish one member of Parliament in whom legislative sovereignty lay, they would have found it difficult not to have selected the King. But at the same time they were accustomed to regard the entire Parliament as the highest and most absolute authority in the land, by which all their most important laws were made. 'How then', asks S. B. Chrimes, 'was the (apparently) absolute power of the king reconciled with the manifest practical indispensability of the parliament in the legislative and fiscal spheres?'

Only in terms of expediency, custom, and royal acquiescence, and these, after all, were the true historical explanations of how these illogicalities had come into being. There was no legal rule that Cowell or any one else could find which laid down that the king *must* make laws or raise subsidies only with the assent of parliament; there was no such legal rule then, and only indirectly is there any such rule now.[1]

Yet objective historical and legal analysis was hardly the forte of the members of the Parliament of 1610. Their superficial confrontation with Cowell's definitions left the impression that the Cambridge professor was intending 'to take away the power and authority of the parliament'.[2] Moreover, Cowell had in the context of his discussion about Parliament volunteered another constitutional opinion which caused even greater consternation at Westminster.[3] He declared that the King was 'above the law by his absolute power'[4]—a status so essential to Cowell's conception of true sovereignty that he admitted 'Of these two one must needs be true: that either the King is above Parliament, that is, above the positive laws of his kingdom, or else he is not an absolute King.'[5]

Cowell did not explore the full implications of his statement. He did not examine all the different ways in which the King was said to be above the law. Since his immediate concern was the relation between the King and Parliament, he was content to establish that

[1] Chrimes, 'Cowell', 480.   [2] Foster, *Proceedings*, i. 18.
[3] Ibid. ii. 38–9. This took precedence as the first of three points raised against Cowell.
[4] Cowell, *Interpreter*, sub 'King'.   [5] Ibid., sub 'Parliament'.

the King's superiority over the laws allowed him to dispense with parliamentary statutes, provided of course that the monarch did not violate the rights of other subjects in the process.[1] He said nothing else about the King's relationship to the law, nor did he refer to the civil law doctrine 'princeps legibus solutus est'.

Where Cowell was reticent, however, Gentili was explicit, and as the Oxford professor allegedly articulated the most extreme absolutist views within England, it is imperative to discover exactly what he meant when he placed the King above the law. The actual text of the civil law by no means freed the King from all restraints whatsoever,[2] and Gentili did labour towards a judicious assessment of that text's true meaning. As a first step he placed himself in complete agreement with those medieval civilians who insisted that the monarch, irrespective of his superiority to the laws of the realm, was not exempt from the dictates of the divine and the natural law:

> For the Prince is still under God and held to the law of God. We speak of the absolute power of the Prince in relation to citizens. God is, by his purely absolute power, not bound by any laws, whether they be his own laws, the laws of nature, or the laws of nations. . . . The Prince, writes Baldus, is above the law, namely the civil law; below the law, namely the law of nature and of nations. He is not above divine law, so write he and Bartolus and Angelus.[3]

This of course was no startling concession from a devoted Christian and a lawyer who took his inspiration from the great medieval civilians of France and Italy. To argue otherwise would have separated him from a consensus among European writers which included even the most convinced champions of absolutism.[4] Subscription to an alternative theory would have required a secularization of political thought which had begun earlier in Italy

[1] Cowell, *Institutes*, p. 5.
[2] See A. Esmein, 'La Maxime "Princeps Legibus Solutus Est" dans l'ancien droit public français', *Essays in Legal History* (ed. P. Vinogradoff, London, 1913), 201–2.
[3] Gentili, *De Potestate*, p. 17.
[4] Bodin, *Six Livres*, pp. 130, 133, 145; McIlwain, *Political Works of James*, p. xliv. Also, Hayward, *Succession*, p. 41.

with Machiavelli but which made no apparent inroads in England until the time of Hobbes.[1]

Not only was the idea that the Prince had to conform to the divine and natural law so universally accepted at this time that Gentili could claim no intellectual courage or ingenuity in making it, but it was so devoid of sanction and in actual political terms so meaningless that it cut no ice with his critics. Instead of amounting to a restriction of the King's power, it served as a euphemistic way of exaggerating it. The way in which Gentili, Hayward, Bodin, and James I all defined the absolute height of power was by proclaiming the law of God to be its only boundary.[2] What was important was not the subjection to God but the freedom from the control of all men. In exposing the irony of this distinction, the Parliamentarian critic of Gentili bitterly reminded his audience that Charles I had frequently appealed to the adage that kings were responsible to God alone in order to justify his policies, which actually violated God's law of justice itself.[3]

Aside from conforming to the laws of God and of nature, the English monarch described and idealized by Gentili accepted one further limitation to his absolute power. When acting in his ordinary and private capacity, he was obliged to observe the positive laws of the kingdom. This obligation was itself hedged by a number of reservations which medieval civilians and theologians had already formulated. Paramount among these was the distinction that the King submitted to the laws voluntarily and not by necessity. Only subjects were constrained to follow the positive laws of the realm, for 'The Prince is within the law, that is, he voluntarily obeys the laws. Subjects are under the law; they act according to the law of necessity, driven by force.'[4]

Once again, the weakness of the theory lay in its inability to

[1] Among lawyers in England reference to a higher law was common until the time of Bentham. See J. W. Gough, *Fundamental Law in English History* (Oxford, 1955), pp. 188–91.

[2] Hayward, *Supremacie*, p. 5; Bodin, *Six Livres*, p. 130; McIlwain, *Political Works of James*, pp. 55, 61.

[3] *Englands Monarch*, pp. 3, 8–9.

[4] Gentili, *De Potestate*, p. 30. For a discussion of the concept of the King's moral authority in Tudor England see F. Baumer, *The Tudor Theory of Kingship* (New Haven, 1940), pp. 192–210.

suggest an adequate means of enforcing the King's observance of the laws. Gentili's critic, writing at the time of the Civil War, was particularly sensitive to this deficiency, and he refused to accept 'that distinction of some divines, who say the Prince to be subject to the directive, but not to the coactive or compulsive power of the law'.[1] Yet the Parliamentarians had themselves applied coercive power against the King to enforce his observance of the laws of the realm only with the greatest hesitation and reluctance. Gentili wrote his treatise nearly forty years before they took this step, at a time when political conflict of such magnitude was inconceivable and when the writings of not one political theorist in England, civilian or non-civilian, furnished an alternative opinion to his own. The reason why the King could not be forced to observe the laws was because he had no superior who could bring action against him. A ruler who 'possesses the power of the laws' in himself could not direct that power against his own person.[2] Accursius,[3] Salicetus,[4] Budé,[5] and other civilians respected this invulnerability of the King without denying his moral obligation to observe the laws. Medieval theologians, such as Thomas Aquinas, were in agreement. 'The Prince is said to be free from the law', wrote Aquinas, 'because no one can pass judgment condemning him if he acts against the law . . . but as regards the directive force of the law the prince is subject to the law by his own will.'[6]

Among English authors Bracton had taken a similar stance. The King was *sub lege* in that he had an obligation to live according to the law, but the only guarantee of his adherence to it was his own good will.[7] The King's physical exemption from the law was recognized universally in England, and the adage 'The King can

[1] *Englands Monarch*, p. 13.

[2] Gentili, *De Potestate*, p. 31. 'Can he who has the laws in his power be within the power of the laws?'

[3] Tierney, 'Bracton', 301-12.

[4] Gentili, *De Vi Civium in Regem Semper Iniusta*, in *Regales Disputationes Tres*, p. 117. Salicetus believed that although the King was not tied to the laws, shame and his conscience forced him into observance.

[5] Gentili, *De Potestate*, p. 32.   [6] *Summa Theologica*, 1. 2. 96. 5.

[7] G. Lapsley, 'Bracton and the Authorship of the "Addicio de Cartis"', *EHR* 62 (1947), 9.

do no wrong' epitomized the rationale for his privilege. As Dr. Gooch told the Parliament of 1621, 'The King can not do a man wrong because there is none higher to complain.'[1] Gentili was on solid constitutional ground when he applied the maxim 'princeps legibus solutus est' to England, as was his successor at Oxford, Richard Zouch, when he echoed the words of his master some thirty years later: 'He [the King] is not bound by the civil laws. For the condition of the Emperor, under whom God places these laws, is exempted in all things. Nevertheless it is fitting, says Paul, that the Prince serve the laws of which he himself is free.'[2]

(d) The problem of resistance

If kings were exempt from the penalties of the laws and obeyed them only voluntarily, it was of the utmost importance that they be just and virtuous men. According to Gentili, absolute power was 'to exist as the will of a virtuous man'. A prince could not exploit that power for intrinsically evil purposes, nor could he by virtue thereof deprive a subject of his property without just cause.[3] But it was still at the discretion of the King to determine when that just cause existed,[4] and there was no way to ensure adequately that the ruler followed the dictates of his conscience. The civilians had to place a great deal of faith and trust in the person to whom they attributed the full height of political power.

As if to dispel all possible doubt, Gentili affirmed that the Prince to whom he had dedicated the treatise qualified as a truly just and virtuous monarch.[5] Yet despite this assurance, Gentili still could not skirt the ultimate question of what recourse the members of a commonwealth had when their prince so blatantly violated the laws of God and of the kingdom as to destroy the faith and trust that they had placed in him. The Oxford professor addressed himself to this problem in the third of his *Regales Disputationes Tres*, which was entitled *De Vi Civium in Regem Semper Iniusta*. As the title suggests, Gentili denied the right of subjects to take violent action against a legal prince regardless how tyrannical his

---

[1] *NRS* vi. 141.   [2] Zouch, *Elementa*, p. 61.
[3] Gentili, *De Potestate*, p. 27.   [4] Ibid.; *Englands Monarch*, p. 11.
[5] Gentili, *De Potestate*, p. 27.

rule might become.[1] In taking this position he placed himself in agreement with a number of his colleagues. Hayward, Sutcliffe, and Crompton, intending to discredit Jesuitical theories of resistance, all declared that the King was the immediate minister of God, that God 'seateth Kings in their state', and that therefore the person of the King is inviolable.[2] No matter how strongly these civil lawyers insisted that the King must obey the divine and natural law or how sternly they inveighed against the evils of tyrannical rule, they would not sanction the people's right to take action against him. Hayward wrote:

If they [Kings] abuse their power, they are not to be judged by their subjects, as being both inferior and naked of authority, because all jurisdiction within the realm is derived from them, which their preference doth only silence and suspend: but God reserveth them to the sorest trial.[3]

Should kings command subjects to commit actions forbidden by the word of God, the subjects were not obliged to obey. But even then, they were still not allowed to remedy the abuses of princely rule. Instead, Hayward recommended to such afflicted souls that 'we must show our subjection by patient enduring.'[4]

Despite the civilians' frequent articulation of the theory of non-resistance in the early seventeenth century, it was by no means the exclusive intellectual property of their profession. It enjoyed widespread and unquestioned support among Englishmen during this period, and the civil lawyers did not distinguish themselves through their public adherence to it. Nor did they attach their own peculiar stamp to the doctrine by justifying it with quotes from the civil law. Instead they fell back upon the well-worn scriptural references and opinions of theologians.[5] Gentili, it is true, did cite medieval jurists to substantiate his opinions. But he relied upon the actual text of the *Corpus Juris Civilis* only indirectly, to the extent that it had already served to establish the Prince

[1] Gentili, *De Vi Civium*, esp. pp. 109–11.
[2] ITL, Petyt MS. 538/38/f. 47; Sutcliffe, *Answer to Libel*, p. 95; *Examination of Survey*, p. 79.
[3] Hayward, *Succession*, p. 45.
[4] Ibid., p. 46.   [5] Ibid., p. 42.

as an absolute monarch. Divine law, historical analogies, and philosophical reflection were the main ingredients of his exposition.

These actually placed him on more certain ground than did the text of the civil law, for a theory of non-resistance did not necessarily proceed from an examination of the code of Justinian. As has already been shown, the one civil lawyer who towards the end of this period did rely heavily upon the prescriptions of the *Corpus* concluded that rebellion against a prince was justified under certain circumstances. Isaac Dorislaus, believing that the *Populus Romanus* never surrendered all of its power to the Emperor but retained some part for itself, virtually admitted the right of the people to defend their share in the sovereignty of the State. Dorislaus phrased his statements cautiously and recommended that before taking any action private citizens should test over-all public opinion on the question and consult as many authors as possible who treated the subject. He inserted a warning, moreover, against the excesses of the Jesuits, who 'absolve subjects from obedience and arm them against the King'.[1] Yet despite these reservations, his approval of direct and violent action against a king under certain circumstances remains quite obvious.

The real heart of Dorislaus's position was his contention that the Prince in question was not an absolute monarch. The people shared sovereignty with the Prince to begin with. Once he established this point, the case for rebellion followed naturally. Even civilians who advocated non-resistance admitted the validity of the deduction, as they themselves pursued the same line of argument in their own works. For while they interpreted the people's concession of power to have been absolute and unconditional, they still had to cope with the distinctions that the civil law suggested between different types of monarchs. Gentili, for example, admitted that his argument was never meant to apply to princes who did not have supreme power, such as the doges of Venice and the Holy Roman emperors.[2] These rulers were mere magistrates and

---

[1] PRO, SP 16/86/87 I, f. 3.

[2] Gentili, *De Vi Civium*, pp. 99, 122–3; Molen, *Gentili*, p. 236; see also Hayward, *The First Part of the Life and Raigne of King Henrie the IIII* (London, 1599), p. 102.

hence could be resisted by all men, should they violate the trust placed in them. Nor did Gentili consider as legitimate sovereigns those princes whose power rested upon an agreement with the people which specified that he observe certain laws.[1] These princes could also be overthrown upon just cause.

This last qualification was intended by Gentili to accommodate the Dutch rebellion against the rule of Spain, a cause that the Professor supported because of his strong Protestant convictions. This was the same international conflict that later figured so significantly in Dorislaus's arrival at a theory of popular sovereignty and lawful rebellion. Gentili did not go as far as Dorislaus, choosing to consider the Netherlands as exceptional rather than normative. Yet in one of his earlier works, entitled *De Jure Belli* (1598), he had been so preoccupied with this one example that this book contained none of the dogmatic declarations of absolutism and non-resistance that characterized his writing in 1605. Foreshadowing the views of Dorislaus, Gentili regarded the two combatants in the Spanish-Dutch war as co-possessors of sovereignty until the conflict was terminated.[2] This gave added justification to English intervention in the dispute—a step approved by Gentili on grounds of both international law and diplomatic expediency.[3] Then to garner more support for the rebels on the Continent, Gentili placed specific restrictions on the power of all princes[4] and recognized the right of magistrates who held office under a tyrannical prince to stage a revolt against him.[5] These opinions he reversed in 1605.

Gentili's inconsistencies reveal how much flexibility the prescriptions of the civil law left to the individual commentator or

[1] Gentili, *De Vi Civium*, p. 99.

[2] Id., *De Jure Belli Libri Tres* (trans. J. Rolfe, Oxford, 1933), pp. 74–8.

[3] Ibid., pp. 75–7. Even if the rebellion were unjust, a third power could intervene to force the power in authority to use moderate force in suppression. Bodin also allowed another sovereign power to interfere when he would not allow the subjects themselves to revolt. The diplomatic justifications presented by Gentili were that intervention would help to bring about peace between England and Spain and would also reflect England's neighbourly goodwill towards the Dutch.

[4] Gentili, *De Jure Belli*, pp. 371–2.

[5] Ibid., p. 51; Molen, *Gentili*, p. 235.

theorist. He possessed considerable freedom to determine where true sovereignty existed in order to satisfy his own personal preferences. The text of the civil law did not tie him to any one set of political theories, nor did it deny him the privilege of ignoring the *Corpus* completely and of resting his case upon theological and philosophical opinions. What most strongly influenced the writings of the English civilians was not any professional ideology but a variety of shifting individual political and religious convictions which often arose independent of their legal thought processes. When Gentili wrote *De Jure Belli* in 1598, he stressed the dangers of absolutism and the right of rebellion because the conflict in the Netherlands was uppermost in his mind and because he wished to justify English foreign policy in that area. In 1605, however, when he wrote *Regales Disputationes Tres*, the political situation had changed. England had concluded peace with Spain and had stopped her aid to the Dutch. And James I, a monarch whose preference for absolute monarchy and whose insistence upon the obedience of his subjects were widely publicized, was on the throne. The security of the Stuart dynasty, moreover, was threatened by the Papists. Gentili, eager to please the new King, upon whose favour his own career depended, shifted the emphasis of his thought.[1] He continued to justify the Netherlands, but he dismissed their case with a passing reference which implied that the circumstances surrounding the dispute were atypical.[2] He devoted nearly all his efforts to exalting the powers of the truly absolute monarch and to denying the subjects of such a ruler any right of resistance whatsoever.

John Hayward appears to have made an even more pronounced shift in his political views after the accession of James I. In 1599, before the Earl of Essex's attempted *coup d'état*, Hayward published a book entitled *The First Part of the Life and Raigne of King Henrie IIII*. While it purported to be a strict narrative of the events of those years, Hayward put into the mouths of the deposers of Richard II arguments which declared that allegiance was to the body politic rather than to the King's person and which

[1] See Molen, *Gentili*, p. 235.
[2] Gentili, *De Vi Civium*, p. 114.

demonstrated the legality of deposing a sovereign.[1] Hayward was cautious not to identify these ideas as his own. He had the 'learned and wise' Bishop of Carlisle deliver a lengthy discourse in favour of non-resistance.[2] But the dedication of the book to the Earl of Essex, to whom Hayward appealed in terms that smacked of royal flattery,[3] and the timing of the publication to coincide with the Earl's arrival in Ireland, suggested that Hayward was indeed looking to Essex to remedy the political ills of the day and providing him with the necessary political theory to justify his actions. As Sir Edward Coke, then Attorney-General, noted, 'He selecteth a story 200 years old and publisheth it this last year, intending the application of it to this time.'[4] Hayward later insisted that he had harboured no ulterior motives in writing the history. Yet it is doubtful that he could have been unaware of the strong historical parallels suggested by his work. Perhaps his main intention was to use the parallels and the dedication to attract attention to the publication, which sold more than 1,000 copies.[5] In any event he had toyed with some officially unacceptable ideas. Elizabeth had already expressed displeasure over the deposition scene in Shakespeare's *Richard II* and she considered Hayward's treatment of the same event to be intentionally controversial. After Essex staged his abortive *coup* in 1601 Elizabeth used Hayward's book as evidence against the peer at his trial, had Hayward imprisoned, and spared him his life only on the intercession of Sir Francis Bacon.[6] When James ascended the throne, however, Hayward sought relief from his public disgrace. He saw in the threat

[1] Hayward, *Life of Henrie*, pp. 84–98; Usher, *Reconstruction*, i. 128. For a complete discussion of the publication and the arguments presented by Coke, Hayward, and Sir Francis Bacon see M. Dowling, 'Sir John Hayward's Troubles Over His Life of Henry IV', *The Library*, 4th ser. 11 (1931), 212–24.

[2] Hayward, *Life of Henrie*, pp. 101–10.

[3] Ibid., dedication. See also J. Bruce, introduction to Hayward, *Annals of the First Four Years of the Reign of Queen Elizabeth* (Camden Society vii), p. xi; L. Strachey, *Elizabeth and Essex: A Tragic History* (New York, 1928), p. 196, for a further analysis of the dedication.   [4] PRO, SP 12/275/25 I.

[5] Usher, *Reconstruction*, i. 128. See also Hayward's defence, PRO, SP 12/278/17.

[6] Bruce, introduction to *Annals*, pp. xii–xiii; Strachey, *Elizabeth and Essex*, p. 197. Bacon had originally dissuaded the Queen from a charge of treason and had recommended the lighter charge of felony. Bacon noted that Hayward had drawn freely from Tacitus.

from the Catholics, for whom he seems to have had a genuine abhorrence, a chance to exalt the authority of the Crown, flatter James, and secure a place at Court. According to one historian, Hayward's writings after 1603 were 'mere ambitious attempts to draw upon their author some share of court notice and favour'.[1] Such ulterior motivation makes it even more difficult to consider Hayward's views simply as a legacy of his theoretical legal training.

While Gentili and Hayward became more respectful of royal authority after James I came to the throne, Calibute Downing moved in the opposite direction during the 1630s. As a young man who hoped to rise to become a bishop, Downing started his career in a way that could not fail to please the party of Charles's supporters. In 1633 he published *A Discourse of the State Ecclesiasticall of this Kingdome in Relation to the Civill*, in which he defended episcopacy as well as the profession of the civil law. Yet shortly thereafter he became impatient with the episcopal government of Laud, and by 1637 he had gained recognition as the Puritan vicar of Hackney, Middlesex. In September 1640 he preached a sermon to the Company of the Artillery in London, counselling them as to what action they should take against the 'Jesuited' faction which was infecting the present government and ruining the nation. He discussed the criteria for a just war and recalled the otherwise authoritarian Bishop Bilson's defence of rebellion by Continental Protestants against their Catholic sovereigns.

Downing then proceeded to handle the difficult question whether by their act of resistance the soldiers would break the law of the land. His answer reassured them that 'where the laws of the land are thus by them made too short for your security, the laws of nations come in for relief, till it can be otherwise provided: for twas never intended by Law-makers to lay them on with so rigid a will, but that still, *salus populi* should be *sola & suprema lex*'.[2] Then Downing called upon the great Dutch jurist Grotius: 'In

[1] Bruce, introduction to *Annals*, pp. xv–xvi. See Hayward, *Succession*, dedication to James I. Hayward refers to his earlier work to support his 'defense of the present authority of Princes and succession according to proximity of blood'.
[2] *A Sermon Preached to the Renowned Company of the Artillery* (1641), pp. 36–7.

such a case rational Grotius is clear: that in the most serious
and certain danger the law of non-resistance does not hold.'[1] He
concluded that when a common enemy prevented the estates of
a kingdom from assembling, the people 'may go very far before
they can be counted rebels'.[2]

Downing's defence of rebellion, one of the first during the
period immediately preceding the outbreak of civil war, was more
explicit than the earlier statements of Gentili and Hayward and
more remarkable than the arguments of Dorislaus. For Downing,
unlike Dorislaus, was a native Englishman, and he meant that his
counsels apply to England rather than to the Netherlands. Of
course it can be argued that Downing, like Dorislaus, was not a
typical civilian. Indeed, he was a Puritan, and this gave him added
incentive to criticize and eventually to oppose the established
government. Even more important, he was one of the few frustrated civilians whom the government was not able to satisfy with
employment in the Court. It might have been easy for James I to
keep Gentili and Hayward happy after 1603, but Charles I did not
have the same fortune with Downing. There is no question that
this civil lawyer had been disappointed in the pursuit of office. Not
only had he failed quickly to ascend the clerical ladder, but he had
also been denied a position as chaplain to the Earl of Strafford
in Ireland. After this setback he received his Hackney vicarage
through the patronage of Lady Mary Vere, a renowned Puritan.
This meant that Downing, unlike almost all of his colleagues, was
not operating within the ambit of the Court. He was of course
subject to the administrative control of his clerical superiors. But
his position was secure, and Puritans survived remarkably well in
the outparishes of London.[3] Downing, as one of the few civilians
who can be regarded as an alienated intellectual, was free to
develop his ideas.

It is possible, therefore, to attribute most of the unorthodox
political views espoused by civilians after 1603 to that tiny group

---

[1] *A Sermon Preached to the Renowned Company of the Artillery*, p. 37. '[I]n
gravissimo et certissimo discrimine lex de non resistendo non obligat.'
[2] Ibid., p. 38.
[3] V. Pearl, *London and the Outbreak of the Puritan Revolution* (London, 1961),
pp. 40–2.

of men who stood on the fringe of their profession. There was, however, one civilian whose break with the government deviates from this pattern. For although his opposition was of the most moderate variety, he articulated his views as one of the most successful and representative of all the civil lawyers, who held a number of choice positions in the King's service. This was Sir Henry Marten.

(e) *Sir Henry Marten and the Petition of Right*

During the early years of the reign of Charles I the political atmosphere was less conducive to statements of absolutism and divine right than it had been at the beginning of the reign of his father. The writings of the Jesuits evoked far less fear than they had in 1603, and the Stuart dynasty seemed secure. The political preoccupation of the entire kingdom was the activity of Charles himself, who was allegedly violating the fundamental liberties of the people. In the Parliament of 1628 M.P.s tried to prevent further unjust encroachments upon their freedoms by passing the Petition of Right—a statement of certain fundamental liberties which, as so many civilians had admitted at the theoretical level, the King was under a moral obligation to respect and maintain.

Sir Henry Marten was right in the thick of the parliamentary debates concerning the Petition of Right. Standing second only to Sir Julius Caesar as the most distinguished member of his profession, Marten represented his fellow civil lawyers in a special way. Not only had he defended their interests in the debates with the common lawyers over the question of prohibitions,[1] but he had also become Dean of the Arches and hence President of Doctors' Commons. He was involved more than any civil lawyer of his day in the work of the central ecclesiastical and Admiralty courts, serving as Judge of both the Court of the Arches and the High Court of Admiralty.

In the Parliament of 1628 Marten sat for the University of Oxford, a constituency renowned for royalist influence during this period. As the judicial representative of Lord Admiral

---

[1] Bodl., Tanner MS. 280, ff. 119ᵛ–120.

Buckingham,[1] Marten was tied to the court party in an additional way. Yet in the debates on the floor of the House, Marten showed himself to be politically independent, highly suspicious of Charles, and unwilling to place in his King the same trust that Gentili had freely conceded to James I.

During the debates over the Petition of Right, the Lords proposed an amendment to the text first drafted by the House of Commons. It stated: 'We humbly present this Petition to your Majesty, not only with a care for preservation of our liberties, but with a due regard to leave entire that sovereign power whereby your Majesty is entrusted for the protection and happiness of your people.'[2] The sovereign power referred to by the Lords was the King's discretionary authority in affairs of state—that part of his prerogative that royalist common lawyers termed absolute as opposed to ordinary, and the civil lawyers equated with *majestas* or sovereign power. According to both schools of thought this power entitled the King to ignore the ordinary rules of the common law in order to promote the welfare of the people, so long as there was just cause. It was, however, left to the decision of the King when just cause actually existed. It was this last part of the theory to which the Commons were objecting. They were trying to prevent the King's use of his discretionary authority under any circumstances to suppress rights that they considered inviolable.

The leaders of the House called upon Marten to formulate and to present their objections to the proposed amendment in a conference with the Lords on 22 April.[3] Marten was selected not on account of his legal training but for his mastery of logic. Another M.P., a common lawyer and ally of Coke, John Glanvill, was instructed to precede Marten with an answer to the 'legal part' of the Lords' declaration. The civilian was to restrict himself to the 'rational part',[4] which he did. But in pointing up the logical

---

[1] In the Parliament of 1626 Marten had 'strode as an officer of the Duke', but tension mounted between him and Buckingham. See J. Forster, *Sir John Eliot* (London, 1864), i. 336; ii. 104 n.

[2] ITL, Petyt MS. 537/23/f. 367.

[3] Ibid., f. 364ᵛ; Gardiner, *History*, vi. 282–3. Marten was to be assisted by Sir N. Rich and Mr. Pym, *CJ* i. 903.   [4] ITL, Petyt MS. 537/23/f. 382ᵛ.

inconsistencies of the text under discussion, he touched upon some of the finer points of constitutional law. He did not deny that the sovereign power existed. By itself the Lords' amendment was harmless. 'Their is never a word in this addition by itself, but I do believe it, nay all of it I admit.'[1] His complaint was simply that, stated in this specific context, the admission constituted such an exception to the terms of the Petition that it rendered the proposals of the Commons meaningless.

The King may not require money but in Parliament, it is a man's head; but add this clause unless it be by Sovereign power; then it is lion's neck, and it mars all. We leave entire a sovereign power. It is with a *terminus diminuens* as was said. I say it is *terminus augens*, and it is danger-ous. It implies the King is trusted with a power for the destruction, and also for the safety of the people. It admits also he may use sovereign power, and if he does we may not refuse it for it is for our protection, so it bounds up my mouth that I cannot but say it is for the good of the people. *Sovereign power is transcending and a high word.*[2]

Marten was trying to show that once sovereign power was granted to the King, he could use that power for malevolent as well as benevolent purposes. The King's subjects had no control over his actions because the possession of sovereign power allowed the King to decide when he should exercise it. To illustrate his point further, Marten mentioned one of Aesop's Fables, 'the moral whereof shall be that when actions are regulated by the Preroga-tive, there is no end'. An ass, a fox, and a lion went hunting, and finding good prey, the ass divided it into three equal piles and gave the lion the prerogative to choose his share. Whereupon the lion, insulted by the even division of spoils, proceeded to gobble up the ass. The fox, seeing the calamity of the ass, wisely gave the lion all of what was left.[3]

Marten found himself in 1628 unable to share Gentili's faith in the moral restraint of a supposedly virtuous king. Aware of Charles I's recent displays of callousness towards individual liberties, Marten was reluctant to trust the King with the right to

---

[1] Ibid., f. 356ᵛ. This was in a speech in the Commons the day before the conference with the Lords.

[2] Ibid., ff. 356ᵛ–357. [3] Ibid., f. 357.

decide when he was entitled to invoke his absolute power. He insisted that at least with respect to the four liberties specified in the Petition of Right the monarch had no choice but to observe the prescriptions of the common law. Marten was of course no radical. Nor were any members of that House.[1] The Commons did not contemplate the use of coercive action to enforce their demands. Penal action was still technically impossible; violence was inconceivable. They chose to rely upon political pressure alone, with the hope of gaining eventual judicial support from the Westminster courts.[2] Even then, Marten was still concerned about the adverse effects of the entire episode and appealed for an end to the discord between the King and his people.[3] He bent over backwards to please the Lords, assuring them that he had no intention of even restricting the sovereign power of the King, since by definition that power existed only for 'the protection, safety and happiness of his people'.[4] His only complaint was that the King had used the same power in contradiction of its very purpose, and this he wished to prevent from happening again.

Marten took one giant step forward in 1628 from the ranks of his profession to meet Sir Edward Coke and his political allies. While not as intensely committed to the movement of parliamentary opposition as that common lawyer, he agreed in substance, though not in rhetoric, with Coke's declaration that 'sovereign power is no Parliament word . . . it weakens Magna Carta and other statutes, for they are absolute without any saving

[1] 'The mildness and moderation of this House I have ascribed to God's hand amongst us.' Massachusetts Historical Society, Debates and Proceedings in the House of Commons, 1627/1628 (typescript), pp. 421, 422. There were of course varying degrees of moderation. See F. H. Relf, *The Petition of Right* (Minneapolis, Minn., 1917), p. 31, for the differences between the 'reformers' and the 'opportunists' of the House. Marten was extremely moderate. See Rex, *University Representation*, p. 119, and Humberstone, *University Representation*, p. 77.

[2] The opportunists wished to be able to bring penal action against Privy Councillors. See Relf, *Petition*, pp. 31, 33, 57–8. See also Kenyon, *The Stuart Constitution*, p. 103.

[3] 'There is a distance betwixt him and us, before we can have his heart we must remove it. . . . I would we could wrestle with the King in duty and love and not to let him go in this Parliament till he comply with us.' John Rushworth, *Private Passages of State* (London, 1659), i. 521.

[4] ITL, Petyt MS 537/23/f. 384ᵛ.

of the sovereign power'.[1] Of all the civilians of the early seventeenth century, Marten best reveals that in regard to political fundamentals the civilians and the common lawyers were by no means as incompatibly antagonistic as they were in matters which concerned their professional advancement and success. Even the most absolutist among them, such as Gentili and Cowell, did not differ all that much from the royalist common law judges in their definition of the royal prerogative, although they did disagree on the question of legislative sovereignty. At the other end of the political spectrum, spirits such as Dorislaus, Downing, and Marten mitigate the force of the generalizations that identify the civilians with the law they studied and that law with political authoritarianism in its most distasteful forms.

[1] Ibid., f. 344.

IV

THE LAWS OF ENGLAND

THE civil lawyers received their education and training in a law that differed both in substance and procedure from the English common law. Their dedication to the preservation of this legal tradition in England and their rivalry with the common lawyers over their respective jurisdictions actually earned them a reputation for hostility towards the common law. This reinforced the prevailing conception of the civil lawyers as the antagonists of constitutional liberty. For members of the parliamentary opposition regarded the common law not only as a legal system but also as a political cause. It embodied and preserved the ancient rights and liberties of the English people.[1] Since James I and Charles I were threatening, if not actually attempting, to violate a number of these rights, the opponents of the Crown appealed to the common law as the foundation of their political freedom.

Common lawyers helped to perpetuate the civil lawyers' reputation as the enemies of the common law and the liberties it protected. When the common law judges issued writs of prohibition against cases pending in the civil lawyers' courts, they were acting in a time-honoured capacity as the 'special conservators of the law'.[2] Not only were they preserving the integrity of common law jurisdiction, which they claimed the civilians were attempting to violate,[3] but they were also guarding the people's

[1] 'The ancient and excellent laws of England are the birthright and the most ancient and best inheritance that the subjects of this realm have; for by them he enjoyeth not only his inheritance and goods in peace and quietness, but his liberty and his most dear country in safety.' Quoted in C. Hill, *Puritanism and Revolution* (London, 1958), p. 65.

[2] See [C. G. Cocke], *Englands Compleat Law-Judge and Lawyer* (London, 1655), pp. 24–5. Cocke argues that the common law judges had surrendered their indifferent status as conservators of the law by becoming a party to the dispute over prohibitions.

[3] Coke, *Institutes*, iv. 135, answers to objections 4 and 5.

liberty. They were either guaranteeing Englishmen their right to have justice administered through the proper channels or protecting them from the use of legal procedures not allowed at the common law.[1] This implied, in no uncertain terms, that the civilians were denying these subjects their rights. Speaking even more directly to this point, the common law judges asserted in the heat of the debate over prohibitions that the civilians and Bancroft were pursuing a course 'which tendeth to the overthrow of the common law and to deprive His Majesty's subjects of their Birthright'.[2] This cast the civilians, who were by all outward appearances the victims of the common lawyers' superior power, in the role of the political and legal aggressors. Indeed, when James I applauded the publication of Sir Thomas Ridley's *View of the Civile and Ecclesiastical Law*, Sir Edward Coke 'undertook from thence to prophecy the decay of the Common Law'.[3] More recently Charles McIlwain has claimed that the civilians were actually hoping to execute a veritable legal revolution, whereby the principles and procedures of the civil law, less sensitive to the individual's rights, would have undermined the storehouse of English liberties:

For there is some evidence, not often noticed, that in James's first years a conscious and determined effort was being made, not altogether without the sympathy of the King, to weaken the immemorial custom of the courts of common law by a 'reception' more or less complete— more rather than less the lawyers feared—of the principles and procedure of Roman law, already employed in the courts of Scotland and in various jurisdictions in England, particularly the ecclesiastical.[4]

This then was the concrete political danger that lay beneath the controversy over prohibitions and the civilians' exaltation of the royal prerogative. If the civil lawyers could escape the control of

---

[1] Coke's justification for the prohibition in *Cheekitt's Case* (1611) was that 'Cheekitt is a free man and a lay subject and so hath been all his life time and ought to enjoy all liberties and customs due to all subjects.' Quoted in Usher, *High Commission*, p. 209.

[2] BM, Cotton MS. Cleo. F II, f. 121.

[3] D. Lloyd, *State-Worthies or the Statesmen and Favourites of England Since the Reformation* (London, 1670), p. 923.

[4] McIlwain, *Political Works of James I*, pp. xl–xli.

the common law judges, they would undermine the common law and endanger the liberties of all English subjects. This reception never occurred, but the problem remains whether or not the civilians intended to bring it about. How did they, as students and professors of the civil law, view this rival legal system, and in what ways did they actually challenge it during the early seventeenth century?

(a) *The civil lawyers and their rivals*

The threatened reception of civil law during the reign of James I had a precedent which occurred early in the sixteenth century. First suggested and described by F. W. Maitland at the turn of this century,[1] the actual threat has been reduced both in size and importance through subsequent historical investigations.[2] There has persisted a school of thought that believes that in the realm of public as opposed to private law—the law of the Constitution and not the law of the English courts—Tudor statesmen had indeed hoped to establish a more autocratic form of government inspired by the principles of the civil law.[3] But in the area of private litigation there exists no substantial evidence that either civil lawyers or the system of law that they studied and practised ever seriously challenged the ascendancy of common lawyers or the common law during these years. It is true that the business of the common law courts did, as Maitland claimed, register a temporary decline;[4] but this did not redound to the advantage of the civilians alone. The civil lawyers and civil law procedure held complete sway only in the ecclesiastical, Admiralty, and Chivalry courts,

[1] Maitland, *English Law and the Renaissance*. See also Senior, *Doctors' Commons*, pp. 64–6.

[2] Holdsworth, 'The Reception of Roman Law in the Sixteenth Century', *Law Quarterly Review*, 27 (1911), 387–98; 28 (1912), 39–51, 131–47, 236–54; D. Ogg (ed.), *Ioannis Seldeni Ad Fletam Dissertatio* (Cambridge, 1925), xlvi-lxv; H. E. Bell, *Maitland: A Critical Examination and Assessment* (Cambridge, Mass., 1965), pp. 131–7.

[3] W. H. Dunham, 'Bell: Maitland: A Critical Examination and Assessment', *The Yale Law Journal*, 75 (May 1966), 1063–64; L. Stone, 'The Political Programme of Thomas Cromwell', *Bulletin of the Institute of Historical Research*, 24 (1951), 9; Ogg, *Dissertatio*, p. lviii.

[4] Ives, 'Common Lawyers', 165–7.

which were such specifically defined jurisdictions that they could never encroach extensively upon the areas of litigation pre-empted by the common law. The legal business that the common law courts lost went instead to the newly created tribunals such as the Court of Star Chamber, the Court of Requests, the Council of the North, and the re-invigorated Court of Chancery.[1]

Yet these were not distinctly civil law institutions. In none of these courts were all the judges, masters, or commissioners civil lawyers. Common lawyers were always joined with Doctors of Laws. And in matters of procedure the prerogative courts were exposed to strong common law influences, especially in Chancery and Star Chamber.[2] Their adoption of civil law procedure in some instances, as in the examination of witnesses and the admission of written evidence, is clear; but as David Ogg warns:

[I]t would be wrong to assume therefrom that there was a 'reception' of Roman Law in sixteenth-century England. The characteristic of these courts was not that they could use civil law doctrines but rather that they were not bound by any stereotyped procedure at all: in their methods they were eclectic, and they subordinated judicial conventions to what they conceived to be the interest of the state. Where they had to deal with a case involving principles outside the common law, they did not hesitate to employ civilians or canonists, but this practice did not diminish, to any appreciable extent, the scope of common law jurisdiction.[3]

Indeed, G. R. Elton has made the point that far from encroaching upon common law jurisdiction, the Tudor prerogative courts were intended to supplement and correct the common law in areas where its authority was lacking or its means of enforcement were weak, not to establish an alternative to its predominant position in the State.[4]

For the purposes of this study, the most important feature of the alleged threat to the common law, however real, was its unquestioned failure. The net result of the entire episode is that the

---

[1] Ogg, *Dissertatio*, pp. 1 ff.   [2] Ibid., pp. 1, liii; Jones, *Chancery*, p. 301.
[3] Ogg, *Dissertatio*, p. lvii; see also Ives, 'Common Lawyers', 165.
[4] G. R. Elton, 'The Political Creed of Thomas Cromwell', *Transactions of the Royal Historical Society*, 5th ser., 6 (1965), 78.

common law remained virtually unchallenged as the dominant legal system in England throughout the sixteenth century. The civil lawyers, from whom the threat was supposed to have come, contented themselves with a distinctly minor and relatively isolated area of jurisdiction which was exclusively their own. The civil lawyers were 'shut up, as it were, into a narrow corner of their profession'.[1] From such a small base of operations, an assault against the common law would have been difficult to muster.

Even in the midst of the fury of the debate over prohibitions, civil lawyers did not attempt to invade the common lawyers' proper domain, much less advocate a full-scale reception of the civil law.[2] It is true that the civil lawyers tried to adjudicate cases that did not fall within a clearly defined jurisdiction, such as those arising from maritime contracts concluded in foreign countries. One might also argue that the civilians on the High Commission attracted suits that would otherwise have found their way into the common law courts.[3] But on balance, it is difficult to conclude that the civilians were conducting an offensive against the almost impregnable bulwark of the common law.

Actually too much has been made of the civilians' hostility towards the common law and common lawyers. Certainly civil lawyers did not like prohibitions, and they protested bitterly that these writs were issued far too often. But in other circumstances civilians worked harmoniously with their rivals. Civil lawyers were often involved in legal work with common lawyers in the Courts of Chancery, Requests, and Delegates, in many royal commissions, and even in Parliament. In this way they developed

[1] Ridley, *A View*, p. 106.
[2] The first civil lawyer to recommend what amounted to a reception was Robert Wiseman in 1656. See D. Veall, *The Popular Movement for Law Reform* (Oxford, 1970), pp. 109–10.
[3] See P. Tyler, introduction to Usher, *High Commission* (2nd edn., 1968), pp. xxxi–xxxii. Tyler claims that the High Commission was depriving the lesser Church courts of a large portion of their business and that prohibitions were not frequent enough to prevent the common law courts from losing business that would have come to them by way of appeal. None the less, the lawyers who lost the greatest volume of litigation to the High Commission were not the common lawyers, but the officials of the lower Church courts, many of whom were civilians.

a spirit of co-operation which is often overlooked because of the hostility that prevailed between the same groups of lawyers over the question of prohibitions.[1] On the Court of Delegates, where common lawyers were often joined with civilians to test appeals from the Admiralty and ecclesiastical courts, conflict was the exception, not the rule, and the court's one historian has referred to the early seventeenth century as a period of special equanimity among its members.[2] The arena of co-operation was even transferred on occasion to the Westminster courts, where the common law judges called upon the civilians to give legal opinions which they were especially well qualified to present.[3]

At the local level civilians often worked hand in hand with common lawyers. Sometimes they acted together as commissioners of the peace. At other times the civilians looked to the common lawyers to reinforce the limited authority that they possessed in their own capacities as ecclesiastical and Admiralty judges.[4] In Essex officials of archdeaconry courts corresponded with justices of the peace who were common lawyers whenever they both were interested in the same case.[5] One area of continually overlapping concern was witchcraft, and it is noteworthy that Richard Bernard dedicated his *Guide to Grand Jury Men . . . in Cases of Witchcraft* to both common and civil lawyers.[6] Seditious heresy could also arouse concern from both branches of the legal profession. After proceeding against a separatist and Anabaptist named Sayey in the diocese of Norwich, Chancellor Robert Redman

[1] J. P. Dawson, *A History of Lay Judges* (Cambridge, Mass., 1960) p. 162. Dawson argues that Coke's attack upon Chancery in 1616 was a brief eruption which distorts the true picture of harmony that usually prevailed between the common lawyers and the Chancery Bench.

[2] Duncan, 'Delegates', pp. 316–18.

[3] BM Lansdowne MS. 161, f. 265; *Dodson* v. *Lynn* in Croke, *Reports . . . Charles I*, p. 476.

[4] See for example the Admiralty's reliance upon local justices in *CSPD 1590–1594*, p. 232.

[5] Repent Savage frequently sought advice from Sir Nicholas Coote and Thomas Edwards. Quintrell, 'Government of Essex', p. 187.

[6] Richard Bernard, *A Guide to Grand Jury Men . . . In Cases of Witchcraft* (London, 1627), dedication. The first dedication was to Sir John Walter and Sir John Denham of the Court of the Exchequer; the second to Gerard Wood, a Doctor of Divinity, and to Arthur Duck.

turned to the common lawyers to handle the further charge of disloyalty to the established government. 'I would the temporal magistrate had him in his jurisdiction,' wrote Redman to his bishop, 'and if it please your Lordship to make known his opinions to the Honourable the Lord Coke, happily he will proceed against him at the next assizes.'[1]

So often involved with the same cases and procedures proper to the common law, civilians found the study of that law to be desirable if not indispensable, for their work. For Masters in Chancery, Justices of the Peace, and Members of Parliament it was an absolute necessity.[2] It is no wonder therefore that officials at Cambridge recommended in the university statutes of 1570 that 'A Doctor of Laws will study the laws of England soon after the doctorate so that he will not be unacquainted with those laws which his country has; and he will know the differences between the law of his country and those of other lands.'[3] Circumstantial evidence suggests that at least some of the civil lawyers did indeed follow the advice of the statute. In their published works John Cowell, Richard Zouch, and Thomas Ridley all displayed an ample, if not commanding, knowledge of the common law.[4] Sir Henry Marten boasted to the Parliament of 1628 how much common law he had read.[5] According to a sympathetic biographer, Thomas Ryves was 'so skilled in the common law as well as the civil law that he could practice at Westminster as well as at Doctors' Commons'.[6]

As erudite as he may have been, Ryves could never have actually pleaded in a common law court because he was not a

---

[1] *Registrum Vagum*, ii. 342. A similar appeal is implicit in Matthew Sutcliffe, *An Answere to a Certaine Libel*, dedication to Sir Edmund Anderson, Chief Justice of Common Pleas.

[2] G. Carew, 'A Treatise', p. 313; Jones, *Chancery*, p. 266, and Dawson, *Lay Judges*, p. 149.

[3] J. Heywood and T. Wright, *Cambridge University Transactions During the Puritan Controversies of the Sixteenth and Seventeenth Centuries* (London, 1854), i. 10.

[4] Cowell, *The Interpreter* and *The Institutes*; R. Zouch, *Descriptio Juris et Judicii Temporalis Secundum Consuetudines Feudales et Normannicas* (Oxford, 1636); Ridley, *A View*.

[5] William Borlase, 'Some Notes Taken in the Sessions of Parliament . . . 1628', BM, Stowe MS. 366, f. 94.   [6] Lloyd, *Memoires*, p. 592.

qualified barrister. His education in the common law had been completely informal. A number of his colleagues did, however, become members of the Inns of Court either before or after they received their doctorates in civil law. Of the entire group of 200 civil lawyers, thirty entered the legal societies, most of them finding places at Gray's Inn.[1] Julius Caesar actually rose to become Bencher and Treasurer of the Inner Temple, and James Littleton became Associate to the Bar and Assistant to the Bench of the same Inn in 1639.[2] It is true that the admissions of all but four civilians to the Inns were honorific and that none was actually called to the Bar, although Walter Walker did seek this privilege in 1642.[3] Yet even if the civilians did not undertake a formal study or practice of the common law, their admission to the Inns does indicate an absence of hostility between the two branches of the legal profession and a certain respect among the civilians for the common law.

Really, there was little reason for the civilians to have detracted from that law. Ridley wrote that he could not 'derogate from the credit of that law under which I was born, and by which I hold the small maintenance that I have'.[4] Henry Marten admitted defensively in 1628 that 'No man loves the Common Law better than I. I am an Englishman, married to a daughter of a common lawyer.'[5] The civilians were not extraneous or foreign agents within the legal profession who were promoting an alien legal system as a rival to customary English law. They were almost to the number native Englishmen of many generations standing—'not strangers or foreigners but home-born subjects, of the same faith, of the

[1] Nineteen registered at Gray's Inn, five at the Inner Temple, four at Lincoln's Inn, and two at the Middle Temple. J. Foster (ed.), *The Register of Admissions to Gray's Inn 1521–1889* (London, 1889); ITL, Admissions to the Inner Temple; *The Records of the Honourable Society of Lincoln's Inn: Admissions from 1420 to 1799* (London, 1896); *Middle Temple Admissions*.

[2] *Students Admitted to the Inner Temple* (London, 1887), p. 95; F. A. Inderwick (ed.), *A Calendar of Inner Temple Records* (London, 1898), ii. 250–1; Prest, 'Inns of Court', p. 85.

[3] *Inner Temple Records*, ii. 268. There is no record of his having been called to the bar.

[4] Ridley, *A View*, p. 276; see also Coke's statement, ITL, Petyt MS. 537 23/213^v.

[5] BM, Stowe MS. 366, f. 94^v.

same religion, of the same kindred and family, of like allegiance to the Prince and service to the commonwealth as other his good subjects are'.[1] Only three—Alberico Gentili, Isaac Dorislaus, and John Hotman—were Continental emigrants.[2] Another six received their doctorates at foreign universities such as Leyden, Paris, and Vienna after obtaining undergraduate degrees in England;[3] while still more sojourned abroad to study briefly at these and other institutions, like Padua.[4] But what they learned abroad was, like the Roman law which their colleagues studied at Oxford and Cambridge, still mainly juristic theory rather than the law of any one European country. And the law that the civilians eventually practised when they returned to England was, contrary to some strong popular prejudices,[5] thoroughly anglicized. The originally foreign ecclesiastical and maritime law had been augmented by so many statutes, decrees of Convocation, and practices of English merchants that they had lost much of their international character.[6] The law of arms which the civilians upheld in the Court of Chivalry was an entirely indigenous creation and owed nothing to Continental influences.[7] All these legal codes, moreover, had been in use so long within England that they had acquired a status, albeit a minor one, at the common law itself. The only distinctly Roman, Continental, or foreign attributes they possessed were the procedures that civilians used to enforce them.

[1] Ridley, *A View*, p. 274. See also CUL, MS. Mm VI.57, f. 14ᵛ.

[2] Gentili was an Italian from the University of Perugia, Dorislaus a Dutchman from the University of Leyden, and Hotman a Frenchman from the University of Valence. See below, p. 203.

[3] These were J. Caesar (Paris), Carew (Louvain), Covert (Leyden), Parkins (unknown), Spicer (Leyden), Vaughan (Vienna). For the period 1558–1642 Curtis's *Oxford and Cambridge*, p. 154, counted twelve foreign degrees. For Parkins see *HMCS* vi. 122.

[4] Mullinger, *Cambridge*, pp. 57–8; Dewar, *Smith*, pp. 21–2.

[5] For contemporary opinions that the laws that the civilians practised were foreign see BM, Cotton MS. Cleo. F I, f. 120; Stoughton, *An Assertion*, pp. 37–45.

[6] Holdsworth, *History of Law*, i. 594–5; N. Figgis, 'Bartolus and the Development of European Political Ideas', *Transactions of the Royal Historical Society*, n.s., 19 (1905), 168; R. Zouch, *Descriptio Juris et Judicii Ecclesiastici Secundum Canones et Constitutiones Anglicanas* (Oxford, 1636), preface.

[7] Squibb, *Chivalry*, p. 166.

(b) *Academic attitudes towards the common law*

None the less the ancient Roman law of Justinian, while not in force in any English courtroom, still commanded high respect and even veneration among English civilians.[1] As a fund of legal wisdom it invited comparison with the customary or common law under which the civilians lived. A similar assignment occupied the interests of Continental jurists, since the law they practised, although indebted to definite Roman influences, was also largely a body of native customary law and differed markedly from the prescriptions of the *Digest* and the *Institutes*.[2] These lawyers developed two distinct theories which treated the relationship between the ancient law of the Roman Empire and the laws of the various European states. The first belonged to those lawyers and scholars who regarded themselves as humanists; the other to those jurists who adhered to the older tradition of Bartolus. Although both schools of thought were of Continental origin, each claimed adherents at the English universities, and not only among those civilians who had studied abroad.[3] The ascendancy that the Bartolists achieved towards the end of the sixteenth century defined the attitude of the great majority of English civil lawyers towards their own common law.

The humanists began to command some influence in England during the second quarter of the sixteenth century, and it was their contempt for the common law that first led Maitland to detect a challenge to that law's supremacy.[4] The pioneers in humanist jurisprudence—Alciatus of Italy and of France, Budé of France, and Zasius of Germany—had indeed ascribed little value or function to native customary law. Their purpose was to extricate

---

[1] J. Hayward, *A Treatise of Union of the Two Realmes of England and Scotland* (London, 1604), p. 43. The most laudatory was Wiseman, *Law of Lawes*, p. 166, 'The Roman Civil Law has not the pre-eminence of other laws in title and denomination only, but it is thought also, that in the books thereof there are laid up such treasures of human Wisdom, Policy, Justice, Equity and natural Reason that the art of doing equal justice and the doctrine of true and uncorrupted right is taught by them only.'

[2] See Squibb, *Chivalry*, pp. 163–4.

[3] Holdsworth, 'Reception', pt. i, 395–6; *History of Law*, iv. 239.

[4] Maitland, *English Law*, pp. 6–7.

the pure texts of Justinian from beneath the turgid and burden-
some medieval commentaries that had brought Roman law to
bear on medieval customary and feudal law.[1] As true humanists
these scholars placed faith only in the wisdom of the ancients, and
therefore they tried to establish the exact meaning the Roman laws
had in the minds of those who formulated them.[2] The humanists
believed that the principles that they were discovering were more
enlightened than the 'barbarous' prescriptions of the various
systems of European customary law.

First advertised in England by the European humanist Johannes
Ludovicus Vives,[3] who settled in Oxford in 1523, received a
doctorate in law, and became a fellow of Corpus Christi College,
the humanist approach was introduced at the universities. It became dominant in the 1540s when Thomas Smith, a devotee of
the new school, served as Regius Professor of Civil Law at Oxford.[4] Although the energies of the humanist civilians were confined to the strictly academic work of searching for a purified
version of the ancient texts, their exaltation of the code that they
were discovering did foster a certain amount of disdain for the
common law both among civilians and other educated Englishmen. And the provincial character of English law, the imperfec-
tions and inequities that it tolerated, its lack of systematic
arrangement, and its uncouth language all served to discredit it
in their eyes.[5] Thomas More, though himself a common lawyer
by training, was well aware of that legal system's drawbacks.[6]
Thomas Starkey condemned the common law for being as
'barbarous' and 'tyrannical' as the law French used in its courts;[7]

---

[1] Molen, *Gentili*, p. 30; Holdsworth, 'Reception', pt. i, 395; Mullinger,
Cambridge, 125.

[2] Pocock, *Ancient Constitution*, pp. 8–9, 14.

[3] *DNB* xx. 377–8; Johannes Vives, *Io. Lodovici Vivis Valentini Opera* (Basel,
1555), i. 426–35; Senior, *Doctors' Commons*, p. 65.

[4] Dewar, *Smith*, p. 21. Malden, *Trinity Hall*, pp. 70–2, reports that at least at
Cambridge the new approach to law was slow in taking root.

[5] Curtis, *Oxford and Cambridge*, p. 156.

[6] J. H. Hexter, *More's Utopia: The Biography of an Idea* (Princeton, N.J., 1952),
pp. 148–50.

[7] Thomas Starkey, *A Dialogue Between Reginald Pole and Thomas Lupset* (ed.
K. M. Burton, London, 1948), pp. 174–5.

and Thomas Smith himself referred in one of his lectures to 'such barbaric and semi-gallic laws of ours.'[1]

Humanist attitudes towards the relative merits of the civil and common laws persisted into the early seventeenth century. Both King James I and Matthew Sutcliffe equated the threatened extinction of the civil law with the introduction of barbarism into the kingdom,[2] while Thomas Ridley located the source of true equity in the civil law, not the law of the English.[3] In 1615 some Cambridge undergraduates satirized bitterly the language of the common law in a play entitled *Ignoramus*.[4] The intentions of all these comments and criticisms must not be overlooked. Only Starkey ever advocated more than a reform of the abuses of the system. He suggested that the Tudor government should 'receive the law of the Romans'. But he placed his recommendation within the context of a staged dialogue, in which he allowed the speaker's opponent to pass off the suggestion as a completely impracticable fancy of the mind.[5] None of the other critics ever even considered the possibility of a reception. James actually admitted to a great love for the common law, according to whose sanction he had received his kingship.[6] And Smith in his famous treatise *De Republica Anglorum*, Maitland concedes, 'certainly did not underrate those traditional, medieval, Germanic and Parliamentary elements which were still to be found in English life and law under the fifth and last of the Tudors'.[7] It appears that the attitude which the humanists fostered towards the English common law was often little more than a simple reflection of their cosmopolitan snobbery at anything provincial or medieval and of their belief in the superior wisdom of the civil law; at most it was an appeal to correct and to reform, not to replace, the inherited treasure of English law and legal institutions.

[1] Text of Smith's lecture in Maitland, *English Law*, p. 90, n. 61.
[2] Sutcliffe, *Answere to Libel*, p. 94; McIlwain, *Political Works of James*, p. 310.
[3] Ridley, *A View*, p. 275. See also Cowell, *Institutiones Juris Anglicani* (London, 1605), preface, p. 1.
[4] George Ruggles, *Ignoramus: A Comedy* (trans. R. Codrington, London, 1662). See also Simon, 'Dr. Cowell', 270–1.
[5] Starkey, *Dialogue*, p. 175.   [6] McIlwain, *Political Works of James*, p. 310.
[7] Maitland, *English Law*, pp. 16–17.

In any event, the humanists' influence among the civilians began to wane towards the end of the sixteenth century. Anthony Wood reported that Peter Pitheus, one of the disciples of the great French humanist Cujas, was incorporated at Oxford in 1572 and resided at that university for several years.[1] Pitheus's influence was limited, however, since he never became a lecturer in his field. As it was, the two civilians who did secure chairs in civil law at the end of Elizabeth's reign belonged to a school of jurisprudence that rivalled that of Pitheus and Cujas. Both Alberico Gentili and John Cowell identified themselves with the older school of Bartolus, against which the humanists had reacted.[2]

The Bartolists had in turn arisen in response to the shortcomings of the Glossators, the first civilians to attempt a formal study of the *Corpus Juris Civilis*. These scholars had established the complete and accurate text of Justinian's compilation and had attempted to explain its meaning.[3] Yet as precise and as valuable as the work was, the Glossators did not supply a body of positive legal doctrine capable of effective application in courts of law. To achieve this goal the fourteenth-century Italian jurists, Bartolus de Sasso-Ferrato and his protégé, Baldus de Ubaldis, instead of continuing the interpretative work of the Glossators, undertook a systematic arrangement of the texts under proper headings. They strove, moreover, to blend Roman law, canon law, and customary feudal law into one corpus of legal rules which met the needs of the time. The product of their scholarship became the law of most European court-rooms in the fifteenth and sixteenth centuries.[4]

The Bartolists were despised by the humanists not only for their corruption of the pure texts of Justinian but also for their unpolished and garbled style of writing, which won them the

[1] Wood, *Fasti*, i. 190.

[2] Maitland, *English Law*, pp. 14, 60, n. 30; C. Phillipson, *Albericus Gentilis* (1911), pp. 6–7.

[3] For a brief discussion of the Glossators see P. Vinogradoff, *Roman Law in Medieval Europe* (2nd edn., Oxford, 1929), pp. 60–9.

[4] Holdsworth, 'Reception', pt. i, 391–3; Hall, 'Calvin', 205; Molen, *Gentili*, p. 28; M. P. Gilmore, *Humanists and Jurists* (Cambridge, Mass., 1963), pp. 62–3; T. F. T. Plucknett, *A Concise History of the Common Law* (5th edn., Boston, 1956), p. 296.

nickname of the 'scribblers'. The Bartolists replied with the argument that the humanists, or as they chose to call them, 'grammarians', were simply etymological experts and ministers of nothing but ancient jurisprudence, which hardly touched upon the problems handled in a court of law.[1] They were purely scholars and not really lawyers at all.[2] This critique exposed the major defect in the entire humanist approach. The humanists were idealizing a code that was intended for a society that their research concerning Roman life and institutions revealed was totally different from their own. What value could there be in the ancient law of the Roman Empire for sixteenth-century Europeans if the two societies were totally dissimilar? Even the humanists became aware of this problem, and the last great member of the school, François Hotman, came to the very same conclusion in his study entitled *Anti-Tribonian*.[3]

With the virtues of relevance and practicality in its favour, the Bartolist tradition survived, and it never lost its predominance in the law faculties of Italian universities. At Perugia Gentili studied under professors committed to this line of thought, and after he emigrated to England for religious reasons, he took up the pen against his humanist opponents. Although in his published work he never directly applied the Bartolist theories concerning the relationship between Roman and customary law to England, it can be assumed from the writings of his protégés that he never passed on to any of the civil lawyers who studied under him the contempt for customary law so characteristic of the humanists.[4] In fact, the humanists at this time, under the direction of Hotman, were themselves arriving at a new-found respect for customary law which led them to enunciate the principles of what J. G. A. Pocock terms 'neo-Bartolism'.[5] Aware of the irrelevance of the ancient Roman law, Hotman in his later work advocated the

---

[1] William Fulbecke, *A Direction or Preparative to the Study of the Lawe* (London, 1600), p. 20; Holdsworth, 'Reception', pt. i, 395–7.

[2] Molen, *Gentili*, p. 207; see Gentili, *De Juris Interpretibus Dialogi* (London, 1582).

[3] See Pocock, *Ancient Constitution*, pp. 11–15.

[4] Zouch, *Descriptio Juris et Judicii Temporalis*, preface; Duck, *De Usu*, pp. 323–9.

[5] Pocock, *Ancient Constitution*, pp. 23–4.

forging of a new mixture of customary law with the relevant and universally applicable principles of the Roman Law, much in the same way that Bartolus had two centuries earlier.[1]

It is not certain how much of a favourable response Hotman's approach evoked in England, but it is significant that his son, also a jurist trained in his father's tradition, settled in England at Oxford during the late sixteenth century and developed a friendly professional relationship with Gentili.[2] Naturally, the English Bartolists could not have achieved or even proposed a fusion of the civil law and the common law of England in the same way that their Continental counterparts blended the ancient Roman code with their native customary laws. The law of the Roman Empire still constituted an essential ingredient in the law of most European nations but held no place whatsoever in the common law of the English. But it was possible to advocate a reconciliation between the two legal traditions, to show that they agreed upon a number of fundamentals and to view them both as derivatives of a higher natural law.

The first scholar who actually did apply the theories of the neo-Bartolists to English customary or common law was not even a fully accredited civilian. William Fulbecke, after receiving both the B.A. and M.A. degrees from Oxford, became a member of Gray's Inn in London and then went abroad for a number of years, where he claimed to have earned a doctorate in civil law at an undesignated Continental university.[3] Although neither English university ever acknowledged his status as a doctor of law, Fulbecke still considered himself eminently qualified, having studied both the law of the Romans and that of the English, to compare the two. Committed to the Ciceronian theory that 'the law' was 'a principal reason ingrafted in us by nature', Fulbecke believed that 'all the particular and several laws of divers nations are but the branches of this law'.[4] Accordingly he set out to show, in his book entitled *A Parallele or Conference of the Civill Law, the Canon Law and the Common Law of England*, how few differences

---

[1] Pocock, *Ancient Constitution*, p. 23; Plucknett, *History*, p. 296.
[2] Molen, *Gentili*, pp. 46–7, 209.   [3] *DNB* vii. 743.
[4] Fulbecke, *Direction*, p. 8ʳ.

actually did exist between the three legal systems. In the introduction he explained that

> it seemed strange unto me that these three laws should not as the three Graces have their hands linked together and their looks directly fixed the one upon the other, but like the two faces of Janus, the one should be turned from the other and should never look toward or upon the other; and weighing with myself that these laws are the sinews of a state, the Sciences of government and the arts of a common weal, I have seriously and often wished that some joint discourse might be made of these three excellent laws, whereby the agreement or disagreement of them, and the grounds and reasons thereof might evidently appear by some very skillful in these laws well grounded, and if it might be, which I never yet saw, professed in the same.[1]

While Fulbecke's work testifies adequately to the actual application of Bartolist jurisprudence to the study of English law, the author's attachment to the Inns of Court and his lack of association with Doctors' Commons detracts from the significance of his pioneering efforts. But John Cowell's adoption of Fulbecke's approach just a few years after the *Parallele* appeared leaves no doubt that among bona fide English civilians the idea of reconciling their native law with the law they studied and practised had indeed taken hold. *Institutiones Juris Anglicani ad methodum et seriem institutionem Imperialum compositae et digestae* (1605) was Cowell's first major book.[2] With the intention of providing the students of the civil law with a more thorough understanding of both their own native law and that part of their discipline that approximated to the universal reason of natural law, the author set out to illustrate the similarity and unity of the two laws.[3] Cowell was firmly convinced that the two legal codes 'both be raised as one foundation' and that the common law was just as close to the ancient law of Rome as the law of any European nation.[4]

---

[1] Fulbecke, *A Parallele or Conference of the Civill Law, the Canon Law and the Common Law of England* (London, 1601), preface.

[2] A slightly altered but serviceable translation appeared in 1651, ironically by order of Parliament. Hereafter referred to as Cowell, *Institutes.*

[3] Cowell, *Institutiones*, preface, p. 2.

[4] Cowell, *Interpreter*, preface, mentions that the author had 'in some towardness' a tract which was to illustrate this common foundation, but the tract never

His attempt was only partially successful. Under each title of Justinian's *Institutes* Cowell referred to the English counterparts of the prescriptions of the Roman text. He did point up a number of interesting parallels between the two bodies of laws,[1] yet correspondence was the exception and not the rule. Beneath some titles, such as 'The Excuses of Guardians' and 'The Orphitian Decree',[2] Cowell had to admit that there had never been any need for English equivalents. With reference to other matters, such as 'The Taking Away of Devises',[3] the two laws had made entirely antithetical provisions. At least one contemporary was aware of the limitations of the doctor's undertaking. In some notes concerning the civil law preserved at the Inner Temple Library, the anonymous author recommended that one 'read Mr. Doctor Cowell's little book of Institutes for the matters of every chapter in the 4 books of Institutes, where is shown how little of those institutes is now our law'.[4] More recently, an English lawyer has compared Cowell's project to 'crushing an ugly sister's foot, bunions and all, into Cinderella's glass slipper'.[5]

Despite its shortcomings, Cowell's work does offer some evidence that the Bartolists' respect for, and interest in, customary law and their desire to reconcile it with the law of Rome had begun to rub off on the English civilians' attitudes toward their own common law. While no civilian was foolish enough to enlarge upon Cowell's hopeless efforts to fuse the two laws, Richard Zouch did conduct collateral investigations of both legal systems in which he accentuated the superior jurisdiction of the Roman Law and the Continental contributions to the common law.[6] There were other signs of the new outlook. John Hayward,

---

appeared. As for the laws of other nations, Cowell exaggerates the customary nature of Italian, Spanish, French, German, and Scottish laws, *Institutiones*, preface, p. 1.

[1] Cowell, *Institutes*, pp. 118–19, for example, points out some similarities concerning the qualifications for witnesses. Yet even this is somewhat defensive, since the two laws differed markedly on the number of witnesses required for such an important consideration as proving a will.

[2] Ibid., pp. 50, 160.   [3] Ibid., p. 147.

[4] ITL, Petyt MS. 538/55/190ᵛ.   [5] Simon, 'Dr. Cowell', 263

[6] Zouch, *Elementa Jurisprudentiae* and *Descriptio Juris et Judicii Temporalis*.

in arguing for the union of England and Scotland, insisted that
the law of Scotland, which was heavily influenced by Roman law,
could easily be combined with the English common law, since
the two agreed in fundamentals.[1] Sir Henry Marten gave public
expression to the Bartolist attitude when he told the Parliament of
1628 that 'The common law is the daughter, the civil law is the
mother. I am sorry to see such a strangeness between them.'[2]

It is especially significant that it was Cowell who became the
first member of the profession to advocate publicly the idea of
harmony or unity between the two laws. For Cowell was taken
to epitomize his colleagues' supposed contempt for the common
law that led McIlwain to suspect that they wished to bring about
a reception. Cowell was, after all, one of the authors of Archbishop
Bancroft's *Articuli Cleri*, the official list of complaints against the
common law judges. And one of the accusations against this
civilian in the Parliament of 1610 was that in his second book, *The
Interpreter*, he had 'spoken irreverently of the common law of
England'.[3] Even King James, acting under considerable political
pressure, conceded that the Regius Professor was 'in some things
too bold with the common laws of the realm'.[4]

The criticisms were greatly exaggerated. *The Interpreter* made
a number of claims about the King's relationship to the law which
did not exactly enthral Parliament. But except for a few harsh
words about Littleton,[5] there were few passages in that work that
spoke disparagingly of the common law or its judges.[6] In fact,
Cowell's rationale for drawing up the dictionary was similar to
the one he had formulated for writing *Institutiones*. He wished to
bring his extensive knowledge of the civil law to bear upon the
common law in order to offer English civil lawyers a fuller understanding of the latter. The German civilian whose work Cowell

---

[1] Hayward, *Treatise of Union*, p. 43. Cowell and Gentili also argued for the
union. See Cowell, *Institutiones, Epistola Dedicatoria*; Gentili, *De Unione Regnorum
Britanniae* in *Regales Disputationes Tres*, pp. 39–98.

[2] BM, Stowe MS. 366, f. 94.

[3] James I, 'This Later Age'; Chrimes, 'Cowell', 478. *The Interpreter* was
regarded by the House as 'tending to the Disreputation of the Honour and
Power of the common laws', *CJ*, i. 399.

[4] Foster, *Proceedings*, ii. 49.

[5] Cowell, *Interpreter*, sub 'Littleton'.   [6] Chrimes, 'Cowell', 478.

imitated was one Kahl or Calvinus, who had compiled a *Lexicon Juridicum Juris Caesarei simul et Canonici Feudalis item Civilis Criminalis, theoretici ac practici.*[1] The title indicates that Kahl was one of the Bartolist school, and the text confirms that he did indeed draw freely from a variety of legal traditions in the forming of his definitions. By employing a similar technique Cowell once again found an opportunity to expose the similarities between the civil and the common laws.[2] Thus under the term 'abeyance' Cowell wrote 'So that (*as the civilians say*) goods and lands do *iacere* whilst they want a possessor, and yet not simply because they had lately one, and may shortly have another: *so the common lawyers* do say that things in like estate are in abeyance'.[3] The author drew similar parallels under such words as 'easement', 'custom', 'record', and 'prerogative of the King'. Cowell was elaborating upon the work Fulbecke had begun seven years earlier when he had published a 'table of certain words in the interpretation whereof the common law and the civil law do seem to agree'.[4] The doctor was mediating between the common and the civil laws, trying to render them more compatible by exposing one common foundation.[5] In the introduction to the *Interpreter* Cowell explained that he felt the two laws differed 'more in language than in substance'.

(c) *The challenge to the common law*

If the most politically discredited civilian of the entire profession used the civil law only to amplify rather than to disparage the common law, and if so many other civilians displayed the greatest apparent respect for their native English law, it is difficult to accept the thesis that they were intending either to 'overthrow' the law of the land or to weaken its 'immemorial custom' and to

[1] First published in Frankfurt, 1600. I have used the 1645 edition.

[2] Despite the comparisons he drew, Cowell was still not fully aware of all the Continental influences, especially the feudal ones, that had contributed to the formation of the common law and hence made the comparisons possible. See Pocock, *Ancient Constitution*, p. 91.

[3] Cowell, *Interpreter*, sub 'abeyance'.

[4] Fulbecke, *A Direction*, pp. 72^v–81^v.

[5] Chrimes, 'Cowell', 462; Mullinger, *Cambridge*, p. 498.

pave the way for a 'reception'. Yet during the years of their professional dispute with the common lawyers, the civilians did present a fairly well-defined challenge to both the supremacy and the antiquity of that law.[1] Their opinions in this context represent the full extent of their allegedly hostile intentions towards customary English law.

As lawyers who were especially proud of both their educational background and the cosmopolitan nature of the law they practised,[2] the English civilians did not take lightly any manifestation of common lawyers' assumed superiority over them. Thomas Eden once complained that whenever a few civil lawyers met with any of the King's common law counsel, the latter 'do so overbear us all as we stand but for ciphers',[3] and John Lambe protested that when the same groups met as members of the Court of Delegates, the common lawyers often made the civilians humbly attend upon them at Serjeants' Inn to hold the sessions of the court.[4] Civil lawyers were also sensitive to displays of protocol which acknowledged precedence of common lawyers before them. They became involved in a heated dispute with the serjeants-at-law as to which of them held higher rank in the State.[5] At the more personal level, Cowell seems to have brought dishonour both to Cambridge University and the civilians by relinquishing the place of the Vice-Chancellor at dinner to Sir Edward Coke during a visit of the justice there in 1604.[6]

Even more irritating to the civilians than their symbolic subordination to the common lawyers was the latter's claim to the sole right of interpreting parliamentary statutes. The common lawyers first asserted this exclusive prerogative in reference to the statute of 23 Henry VIII, c. 9, which restricted the Archbishop of Canterbury's right to cite accused parties outside their dioceses

---

[1] Holdsworth, 'Reception', pt. iv, 244, claims that the supremacy of the common law was under attack in the sixteenth century as well.

[2] W. Senior, 'The Advocates of the Court of Arches', *Law Quarterly Review*, 39 (1923), 495.

[3] Bodl., Tanner MS. 86, f. 202.   [4] PRO, SP 16/442/37.

[5] Bodl., Barlow MS. 9, pp. 1–10. The Masters in Chancery became involved in a similar dispute with the serjeants, PRO, SP 14/26/30.

[6] Cooper, *Annals* iii. 7–8.

to the Court of the Arches in London. The judges interpreted this as a denial of the Archbishop's right to cite men from London diocese, since the Arches was not a diocesan court, even though geographically it was located in London. Accordingly the common law judges issued a prohibition on this basis and justified their action by claiming that 'Acts of Parliament are parcel of the laws of England although they be of matters of ecclesiastical cognizance, and therefore the interpretation of them do belong to the judges of the laws of England and not to the civilians.'[1]

Sir John Bennet contested this point on behalf of his fellow civilians. Appealing to the Henrician statute which declared that the Kingdom of England was a body politic composed of a spirituality and a temporality, he deduced therefrom that each part of this corporate entity had the right to regulate its own affairs. While the common lawyers could legitimately interpret ambiguous legislation that touched upon temporal matters,[2] the civilians possessed the corresponding right to clarify statutes that dealt with ecclesiastical affairs.[3] Bennet was elevating the ecclesiastical law to a position of parity with the common law.

Prohibitions, however, were the crucial issue upon which the superiority of the common law judges stood or fell. Each writ implied an unequal relationship between the two groups of lawyers. The right to issue them gave one party complete control over the legal activity of the other. The common law judges, as the specially appointed conservators of the law of the land, tolerated the functioning of the civil law courts only to the extent that they did not infringe upon the jurisdiction of the common law.[4] The civil law judges, on the other hand, possessed no corresponding power of review over the actions of the common law courts at Westminster. 'We could do nothing without them [the common lawyers]', wrote Sir John Lambe, 'but they did what they pleased without us.'[5] In a decision handed down in

---

[1] BM, Cotton MS. Cleo. F II, f. 431; Lansdowne MS. 161, f. 264.

[2] Julius Caesar admitted as much in the Parliament of 1610, *CJ* i. 430.

[3] 'Sir John Bennet's Treatise of Interpretation of Statutes Concerning Ecclesiastical Affairs', Bodl., Barlow MS. 9, ff. 53-5. See also BM, Lansdowne MS. 160, ff. 423-4. See also Cardwell, *Annals* ii. 116 n.

[4] BM, Cotton MS. Cleo. F I, f. 120ᵛ.   [5] PRO, SP 16/442/37.

Roberts's Case (1611) Coke drew attention to this unbalanced relationship:

In divers cases the judges of the common law write to the ecclesiastical judges, commanding them to certify some thing put in issue: and the judges of our law prohibit the judges ecclesiastical to hold plea of some things which are determinable at common law: But the court ecclesiastical hath not power to write to our judges, or to command them, or to prohibit them when they hold plea of things determinable by the ecclesiastical judges; but this is erroneous, and shall be reversed by error.[1]

Irked by the common lawyers' apparent abuse of the superior legal powers entrusted to them, the civilians began to formulate an alternative theory of parity between the two groups of lawyers and the laws that they administered. Julius Caesar laid the groundwork for this new approach when he declared that civil law and common law judges were authorized to govern 'by several laws in like immediate degree from the Prince'.[2] Each civil law judge was just as much a direct representative of the King as a justice of a common law court; each body of civil law just as much his law and hence the law of the land as the common law itself. 'The Admiral jurisdiction is *lex terrae* to the subject in all Admiral Causes' the civilians declared in their articles against prohibitions in 1598.[3] They claimed the same for ecclesiastical jurisdiction, which ever since the Reformation had been firmly attached to the King himself.[4] The ecclesiastical law had become, like the maritime law and the common law, just one more facet of the King's justice and another component of the law of the land.[5] Since it had achieved the same status and authority as the common law itself, there remained no reason, as there had been in the days of papal authority, for the common law judges to issue prohibitions to the Church courts.[6]

The civilians' arguments to establish parity between the various jurisdictions and laws of the realm were as politically explosive as

[1] Mich. 8 Jac., Coke, *Reports*, xii. 68. [2] See above, p. 83.
[3] BM, Lansdowne MS. 142, f. 453ᵛ. [4] 26 Henry VIII, c. 1.
[5] See speech of Marten in 1628 Parliament, ITL, Petyt MS. 537/23, f. 217.
[6] BM, Harl. MS. 358, f. 186ᵛ; Cowell, *Interpreter*, sub 'Prohibition'; Usher, *Reconstruction*, ii. 211, 227. For the common lawyers' opinion see Usher, *High Commission*, p. 226.

their theory that the royal prerogative stood above the law. Once again their constitutional views identified them with royalists who, in defending the King's violation of the common law in certain instances, appealed to other legal codes to justify the monarch's actions and then ascribed to those other laws a status equal to the common law itself. Thus Sir John Davies, a common lawyer who justified the King's right to levy impositions by referring to the law merchant, broadened the definition of the 'law of England' to include:

such other laws also as be common to other nations as well as to us, have been received and used time out of mind by the kings and people of England in divers cases, and by such ancient usage, are become the laws of England in such cases; namely the general law of nations and the law merchant, which is a branch of the law, the imperial or civil law, the common or ecclesiastical law . . .[1]

In the Parliament of 1628 John Coke, the Secretary of State, and Serjeant Ashley presented essentially the same argument in an attempt to justify arbitrary arrest according to the martial law and the law of State. Coke regarded the martial law as 'an essential law of the kingdom', as 'the whole government consists not in the common law but in others'.[2]

For both professional and political reasons, the common lawyers who were engaged in the controversy with the civilians refused to subscribe in any way to the theories of the civilians, Davies or John Coke. For these ideas did contradict the cherished belief of most common lawyers that the common law and the law of the land were conterminous.[3] In the preface to one of their replies to Archbishop Bancroft's complaints concerning prohibitions, the common law judges made it sufficiently clear that they regarded the common law alone to comprise the laws of England, which were 'superior over the civil and canon laws of the realm'.[4] John

---

[1] Davies, *Impositions*, pp. 2–3; Judson, *Crisis*, pp. 134–5.

[2] *LJ* iii. 758–9; Gough, *Fundamental Law*, p. 62; ITL, Petyt MS. 537/23, f. 222. For Bacon's views on this subject see M. Ashley, *Magna Carta in the Seventeenth Century* (Charlottesville, Va., 1965), p. 9.

[3] It is true that both Cowell, *Institutes*, pp. 3–4, and Duck, *De Usu*, pp. 324–6, do use the term 'the law of England' to distinguish it from the civil law.

[4] BM, Cotton MS. Cleo. F I, f. 120.

Selden, who entered the verbal war against the civilians with as much vigour as had Sir Edward Coke, declared explicitly in the Parliament of 1628 that 'If the question were what the law of England is, we must say what is done in the courts at Westminster.'[1]

While refusing to accept the ecclesiastical and maritime laws as autonomous components of a *lex terrae* which comprehended more than just the common law, Sir Edward Coke and his associates did try to accommodate the law of the civilians' courts within the broad structure of the common law itself. Judging the case of *Bird* v. *Smith* (1607), Coke actually went so far as to maintain that 'the temporal law and the ecclesiastical law have been so coupled together that they cannot exist the one without the other'.[2] As he explained further on in his decision, this meant only that the sentences of Church courts were binding in courts of common law and could not be questioned by the common law judges, provided of course that the ecclesiastical courts had not in the process exceeded the bounds of their jurisdiction.[3] Coke was fully recognizing the validity of ecclesiastical justice and giving it a status at the common law.[4] He was indeed incorporating it to some extent within the common law itself. But he was awarding it an ostensibly subordinate position therein. The common law was the distinctly superior element of the symbiosis. As he explained later, 'The common law is the great and principal law, taken in a case mixed with the civil law, the common law carries it.'[5]

John Selden ascribed to civil law jurisdictions an even closer relationship to the common law than did Coke. He held that not only the sentences of ecclesiastical and Admiralty courts but the entire substance of the laws that civilians administered in England

---

[1] BM, Stowe MS. 366, f. 93ᵛ. Yet in another context Selden was willing to allow that the law merchant was *a* law of the land. ITL, Petyt MS. 537/23, f. 216. Note that the idea of the common law as *the* law of the land held the greatest appeal among those political opponents of the first two Stuarts who, like the Puritans, found their case best served by the common law and not by any other. See Stoughton, *An Assertion*, p. 37.

[2] Sir Francis Moore, *Cases Collect & Report* (London, 1663), p. 782.

[3] He admitted this in *Cawdrey's Case*, Coke, *Reports* v. vii.

[4] See Usher, *High Commission*, p. 228.

[5] ITL, Petyt MS. 537/23, f. 213ᵛ.

had a place at the common law. Since the common law was a body of English customs, augmented by occasional statutory declarations, the civil law as it was traditionally applied in England was subsumed within that law as custom, not as written law. In the Parliament of 1628, a few days after he had gone on record that the common law alone comprised *lex terrae*, Selden was still able to state that 'As the canon law, the laws of marrying, and the law merchant does stand with the common law, so they say does the martial law. There are but two ways of making laws, customs and acts of Parliament. These are laws of custom.'[1] The formal enunciation of this theory was left to Blackstone, who simply included all civil law as practised in England within the category of 'particular customs', and thereby fully integrated it within the common law; but Selden proposed the substance of it a century earlier.[2] The thesis had the merit of ascribing full recognition to the civil law without compromising the superiority of the common law within which it was incorporated.[3]

In 1610 Sir Henry Hobart, the Attorney-General, had proposed the most certain ground of that superiority. In the aftermath of the attack on Cowell he was ostensibly trying to eliminate tension when he said 'We desire not to have any emulation betwixt the common and civil law; these two laws are brethren, but the civil the younger brother.'[4] In effect, he was suggesting there was no reason why the civil and the common law should not function harmoniously together within the same legal structure so long as the civil law recognized its subordinate status. And it was age that had determined the relationship between the two jurisdictions.

To be sure, common lawyers placed a great emphasis upon the antiquity of their law. The lawyers of Coke's day assumed without question that their customary law, being the only law England had ever known, was immemorial: that it pre-dated the historical memory of man and could be assumed therefore not to have been the work of any one legislator at any one point in time. Oblivious

---

[1] BM, Stowe MS. 366, f. 94.   [2] Blackstone, *Commentaries*, i. 74–80.
[3] It is some credit to Selden's rhetoric that a civilian in 1656 accepted his theory. See Wiseman, *Law of Lawes*, pp. 139–40.
[4] Foster, *Proceedings*, i. 24.

to the substantial alterations that the Normans' introduction of feudalism had brought about in their law, and convinced that the civil law had had no impact at all upon their law's development, the common lawyers set out to prove that the law that they administered in their courts had originated 'time out of mind' and had persisted in generally unaltered form to the present day.[1] Their most challenging task was to discredit the notion that William the Conqueror had actually imported and effectively established a law different from that of the Anglo-Saxons. In his *Ad Fletam Dissertatio* Selden illustrated this by tracing the common law's long tradition:

First the Anglo-Saxons, then the Danes, and lastly the Normans (all well enough comprehended under one and the same line of Kings) had from the end of the Roman government here, that is for seven hundred years or upwards, made use, without any mixture of the Roman or Imperial Law, of their own peculiar laws, now called by us the common law of England, though variously, as it must always happen, altered according to the different state of affairs.[2]

In order to support the claim that their jurisdictions possessed equal status with the common law, the civil lawyers had to establish that equally great antiquity inhered in their courts. But this was not the case. The civil law itself was undoubtedly more ancient than the common law;[3] but civil law jurisdictions in England were of notably more recent origin. Only the Court of Chancery could even hope to rival the common law courts in antiquity. Sir Julius Caesar, in his unpublished treatise 'De Cancelleria', placed that court's origin in the legendary past of King Arthur's reign, and he drew attention to an affirmation by all the judges of the realm in 1470 that 'Chancery, King's Bench,

---

[1] Pocock, *Ancient Constitution*, pp. 30–55. Pocock claims that the common lawyers believed their law to be *exactly* the same as it always had been, but Selden does not seem to have held to that theory. Blackstone presented a modified version of this theory in his introductory Vinerian lecture, quoted in Howe, *Studies in the Civil Law*, p. 37.

[2] Selden, *The Dissertation of John Selden Annexed to Fleta* (London, 1771), p. 141. I have relied upon this translation.

[3] In the Parliament of 1628 Marten referred to the civil law as the mother and the common law as the daughter. BM, Stowe MS. 366, f. 94.

Common Pleas, and Exchequer be all the Kings' Courts and have been time out of memory of man, so as no man knoweth which of them is the most ancient'.[1]

The same, however, was not true of the other courts in which the civilians practised. An admiralty jurisdiction had arisen only when foreign trade was voluminous enough to necessitate it, and no civilian or other historian of the Admiralty Court was able to place the date any earlier than the reign of King John.[2] Ecclesiastical jurisdiction had of course been in force much earlier, but it had first acquired autonomous status during the reign of William the Conqueror and its rules had changed drastically since that time. It was common knowledge that the law and procedure of the Court of the Arches underwent notable revision in 1272;[3] and even the civilians themselves made mention of only 400 years of past history when they appealed to the antiquity of that court.[4] They did nevertheless, like Sir John Davies, use the phrase 'time out of mind' to characterize the laws and procedures of these and even of some of their more recently erected courts, such as the High Commission.[5] But the term did not mean, in those contexts, of unknown origin. It had acquired the diluted connotation of 'very old', or 'beyond the memory of any *living* man'.[6]

Put at such disadvantage in trying to beat the common lawyers at their own game, the civilians and their supporters resorted to more negative but at the same time more damaging tactics. With no cohesive plan of attack, a few of them began to undermine the myth of antiquity upon which the common lawyers had rested the authority of their law. They advocated the heretical view that William the Conqueror had imported the common law from

---

[1] BM, Lansdowne MS. 132, f. 216.

[2] Only Cowell, *Interpreter*, sub 'Admirall' placed it as early as John's reign. For more accurate estimates see Coke, *Reports*, xii. 79–80; Sir Henry Spelman, *Of the Admiral Jurisdiction and the Officers Thereof*, in *The English Works of Sir Henry Spelman* (London, 1723), ii. 222.

[3] H. Consett, *The Practice of the Spiritual or Ecclesiastical Courts* (London, 1685), p. 4.

[4] BM, Harl. MS. 358, ff. 184–5.

[5] John Strype, *The Life and Acts of John Whitgift, D.D.* (Oxford, 1822), ii. 32; Coke, *Institutes*, ii. 135, objection 3.

[6] Cowell, *Interpreter*, sub 'Custom'.

Normandy and that his legal baggage differed from the customs of the Anglo-Saxons. The idea was not original. Early in the sixteenth century Thomas Starkey had placed the 'first institution of our common law' at the time when William the Conqueror had 'subdued the country' and had 'established its laws'.[1] William Fulbecke presented a modified version of Starkey's theory by crediting the Norman kings with having preserved some of the Anglo-Saxon customs while at the same time altering many more.[2] Cowell seems to have been of the same opinion.[3] John Hayward added that William had not only changed 'the greatest part' of the laws but had also introduced a new legal language into the land.[4] Finally, after antiquarians like Henry Spelman showed that the *feudum*, to which so much of the common law referred, was a Norman novelty, the civilians Richard Zouch and Arthur Duck were able to use this knowledge to cut the common law completely down to size.[5] Duck was the most explicit:

But as soon as he [William] had got the Crown upon his head, *he made several alterations in their laws, and instituted new forms and methods in the courts of justice*; turning many of the allodial lands belonging to the English into feudal tenure, and imposing many taxes and tributes, to which the English had been strangers till his time ... But the kingdom being quieted, when he applied himself to make new laws out of those observed by the Mercians, Danes and East Saxons, which were the chief people in this nation, he preferred those of the Danes, because they came nearest to the laws of the Normans, who were originally descended from the Danes; these *he mixed with the laws of Normandy*, and then published them in his own name, and many of them are still in force among us.[6]

---

[1] Starkey, *Dialogue*, p. 110.

[2] Fulbecke, *Parallel*, ix–lxv; *Direction*, p. 23.

[3] Cowell was far from explicit but he did refer to Norman parallels if not direct influences upon English law, *Interpreter*, sub 'Fee', 'Maner', 'Record'.

[4] John Hayward, *The Lives of the III Normans, Kings of England* (London, 1613), p. 96. See also Hayward, *Succession*, p. 34, and *A Treatise of Union*, p. 11.

[5] Pocock, *Ancient Constitution*, p. 91; Zouch, *Descriptio Juris et Judicii Temporalis*, pp. 7–8, 15–17, 20–2, as well as preface.

[6] Duck, *De Usu*, pp. 300–2. I have relied upon the eighteenth-century translation, pp. xv–xvi. Duck, however, did not deny that the English in large measure resisted Norman attempts to abrogate English laws and to introduce Norman manners and customs, pp. vii–viii.

By arguing that William made substantial changes in the common law the civil lawyers did not intend to expose its authoritarian character and tyrannical purpose, as did the Levellers. For they did not share the intention of the Levellers to reform the entire legal system.[1] But by arguing that the common law was not in fact immemorial, the civilians lent academic support to their instinctive professional assumption that the civil law was an equal partner to the common law. It allowed them to assert with greater conviction that ecclesiastical and maritime law were not subordinate legal codes, acceptable only to the extent that they were customs of the realm, but integral and autonomous components of the *lex terrae*, proceeding directly from the fountain of justice himself.

(d) *The procedures of the civil law*

Even if the civil lawyers had been able to convince the common lawyers that their respective jurisdictions were on a par, one source of tension between the two legal systems would have remained. For the civil law courts employed distinctly Continental procedures which were not used in the common law courts. The most highly criticized of these was the oath *ex officio*, whereby the judges of the spiritual courts required defendants in official prosecutions to swear to answer articles concerning their religious beliefs before the accused knew what those articles were. The oath played an important and time-honoured role in the administration of ecclesiastical discipline and in some cases it was the only means of bringing a 'criminal' to justice.[2] But the common law judges did not recognize any such procedure in their courts and even granted prohibitions in cases when the oath had been used against

---

[1] C. Hill, *Puritanism and Revolution*, pp. 75–87. See also Prall, *Agitation for Reform*.

[2] The best defence of the oath appears in a late Elizabethan memorandum by eight civilians, LPL, MS. 2004, f. 65. See also Strype, *Whitgift*, ii. 32; iii. 323–5; Edward Lake, *Memoranda Touching the Oath Ex Officio* (London, 1662). For discussion of the oath see M. H. Maguire, 'The Attack of the Common Lawyers on the Oath Ex Officio as Administered in the Ecclesiastical Courts in England', *Essays in History and Political Theory*, pp. 199–229, and L. Levy, *Origins of the Fifth Amendment* (New York, 1968), pp. 123–6.

the wishes of the defendant. Their rationale in such instances was that the oath had denied the litigant his rights and liberties held at the common law.

The political implications of such a charge are clear. The civilians were threatening to deprive 'his Majesty's subjects of their Birthright'. Indeed, there has persisted a belief even into the present century that the common lawyers had good reason to regulate the proceedings of the civil law courts because the procedures in force there did in fact constitute a threat to English liberties. Since the common law and its American derivative have survived as the structures within which individual rights find definition, the equation of those rights with the structure itself has become the historical by-product of the survival. Any rival or alternative to the structure has been, therefore, by the internal, logic of the equation, not as just. This was certainly true for seventeenth-century English society, which located all its rights within the common law and therefore identified that law as a whole with the cause of justice itself. Because they made this identification, the common lawyers of the day were able to argue convincingly that the civil law potentially could and at times actually did ride rough-shod over the liberties of the English people. Such attitudes die slowly. As late as 1954 one historian referred to Roman law procedure 'as the instrument adopted *par excellence* for governments that propose really to control the lives of their subjects'.[1]

Admittedly there is a strong case against the civilians for their use and abuse of the *ex officio* oath. Even if the right against self-incrimination was not clearly established at that time, civil law judges, in using this procedure, were far from solicitous of the rights of the accused. Yet it would be precipitate to reach any general conclusions about the relative merits of civil law and common law jurisdiction simply on the basis of the oath, especially since the oath was not used in the great majority of court cases. Ronald Marchant has argued convincingly that by the standards of the sixteenth and seventeenth centuries, the Church courts were far from arbitrary and that defendants enjoyed certain advantages

---

[1] P. Hughes, *The Reformation in England* (London, 1954), iii. 200. See also Levy, *Fifth Amendment*, p. 5.

that were not given to persons accused in the secular courts. They could, for example, compel attendance of witnesses on their behalf and give evidence to an impartial registrar outside the court-room.[1]

Nevertheless there were respects in which civil law procedure appeared to deny defendants the full protection of the law. In most cases they relate to the wide discretionary powers vested in the civil law judge. Especially in making his legal decisions that judge observed few technical restrictions. Since the civil law was written, precedents did not constitute the basis of judgment as they did at the common law. The judge was supposed to refer to the text of the law itself,[2] but since this was terse and in places vague, the civilian could pick freely from a host of available commentaries to support his pronouncement. Instead of appearing to declare what the law really was, he gave the impression of almost creating the law to suit his own desires, except of course when specific statutes or canons applied.[3] Coke located the reason for the judge's wide-ranging freedom of decision in the uncertainty of the civil law itself:

Upon the text of the civil law there be so many glosses and interpretations and again upon those so many commentaries and all these written by doctors of equal degree and authority, and therein so many diversities of opinions; as they do rather increase than resolve doubts and incertainties, and the professors of that noble science say that it is like a sea full of waves. The difference between those glosses and commentaries and this which we publish, is that their glosses and commentaries are written by doctors, which be advocates, and so in a manner private interpretation. And our expositions or commentaries upon Magna Carta and other statues are the resolutions of judges in courts of justice in judicial courses of proceeding, either related and reported in our books, or extant in our judicial records, or in both, and therefore being collected together shall (as we conceive) produce certainty.[4]

---

[1] Marchant, *Church Under Law*, pp. 6–7. [2] Oughton, *Forms*, p. 14.
[3] Squibb, *Chivalry*, p. 163; Vaisey, *Canon Law*, p. 57; Collinson, *Puritan Movement*, p. 39. See for example Marten's sources in *Wyer* v. *Atchley*, Bodl., Tanner MS. 427, f. 148; *Heraldic Cases* (Harl. Soc. cvii), p. v.
[4] Coke, *Institutes*, ii, proeme, p. vi. See also Clerk, *An Epitome of Late Aspersions Cast at Civilians* (Dublin, 1631), pp. 1–8. In the pronouncements of one civilian,

The certainty of the common law was valued because it protected the subject from the exercise of arbitrary authority. In the Parliament of 1628, Mr. William Coryton, M.P. from Cornwall,[1] appealed to that law as a defence against the abuse of martial law, which was itself considered part of the civil law: 'I desire to live under a known law. The common law gives every man his due and every offence that deserves death is punished by it. This martial law strikes to every subject, we are all soldiers to serve the King.'[2]

The case against the civil law, however, is not airtight. For the common law, which Coke esteemed as the paragon of precision, allowed its judges just as much dangerous flexibility in its application as did the civil law. The common law was, after all, case law, and the judges could draw upon an infinite variety of precedents with as much discrimination as civilians did upon their commentaries.[3] King James himself explained to the Parliament of 1610 how this freedom could be used to harmful political effect:

[T]he common law is but *responsa prudentum*, depending upon the reports of judges, which I would have in Parliament set down directly what are laws, and in one and the selfsame case the judgments, and no superfluous and idle acts of parliaments (which are but to ensnare subjects) to stand in force and be records, for now no subject, as the law standeth, can either avoid or escape a tyrannous or an avarice King.[4]

These are ironic words for the first of the Stuart kings, against whose power the judges appealed to their law as the bulwark of English liberties; but John Lilburne was to say virtually the same thing in 1646.[5] The civil law judges claimed no monopoly of

---

Sir Henry Marten, the uncertainty of the civil law was even more apparent since Marten would not put his judgments into writing. Hence he earned the nickname of the 'Delphian Oracle' or the 'Sphinx'. *CSPD 1638–1639*, p. 32.

[1] A political ally of John Selden and John Eliot. See H. Hulme, *The Life of Sir John Eliot 1592 to 1632: Struggle for Parliamentary Freedom* (London, 1957), p. 308.

[2] ITL, Petyt, MS. 537/23, f. 223.

[3] A. Harding, *A Social History of English Law* (London, 1966), pp. 220–4. R. Wiseman claimed that one great attribute of the civil law was its certainty, since it was written and codified, *Law of Lawes*, p. 177.

[4] Foster, *Proceedings*, i. 47.

[5] C. Hill, *Puritanism and Revolution*, p. 76.

arbitrary legal power. There was no safeguard built into either legal system to protect the subject from a politically partial or captive judge.

The common law courts, however, still had a jury which might prevent the judge from giving an unjust decision. The civil law courts, in imitation of the standards of legal procedure that had developed on the Continent, dispensed completely with the participation of 'lay judges' in their proceedings.[1] Unlike the common law courts, which preserved and expanded the use of the jury under the Norman kings, Continental legal systems assigned complete responsibility for the judicial proceedings to professional judges.[2] During the course of a trial one judge remained in full command, weighing the value of witnesses' testimony according to certain rules of evidence before reaching his final decision. His control of the proceedings was even more pronounced when the court resorted to summary process, wherein the judge operated more secretly, independently, and expeditiously than in the alternative plenary process.[3] The net effect of this concentration of authority upon the civil law judge was, as Coke claimed, that it was 'at the will of the judge with which party he shall give his sentence'.[4]

There were reasons of convenience and of justice for the judges to have acted without the assistance of a jury and in a summary fashion. Juries were, even by Coke's own admission, terrible inconveniences.[5] They invariably slowed down the judicial process and could actually deter the course of justice itself, when the volume of business was heavy, as in the ecclesiastical courts.[6] They were also legally ignorant bodies of men who required instruction in matters of law by the judge before they reached their verdict.

[1] Dawson, *Lay Judges*, pp. 175–6.

[2] Ibid., pp. 87–8, 293.

[3] Ritchie, *Ecclesiastical Courts*, pp. 155–7; Usher, *High Commission*, p. 108; Francis Clerke, *The Practice of the High Court of Admiralty*, trans. in John Hall, *The Practice and Jurisdiction of the Court of Admiralty* (Baltimore Md., 1809), pp. 34–5; O. J. Reichel, *A Complete Manual of Canon Law* (London, 1896), ii. 237–8.

[4] Coke, *Reports*, xiii. 44, Case of *De Modo Decimandi* Trin. 7 Jac. I.

[5] Ibid.

[6] 'One learned civilian will dispatch more business in a day than the present ᶦudges can in a term.' BM, Add. MS. 32093, f. 389.

There was, however, no guarantee that they would not ignore that law to suit their own personal prejudices.[1] Moreover, when the law involved such technical matters as ecclesiastical doctrine and mercantile custom, confusion among jurymen could easily have resulted. For this reason the common law, after it did incorporate maritime jurisdiction within its boundaries, appointed juries of knowledgeable merchants to sit in judgment of such cases.[2] In the present century English courts have found juries to be so inadequately versed in the technicalities of the law and so inessential if not prejudicial to the course of justice in certain types of hearings that they have excluded them in most civil proceedings.[3]

The employment of summary process in the seventeenth century had particular advantages in the Admiralty Court, where it was employed frequently. Swift justice by a judge, based upon written testimony which could be taken even in foreign Admiralty courts, freed travelling mariners and busy merchants from the inconveniencing plenary process and even more so from the delays so characteristic of the common law courts. An Admiralty court could sit at any time and did not have to postpone urgent business until the beginning of the next law term.[4] This convenience, coupled with the relative competency of the civilians in maritime law, helps to explain the preference of merchants and mariners for the Admiralty Court over the common law courts even during the period of the Civil War.[5]

The absence of a jury and the use of summary process, therefore, by themselves do not seem to have restricted the course of justice but on the contrary often expedited it. The main requirement for justice when such procedures were employed was the impartiality of the judge, who controlled and directed all legal proceedings and delivered the verdict himself. And it was the inability of the

[1] Lord Chancellor Ellesmere thought that 'it is somewhat hard that the validity of a Church should be tried by an ignorant jury'. Bodl., Tanner MS. 280, f. 121ᵛ.

[2] C. H. S. Fifoot, *Lord Mansfield* (London, 1936), pp. 104–5.

[3] Harding, *Social History of Law*, p. 406.

[4] Wynne, *Life of Jenkins*, p. lxxiv; Zouch, *The Jurisdiction of the Admiralty of England Asserted* (London, 1663), p. 129.

[5] *CJ* iv. 720; petition of merchants to the King 1660, Lincoln's Inn Library, pamphlet 1839 appended to *The Jurisdiction of the Court of Admiralty Settled*, pp. 19–21.

civilians of the late sixteenth and early seventeenth centuries to meet this criterion of fairness as judges that lends credence to the complaint that they did actually pass down arbitrary decisions in their courts. The civil lawyers displayed a prejudice in favour of, and at times an institutional identification with, the prosecution in many of the criminal cases they adjudicated, especially in the ecclesiastical courts. The civilians' initial presumption in these cases that the accused was guilty serves as only one indication of their partiality.[1] Even more important was their involvement in the detection of the crimes they tried and their assumption of the role of accuser in official prosecutions. For when an ecclesiastical court proceeded by inquisition, the judge himself presented articles against the accused on the basis of personal knowledge or common rumour.[2] Thus the same individual who made the initial accusation delivered the final judgment. As Professor Levy has argued, the ecclesiastical judge combined in his own person the roles of 'accuser, prosecutor, judge, and jury'.[3] This heavy concentration of judicial power in the civil law judge often put the accused at a serious disadvantage. In 1590 John Elvin, the Puritan minister of Westwell, Kent, objected to his legal treatment at the hands of Dr. Stephen Lakes, the Commissary of Archbishop Whitgift. 'I think it in like manner hard cause', wrote Elvin, 'that a judge (who by the law ought to make himself no business as I have heard) having no presentment (that I can hear of) should upon mere surmise commence new articles against me and therein seek all advantages that any way may be afforded him.'[4]

---

[1] Usher, *High Commission*, p. 118. On the presumption of guilt in civil law procedure see Holdsworth, *History of Law*, i. 316; J. H. Merryman, *The Civil Law Tradition* (Stanford, Calif., 1969), p. 138.

[2] When the court proceeded by denunciation the judge acted in similar fashion on behalf of a secret or unknown accuser.

[3] Levy, *Fifth Amendment*, p. 23. In a different way the position of judge also became confused with that of advocate. Advocates often served as surrogates to the judges of the courts in which they practised, especially in the Court of Delegates. 'All the doctors are engaged at the same court, both as judges and advocates, and so the same person now a judge, presently an advocate, then a judge again.' [Cocke], *Compleat Law Judge*, p. 25.

[4] LPL, MS. 2014, f. 81.

The active and partial role that judges like Dr. Lakes played in official prosecutions had wide-ranging political implications. The civil lawyers were engaged in an administrative as well as a judicial process. They were not only arbitrating disputes between parties, but enforcing the law upon subjects in accordance with the policies established by their superiors. This was especially true of their service as Commissioners for Ecclesiastical Causes. Of course it might be argued that the common law judges could just as easily have allowed the policies of those upon whom they depended for their livelihood to influence their legal decisions. But there was a difference between the common lawyers and the civilians, for the former were not entrusted with any judicial powers whereby they could bring action against offenders of their own initiative, or pass judgment against them without the assistance of the local community.

The real case against the civilians, therefore, was not their callous disrespect for Englishmen's legal rights or even the intrinsic authoritarianism of the legal system that they administered, but the purpose for which they exercised the discretionary powers vested in them. Especially in proceeding against non-conformists some of them did use the law as an instrument of political and religious policy. The Puritans recognized this, and it underlay their objections to ecclesiastical jurisdiction and to the *ex officio* oath. It was the broader issue that aligned them with the common lawyers against the civilians on the question of prohibitions. This alliance was too strong for the civilians, and it brought about the virtual destruction of their profession in 1641. To understand how this came about, however, it is necessary first to study the role the civilians played in ecclesiastical politics.

V

ECCLESIASTICAL POLITICS

THE Puritans of the early seventeenth century were the most steadfast and, in the final analysis, the most successful opponents of the English civil lawyers. Their criticism of the civilians as the legal officers of the ecclesiastical hierarchy and hence as the custodians of religious orthodoxy was contemptuous and at times even crude. In their view the civilians were as responsible as bishops themselves for preventing the introduction of the 'government of Christ' into the kingdom.[1] For the Puritans considered the correction of Church manners, which the civilians undertook in the name of episcopacy, to be a matter of congregational rather than diocesan or archdiocesan concern.[2] The civilians moreover, seemed to display a deep personal hostility towards Puritan activities. 'The very sight of a Puritan (as they brand them) in their courts', wrote one bitter Parliamentarian in 1641, 'makes their blood rise and their spirits rage and swell as against the mortal enemies of their dominion.'[3] To alienate them further from their Puritan detractors, the civil lawyers relied upon the unreformed and hence suspect canon law of Rome for many of their legal decisions and administered the unpopular *ex officio* oath in their courts.

Because of their association with an allegedly unreformed episcopacy and because of their reliance upon the canon law of Rome, the civilians fell victims to the traditional Puritan curse of

[1] See, for example, *The Marprelate Tracts*, pp. 248–51. For a balanced view of Puritan attitudes towards the episcopacy see P. Collinson, 'Episcopacy and Reform in England in the Later Sixteenth Century,' *Studies in Church History* (ed. C. J. Cuming, Leiden, 1966), iii. 91–125.

[2] Collinson, *Puritan Movement*, pp. 346–7; Stoughton, *An Assertion*, pp. 366–93.

[3] [U.N.V.], *The Downfall of the Pretended Divine Authority of the Hierarchy Into the Sea of Rome* (London, 1641), p. 10.

being tainted with popery. The authors of the *Marprelate Tracts* referred to the civilians in passing as the 'popish doctors of the bawdy courts',[1] while another Elizabethan Puritan observed that both the bishops and their civilian chancellors, working by the canon law, reveal that 'the Pope hath his horse ready sadled and bridled, watching but the time to get up again.'[2] The civil lawyers never lost this stigma of papal affiliation. The Puritans applied it to them with special delight during the period of Laud's supremacy, when the episcopacy was largely Arminian in sentiment and when the civilians either enthusiastically or acquiescently provided legal support for Laud's policies. Puritan pamphleteers had a field day at the time of the Long Parliament, linking together Laud, the bishops, and the civilians as members of one large popishly affected conspiracy to subvert the true religion.[3] William Prynne included in a list of 'popish books' which had appeared during the reign of Charles not only Bishop Montague's controversial *Apello Caesarem* but also the second edition of Dr. Ridley's *View of the Civile and Ecclesiastical Law*.[4] Another Puritan author, in a scathing attack upon the crumbling Laudian Church, entitled *The Downfall of the Hierarchy Into the Sea of Rome*, best summarized the nature of the alleged conspiracy:

But archbishops, diocesan bishops, deans, archdeacons, chancellors, officials, etc. their names, offices, and practices are such; as in one word appears in that they have their foundation in that filthy dunghill of the canon law, and thence their practices, *ex mero officio*, are only warranted

[1] *Marprelate Tracts*, p. 51.

[2] LPL, Lambeth Lib. Revel. 3.20. Quoted in Ritchie, *Ecclesiastical Courts*, p. 215, n. 52.

[3] Senior, 'Advocates of Arches', 504–5; *A True Description or Rather a Parallel Betweene Cardinal Wolsey, Archbishop of York and William Laud, Archbishop of Canterbury* (London, 1641), p. 7; *The Proctor and the Parator*, pp. B2ᵛ–B3; *St. Paul's Potion Prescribed by Doctor Commons, Being Very Sick of a Dangerous Fulnesse* (London, 1641), pp. A2ᵛ–A3; *The Organ's Echo to the Tune of a Cathedral Service* (London, 1641), Stanzas 7, 8, 10, 11; 'The Last Will and Testament of Doctors Commons', appended to *The Pimpes Prerogative* (London, 1641), displays a woodcut of a number of bishops and civilians at a table. One bishop says 'What, no Commission', while another replies, 'Then woe to Rome and us.'

[4] Prynne, *Canterburies Doome*, pp. 186, 218. The 'popish' parts to which Prynne referred were such matters as a bishop's right to pull down a church built by a patron without episcopal consent.

to uphold and propagate the kingdom of Antichrist, and bring in popery again.[1]

(a) *The civilians and the ecclesiastical hierarchy*

While the Puritans grossly misrepresented the true nature of the civilians' religious allegiances, their rhetoric did bring into focus one aspect of their enemies' careers which provides the best single explanation of the civilians' politics. The association of the civil lawyers with the ecclesiastical hierarchy—whether Arminian, orthodox, or moderately pro-Puritan—was the most distinctive feature of their entire professional life. It provided a common bond not just among all the fellows of Doctors' Commons, who by virtue of membership in that society entered the service of the Archbishop of Canterbury, but also among those other civilians who did not practise in the central courts but who none the less participated in the official life of the Church as either diocesan chancellors, commissaries of archdeacons, or members of cathedral chapters. Of the entire group of 200 civilians, only a small group of seven university fellows and professors and a few civil lawyers who avoided all forms of official employment pursued careers that were completely divorced from ecclesiastical affairs.

The alliance between the profession of the civil law and the Church of England was, however, far from hard and fast. For most civilians it was, from the outset, a strictly professional and not a clerical attachment. Only twenty-seven civil lawyers included in this study are known to have taken holy orders, while three others took minor orders.[2] The number had been higher among their fourteenth- and fifteenth-century predecessors.

[1] *The Downfall of the Hierarchy*, p. 3.

[2] In determining clerical status, I have relied upon the evidence that the twenty-one were either vicars of parish churches or are known to have actually taken orders. The number of clerics does not include those who, like David Yale, Repent Savage, and Nicholas Nevill, took minor orders. Concerning the general assumption by many historians that all civilians were laymen see Mullinger, *University of Cambridge*, p. 423, n. 3. The reason for this assumption might have been that legal education was coming to be regarded as an alternative to clerical training rather than its complement. See H. G. Owen, 'The London Parish Clergy in the Reign of Elizabeth I' (London University, Ph.D. thesis, 1957), p. 27, and V. H. H. Green, *Religion at Oxford and Cambridge* (London, 1964), p. 100.

Before the Reformation it was not at all uncommon for a civilian to be in holy orders. Within the Church there had existed a heavy demand for clerics who were qualified to administer ecclesiastical jurisdiction, which was based upon canon law. Since it had been customary for Doctors of the Civil Law to extend their stay at the university for an additional two or three years and to become Doctors of Canon Law as well, the civilian-canonist who was also a cleric possessed high potential for upward mobility within the hierarchy of the English Church.[1] Knowledge of the canon law became a criterion for promotion to such important positions as archdeaconships, diocesan chancellorships, and even bishoprics. Skill as a civilian was an added asset for the aspiring cleric, especially during the fifteenth century, when his exposure to problems of international law recommended him as a negotiator with the Papacy on such increasingly complicated matters as papal taxation.[2] The study of the civil law was also believed to cultivate the art of statesmanship, and for this reason, as well as for their knowledge of the canon law, a growing number of civilian-canonists joined the ranks of the episcopacy in the late fifteenth and early sixteenth centuries.[3]

Despite the opportunities that a clerical career offered, some civilians chose to eschew the clerical state and to rely completely upon their non-ecclesiastical service as diplomats, Masters in Chancery, and judges in the Admiralty Court.[4] It appears that even some of the advocates of the Court of the Arches in pre-Reformation England were laymen, a situation that was perfectly in accord with Church law, since the advocates only pleaded for clients and were not entrusted with ecclesiastical jurisdiction.[5] But it was not until after the Reformation that the lay civilians commanded the same employment opportunities as their clerical counterparts. Following upon his break with Rome, Henry VIII

---

[1] Smith, *Tudor Prelates and Politics*, pp. 23, 39–40.
[2] Charlton, *Education*, p. 46.   [3] Williams, *Welsh Church*, p. 301.
[4] Senior, *Doctors' Commons*, pp. 37–58, describes the opportunities open to them.
[5] See 21 Henry VIII, c. 13, art. xvii, which refers to 'as many of the xii Masters of the Chancery and xii advocates of the Arches as be or hereafter shalbe spiritual men', clearly implying thereby that some were not. In 1295 no priests were allowed to plead in the Arches. LPL MS. 958, p. iii.

discouraged the study of canon law at Oxford and Cambridge, intending eventually to supplant that body of jurisprudence with a code of English ecclesiastical law.[1] With their supply of canonists from the universities thus discontinued, the hierarchy of the English Church had to rely upon the civilians to staff their courts, which followed civil law procedure. Parliament gave official sanction to this shift in personnel by a statue of 1546 which opened all posts of ecclesiastical jurisdiction to Doctors of Civil Law, whether they be clerical or lay.[2] This allowed civilians to take advantage of the numerous professional opportunities open to them within the Church without assuming the additional responsibilities of clerical life.

During the reign of Elizabeth the membership of the profession of civil law became gradually less clerical. Then towards the end of the sixteenth century Archbishop Whitgift relieved the fellows of All Souls College, sixteen of whom were students or professors of the civil law, of their customary obligation to take holy orders.[3] After this time only two clerics, John Tuer and Jonathan Browne, entered Doctors' Commons, and neither of these was granted full admission.[4] The other Doctors of Laws who elected to become clerics in the early seventeenth century never established any connection with the College of Advocates. Most of these clerical civilians were rectors or vicars of parish churches who regarded their degrees as a culmination or an embellishment rather than a prerequisite of their careers and manifested no desire to advance in the King's service. The one exception to this pattern was William Juxon, who as the only bishop among the civilians of

[1] Senior, 'Advocates of the Arches', p. 503. Degrees ceased to be taken as a separate faculty in 1535. Only seven or eight students after that date received degrees in the canon law. 'It obviously required some boldness at the time to devote oneself to the study of a system of jurisprudence whose fundamental principle was the universal supremacy of the papal see.'

[2] 37 Henry VIII, c. 17.

[3] M. Burrows, *The Worthies of All Souls* (London, 1874), pp. 9, 106. See also C. T. Martin, *A Catalogue of the Archives in the Muniment Rooms of All Souls' College* (London, 1877), p. 305.

[4] For Tuer see LPL, Bancroft Register, f. 157; for Browne see Borth. Inst., R. VII. PR 108. Regarding the lay status of those who were full members of Doctors' Commons see LPL, MS. 958, preface, p. 2.

this period relied upon his qualifications as a civilian to ascend through the ecclesiastical hierarchy to the eventual rank of Archbishop of Canterbury. Juxon was accepted by the fellows of Doctors' Commons as an honorary member.[1]

Some civilians were particularly emphatic in their rejection of the clerical way of life. Matthew Carew overcame considerable pressure to take holy orders. Soon after he received a B.A. from Cambridge at the age of twenty-one, the Bishop of Norwich tried to lure him into the priesthood by appointing him Archdeacon of Norfolk on the condition that he enter the priesthood within a three-year period. Carew, however, realizing that there was equal if not superior opportunity as a lay civilian, never followed the bishop's wishes.[2] Barnaby Gooch seems to have been just as alert to the drawbacks of clerical life. By his will he endowed two fellowships at Magdalene College, Cambridge, for students of the civil law who were not to be 'tied to enter any order of the Church or to perform any exercise in divinity'.[3]

Yet despite their avoidance of the clerical state the civilians still managed to secure numerous and often prominent 'spiritual' employments within the English Church. For in addition to claiming the legal offices which were reserved for the members of their profession, such as the diocesan chancellorships, the civilians often accumulated ecclesiastical preferments which were traditionally the preserve of clerics. It was not at all unusual for a civil lawyer to serve as a lay rector, prebendary, or dean.[4] Until 1663 there was no impediment for him or any layman to become a rector, provided he supplied a spiritual vicar for the cure of souls.[5] Before accepting a prebend or a deanship, however, it was necessary for him to obtain a dispensation. Henry Mountlowe, for example, was careful to obtain two dispensations, one by a letter

[1] Ibid., list of honorary members of Doctors' Commons.
[2] Blomefield, Norfolk, iii. 644.
[3] PRO, will of Gooch, PROB 11/149/71.
[4] Occasionally the civilians' lay status was noted in official records, as was Barker's when he was installed in Highleigh prebend in Chichester Cathedral. See Peckham, Acts of the Dean and Chapter of Chichester, no. 903.
[5] Sir Robert Phillimore, The Ecclesiastical Law of the Church of England (London, 1895), i. 310–11.

patent from Queen Elizabeth and another from Archbishop Whitgift in his Court of Faculties, before his installation as a prebendary of York.[1]

The civilians became, therefore, something of an anomaly within the late Elizabethan and early Stuart Church. As laymen serving in clerical posts, their peculiar status gave rise to considerable animosity towards them. Puritans in particular resented the assignment of what appeared to be essentially spiritual powers to men who were not invested with priestly dignity or who were not at least lay presbyters of a local community.[2] The Puritans, it is true, did not object to the use of laymen in matters of 'spiritual' jurisdiction which to their minds were really temporal concerns. These they desired to be handled by common lawyers or, as William Stoughton suggested, by civilians who received their powers directly from the King and not from the bishops.[3] But spiritual powers belonged with spiritual men, not lay administrators and lawyers. It is interesting to note in this context that one of the few reforms undertaken by the abortive Canons of 1640 was the stipulation that all excommunications and suspensions be pronounced either by a bishop or by an episcopal representative who possessed ecclesiastical jurisdiction and who was in holy orders.[4] Understandably the civilians protested against this restriction of their judicial powers.[5]

---

[1] HMCS ix. 421. For the dispensation of Wilkinson see HMCS xi. 437.

[2] The claims of the Puritans are epitomized and countered by Downing, A Discourse of the State Ecclesiasticall, pp. 33–42. The Puritans were concerned mainly over the excommunicative powers that the lay civilians exercised. See W. Barlow, The Summe and Substance of the Conference, pp. 8–9; the Millenary Petition of 1603, quoted in S. B. Babbage, Puritanism and Richard Bancroft (London, 1962), p. 45; P. Tyler, 'Ecclesiastical Commission', p. 12, minimizes the extent of the grievance, especially during the early Elizabethan period, when more civilians were clerics. For a good discussion of excommunication see Quintrell, 'Government of Essex', pp. 179–80.

[3] Stoughton, An Assertion, pp. 78–90; Usher, High Commission, p. 188.

[4] Cardwell, Synodalia, i. 410, article xiii. Note that there had been an earlier injunction to this effect in 1584, but it had not commanded adherence. See Stoughton, Assertion, pp. 386–7.

[5] The civilians protested to the King against a number of canons which they claimed were prejudicial to their profession. See Bodl., Tanner MS. 65, f. 82; PRO SP 16/456/44.

The Puritans were not the only Englishmen who disliked the civilians for their position within the Church. The Anglican clergy frequently found themselves at odds with the civil lawyers. No fewer than sixteen civilians included in this study became embroiled in disputes either with members of cathedral chapters or with bishops of their dioceses. The reasons for the disagreements varied, but in each case the offending civilian appeared as an intruding outsider, who either threatened to encroach upon the clergy's privileges or refused to follow the clerical way of life.[1] The encounters leave the distinct impression that the civilians were both unwelcome and uncomfortable members of the ecclesiastical establishment.

The most common complaint was that the civilians controlled far too great a share of the ecclesiastical jurisdiction of the dioceses. Thus the Canons of Exeter Cathedral delayed their confirmation of the patent of Dr. Gooch as chancellor of their diocese for almost a full year because they feared the action 'may be prejudicial to the jurisdiction of the Dean and Chapter, the Dean, the four archdeacons, and the Vicars'.[2] Bishop Scrambler of Norwich laid a similar claim against Peter Withypoll's patent as Commissary for the Archdeaconry of Suffolk and brought his protest before the Privy Council.[3] In Ireland, the English civilian Thomas Ryves met a cool reception from the Archbishop of Armagh and the Bishop of Neath, who challenged the wide terms of Ryves's patent as Judge of the Prerogative Court there.[4]

In York a different problem arose when Queen Elizabeth dispensed John Gibson not only to hold a prebend in the cathedral but also to derive all the benefits of a canon residentiary without keeping twenty-six weeks of required residence in the Cathedral

---

[1] Mullinger, *Cambridge*, pp. 423–4. On the other hand, civilians like Edward Mottershed did not trust the local clergy. See Marchant, *Church Under Law*, pp. 196–7.   [2] Exeter Cathedral Library, MS. 3553, f. 53.

[3] J. Strype, *Annals of the Reformation and Establishment of Religion* (Oxford, 1824), iii, pt. 1, pp. 480–1; G. C. Smith, *The Family of Withypoll* (Walthamstow Antiquarian Society, xxxiv, 1936), pp. 60–1.

[4] *CSP Ireland 1615–1625*, pp. 105–6, 173–4. For Archbishop Usher's protest over the renewal of his patent in 1625. See R. Parr (ed.), *The Life of the Most Reverend Father in God, James Usher, Late Lord Archbishop of Armagh* (London, 1686), pp. 327–8.

Close. Dean Matthew Hutton was willing to tolerate the first dispensation, but not the second, which was contrary to the statutes of the cathedral and which, if tolerated, would 'open a window, which (if it not be speedily shut) is like utterly to overthrow the state of our Church'.[1] Gibson's problem was not simply that he was a layman but that he was also a member of the Court and had other pressing obligations in London which prevented him from spending as much time in the vicinity of the cathedral as the other canons were accustomed.

Interests at Court lay at the root of two other civilians' disagreements with their cathedral chapters. Matthew Sutcliffe, although one of the few members of Doctors' Commons who actually had taken orders, none the less could not get along with his chapter. Legal and ecclesiastical business in London had required him to request repeated dispensations from residence at Exeter Cathedral,[2] and whenever he did manage to remain in the diocese, coexistence with his colleagues was difficult. Tensions mounted so high after Sutcliffe supported a litigant against whom the members of the chapter had brought action[3] that in 1608 the canons petitioned the Privy Council concerning Sutcliffe, 'touching all his molestations and grievances unto us and his misgovernment in our church and chapter business'.[4] It appears that similar differences between dean and chapter prevailed at Wells Cathedral, where the dean was Sir John Herbert, a lay civilian, Privy Councillor, Second Secretary of State to Queen Elizabeth, and a courtier *par excellence*. Corresponding with his chapter from London, Herbert tried in 1590 to install a chancellor, another civilian, through the influence of the Privy Council against the wishes of the canons themselves.[5]

Yet despite their lay status, their interests at Court, and their differences with diocesan clergy, the civilians remained firmly

[1] Matthew Hutton, *The Correspondence of Dr. Matthew Hutton, Archbishop of York* (Surtees Society, xvii, 1843), pp. 18–19, 63–4.

[2] Exeter Cathedral Library, MS. 3553, ff. 39, 45ᵛ, 49. Sutcliffe was referred to as being employed in 'Negotiis Publicis Ecclesiae'.

[3] Cassidy, 'Episcopate of Cotton', pp. 36–7; Exeter Cathedral Library, MS. 7155/1, f. 71. See also ff. 4–4ᵛ, 299, 372.

[4] Exeter Cathedral Library, MS. 3553, f. 8.

[5] HMC, *Calendar of the Manuscripts of the Dean and Chapter of Wells*, ii (London, 1914), p. 319.

attached to and identified with the Anglican Church. Professional considerations explain this almost completely. No matter how unpleasant the civil lawyers' clerical associations might have been, the episcopacy controlled not only a majority of the positions in which they could find employment but also the occupational stepping-stones to lucrative non-ecclesiastical positions in the King's service. This was not readily obvious to all Englishmen. During the late Elizabethan and early Stuart periods, a number of Puritans, desirous of destroying the episcopal system of Church courts, tried to convince the civilians that the courts were not necessary for their economic well-being. The Puritans alluded to the relatively poor financial returns that offices of ecclesiastical jurisdiction yielded to their incumbents and suggested that the civilians could prosper much more favourably in secular employments.[1] Their appraisal of the civil lawyers' economic plight was in some respects accurate. It has already been shown that officials of archdeacons and even a fair number of chancellors were reaping mediocre, if not paltry, profits from their judicial offices. Even the active advocates in the London courts could not match the wealth of many common law barristers and might easily have agreed with the logic of the Puritans' argument. But the polemicists failed to observe that the most lucrative as well as the most unprofitable positions that the civilians filled were at the disposal of the Archbishops of Canterbury and of York. The plums of the profession, which help to account for the wealth of civilians such as Stanhope, Bennet, James, and Marten, were the judgeships of the archiepiscopal courts. Supplementary ecclesiastical preferments which often made the difference between a low and a comfortable economic standing for a number of diocesan chancellors, were also controlled by the higher clergy. The Archbishop of Canterbury, moreover, exercised a power of review over the membership of Doctors' Commons, and it was from the ranks of this society

[1] Stoughton, *An Assertion*, pp. 69–77. For an earlier statement of the same opinion see *The Marprelate Tracts*, pp. 250–1. Both were replies to the statement of Bishop Thomas Cooper of Winchester that 'the civilians in this realm live not by the use of the civil law but by the offices of the canon law, and such things as are within the compass thereof'. *An Admonition to the People of England Against Martin Marprelate* (London, 1589), p. 77 (p. 67 in the second edition of that year).

that the candidates for higher positions in Church and State were customarily chosen.

The average civilian, therefore, instead of weighing alternatives to ecclesiastical employment, gravitated naturally towards the Church as the main source of his professional advancement. Early in his career he became assimilated within the upper ranks of the Anglican clergy. Some civilians, such as Francis James, Giles Fletcher, George Parry, and Morgan Goodwyn had a preliminary advantage in this pursuit, since they had blood relatives within the episcopacy.[1] Others established ties with bishops through the patronage of the latter. John Cowell owed his decision to become a civil lawyer and the success of his entire career to Archbishop Bancroft, who became his close friend and confidant.[2] Robert Aylett stood in a similar relationship to John King, the Bishop of London. Looking back on his long career as the official of the Archdeacon of Essex, Aylett addressed one of his poems to his patron and friend:

> Your Lordship's worthy favours did invite
> Me to this boldness, when you first did raise
> My lot which in obscurity was light,
> In better fortunes for to spend my days,
> For which I blesse your bounty, and my Maker praise.[3]

Thomas Ridley was benefited by the assistance of two episcopal patrons. William Day, the Bishop of Winchester, acted as a second father to the young Ridley, saw him through Cambridge and raised him to his first ecclesiastical position as his own diocesan chancellor. After Day's death, Archbishop Abbot advanced Ridley through the higher ranks of the ecclesiastical hierarchy to the position of his vicar-general.[4]

---

[1] See the biographies of these civilians in the appendix. See also the biographies of Francis Alexander, Nicholas Darrell, William Griffith, Edmund Merrick, Sir William Merrick, and Tobias Worlich.

[2] See Cowell's dedication to Bancroft in *The Interpreter*. Cowell assisted the Archbishop in the drawing up of the Canons of 1604 and became his vicar-general in 1608.

[3] Quoted in F. M. Padelford, 'Robert Aylett', *The Huntington Library Bulletin*, 10 (1936), 3. John Hoskins had a similar relationship with Bishop Robert Bennet of Hereford. See SP 14/174/70.   [4] HPT, biography of Ridley.

Marriages often conveniently reinforced professional ties between civilians and bishops. Ridley married Day's daughter, while Nathaniel Brent wedded the niece of Archbishop Abbot, whom he served as commissary and vicar-general.[1] Zachary Babington married the daughter of Bishop Overton of Lichfield diocese, who proceeded to advance his son-in-law's interest there at the expense of another civilian, William Becon.[2] To cement relationships that they had already established through years of professional association, both David Yale and John Weston gave their children in marriage to the bishops of their dioceses.[3]

Doctors' Commons assisted in the cultivation of social ties between the civilians and prominent ecclesiastics by welcoming bishops such as George Abbot, Lancelot Andrewes, and Richard Neile into its halls as honorary members.[4] The prelates paid an annual contribution of 6s. 8d. and were invited to dine with the fellows.[5] Outside Doctors' Commons, professional necessity fostered a great measure of cohesion between the two. This was especially true of diocesan chancellors, who were the official representatives of their bishops. Not only did they serve as the officials of their bishops in the diocesan consistory courts, but they also acted as their superiors' vicars-general in spirituals and in that capacity administered much of what was comprised within the bishops' personal or 'voluntary' jurisdiction. Since this involved them in the visitation of parish churches, the institution and deprivation of ministers, and the collection of tenths and other fees from all the clergy of the diocese,[6] chancellors assumed the

[1] G. C. Broderick, *Memorials of Merton College* (Oxford, 1885), p. 75.

[2] *Marprelate Tracts*, p. 156, n. 1. See also the biography of Alexander Hyde in the appendix.

[3] Yale's daughter married Bishop Lloyd of Chester, while Weston mentioned in his will that his eldest daughter Anne had married the Bishop of Peterborough, William Piers. Piers had been Weston's associate as prebendaries of Oxford. See Le Neve, *Fasti*, ii. 518, 525. [4] Reg. Doc. Com., ff. 46–7.

[5] Doc. Com. Treas. Bk. lists those paying this fee for each year. This group, which included civilians as well as honorary members, was referred to collectively as being 'out of Commons'.

[6] For instances of civilians serving as collection agents of the hierarchy see *CSPD 1611–1618*, p. 432; *1619–1622*, p. 431; *1623–1625*, pp. 150, 295, 436; CUL, MS. Mm I. 49, pp. 327–8.

role of mediator between their bishops and the lower clergy.[1]
Some became as attached to the latter group as to the bishops
themselves, defended their common interests,[2] and even used their
powers of patronage to advance the fortunes of a few promising
ministers.[3]

Civilians at both the lower archidiaconal and higher archiepiscopal levels of ecclesiastical jurisdiction became as involved with
clerical life as the diocesan chancellors. Even the advocates of
the Arches, who in their normal routine represented only their
clients and not their ecclesiastical superiors, stood at the continual
call of the Archbishop of Canterbury to serve as surrogates to the
judges of the archiepiscopal courts, to assist in metropolitican
visitations, to exercise jurisdiction during the vacancy of episcopal
sees, and to confirm the election of bishops.[4] Most of the advocates, moreover, worked in close co-operation with the episcopacy
as Commissioners for Ecclesiastical Causes and less frequently as
members of the Court of Delegates.

(b) The defence of the Church

So intimately involved in the work of the ecclesiastical hierarchy, the civilians acquired a reputation as staunch champions of
the liberties, doctrine, and laws of the Anglican Church. Their
commitment to this cause was so deep that Sir Francis Knollys,

[1] See, for example, the letter of Robert Redman as Chancellor of Norwich to
the doubly beneficed clergy of the diocese. *Registrum Vagum*, i. 151–2.

[2] On the question of tithes the civilians gave the lower clergy the clearest vote
of support. See Thomas Ryves, *The Poore Vicars Plea* (London, 1620); Ridley,
A View, pp. 217–23; and Gooch's defence of tithes for fishing voyages in the 1621
Parliament, *NRS*, ii. 136.

[3] Sir Henry Marten, as Official Principal to the Archbishop of Canterbury,
seems to have used his patronage most generously. See the dedications to him in
Henry Mason, *The Cure of Cares* (London, 1630); John Blinkow, *Michaels Combat
with the Divel* (London, 1640); and Lewis Owen, *Speculum Jesuiticum* (London,
1629); see also the dedication of Robert Lovell, *Publican Becoming a Penitent*
(London, 1625), to Ryves and the less revealing dedication of John Gore, *Un-
knowne Kindnesse* (London, 1635), to Arthur Duck, Chancellor of London diocese.

[4] Note for example how Bancroft employed Drs. Ferrand and Amye in
conjunction with his vicar-general, Edward Stanhope, in such capacities. LPL,
Bancroft Register, ff. 10ᵛ, 15ᵛ, 16ᵛ, 28ᵛ–29, 59. As for the important role of
civilians in the confirmation of bishops see Notestein and Relf, *Commons Debates
for 1629*, pp. 36, 134–5.

one of Elizabeth's Puritan privy councillors, publicly censured
the civilians in the Parliament of 1592 for seeking to make the
Church virtually autonomous within the State. In response to the
objection of the civilian Dr. William Lewin to a bill designed
to correct certain abuses perpetrated by the High Commission,
Knollys complained:

These civilians and other confederates of the clergy government would
fain have a kind of monarchy in the said government, as was in the
temporality. The which clergy government they would have to be
exempted from the temporal, saying they spake not against the Prince's
government touching the supremacy.[1]

Knollys's concern was legitimate. The civilians did not, as he
admitted, have any intention of reversing the break with Rome.[2]
But they did wish to preserve the integrity of the Church as an
institution subordinate only to the King himself. Their goal was
not as revolutionary as Knollys made it out to be. It was essentially defensive—a rear-guard action against a mounting assault
upon the institution with which they identified a good portion of
their professional life and personal fortune. The tide was turning
against the Reformation Church, as both Puritans and common
lawyers were trying to deprive it of its autonomous powers. The
period of the Church's greatest independence had already passed,
during which the Crown had assisted landed society in the plun-
dering of ecclesiastical wealth. The dependence of the Church
upon the temporal government had gradually increased to the
extent that the Crown had begun to protect the Church and to
employ it as an ally in the preservation of the social order.[3] The
Church's problem at this time was to prevent any further encroachments upon the independence which it still retained.

The civilians gladly assisted in the 'reconstruction' of the English Church, not only because of their general identification with
the ecclesiastical hierarchy but also because of their immediate

[1] Strype, *Whitgift*, ii. 123–4; Neale, *Parliaments 1584–1601*, pp. 271–2.
[2] F. W. Maitland, *Roman Canon Law in the Church of England* (London, 1898),
p. 94, emphasizes the civilians' firm acceptance of the royal supremacy and in this
sense their desire for a Church dependent upon rather than independent of the
State.
[3] Hill, *Economic Problems*, p. 133.

involvement in one of the Church's most pressing problems. The attack of the common lawyers upon the ecclesiastical courts threatened both to deprive the civilians of their livelihood and to destroy the entire administrative structure of the Church. The civilians, in coming to the defence of their own interests, called for the preservation of the Church's integrity as well as that of their own profession. Thomas Ridley argued that to deny a 'free course' to the civil and ecclesiastical law not only would weaken the civilians' profession and deprive the State of their valuable talents, but would also 'disarm the Church of her faithful friends and followers and so to cut the sinews . . . of ecclesiastical discipline and to expose her to the teeth of those who for these many years have sought to devour her up'.[1] In a petition to Archbishop Bancroft concerning the problem of prohibitions the civilians identified the cause of the Church with their own,[2] while Thomas Crompton castigated the common lawyers not only for hampering the proceedings of the civilians' courts but also for failing to abide by their oaths 'to maintain the liberties of the Church'.[3]

Intense commitment to the cause of the Church became a common political characteristic of those civilians who served as M.P.s. Nearly all of them, it should be recalled, were engaged in the service of the Church in at least one capacity, and a number of them even owed their parliamentary seats to the patronage or influence of their ecclesiastical superiors. In this light their defence of clerical practices which Puritans and other members of Parliament considered to be grievances of the entire commonwealth is entirely comprehensible. In the parliaments of Elizabeth, James, and Charles, numerous bills called for reforms in such matters as pluralities and non-residence, the presence of scandalous and unworthy ministers in the Church, the unsparing use of excommunicative powers, abuses of ecclesiastical jurisdiction, and the 'more due execution of Church government'.[4]

[1] Ridley, *A View*, p. 276.   [2] BM, Harl. MS. 358, ff. 184–5.
[3] BM, Cotton MS. Cleo. F II, f. 427.

[4] See ibid., f. 218 for one summary of bills presented to a late Elizabethan Parliament. See also *CJ* i. 173, 235, 236, 237, 274, 277, 291, 296, 311, 329, 350, 374, 375, 410.

Civilians in the House, on account of their first-hand knowledge and experience in ecclesiastical affairs, were usually assigned to the committees that discussed the proposed measures. Almost invariably they represented the position of the ecclesiastical hierarchy.

The civilians' defence of pluralities in the Parliament of 1601 pitted them against the majority of the House. A group of Puritans had sponsored a bill which demanded the surrender by all double-beneficed clergy of all but one of their livings. Legislation during the reign of Henry VIII had already lowered the incidence of such ecclesiastical aggrandizement but had made numerous exceptions for Church and Crown dignitaries, peers, and men of learning.[1] Included in this latter group were Doctors of Divinity and civilians themselves, many of whom relied upon additional preferments to supplement their relatively low incomes from their main posts. Three of the most prominent and wealthy civil lawyers, Dun, Crompton, and James, rose to defend both the Church and themselves. Dun argued somewhat arrogantly that 'men of unequal desert should not be equally beneficed' and that pluralities were necessary to provide adequate reward for the worthy. In a more conciliatory mood Crompton posed the simple economic consideration that the freedom of the clergy to marry had rendered the profits of one benefice inadequate for the support of a family. James extended this argument, showing that of 8,000 benefices in England, only 600 offered a competent living. Elimination of pluralities would have invited corruption among those who were not provided for and would have discouraged learned preachers from studying divinity and joining the clergy. James could easily have applied the same argument to the profession of which he was a member.[2]

Other members of the House had no sympathy for the civilians' rationalization of what appeared to them to be a flagrantly unjust and unbalanced distribution of ecclesiastical income. Their

[1] 21 Henry VIII, c. 13.
[2] Sir Simonds D'Ewes, *The Journals of All the Parliaments During the Reign of Queen Elizabeth* (London, 1682), pp. 639–40; Townshend, *Historical Collections*, p. 218; Neale, *Parliaments, 1584–1601*, pp. 407–8.

reaction to the speech of one unnamed 'old Doctor of the Civil Law' towards the end of the debate conveyed their disrespect for the arguments of the whole group. Since the old doctor 'was too long and spake too low, the House hawked and spat and kept a great coil to make him make an end'.[1] Thomas Crompton met with almost as unfavourable a reception in the first parliament of James I's reign when he spoke a few words in defence of the courts of commissaries to bishops and officials to archdeacons, many of which were staffed by civilians. Crompton's apology for the courts was unpopular enough, but his admission that he had conferred with some bishops concerning the proposed legislation was as indiscreet as it was unnecessary. It only confirmed the suspicions of many M.P.s that an alliance existed between the civilians and the 'clergy government'. Crompton was accused of disclosing the secrets of the House and avoided having to answer at the Bar for contempt only by offering the further explanation that his conference with the bishops had been nothing but 'a project . . . in his own head'.[2]

One excerpt from the *Commons' Journal* for 1606 reveals how the civilians' resistance to ecclesiastical reform distinguished them as members of the Court and set them at odds with the members of the parliamentary opposition. The *Journal* recorded the division of opinion concerning a 'grievance touching the Church':

The two High Commissions: the one to be executed within — miles of London; the other within — miles of York.
Mr. Fuller expounds it.
Sir Daniel Dun: No fit grievance to be presented.
Mr. Wentworth defends the article.
Sir John Bennet against it.[3]

Again and again religious issues tied the civilians to the King's party within the House of Commons. In a retrospective analysis of the Parliament of 1628, Sir Simond D'Ewes blamed 'some civil law doctors of the House' for thwarting the success of that

---

[1] Neale, *Parliaments, 1584–1601*, pp. 407–8.
[2] *CJ* i. 173; Rex, *University Representation*, p. 47.
[3] *CJ* i. 286. For a similar division of opinion over the question of awarding costs in a prohibition see ibid. 229.

assembly by having not 'voted well in the cause of religion'.[1] It is true that one of the two civilians in that House, Sir Henry Marten, despite an otherwise admirable record of support for the opposition, did none the less object to a bill designed to entrust the justices of the assize with the punishment of scandalous, drunk, and adulterous ministers. Marten's complaint was that the bill would 'at one blow take away Magna Carta from the clergy', who had a right to be presented before their own spiritual courts.[2] The other civil lawyer in that Parliament, Thomas Eden, defended the right of Church officials to issue marriage licences, which a number of M.P.s wished to see 'swept away' as 'plain remnants of popery'.[3] In 1640 Eden offered an even more emphatic endorsement of ecclesiastical authority when, in the face of strong opposition, he defended the Laudian Canons of 1640.[4]

Civilians who served as M.P.s were not the only members of the profession who found themselves at variance with the religious predilections of the parliamentary opposition. Complaints concerning excessive fees in spiritual courts, the use of the *ex officio* oath, the 'irreligious use of excommunication', and diocesan chancellors' reliance upon their role as justices of the peace 'to strike with both swords'[5] subjected the civil lawyers to collective criticism. Occasionally individual civilians were summoned before Parliament to answer charges concerning their responsibility for such practices, as John Lambe had been in 1621. John Hayward and Edmund Pope were both called before the House of Commons in 1626 to testify concerning their share as High Commissioners in the trial, imprisonment, and excommunication of Sir Robert Howard, an M.P. who had claimed parliamentary privilege against the proceedings.[6] Another seven civilians faced

---

[1] J. Halliwell (ed.), *The Autobiography and Correspondence of Sir Simonds D'Ewes, Bart. During the Reigns of James I and Charles I* (London, 1845), i. 405–6.

[2] ITL, Petyt MS. 537/23 ff. 327ᵛ–328. Marten had opposed a similar bill in 1626. CUL, Bulstrode Whitelocke's Journal of the Parliament of 1626, ff. 86ᵛ–87ᵛ.

[3] BM, Stowe MS. 366, ff. 97ᵛ–98.

[4] Notestein, *D'Ewes*, pp. 125–6. Eden was joined by the other two civilians in that House, Chaworth and Parry.

[5] *NRS* iv. 254. As further evidence that this practice did actually exist see *Registrum Vagum* i. 124.

[6] CUL, Whitelocke Journal, ff. 175ᵛ–177.

impeachment proceedings in 1641 for their share in the High
Commission's earlier trial of John Bastwick,[1] while Drs. Corbett,
Duck, Eden, Farmery, and Peirce submitted to individual accusa-
tion, interrogation, or censure by the Long Parliament.[2]

At the base of all this criticism of the civil lawyers was a protest
against not only the procedures that the civilians employed to
bring spiritual delinquents to justice, but the very grounds upon
which the lawyers brought charges and passed judgment against
them. The civilians were held responsible for the enforcement of
far too rigid standards of religious conformity. Especially during
the archiepiscopates of Whitgift and Laud the civilians' staunch
defence of religious orthodoxy in their capacity as ecclesiastical
judges became a matter of intense public concern. A good number
of the 200 civilians included in this study acquired the reputation
for implacable opposition to Puritanism through their support of,
or at least compliance with, the forays of both prelates against
nonconformity. When Whitgift inaugurated his campaign
against Elizabethan Puritanism in the 1580s he relied upon civil
lawyers for political support as members of his 'little faction' in
Parliament, intellectual assistance in the refutation of Presbyterian
doctrine, and legal service as members of the High Commission.[3]
In connection with this campaign Edward Stanhope gained his
reputation for 'blowing all Puritanism out of the city and diocese
of London';[4] Stephen Lakes won renown as Whitgift's commissary for his indefatigable investigation of Puritan activities;[5] and
all the civilians became identified with the *ex officio* oath, which
they administered frequently in their courts in order to detect
concealed Puritan practices and beliefs.

The civilians' vigilance in the preservation of ecclesiastical
conformity abated somewhat during the archiepiscopates of Bancroft and Abbot. The relative moderation of the Puritan movement, the Church's preoccupation with the Catholic threat, and

[1] PRO, SP 16/477/62.
[2] For the articles presented against Dr. Eden see Bodl. Tanner MS. 65, ff. 4–5.
For the petitions against Duck, Peirce, Corbett, and Farmery, see Notestein,
D'Ewes, pp. 38, 173, 414, 476.
[3] Collinson, *Puritan Movement*, p. 387; Levy, *Fifth Amendment*, pp. 124–6.
[4] Stoughton, *An Assertion*, p. 370.   [5] Strype, *Whitgift*, i. 276–80.

Abbot's leniency towards Puritans all contributed towards a reduction in the intensity of prosecutions against non-conformists.[1] But the High Commission remained active[2] and the civilians had little difficulty in perpetuating the reputation for anti-Puritanism that civilians such as Stanhope had given to the entire profession. In the diocese of Chichester, the Chancellor, John Drury, investigated a petition from some 'hot reformers' of Sussex at the request of the Privy Council.[3] John Cowell, as Master of Trinity Hall, Cambridge, kept his eye on the preachers at St. Mary's University Church to ensure that no non-conformist be given an opportunity to propagate his views.[4] Robert Redman continued to seek out Puritans in Norwich diocese with a vengeance even when the people he prosecuted were hardly guilty of nonconformity.[5] Late in King James's reign, John Farmery, Chancellor of Lincoln, contended with more deliberate manifestations of Puritan recalcitrance,[6] while in the same diocese John Lambe tried unsuccessfully to pressure his more tolerant bishop to allow him to proceed against suspected Puritans.[7]

Yet it was not until the archiepiscopate of Laud that the civilians were recruited actively and collectively once again to enforce adherence to specific standards of religious conformity. Nearly all of the civilians included in this study who survived into the Laudian period became involved in the implementation of the Archbishop's programme. Arthur Duck and John Lambe, two of the most active High Commissioners during this period, won national recognition as 'Canterbury's agents' and as symbols of the Laudian regime through the derisive attention given to them by Puritan pamphleteers in 1641.[8] They and their colleagues

---

[1] S. B. Babbage, *Puritanism*, pp. 374-5, notes none the less that Puritanism was expanding and that it was more widespread than court records might indicate, since many Puritans chose to conform sufficiently to escape official censure.

[2] Hill, *Society and Puritanism*, p. 349.

[3] *HMCS*, xv. 262-3; Babbage, *Puritanism*, pp. 192-3.

[4] *HMCS* xvii. 9; Babbage, *Puritanism*, pp. 118-19.

[5] *Registrum Vagum* ii. 279-80. For the activity of Otwell Hill, Chancellor of Lincoln, see J. W. F. Hill, *Tudor and Stuart Lincoln* (Cambridge, 1956), pp. 113-14.

[6] *CSPD 1623-1625*, p. 347.   [7] Rushworth, *Historical Collections*, i. 420-1.

[8] *Parallel Between Wolsey and Laud*, p. 7; *A Letter from Rhoan in France*, p. 8; *The Organ's Echo*, stanzas 7, 8.

regularly proceeded against members of the clergy and the laity for such Puritan practices as refusing to bow at the name of Jesus, standing at the reception of communion, placing the communion table in the centre of the church, and removing the communion rail. In the archdeaconry of Essex Robert Aylett corresponded with Lambe and Laud concerning the desired elimination of 'godly sermons' and other Puritan congregational activities.[1] Clement Corbett, the Chancellor of Norwich, sought to discover the best means of investigating conventicles within his jurisdiction and of controlling 'that ratsbayne of lecturing out of his churches the virulency whereof hath intoxicated many thousands of this kingdom'.[2] Doctors Eden and Farmery abused their powers of excommunication in proceeding against Puritans in Ely and Lincoln dioceses respectively;[3] while in Lichfield the Chancellor, Charles Twysden, followed Laud's directives closely.[4] In York William Easdall revitalized the Church courts to assist in the administration of the northern province along Laudian lines.[5]

(c) Papists and Puritans

The civilians' zealous enforcement of the policies of Whitgift and Laud and their determined opposition to Puritanism gave rise to charges that they were popishly affected. These accusations were mainly rhetorical, intended by the Puritans to discredit the civilians and the laws they administered. But there were enough instances of Catholic sentiment among the civil lawyers to give some credence to the Puritan contention. In 1582 Lord Burghley accused Dr. Legge, Master of Caius College, Cambridge, and his

[1] CSPD 1629–1631, pp. 197, 220. This correspondence took place when Laud was Bishop of London. For Aylett's attitudes toward Puritans see CSPD 1636–1637, p. 514.

[2] Bodl., Tanner MS. 68, f. 2. For the entire correspondence between Corbett and his episcopal superior, Matthew Wren, see ff. 1–11ᵛ. Corbett actually encouraged Wren to be more severe with the Puritans. See R. W. Ketton-Cremer, Norfolk in the Civil War (Hamden, Conn., 1970), pp. 70–1.

[3] Notestein, D'Ewes Journal, pp. 38–9. Bodl., Tanner MSS. 65, ff. 4–5; 68, ff. 200, 202, 223, 226.

[4] J. R. Twisden, The Family of Twysden and Twisden (London, 1939), p. 131.

[5] Marchant, Puritans in York, pp. 44–5; Tyler, 'Ecclesiastical Commission', p. 172.

associate, Dr. Swale, of having 'maintained covertly in the College a faction against the true religion received, corrupting the youth there with corrupt opinions of Popery'.[1] Articles were subsequently brought against Legge, including the accusation that he had frequented the houses of papists in the country.[2] Later in the Elizabethan period three unnamed Doctors of the Civil Law were sent to the Fleet for encouraging a group of suspected recusants to refuse the *ex officio* oath, a step that was all the more remarkable in view of the civilians' frequent reliance upon, and defence of, the use of the oath in their courts.[3] A few civilians admitted to a flirtation with the Roman faith early in their careers. Christopher Parkins had actually entered the Society of Jesus while studying in Rome before he converted to the Anglican faith and entered the Queen's service.[4] Thomas Crompton had to delay the receipt of his doctorate in law at Oxford for six years because he was suspected of 'backwardness in religion'.[5] Richard Trevor converted to Catholicism shortly before his death in 1614,[6] and in 1632 Richard Hart was expelled from Doctors' Commons because he confessed to be a popish recusant.[7] During the period of the Commonwealth Thomas Read professed the Catholic faith at Douai and entered a Carthusian monastery,[8] while Thomas Heath, after losing the chancellorship of Peterborough, fled to the Netherlands, converted to Catholicism, and found refuge with a society of English nuns at Ghent.[9]

It is difficult to consider these scattered instances of Catholic sentiment as representative of the religious predilections of the entire profession, especially in view of the conversion or reconversion of Parkins, Crompton, and Hart. Crompton and Parkins

---

[1] N. H. Nicolas, *Memoirs of ... Sir Christopher Hatton* (London, 1847), p. 261.

[2] Heywood and Wright, *Transactions*, i. 314–41.

[3] Richard Cosin, *An Apologie for Sundrie Proceedings by Jurisdiction Ecclesiastical* (London, 1593), section iii, p. 107; Coote, *Eminent Civilians*, pp. 57–8.

[4] *Al. Oxon.* iii. 1117.   [5] Clark, *Register*, i. 38, 157.

[6] Sarmiento to Philip III, 30 June 1614, Archivo General de Simancas, Seccion de Estado Legajo 2592/77. I am indebted for this reference to Revd. A. J. Loomie, S.J. Trevor's brother John claimed to be an adherent of Rome as late as 1574. *DWB*, p. 980.   [7] LPL, MS. 958, Appendix F.

[8] J. Gillow, *Bibliographical Dictionary of the English Catholics* (1885), v. 399.

[9] *Al. Oxon.* ii. 687.

actually distinguished themselves as champions of the cause of anti-papalism in the early seventeenth century[1] and in that capacity, rather than as Catholic sympathizers, they reflected the views of the majority of their colleagues. Reference has already been made to the intellectual attacks of Hayward, Sutcliffe, and Cooke upon the designs of the Jesuits. To their number should be added Clement Colmore, whose refutation of 'the Catholic divine' (Robert Parsons) and 'answer to Cardinal Bellarmine' remained unpublished at his death and have since disappeared.[2]

The depth of these civilians' commitment to the defence of their Church against papal pretensions should not be underestimated. Sutcliffe was the architect and chief benefactor of James I's projected College at Chelsea, which was intended to serve as a spiritual garrison where learned divines could study and write against the papists.[3] Sutcliffe, 'that godly and well-disposed member of the Church of Christ',[4] was scheduled to assume the post of provost at the institution, and Hayward had been selected to be one of its two historians. The project collapsed through the combined influences of jealousy from the universities, a dire lack of funds, and suspicion from the Puritans that the professors would defend the religious views of the Court.[5] But Sutcliffe's hatred of Rome was deeply personal and even took precedence over his favour with the King. The civilian became so outspoken in his opposition to the projected Spanish marriage that James had him imprisoned.[6] Sutcliffe died soon after, leaving a final testimony of his contempt for Catholicism in his will:

The wicked decrees of the conventicle of Trent, Constance, Lateran and Nice under the Empress Irene contrary to the doctrine of the Church of England now professed, together with all the heresies,

---

[1] ITL, Petyt MS. 538/38/ff. 47–8ᵛ. For Parkins see HMCS v. 369; vii. 516–17.

[2] Borth. Inst., will of Colmore, Wills 35/435. See also Bodl. Tanner MS. 75, f. 349.

[3] T. Fuller, *The Church History of Great Britain* (Oxford, 1845), v. 387–96; Winwood, *Memorials*, iii. 160–1.

[4] PRO, SP 14/54/91.   [5] Fuller, *Church History*, v. 395.

[6] William Camden, *Gulielmi Camdeni Annales Ab Anno 1603, ad Annum 1623* (London, 1691), p. 73; Roberts, *Diary of Walter Yonge*, p. 41; Coote, *Eminent Civilians*, pp. 54–5.

errors, superstitions, idolatry, tyranny, and wicked practices of the Pope and his adherents contrary to the truth, and the professors thereof I abhor, detest and anathematize.[1]

A strong attachment to the cause of Protestantism and a rejection of Roman Catholicism characterized the writings of numerous other civilians. Thomas Ridley and Giles Fletcher both composed poems to introduce the 1576 edition of Foxe's *Actes and Monuments*, the famed apology of the English Reformation.[2] Dr. John Hoskins, in one of his sermons, stated unequivocally that 'We can not brook that ceremonious, erroneous, superstitious doctrine of devils (so doth the Apostle call it) which out of the chair of Rome sends forth imperious traditions.'[3] Alberico Gentili, who fled Italy so that he could practise his Protestant faith more freely, devoted a good portion of his *De Nuptiis* to refute some irresponsible charges that he harboured Catholic sympathies.[4] One of the more Puritanically inclined of the civilians, John Favour, published a large study entitled *Antiquitie Triumphing Over Noveltie*, the very purpose of which was to refute the papists' claim to having preserved the original Church of Christ.[5] Less extensive, yet no less uncertain traces of anti-papal sentiment appear in Nathaniel Brent's introduction and dedication to the 1625 edition of Francis Mason's *Vindiciae Ecclesiae Anglicanae*,[6] and in Arthur Duck's complimentary history of Archbishop Chichele, who won the author's admiration for having 'asserted the rights of the Crown and the liberties of the Church against the papal usurpation'.[7]

The sessions of Parliament gave a few civilians an opportunity to castigate Catholicism as the enemy of the entire nation. Henry

---

[1] PRO, PROB 11/156/94.

[2] John Foxe, *Actes and Monuments of the Churche* (London, 1576), dedication.

[3] John Hoskins, *Sermons Preached at Pauls Crosse and Elsewhere* (London, 1615), i. 59.

[4] Molen, *Gentili*, pp. 261–4.

[5] London, 1619. For the most strongly anti-papal sections see pp. 10, 18, 57.

[6] London, 1625.

[7] Arthur Duck, *The Life of Henry Chichele, Archbishop of Canterbury* (London, 1699), dedication to Bancroft. The first edition, published in Latin, appeared in 1617.

Marten made a special appeal in the Parliament of 1625 against the 'exhorbitant and irregular power of foreign ambassadors', one of whom had obtained a pardon for Jesuits, while others were peddling 'popish and seditious books'.[1] Marten nursed a bitter animosity towards the Spanish ambassador, whom he had castigated in open court in 1615 with words which caused 'public offence'.[2] The ambassador had become 'exceedingly angry' when Marten succeeded Dun as Judge of the Admiralty two years later because the new judge 'was ever of counsel against him'.[3] Another civilian M.P., Barnaby Gooch, feared the 'great man of Rome' as much as Marten, and in 1621 he sternly warned Parliament that the 'papal monarchy' still threatened the nation.[4] In the same assembly Sir John Bennet, just before his own impeachment for corruption, took special care in the drafting of five articles for the restraint of recusants,[5] a problem with which he had been deeply concerned throughout his career.[6] The willingness of individual civilians to prosecute recusants should always be balanced against the enthusiasm with which they proceeded against Puritans. John Lambe, who sought out Puritans in Northampton with a vengeance, was accused of displaying equal intolerance toward suspected recusants.[7]

Despite their strong Protestant sympathies, the civilians still lay exposed to the Puritans' charge that they were administering the Roman canon law in their courts and hence still accepted the authority of papal regulations and decrees. In 1593 Nathaniel Bacon reported that certain diocesan chancellors were 'so much affected to the canon law that some are infected with popish religion'.[8] The most frequent and the most lasting indictment of the civil lawyers, if not for direct allegiance to Rome, at least for

[1] Gardiner, *Commons Debates 1625*, pp. 39, 69, 144–5; Forster, *Eliot*, i. 356.

[2] BM, Lansdowne MS. 152, f. 356.

[3] PRO, SP 14/93/123.   [4] *NRS* iii. 351.

[5] *NRS* iv. 44; ii. 66–7.

[6] Townshend, *Historical Collections*, p. 320, for Bennet's speech in the Parliament of 1601. For another civil lawyer's concern for the problem of recusancy see Dr. James's statement in Willson, *Diary of Bowyer*, pp. 125–6.

[7] R. M. Serjeantson, *A History of the Church of St. Giles Northampton* (Northampton, 1911), p. 63.

[8] Neale, *Parliaments, 1584–1601*, p. 283.

perpetuating the remnants of its former rule in England, lay in their adherence to the canon law.[1]

Much of the law that the civilians applied in their ecclesiastical courts was the same law that had been in force before the break with Rome. After that split, Henry VIII had provided for the appointment of thirty-two commissioners to sort out the discredited canons of the *Corpus Juris Canonici* and to retain those that did not stand at variance with English law, but the commissioners never completed their assignment. Another group, appointed in 1550 to formulate new canons, had nearly completed its work when the Marian reaction nullified their efforts. After Elizabeth's accession to the throne, John Foxe published a new code of law, the *Reformatio Legum Ecclesiasticarum*, which represented the combined efforts of the Commission, the late Archbishop Cranmer, Peter Martyr, and Matthew Parker. But the new body of ecclesiastical law never met the approval of the Queen, Parliament, or Convocation, so the civilians continued to uphold the unreformed canon law in the spiritual courts.[2] Statutory law had, of course, invalidated and superseded a number of intolerable papal prescriptions, and the Canons of 1604 had provided some additional reform. But the bulk of the old law remained in force, and a seventeenth-century reading list for a prospective civil lawyer recommended the decrees of Gratian, the decretals of Gregory IX, the Sext of Boniface VIII, the rescripts of Clement V, and the Extravagantes of John XXII as some of the most valuable sources of his professional knowledge.[3]

The civil lawyers continued to study the canon law informally after the Reformation,[4] and they made frequent allusions to it as

---

[1] Marchant, *Puritans in York*, p. 1; Ritchie, *Ecclesiastical Courts*, p. 172. As late as 1854 the ecclesiastical courts were criticized as being relics of popery, Cuthbert Conyngham, *Doctors' Commons Unveiled; Its Secrets and Abuses Disclosed* (London, 1854), p. 45.

[2] Vaisey, *Canon Law*, pp. 45–6. J. C. Spalding, 'The *Reformatio Legum Ecclesiasticarum* of 1552 and the Furthering of Discipline in England', *Church History*, 39 (1970), 162–71; Collinson, *Puritan Movement*, p. 38.

[3] Durham Cathedral Library, Hunter MS. 12/1.

[4] William Bingham, for example, dispensed with his books of the canon law in his will, Greater London Record Office, Wills 7 'Hamer', ff. 66ᵛ–69. See also will of Cowell, PRO, PROB 11/118/86 and will of Stanhope, PROB 11/111/22.

the basis of their legal decisions. Dr. William Awbrey, late in the
Elizabethan period, admitted that the actual proceedings of the
High Commission were warranted not by the act of 1559 which
had established the commission, but by the 'old canon law' which
had been in force long before the statute was enacted.[1] Other
civilians freely used the term 'canon law' to designate the main
code of law which they upheld in the ecclesiastical courts.[2] Yet
the civilians never admitted this law to be papal in any way
except in origin. They assumed that the law that they practised
in their courts stood in complete accord with the principles and the
spirit of the Reformation settlement. They subscribed to a constitutional theory which was enshrined in the Reformation
statutes and which for four centuries afterwards commanded
unchallenged acceptance by English theologians and historians:
that the canon law as exercised in England, both before and
after the Reformation, had binding force not by virtue of papal
authority but by the nation's free acceptance of that code as the
customary ecclesiastical law of the land.[3]

This theory first came under attack in 1898 by F. W. Maitland,
who in a penetrating study demonstrated that before the Reformation English churchmen had actually accepted the canon law on
the basis of papal authority and that the Crown, not the English
Church, had exercised the freedom to accept or to reject the Roman
decretals.[4] The civilians of the sixteenth and seventeenth century
then, by an extension of Maitland's argument, were indeed
enforcing genuinely papal prescriptions. But the civilians can
hardly be credited with the historical acumen of Maitland. What
is important is the attitude that these lawyers took towards the

[1] J. S. Burn, *The High Commission: Notices of the Court and Its Proceedings*
(London, 1865), p. 16.

[2] Duck, *De Usu*, pp. 99–103; Gardiner, *Commons Debates 1625*, p. 30. See the
opinion of Dr. Ryves 'according to the canon law', PRO, SP 16/375/59.

[3] Vaisey, *Canon Law*, p. 46. The terminology of Sir Julius Caesar, when he
referred to the 'canon laws of this Realm', reflected his agreement with this
theory. BM, Add. MS. 38,170, ff. 22, 27. See also All Souls College, MS.
CCIII, f. 74.

[4] Maitland, *Canon Law*, passim. See also J. W. Gray, 'Canon Law in England:
Some Reflections on the Stubbs–Maitland Controversy', *Studies in Church History*,
iii. 48–68.

canon law. And Maitland himself reported that they accepted the canon law as completely anglicized.[1] Thus there existed no contradiction between the civilians' personal anti-papal sentiments and the religious standards of the courts in which they practised.

Yet despite the civilians' strict reservations about the nature of the law that they studied and practised and their unequivocal rejection of papal authority in all its manifestations, their assimilation and perpetuation of a large portion of the traditional jurisprudence of the Church did affect their religious views. In a study of the episcopacy during the reign of Henry VIII, L. B. Smith has divided the bishops into the reformers, who tried to push the reformation in religion forward after the break with Rome, and the conservatives, who opposed their efforts. He considers it highly significant that of the eleven bishops who were civilians, not one could be classified as a reformer. The more Protestant religious forces were composed entirely of Doctors of Divinity.[2] In his explanation of this phenomenon, Smith suggested that while the conservatives' training in the canon law did not bring them 'to set forth papistry', it did predispose them to 'regard the legal aspects of the Reformation as equal to the spiritual'. Their reluctance to encourage a spiritual renewal derived from those habits of mind which were cultivated by the 'prolonged absorption of legal principles and papal decrees'.[3]

The analysis applied with equal validity to the civilians of the early seventeenth century. So closely involved in the enforcement of the laws of religion, the civilians tended to develop juridical rather than spiritual criteria for defining religious faith. Like Robert Aylett, they displayed 'the conservatism of the jurist who dislikes any departure from precedent and established authority in either courts or in religious practice'.[4] This reverence for precedent, rather than any addiction to the cause of popery, was what the civilians assimilated from their study and administration of English ecclesiastical law. Since this law included many prescriptions of the old faith, the civil lawyers tended to be conservative

---

[1] See the opinions of Duck, *De Usu*, pp. 99–100, and Molen, *Gentili*, p. 218.
[2] Smith, *Tudor Prelates and Politics*, pp. 43–4.
[3] Ibid., pp. 46–7.   [4] Padelford, 'Aylett', 22.

Anglicans who were unwilling to travel any further along the road of reform than the law allowed.

As a group, the civilians were, like Dr. John Drury, 'in religion known sound, to the present government loyally affected'.[1] The requirements attached to the receipt of degrees and entrance into Doctors' Commons naturally encouraged the predominance of such men among the ranks of the profession.[2] It is true that the formal standards of orthodoxy to which they had to subscribe were intentionally loose and excluded only Catholics, Separatists, and Anabaptists. Civilians, however, not only adhered to the formal standards of orthodoxy but also clustered safely around the centre of the religious spectrum. Gentili arrived in England as a committed Calvinist but soon after conformed to more moderate Anglican views.[3] Sir Julius Caesar was strongly influenced by his mother's Puritanism during his early years, but his more mature theological opinions, embodied in a manuscript tract on the Real Presence in the Eucharist, reflected the most widely accepted Anglican opinion. Doubtless the exigencies of court life pressured these two prominent figures to temper their earlier religious convictions.[4]

There were, surprisingly enough, a sprinkling of Puritans among the ranks of the civilians' profession, although it is interesting to note how exceptional their careers were and how little legal practice they engaged in. Dorislaus, whose membership in the Dutch Reformed Church from birth explains his sympathy with English Puritans, did not enter the service of the State until after the Civil War had begun. Henry Hawkins, whose only public activity as a civil lawyer occurred in the late Elizabethan period when he accompanied Lord Zouch on one of his embassies

[1] Clark, *Register*, i. 157.

[2] Heywood and Wright, *Transactions*, ii. 253–5, 269–70; Bodl., Rawlinson Statutes MS. 62, ff. 12, 14, 16.

[3] Molen, *Gentili*, p. 256.

[4] LPL, MS. 113, ff. 256–258ᵛ. C. W. Dugmore, *Eucharistic Doctrine in England from Hooker to Waterland* (London, 1942), p. 40, uses the views of Lancelot Andrewes as normative. Dugmore, however, exaggerates the contrast between the Puritan and Anglican position. See J. F. New, *Anglican and Puritan* (London, 1964), p. 63. For a general discussion of Caesar's views see Hill, 'Caesar', pp. 18–20.

'beyond the seas', was ostracized from the Court after his implica-
tion in the Essex rising. Tied to the Puritan family of the Yelver-
tons by marriage,[1] Hawkins established contact with one of the
most influential Puritan connections in London and Essex, which
included Rowland Heylin, Richard Sibbes, William Gouge, and
John Davenport.[2] In 1629 he donated £100 to the Foefees for the
purchase of impropriations, a Puritan cause to which he also
bequeathed another £300 by his will two years later.[3] Calibute
Downing, who became a Puritan late in his career, held only one
position as Vicar of Hackney, Middlesex.

One moderate Puritan civil lawyer, John Favour, was not
completely excluded from a legal career. Beginning his career as
the chaplain to the Puritan courtier, the Earl of Huntingdon,[4]
Favour, a cleric, became the Vicar of Halifax in York diocese and
there gained the reputation of being a 'great friend to non-
conformists'. One of his lecturers at Halifax was a Mr. Bayn, who
had been banished from Kent for his radical views.[5] Archbishop
Tobie Matthew of York, one of the most lenient of the bishops
of that period towards Puritanism, saw the value of using Favour
to act as a moderating influence on more radical Puritans with
whom he had contact, to represent the views of the Puritan
faction to the bishops of the northern province, and to convince
the Puritans that they were an accepted wing of the English
Church.[6] Favour became the chaplain to Matthew, Precentor of
York Cathedral and canon residentiary in the Cathedral Close.[7]
He was called upon to assist in the conversion of recusants[8] and
even became a member of the Commission for Ecclesiastical
Causes for York province. Yet despite his service as a commissioner,
Favour's Puritanism, clearly reflected in his West Riding Sermons[9]

---

[1] *The Visitation of Norfolk . . . Anno 1563* (Harl. Soc. xxxii, 1891), pp. 328–9.

[2] PRO, will of Hawkins, PROB 11/159/2.

[3] I. Calder, *Activities of the Puritan Faction of the Church of England 1625–1633*
(London, 1957), p. 33.   [4] *CSPD 1591–1594*, p. 417.

[5] John Newton, 'Puritanism in the Diocese of York (Excluding Nottinghamshire) 1603–1640' (London Univ. Ph.D. thesis, 1955), pp. 37–8.

[6] Marchant, *Puritans in York*, p. 204.

[7] York Cathedral Library, Chapter Acts, f. 756. Favour was admitted in 1619.

[8] Newton, 'Puritanism in York', p. 288.

[9] BM, Add. MSS. 4933A, ff. 60, 76, 88; 4933B, ff. 162ᵛ–163, 174.

and in his published work, involved him in legal difficulties. In 1619 he was presented at the diocesan visitation for not wearing a surplice and for refusing to read the canons.[1]

Moderate Puritan spirits such as Favour were able to survive in the Elizabethan and Jacobean Church only because of the shelter that bishops such as Tobie Matthew provided. In addition to Matthew, the Bishops of Carlisle, St. David's, and Worcester were reported in 1603 to have 'turned Puritan', and the Bishop of Durham was expected to have turned shortly.[2] Archbishop Abbot, Bishop Day of Winchester, and Bishop Williams of Lincoln were also known for their Puritan leanings. It is entirely possible that some of the civilians in the employ of these bishops shared their superiors' religious predilections. But it is certain that none of them belonged to the same category as Downing, Dorislaus, Hawkins, or even Favour, as only those four clearly distinguished themselves as non-conformists.

(d) *The civilians and the Laudian Church*

Civilians responded in different ways when Archbishop Laud tightened the requirements for religious orthodoxy and made 'an attempt to restore sacraments, ceremonies and the priesthood to something like their medieval position of honour'.[3] There is little doubt that some of those civilians who enforced Laud's 'Arminian'[4] standards of ecclesiastical conduct easily combined spiritual and professional enthusiasm for their assignment. John Lambe, who had earlier put pressure upon the pro-Puritan Bishop Williams to treat the non-conformists of his diocese more stringently, required no added incentive as Dean of the Arches to pledge absolute subservience to the wishes of his direct superior.[5] Charles Twysden, it is reported, took a personal as well as an official interest in Laud's programme.[6] Both Clement Corbett

---

[1] Marchant, *Puritans in York*, p. 246.   [2] BM, Sloane MS. 171, f. 23ᵛ.

[3] Hill, *Society and Puritanism*, p. 495.

[4] Arminianism was originally a school of theology that stressed free will. For a discussion of how 'Arminian' Laud really was see Kenyon, *Stuart Constitution*, p. 147.

[5] PRO, SP 16/499/42.   [6] Twisden, *Family of Twysden*, p. 131.

and Robert Aylett lent willing support to Laud's schemes, but more because of their near obsession for uniformity and conformity in the Church than for any spiritual preference for Arminianism.[1] Corbett believed that if the hierarchy could eliminate the 'ratsbayne' of lecturing, 'we shall have such a uniform and orthodox Church as the Christian world cannot show the like'.[2]

Yet personal disagreement with Laud's programme, even among those who were attached to him professionally, was not uncommon. Two civilians who passed away just as Laud was gaining national prominence, rejected his Arminianism as heretical. Matthew Sutcliffe, enemy of Puritans and Papists alike, cast equal aspersions on Arminians:

Those false teachers also among us, that palliate popish heresies and under the name of Arminians seek to bring in Popery and endeavour with all their little skill to reconcile darkness to light, Antichrist to Christ, heresy to the true Catholic faith, holding the modern synagogue of Rome to be the true Church and that Salvation may there be had, where the doctrine of Trent is punctually professed and maintained, I hate as apostate from the faith and traitors to God's true Church.[3]

John Weston, an Oxford civilian, echoed Sutcliffe's remarks in testifying 'I die in the faith established in the Church of England and I do detest all doctrines and opinions, whether Popery or Arminianism, crossing the same.'[4]

More hesitant and subtle disagreement with Laud came from civilians who were actually called upon by him to enforce his policies in their courts. There was an element of personal animosity as well as religious disagreement in Nathaniel Brent's rift with Laud. Early in his career Brent had married into the family of George Abbot, Laud's predecessor, and had thereby acquired

[1] *CSPD 1629–1631*, pp. 197, 220. 'A few such excellent sermons would bring again the people in love with conformity.'

[2] Bodl. Tanner MS. 68, f. 2. See also the statement of Corbett quoted in Notestein, *D'Ewes*, p. 414.

[3] PRO, PROB 11/156/94. Sutcliffe had also composed a response to the Arminian views of Bishop Montague before he died, but it had been suppressed before publication. Its title was *The Unmasking of a Massmonger*. See Fuller, *Church History*, vi. 21.

[4] Oxford University Archives, Wills W–Z.

some of Abbot's dislike for his successor.[1] Considering Abbot's leniency towards Puritans and Brent's hatred of Catholicism, a difference in religious opinion could also have arisen between Brent and Laud. None the less Brent served Laud dutifully as his vicar-general and, according to the scattered evidence that is available, enforced his ecclesiastical policies to the full letter of the law.[2] During Laud's trial in 1641, however, Brent testified against his superior, assigning full responsibility for all of his own legal activity to the Archbishop and accusing him of association with Papists. Brent produced written orders from Laud to refute the latter's allegation that his vicar-general had on his own initiative undertaken such projects as removing and railing in the communion tables of all parish churches in the archdiocese.[3]

Brent's compliance with Laud's directives sheds some doubt upon the sincerity of his retrospective disapproval of the Archbishop's policies, especially since Brent made his protest only when Laud was out of power and he himself was seeking to avoid censure and imprisonment. Yet the power that Laud and his associates wielded was immense, and could persuade even the hesitant to support the Laudian reforms. Civilians were reluctant to cross their bishops. Two ministers from Ipswich, Edward Bedwall and Samuel Duncon, who had been excommunicated for serving communion to those who refused to come up to the rail, looked for legal assistance in the Court of the Arches after they had finally succeeded in having their appeal heard there. No one would take their case. 'When they came to any proctor in the Arches or to any Doctor of the Civil Law, they told them Bishop Wren and the Archbishop were of such power as there was no resisting them.'[4]

One civilian was bold enough and financially secure enough to break with Laud. Sir Henry Marten, who had distinguished himself through his political opposition to Charles in the Parliament

[1] Broderick, *Merton*, p. 75, reports that in 1629 Brent 'could scarcely have been in favour with Laud'. See also pp. 167–8.

[2] CUL, MS. Mm. I. 49 (Baker 38), p. 326; Hill, *Economic Problems*, p. 179; *VCH Warwicks* ii. 41.

[3] Prynne, *Canterburies Doome*, pp. 59, 62, 71, 89, 545.

[4] Notestein, *D'Ewes*, p. 237.

of 1628, displayed the same idealism and independence of mind in the service of the Church. In that Parliament he made clear his attitude towards rival religious faiths. On the surface he was orthodox enough, claiming that he loved the Book of Common Prayer 'best of all others'. But he also indicated that he did 'not derogate from other churches' and with respect to treatment of non-conformists he argued that 'it is better not to let him come in than to cast out him that subscribes not to the government of the Church'.[1] In another instance he showed himself to be more tolerant of the Puritan spirit when he supported a bill that was designed to insure that 'no person be molested or convented for being absent from his own Parish Church so as at the same time he be at some other church or chapel and there hear the word of God'.[2] It is clear, therefore, that Marten was not of one mind with Laud in questions of ecclesiastical policy.

Direct conflict between the two did actually occur in 1632 over the placement of a communion table in the parish church of St. Gregory, Paul's Wharf, in London. The Dean and Chapter of St. Paul's Cathedral, who were the ordinaries of St. Gregory's, had ordered the table to be moved from the middle of the chancel to its upper end and placed there altarwise, as it was in their own cathedral. To the Puritans of the parish this was a denial not only of customary practice but also of radical Protestant doctrine, which regarded the fixture not as an altar, as the papists did, but as a table at which they celebrated the commemorative meal.[3] Accordingly five parishioners petitioned Marten as Dean of the Arches to reverse the order of the Dean and Chapter. Marten paid a visit to St. Gregory's and removed the table from the wall, claiming that in that position it would have made 'a good court cupboard'. But by the next Sunday, which was a communion day, the table was back against the wall again,[4] and before Marten

---

[1] ITL, Petyt MS. 537/23 f. 346.

[2] Ibid., f. 330–330ᵛ. 'It is my duty to tell you that if any ordinary do trouble a man for going to another sermon when he hath none at home it is against law and I have upon appeals given good costs against the ordinary and I will ever do it.'

[3] H. R. Trevor-Roper, *Archbishop Laud 1573–1645* (2nd edn., London, 1962), p. 45.

[4] PRO, SP 16/499/42.

was able to pass sentence in favour of the parishioners, King Charles intervened in the dispute and brought the case before the Privy Council.

In the debate that ensued, Laud, who was then Bishop of London, argued strongly in favour of the Dean and Chapter. According to a subsequent report, he actually claimed that Marten 'had a stigmatical Puritan in his bosom', a statement that he later qualified.

This was many years since; and if I did speak anything sounding this way, 'tis more like I should say schismatical than stigmatical Puritan . . . and which word soever I used, if Sir Henry used the one, he might well hear the other. For a prophane speech it was and little becoming a Dean of the Arches.[1]

The case for the parishioners was based upon the Book of Common Prayer and the eighty-second canon, which allowed the communion table to stand where it was most fit and convenient. But the King, declaring himself opposed to all innovation, decided in favour of the Dean and Chapter of St. Paul's. They, as ordinaries, and not the parishioners, possessed the freedom granted by the Book of Common Prayer to decide what location was most fit and convenient for the placement of the table. Charles ordered Marten to pass judgment against the parishioners' appeal.[2] Marten obliged, but shortly thereafter, when Laud succeeded Abbot as Archbishop of Canterbury, he lost his post as Dean of the Arches to Sir John Lambe.

One historian has interpreted the St. Gregory's case as symbolic of the breakdown in the Elizabethan compromise. Where Elizabeth was willing to allow widely diverse elements to remain within the broad confines of religious orthodoxy, Charles tightened the standards and allowed legal action to be taken against those who did not conform.[3] Another historian has extracted political implications from the episode, noting Charles's insistence upon the strict observance of the old law without regard for his subjects' feelings.[4] For the purposes of this study the

---

[1] Laud, *Troubles and Tryal*, p. 327.   [2] PRO, PC 2/43, ff. 155ᵛ–156.
[3] Trevor-Roper, *Laud*, p. 152.   [4] Gardiner, *History of England*, vii. 312.

significance of the event is twofold. On the one hand it illustrates the degree of control to which civilians had to submit when they assumed their judicial posts. Common law judges, while often put under pressure by the Crown, were never subject to the review of the Privy Council and the arbitrary discretion of their superiors as was Marten. On the other hand, it indicates the depth of the religious differences that prevailed between Laud's Arminian faction and a number of civil lawyers, especially those who had cultivated a more tolerant attitude towards Puritanism during the archiepiscopate of Abbot. These men were hardly Puritans themselves, as Laud claimed that Marten was. But they were virulently anti-papal and located themselves solidly in the centre of the religious spectrum. When it appeared that Laud wished to move the entire Church towards Rome, disagreement arose between them and their superior.

The activities of Brent and Marten, as well as the clearly anti-Arminian protestations of Sutcliffe and Weston, reveal that the religious views of the civil lawyers often transcended the professional pressures under which these men continually operated. But generally the civilians were careful to ensure that their private religious beliefs did not interfere with the performance of their legal duties. It would have been suicidal for Brent to have made clear his disagreements with Laud's religious views, since it would have lost him his position as vicar-general. Therefore he kept silent until Laud had fallen from power. Marten, on the other hand, could afford to jeopardize his position as Dean of the Arches since he was at the same time the Judge of the Admiralty Court and did not, therefore, depend entirely on the patronage of the Archbishop.

Thus once again, within the context of ecclesiastical politics, the civil lawyers appear mainly as professionals or courtiers, whose loyalty to the established Church was necessitated by the hard facts of employment and financial well being. Yet their loyalty was often reinforced by their genuine religious zeal to protect the Church from the attacks of both Puritans and Catholics. It is of course impossible to determine whether their religious views were in any way conditioned by their professional circumstances.

Certainly the harsh realities of unemployment were sufficiently strong to reverse the conversion of Richard Hart one year after his expulsion from Doctors' Commons and to prevent Richard Trevor from announcing his adherence to Rome until the year of his death. Perhaps professional concerns did force the civilians to bottle up their innermost beliefs. But it would be unjustified to regard their orthodox religious views as nothing more than by-products of their professional affiliation with the established Church. On the contrary, it is more likely that the civilians had already formulated their religious views before embarking upon their careers and that only those who could in conscience serve the members of the Anglican establishment proceeded with their degrees. The few Puritans who did finish their doctorates either accepted employment with tolerant bishops, became rectors through Puritan patronage, or avoided all forms of ecclesiastical service whatsoever.

The close identification of almost the entire profession of the civilians with the established Church is, therefore, one of the main aspects of their royalism. For it aligned them with some of the most consistent supporters of the Stuart monarchy and against some of its most determined opponents. It was as ecclesiastical officials, moreover, that the civilians received their most bitter popular criticism. Dr. Francis James could well have been speaking for his colleagues when he observed near the end of his life:

I must here acknowledge (which I have often sensibly found to my great grief) but it was my hard hap to live in those times as a public person in the government of the Church, when with some sorts of people (and those many and of place) the best actions of Church officials could never receive good interpretations but were ever misreported because they proceeded from men of that rank and place.[1]

James was writing in 1616, well before the civilians' service as 'public persons in the government of the Church' made them symbols of Laudian tyranny and the butt of both parliamentary and Puritan criticism. Yet even at that early time James realized that the civilians' association with the Church was their most

[1] PRO, will of James, PROB 11/127/43.

serious political liability. During the Laudian period this liability became more onerous, as the Puritans sought to restrain those civilians who were distinguishing themselves in the Archbishop's service, especially as High Commissioners. One Puritan singled out Dr. Arthur Duck for parliamentary censure:

> Then there is also one Doctor Duck
> The proverb says, What's worse than ill luck
> We hope the Parliament his feathers will pluck
> For being so busy, Doctor Duck.[1]

The Long Parliament did actually pluck the feathers of all the civilians. The House of Commons inaugurated proceedings against Duck and eleven other civilians, while many more civilians suffered when Parliament destroyed the High Commission as well as the criminal jurisdiction of all ecclesiastical courts.[2] With this accomplished, one Puritan pamphleteer thought it safe to consign Doctors' Commons to the grave.[3] As the civilians were shortly to prove, however, his funeral elegy was somewhat premature.

---

[1] *The Organs Echo* (London, 1641), stanza 8.

[2] 16 Car. I, c. 11, see Holdsworth, *History of Law*, i. 611.

[3] 'A Funerall Elegie . . . upon the fall or death of Doctors Commons' in *A Letter from Rhoan in France*, pp. 7–8.

VI

DEFEAT AND SURVIVAL

EIGHTY-THREE of the civil lawyers who form the basis of this study survived to witness the beginning of the Civil War in 1642. In view of their political behaviour during the first four decades of the seventeenth century one might expect that the overwhelming majority would declare for the King. In fact the civilians responded to the outbreak of war in a variety of ways, as the following breakdown of their loyalties indicates:

Active Royalists (gave military, legal or administrative aid to the King's forces)	19
Passive Royalists (lost their offices, fled to the Continent, or compounded for their estates)	21
Active Parliamentarians (gave military, legal, or administrative aid to Parliament)	3
Passive Parliamentarians (served in positions under the auspices of Parliament)	19
Unknown	21

The active Royalists present no problems of interpretation. These included Thomas Read and Rowland Scudamore, who gave direct assistance to Charles's forces, George Riddell and William Lewin, who served as judge-advocates in Royalist armies, and Arthur Duck, who assisted the King in his negotiations on the Isle of Wight. Balanced against these nineteen committed Royalists are three members of the profession who dedicated themselves with equal fervour to the Parliamentary cause: Isaac Dorislaus, the regicide; Walter Walker, the advocate for the Parliamentary fleet; and Calibute Downing, who served as a chaplain in the army of the Earl of Essex.

The majority of civilians did not actively commit themselves to one side or the other. Nevertheless, twenty-one of these passive civilians were clearly Royalists, since they either compounded for their estates, fled to the Continent, or lost their ecclesiastical preferments. More difficult to classify, however, are the nineteen civilians who, while being strongly 'royalist' before the War, stayed on in their former employments or took new positions under the auspices of Parliament. These civilians do appear to have destroyed the royalist consensus that had prevailed among the members of the profession prior to 1642.

The civil lawyers had limited opportunities for employment after the war began. They were no longer needed to correct men's morals on the High Commission and in the ordinary ecclesiastical courts. But they did possess the necessary training and experience to prove wills and to regulate marriages, functions still assigned to the Church courts as part of their civil jurisdiction. The civilians were also pre-eminently suited to advise the government on matters of international law and to administer both Admiralty and Chancery jurisdictions. As contemptuous as Parliamentarians may have been of the entire profession of civil law, they still needed some of these lawyers for the perpetuation of orderly and equitable government.

Given the chance to continue on in their former employments, at least nineteen civilians did. Robert Aylett, Thomas Bennet, and William Child all remained at their posts on the Chancery bench. William Sammes replaced Richard Zouch as Judge of the Admiralty Court and served in that capacity until he died in 1646.[1] Thomas Eden kept his parliamentary seat, assisted in the conduct of Admiralty proceedings and diplomatic affairs, and actually took the Covenant in 1643.[2] Nathaniel Brent, who also took the Covenant, became Judge of the Prerogative Court in 1644 and served on numerous parliamentary commissions.[3] At the local level Clement Corbett continued to adjudicate civil litigation in the Norwich Consistory Court even after the abolition of the episcopacy in 1646.[4]

[1] There is no record of his appointment, but see PRO, SP 21/7, pp. 118, 136.
[2] Ward, *Gresham Professors*, p. 241. PRO, SP 21/7, pp. 61, 118, 136; SP 16/503/41.
[3] C. H. Firth and R. S. Rait (ed.), *Acts and Ordinances of the Interregnum* (London, 1911), i. 186, 456, 487, 488, 498, 542, 842, 925, 972, 1090; ii. 149. PRO, SP 21/8, pp. 41, 97–8.   [4] NRO, DEP 45, ff. 33, 124.

The commitment of some of these civilians to the Parliamentary cause was certainly shallow, if not completely lacking. Robert Aylett, for example, never disavowed his royalism, although he did eventually tolerate Cromwell as a 'power that be'.[1] But Aylett and the others who accepted service under the auspices of Parliament had little difficulty in acknowledging the authority of their new superiors. Entering the service of Parliament did not demand of them a radical change in their political outlook. For many of them the shift was in complete accordance with their earlier political behaviour. Their original attachment to the Crown, it should be remembered, owed a great deal to purely professional considerations. When Parliament gained control of London, which was the main residence for a majority of civilians, and then later established its authority over the entire kingdom, the civilians had to choose between unemployment and the service of Parliament. Those who chose the latter course were simply opting for professional survival by joining the new 'Court' which was subservient to Parliament instead of the King. The civilians displayed a high degree of adaptability to new political circumstances whenever their own interests were at stake. When the King returned in 1660, the deprived and exiled Royalists were not the only civilians to fill the posts that they had held earlier in the century. They were joined by Masters in Chancery like William Child and chancellors of dioceses like Francis Baber, 'trimmers' who had survived all the changes of government from 1641 until 1660 without ever losing their positions.

Because of the lingering demand for their services and the versatility of the civilians themselves, the civil lawyers' profession survived the period of Parliamentary government. For a while it was touch and go. The Civil War, one contemporary observed, 'brought the civil law into contempt' at the universities, and students turned from the study of the law and of divinity to that of physic.[2] In 1646 the profession actually stood on the verge of

---

[1] Padelford, 'Aylett', 29–30, 45–7.

[2] Hill, *Intellectual Origins*, pp. 118–19; Rex, *University Representation*, p. 212. Samuel Hartlib called for the abolition of the law lectures at Gresham College. R. Greaves, *The Puritan Revolution and Educational Thought* (New Brunswick, N.J., 1969), p. 50.

collapse when 'some men . . . would have that whole profession removed and quite eradicated'.[1] By mid-century it had reached the nadir of its fortunes, as Robert Wiseman woefully described:

Now the causes thereof (of the civil law courts) are cantonized, and like a spoil divided; some carried to the courts of common law, some to the Court of Equity, others sent into the country, some left without any rule or regulation at all, and nothing left entire to the civil law; . . . the solid reason of that law is crowded out by vulgar reason, the professors thereof scattered, the study thereof discontinued, the very law books for want of use here, all transported beyond the sea to other nations, and all coercion taken away.[2]

Yet even during this gloomy period, the civilians kept Doctors' Commons alive. In 1656 there were eighteen members of that society, a skeleton force it is true, but none the less a professionally active group.[3] These men were sensitive to the lingering popular and parliamentary contempt for their profession, and in order to make themselves more acceptable to their critics they deliberately dissociated themselves from the ecclesiastical affiliations which had previously contributed so much to their unpopularity. In 1657 a number of civilians tried to eradicate prejudice against them by explaining that the law they studied 'is a definite body from the canon law and hath no relation to archbishops, bishops, and archdeacons' and that its proper areas of application were the conduct of foreign trade and diplomacy, the probate of wills, and the regulation of marriage.[4] These were the words of men who were trying desperately to survive in a political climate that was hostile to them and their occupation. In an attempt to salvage some part of their professional life they were willing to jettison those clerical associations which had previously been a main source of their employment.

The Petition of 1657 was a compromise necessitated by the politics of the Commonwealth and of the Protectorate. Soon after

---

[1] Parker, *Reformation in Courts and Cases Testamentary*, p. 3.
[2] Wiseman, *Law of Lawes*, p. iii.
[3] PRO, Doc. Com. Treas. Bk., f. 188.
[4] Bodl., Tanner MS. 51, f. 8. See also Wiseman, *Law of Lawes*, pp. 29–30, 184–9.

the Restoration civilians once again entered the service of archbishops, bishops, and archdeacons and administered canon law in
their courts. Once again they behaved as they had been accustomed
throughout the early seventeenth century, as men who were
concerned mainly for their own professional survival and who
could readily subordinate their principles and ideals to the dictates
of economic necessity.

This view of the civilians as essentially courtiers or even
opportunists has much to recommend it. Indeed, this study has
emphasized those aspects of the civilians' careers that reflect their
official attachment to the King, their complete dependence upon
him to solve their problems, and their close professional association with the hierarchy of the established Church. It has not
denied, however, that principles of ideas motivated at least some
aspects of their political behaviour. To view, for example, the
theoretical writings of Cowell, Zouch, or Gentili as nothing more
than responses to professional stimuli would be misrepresentative
of their true intentions. Certainly these professors of law cared
not only for their own well-being but also for the advancement
of the study of the law and of government. It is true, of course,
that the distinction between principles and self-interest is often
a fine one and that civilians easily equated ideals such as the
integrity of the Church, the defence of the royal prerogative, and
the preservation of the legacy of Roman law, with their own
professional advancement and security. Rather than attempting
the impossible task of determining what their real or underlying
motivation was, this study has simply analysed the various social,
economic, professional, and intellectual influences civilians were
exposed to when they defined their political position. Unless one
recognizes the full complexity of these forces and the ways in
which different motives reinforced one another, the royalist consensus that the civilians represented does not make complete sense.

The civil lawyers acquired their reputation for royalism not
only by their activities as courtiers and their apologies for absolutism but by public charges and accusations made by their enemies:
Puritans who contended that the entire profession was popish;
common lawyers who portrayed the civilians as enemies of the

common law and of individual liberty; and critics of royal absolutism who considered the civil law to be the antithesis of parliamentary freedom. Opposition to the civil lawyers on these grounds was often unjustified. The civilians did not believe that they were upholding the canon law of Rome; they did not attempt or even desire to overthrow the common law or the freedoms that it embodied; and they certainly did not attempt to ascribe to the English monarch the powers of the ancient Roman emperors.

None the less there were elements of truth in the allegations and insinuations of the Puritans, the common lawyers, and the Parliamentarians. The ecclesiastical law which the civilians upheld in the Church courts did include a large residue of Papal legislation; civil law procedure was inquisitorial and hence did prejudice the cause of the defendant; and the study of the civil law encouraged the civilians to ascribe the attributes of an absolute monarch to the English King. This was enough to confirm the suspicions of the civilians' enemies and to give them sufficient evidence to slander the civil lawyers publicly and collectively.

Thus the civilians, already tied to established authority by the nature of their occupational pursuits, were tainted with popery, legal authoritarianism, and constitutional heresy by virtue of their attachment to the civil and ecclesiastical laws. As a further political liability the civilians' primary institutional affiliation was the Church, which was particularly vulnerable to political criticism in the early seventeenth century. In this way the civilians acquired a collective political reputation which did permanent harm to their profession in 1641. After the Civil War the civilians never regained the position of honour they held in society during the Middle Ages and the later Tudor period. The common lawyers never relinquished the supremacy they achieved over the civil lawyers in 1641, and the civilians entered a period of gradual decline which culminated in the reform of the ecclesiastical and Admiralty courts and the destruction of Doctors' Commons in 1867. The reasons for this later decline remain a separate concern.[1]

[1] A. H. Manchester, 'The Reform of the Ecclesiastical Courts', *The American Journal of Legal History*, 10 (1966), 51–75.

But if one wishes to plot the descent of the civil lawyers from the height of Renaissance glory to the destruction of their profession in the nineteenth century, he must give serious attention to the political reputation these men acquired in the early seventeenth century.

BIOGRAPHICAL DICTIONARY

THIS dictionary provides information concerning the origins, education, official and legal careers, literary works, political activities, and financial affairs of the 200 civil lawyers who form the basis of this study. While the individual entries present only a broad outline of their lives, the sources cited supply additional information. I have included all those civilians who received their doctorates before 1641 and who resided in England between 1603 and 1641. I have excluded Henry Dethick, who supplicated for his degree but did not incept.[1] Those who received their degrees abroad but were never incorporated at either Oxford or Cambridge, such as Robert Taylor,[2] I have also excluded. James Baylie,[3] John Vaughan,[4] and Philibert Vernat,[5] who were incorporated after receiving degrees on the Continent, and Eitzo Tiarda, who received his degree at Oxford,[6] do not belong to the group because they did not remain in England after accepting their degrees. Finally I have excluded Richard Hudson from the group because it is uncertain whether he survived the year 1603.

The dates listed for the civil lawyers' receipt of their degrees refer to the date of admission or inception, not supplication. I have taken each year to have begun on 1 January, not 25 March. The dates given for the period during which each civilian was 'in commons' or 'out of commons' are derived from the Treasurer's Book of Doctors' Commons.

[1] *Al. Oxon.* ii. 759; Marchant, *Church Under Law*, p. 249. Marchant also lists Edmund Parkinson as D.C.L., but Wood does not record his degree. See also *HMCS* ix. 397; xv. 394.

[2] A. J. Loomie, 'Sir Robert Cecil and the Spanish Embassy', *Bulletin of the Institute of Historical Research*, 42 (1969), 36 n.

[3] Wood, *Fasti*, i. 404.

[4] *Al. Oxon.* iv. 1536.

[5] Wood, *Athenae*, i. 351; *Al. Oxon.* iv. 1541.

[6] *Al. Oxon.* iv. 1485.

BIOGRAPHICAL DICTIONARY

ABBREVIATIONS

Adm.	admitted
b.	born
bur.	buried
c.	approximately
Com.	Commission
Comr.	Commissioner
Comr. Adm.	Commissioner of Oyer and Terminer for Criminal Admiralty Causes
Comr. Eccles. Causes	Commissioner of Ecclesiastical Causes
Comr. Pol. & Ass.	Commissioner of Policies and Assurances
d.	died
dau.	daughter
Doc. Com.	Doctors' Commons
esq.	esquire
gent.	gentleman
HCA	High Court of Admiralty
inc.	incorporated
m.	married
matric.	matriculated
mess.	messuage or messuages
Parlt.	Parliament
PCC	Prerogative Court of Canterbury
pens.	pensioner
pr.	proved
Preb.	Prebendary
prob.	probably
reg.	register
res.	residence
ten.	tenement or tenements
v.	against
VCC	Vice-Chancellor's Court
w.	with
Warrant Doc. Com.	receipt of warrant from Archbishop of Canterbury for admission into Doctors' Commons

ACRED (AKEROYD, AKEROYDE, AIKEROYDE, AYKEROD), AM-
BROSE, 2nd son of John of Foggathorpe, Yorks., gent. (d. 1592), by Elizabeth
Blanchard. Elder brother Henry admitted to Inner Temple 1593 and grantee of
arms 1614. Matric. pens. Trinity College, Cambridge, c. 1595; B.A. 1597;
M.A. 1600; LL.D. 1630. Fellow of Trinity until death. Held lands, ten. in
Marton and Bothorpe, Yorks.; lease of lands in Skelton, Yorks. Will: Cam-
bridge VCC, pr. 25 June 1640. Lands in Marton and £250 debt to Fellows of
Trinity; £649 in cash to friends and relatives; lease at Skelton to nephews
Henry and Richard; lands in Bothorpe to Cressy Burnet of York. Unmarried.

Al. Cant. i. 3. *Yorkshire Pedigrees* (Harl. Soc. xciv, 1942), pp. 3–4. J. Foster, *The
Visitation of Yorkshire* (London, 1875), p. 485. ITL, Admissions to Inner Temple, i.
247. Cambridge Univ. Archives, Wills, 3/256.

ALDERNE, EDWARD, prob. younger son of Thomas of city of Hereford, esq.
Not to be confused with Edward of the Middle Temple, son and heir of his
brother Thomas. B.C.L. Exeter College, Oxford, 1634; D.C.L. 1638. Warrant
Doc. Com. 1640; full admission 1660. Chancellor of Rochester diocese w.
Robert Mason (q.v.) 1661–2; alone 1662–71. d. 1671. Will: PCC 72 Duke, pr.
5 June 1671. Divided estate among nephew Edward, niece Bridget, and godson
Edward Willoughby. Provides for their education. Had already provided
sufficiently for wife Helen.

Al. Oxon. i. 12. LPL, Reg. Doc. Com. ff. 51, 111. PRO, PROB 11/336/72; SP 16/
442/125. Kent Archives Office, Rochester Episcopal Register, DRc R9, ff. 113–113ᵛ,
115, 124ᵛ.

ALEXANDER, FRANCIS, b. 1579, only son of John of Hartley Wespall, Hants,
esq., by Amye, dau. of Harmann Bilson and sister of Thomas Bilson, Bishop of
Winchester. Winchester College. Matric. as son of commoner New College,
Oxford, 1597; dispensed of 16 terms of residence because he had a cure of souls
in country; fellow 1599–1606; B.C.L. 1605; D.C.L. 1610. Rector of Birdham,
Sussex, 1607; Crawley and Hinton, Hants, 1609; Overton, Hants, 1610–14;
Houghton, Hants, 1613. Preb. of Winchester 1613; Treasurer 1628. Surrogate in Winchester Consistory Court 1627–35. Sequestered from Crawley
rectory and prebend 1647. Res.: Winchester. Will: PCC 503 Wootton, pr. 2
July 1658. £1,000 in trust of John Worsley of Isle of Wight to wife; £300 to
son Gerard; £100 to sons George, William, and James; £300 to dau. Susan.
m. (1) Dorothy, dau. and coheir of R. Johyner, Doctor of Physic; (2) Ann, dau.
of T. Dillington of Isle of Wight.

Visitation of Hampshire (Harl. Soc. lxiv, 1913), pp. 187–8. *Al. Oxon.* i. 13. Clark,
Register, i. 116, 186; ii. 223; iii. 260. Bodl. MS. Top. Oxon. e. 105/2, f. 85. T. F.
Kirby, *Winchester Scholars* (London, 1888), p. 155. HRO, Consistory Court Books
100–18, *passim.* Winchester Cathedral Library, Chapter Book 1622–45, f. 21; Alpha-
betical Index of Hants Clergy (Beneficed), f. 7. *Walker Revised,* p. 179. PRO,
PROB 11/281/503.

AMYE (AMY), Sir John, 6th son of John of Great Abington, Cambs., yeoman. Matric. pens. Clare College, Cambridge, 1564; B.A. 1568; M.A. 1571; taxor 1581–2; LL.D. 1583. Warrant Doc. Com. 1585; full admission 1590; out of commons 1603–20. Honorific adm. Gray's Inn 1590. Active as advocate in London courts 1590–1621. Master in Chancery 1597–1621. Delegates 1595–1620. Comr. Sewers 1606. Comr. Adm. Middx. etc. 1603, 1609, 1614, 1619. Comr. Piracy London 1603–21. Comr. Pol. & Ass. London 1609, 1611, 1616. Chancellor of Worcester diocese c. 1605. J.P. Worcs. 1608. Knighted 1619. Co-author of memorandum on oaths in ecclesiastical courts c. 1590. Patrimony: £200. Grant of Arms 1593. Lease of land in Abington. Res.: Doc. Com. Will: PCC 49 Dale, pr. 5 June 1621. Lease to sister; £5 to Doc. Com. Father of Edward.

> Al. Cant. i. 28. Visitation of Cambridge (Harl. Soc. xli, 1897), p. 61. LPL, Reg. Doc. Com. ff. 44, 105ᵛ; Whitgift Reg. i, f. 113; Bancroft Reg. f. 187ᵛ. Bodl., Tanner MS. 427, passim. Exeter Cathedral Library, MS. 7155/1, f. 23ᵛ. BM, Stowe MS. 558, f. 17ᵛ; Lansdowne MS. 168, f. 152. PRO, C 181/2, passim; DEL 5/2–6 passim; HCA 1 32/1, ff. 29, 38, 55, 90; E 179/146/399, f. 5. Quintrell, 'Government of Essex', p. 164. Haydn, Dignities, p. 395. Gleason, Justices, pp. 51, 213–14. LPL, MS. 2004, f. 65. PRO, PROB 11/73/61; 11/137/49.

AUNGIER (AUNGER, ANGER, AUGIER), John, 2nd son of Richard of Cambridge, esq., by Rose, dau. of William Steward of Cambridge. Elder brother Francis was Master of the Rolls in Ireland and Baron of Longford 1624. Matric. pens. Trinity College, Cambridge, 1583; B.A. 1588; fellow 1589–1614; M.A. 1591; taxor 1607; proctor 1610–11; LL.D. 1616. Preb. of Peterborough 1615. Owned ten. in Cambridge and copyhold lands in St. Ives and Hemingford Abbots, Hunts. Bur. 17 Aug. 1630. Will: Cambridge VCC and PCC 84 Scroope, pr. 12 Oct. 1630. Lands in Hemingford Abbots to nephew Francis; other lands and ten. to wife Anne and then to nephew Gerald.

> Visitation of Cambridge, pp. 17–18. Al. Cant. i. 32. LeNeve, Fasti, ii. 550. Cambridge University Archives, Wills 3/183. PRO, PROB 11/158/84.

AWBREY, William, b. 1562, 2nd son of Richard of Aber-Cynrig, Brecon, gent. Cousin of William Awbrey, D.C.L. (d. 1595). Matric. Christ Church, Oxford, 1581; B.A. 1583; M.A. 1586; proctor 1593; B.C.L. and D.C.L. 1597. Warrant Doc. Com. 1599; full admission 1611; in commons 1611–22; out of commons 1623–41. Elected M.P. Cardigan borough 1601 but never sat. Comr. Adm. Cornwall 1601; Carmarthenshire, Pembrokeshire, and Cardigan 1609; Middx. etc. 1614. Comr. Piracy London 1614; Carm. 1616. J.P. Brecon. Chancellor of St. David's Cathedral 1614–26. Res. London and Broxbourne, Herts. m. (2) Anne, widow of one Bayley of Broxbourne, gent.

> BM, Harl. MS. 5058, f. 75. Clark, Register, i. 182; ii. 102; iii. 109. LPL, Reg. Doc. Com. ff. 47, 107ᵛ; Whitgift Reg. iii, f. 111; Abbot Reg. i, f. 252ᵛ. PRO, C 181/1, f. 5; 181/2, f. 273; C 193/13/1, f. 110; HCA 1/32/1, ff. 38, 57; SP 16/3, ff. 39, 55; LeNeve, Fasti (1716 edn.), p. 516. J. Foster, London Marriage Licences, 1521–1869 (London, 1887), p. 55.

AYLETT, ROBERT, b. 1583, 2nd son of Leonard of Rivenhall, Essex, gent., by Anne Pater. Related by marriage to Sir John Lambe (q.v.). B.A. Trinity Hall, Cambridge, 1605; M.A. 1608; LL.D. 1614. Warrant Doc. Com. 1616; full admission 1617; in commons 1618-42. Proctor and surrogate in Archdeacon of Colchester's court 1608-17; Official of Archdeacon of Colchester 1617-41. Bishop of London's Commissary for Essex and Herts. 1619-41. J.P. Essex 1622. High Com. 1629. Active as advocate in London courts by 1633. Comr. Piracy London 1633, 1635, 1638. Master in Chancery 1638-55. Investigates non-conformity in Essex under direction of Laud and Lambe. Fined by Long Parlt. for illegal sentence as High Comr.; impeachment proceedings brought *v*. him 1641. Master of Faculties 1642. Of Royalist sympathies but serves Parlt. and tolerates Cromwell. Wrote collection of poems, *Divine and Moral Speculation* (1654). Copyhold lands in Feering and elsewhere in Essex. Assessed for ship money at Thornwood, High Roding, Braintree, Felsted, Kelvedon, Waltham, and North Weald, Essex. Res.: house at Feering belonging to Bishop of London. d. 15 Mar. 1655. Will: PCC 236 Aylett, pr. 22 March 1655. Lands to two nephews William and Thomas; rest to wife. m. (1) Judith, dau. of John Gaell of Hadleigh, Essex; (2) Penelope, dau. of William Wiseman, gent.

Al. Cant. i. 59. *Visitations of Essex*, i (Harl. Soc. xiii, 1878), 339. LPL, Reg. Doc. Com. ff. 48, 108; Abbot Reg. i, f. 199ᵛ; ii. ff. 253ᵛ-254. PRO, C 181/3, f. 69; 181/4, f. 139; 181/5, ff. 26ᵛ, 130ᵛ, 251ᵛ; C 193/13/2, f. 27; SP 16/421/108; 16/477/62; 16/483/59; index 16818, p. 46; *CSPD 1629-1631*, pp. 197, 220; *1631-1633*, pp. 352, 410; *1636-1637*, pp. 513-14. Usher, *High Commission*, p. 345. Hill, *Society and Puritanism*, p. 338. Quintrell, 'Government of Essex', pp. 149-50. ERO, T/A 42, nos. 14, 42, 56, 67, 101, 121; D/ABA 1, *passim*. Padelford, 'Aylett'. J. H. Round, 'Dr. Robert Aylett', *Transactions of the Essex Archaeological Society* 10 (1909), 26-34; 'Robert Aylett and Richard Argall', *EHR* 38 (1923), 423-4. PRO, PROB 11/247/236.

AYLWORTH, MARTIN, b. 1592, 2nd son of Anthony, M.D. of New College, Oxford, and physician to Elizabeth I. Matric. Hart Hall, Oxford, 1610; fellow 1611-48; B.C.L. All Souls 1615; D.C.L. 1622. Warrant Doc. Com. 1622; full admission 1622; in commons 1622-42. Comr. Adm. Middx. etc. 1625; Comr. Piracy London 1629, 1633, 1635, 1638. Delegates 1627-39. Royalist during Civil War; expelled for not submitting to Parliamentary Visitors at Oxford 1648. Patrimony: goods and chattels. Res.: Oxford, London. d. 11 Jan. 1658. Will: PCC 350 Wootton, pr. 7 May 1658. £500 to nephews and nieces; *Corpus Juris Civilis* to Bath Library; other law books to Dr. Baldwin.

Al. Oxon. i. 49. Clark, *Register*, ii. 312; iii. 342. LPL, Reg. Doc. Com. ff. 48ᵛ, 108; Abbot Reg. i, f. 296. PRO C 181/4, ff. 37, 139; 181/5, ff. 27, 130ᵛ; DEL 8/70, *passim*; HCA 1/32/1, f. 13; PROB 11/50/58; 11/278/35; M. Burrows, *The Register of the Visitors of the University of Oxford* (Camden Soc. n.s. xxix, 1881), pp. 41-2, 90, 473, *Walker Revised*, p. 23.

BABER, FRANCIS, b. 1600, 2nd son of Francis of Chew Magna, Som., esq. and J.P. (d. 1643), by Anne, dau. of W. Whitmore of London and Salop. Grandson of Edward Baber of Chew Magna, Serjeant-at-law. Matric. Trinity College, Oxford, 1616; B.A. 1620; M.A. 1622; B.C.L. 1624; D.C.L. 1628. Full admission Doc. Com. 1629. Chancellor of Gloucester diocese 1627–31 w. Dr. Sutton; alone 1631–69. Delegates 1630–6. Joins other ecclesiastical judges residing at Doc. Com. in legal opinion 1636. Judge of Vice-Admiralty Court for Glos. 1636. Candidate for clerk of Convocation 1640. d. 17 June 1669. m. Elizabeth, dau. of John Adderley of Middlesex, esq.

> *Al. Oxon.* i. 51. Clark, *Register*, ii. 357; iii. 381. *Visitation of Somerset* (Harl. Soc. xi, 1876), p. 5. LPL, Reg. Doc. Com., ff. 49ᵛ, 109. *CSPD 1629–1631*, p. 84; *1635–1636*, p. 466; *1639–1640*, p. 583; *1640*, p. 367. Gleason, *Justices*, p. 197. J. Collinson, *The History and Antiquities of the County of Somerset* (Bath, 1791), ii. 97. Rudder, *Gloucestershire*, p. 164.

BABINGTON, ZACHARY, b. 1549, younger son of Thomas of Cossington, Leics., esq. (d. 1567), by Eleanor, dau. of Humphrey of Barton. B.A. St. Alban's Hall, Oxford, 1570; M.A. 1573; B.C.L. and D.C.L. Merton College 1599. Official of Archdeacon of Nottingham 1577–81 at £23 p.a. Chancellor of Lichfield diocese 1581 upon purchase of office from Bishop Overton; held chancellorship w. Dr. Becon until Overton removed Becon. Referred to as 'the good chancellor' in *The Marprelate Tracts*. Preb. of Lichfield 1584–9; Precentor 1589–1605. Rector of Sudbury, Derbys., 1583; Hoggeston, Bucks., 1588; Langwith, Derbys., 1595; Cossington, Leics., 1603. J.P. City of Lichfield 1611. Part-owner of land in Staffs. valued at £41. d. 1613. 'A graceless person by all accounts.' m. Thomasin, dau. of John Lowth, Archdeacon of Nottingham.

> *Al. Oxon.* i. 52. *Visitation of Leicestershire* (Harl. Soc. ii, 1870), pp. 205–6. C. W. Boase, *The Register of the University of Oxford* (Oxford, 1885), p. 276. Clark, *Register*, i. 79; ii. 40; iii. 31. *Marprelate Tracts*, pp. 155–6. Bodl., Tanner MS. 427, f. 13ᵛ. PRO, C 181/2, f. 165; PROB 11/50/1. S. Shaw, *The History and Antiquities of Staffordshire* (London, 1798), i. 300. Marchant, *Church Under Law*, pp. 159–63, 252. *CSPD 1603–1610*, pp. 504–5. *Collections for a History of Staffordshire*, iv. 51.

BAILEY (BAYLEY), JAMES. Birth and parentage obscure. B.C.L. All Souls College, Oxford, 1594; Bursar 1598; D.C.L. 1599. Warrant Doc. Com. 1599 but not fully admitted. Chancellor of Hereford diocese. Preb. of Hereford. J.P. Hereford 1609. Assessed for subsidy in Hereford at £8 in goods only 1609. Res.: house called 'Fyers' in suburbs of Hereford. Will: PCC 102 Lawe, pr. 19 Oct. 1614. £100 to each of five daus. Profits from preb. to wife Jane, but £20 from those profits to son Richard after 16 years and £30 after 21 years.

> *Al. Oxon.* i. 90. Clark, *Register*, i. 183; iii. 186. Wood, *Fasti*, i. 182. LPL, Whitgift Reg. iii, f. 111ᵛ. Gleason, *Justices*, p. 252. PRO, PROB 11/124/102. *Catalogue of All Souls Archives*, p. 307.

BARKER, HUGH, b. 1565, 2nd son of Robert of Culworth, Northants., gent., by Mary, dau. of William Danvers. Related to Robert Dillon (q.v.) through Danvers family. Cousin of Samuel Gardiner (q.v.). Winchester College. Matric. New College, Oxford, 1586; fellow 1585–91 (founder's kin); B.C.L.

1592; D.C.L. 1605. Warrant Doc. Com. 1605; full admission 1607; in commons 1608–30. Master of Free Grammar School at Chichester. Commissary to Dean of Chichester 1602. Right of presentation to Birdham rectory, Sussex 1610. Chancellor of Oxford diocese. Official of Archdeacon of Oxford 1618. Proctor in Convocation 1625. High Commission 1625–32; accused of false imprisonment in that capacity. Active as advocate in London courts. Delegates 1608–32. Comr. Adm. Middx. etc. 1622, 1624, 1625; Piracy 1629. Bishop of Oxford tried unsuccessfully to remove him from chancellorship 1624. Owned one mess. and 38 acres pasture in Piddington, Oxon., and one tenement in Chichester Close; leased manor of Fritwell, Oxon. d. 1632. Will: PCC 102 Audley, pr. 10 Oct. 1632. £200 to relatives and charity; Piddington and two-thirds of other lands to wife, then to dau. and heir Mary with all other lands. m. Mary, dau. of Richard Pyott, London alderman.

Metcalfe, *Visitations of Northamptonshire*, p. 164. *DNB* i. 1121. *Al. Oxon.* i. 70. Clark, *Register*, ii. 149; iii. 174. LPL, Reg. Doc. Com., ff. 46ᵛ, 107; Bancroft Reg. f. 135ᵛ. Kirby, *Winchester Scholars*, p. 147. Bodl., MS. Top. Oxon. e. 105/2, f. 77. PRO, C 181/4, f. 37; C 142/490/184; DEL 5/4, f. 37; 8/70, pt. ii, *passim*; PROB 11/162/102; HCA 1/32/1, ff. 13, 19, 21. Burn, *Ecclesiastical Law*, i. 294. Peckham, *Chichester Chapter Acts*, nos. 903, 994, 1072, 1090, 1184. Usher, *High Commission*, p. 346. *CSPD 1631–1633*, p. 232. Queen's College Deeds, 2.P.3.

BELLEY (BELLAY, BELLY), JOHN, 2nd son of John of Haselbury, Som., yeoman. B.A. Oxford 1555; Fellow of Oriel College 1556; M.A. 1559; B.C.L. and D.C.L. 1567. Provost of Oriel 1566–73. Warrant Doc. Com. 1569; full admission 1569; out of commons 1603–9. Preb. of Lincoln 1574. Chancellor of Lincoln diocese until 1609. Perhaps Master in Chancery before 1569. Estate at Great Paxton, Hunts.; mess. and land in Derneford and Buckden, Hunts. Grant of Arms 1602. Will: PCC 95 Dorset, pr. 30 Oct. 1609. £200 a piece to daus. Judith, Susan, and Mary; rest to son Thomas. m. Elizabeth, dau. of Bishop Cooper of Winchester.

Visitation of the County of Huntingdon (Camden Soc. xliii, 1849), p. 122. PRO, will of William, PROB 11/116/105. *Al. Cant.* i. 130. LPL, Reg. Doc. Com., ff. 40ᵛ, 103; Parker Reg., f. 278. S. Cassan, *The Lives of the Bishops of Winchester* (London, 1827), p. 44. Boase, *Register*, p. 227. Cooper, *Athenae*, ii. 481. LeNeve, *Fasti*, ii. 147. PRO, C 142/330/65. Haydn, *Dignities*, p. 395. *Grantees of Arms*, i. 20. PRO, PROB 11/114/95.

BENNET (BENET), SIR JOHN, 2nd son of Richard of Wallingford, Berks., gent. Matric. Christ Church, Oxford, 1573; B.A. 1578; M.A. 1580; proctor 1585; B.C.L. and D.C.L. 1589. Warrant Doc. Com. 1590; full admission 1604; in commons until 1611; out of commons 1611–27. Honorific admission Gray's Inn 1599. Preb. of York 1590–1608. Judge of Exchequer and Prerogative Court at York 1590. Chancellor of York diocese 1590. Comr. Eccles. Causes York 1590–1620; quorum 1590–1603. Negotiated with Scots at Carlisle 1597. J.P. Yorks. 1603. Council of North 1599–1613. Comr. Piracy Cumberland and Durham 1603; Norfolk 1603; London 1609. Knighted 1603. Delegates 1605.

Master in Chancery 1608–22. High Com. 1611, 1613, 1620. M.P. Ripon, Yorks., 1597, 1604; York 1601 through influence of Archbishop of York. M.P. Oxford 1614, 1621. Warns Parlt. not to debate royal prerogative 1601. Supports bill for stricter enforcement of Act of Uniformity 1601. Charged with bribery and corruption 1621; placed under house arrest; pardoned 1624. Speaks against prohibitions in conference with common lawyers 1609. Composed tract on right to interpret statutes (Bodl., Barlow MS. 9, ff. 53–5). Advocated stricter measures *v.* recusants. R. Crankanthorp, *Justinian The Emperor Defended* (1616), and T. Bell, *A Counterblast* (1603), dedicated to him. Owned manors of Harlington and Dawley, Middlesex. Res.: York, London. Invested in Virginia Company 1610. d. 1627. Administration 3 May 1627 to Francis Gregory, heir of wife Elizabeth. m. (1) Ann Weeks of Salisbury; (2) Elizabeth Lowe, dau. of Sir Thomas, governor of Merchant Adventurers and Mayor of London; (3) Leonora Vurendeels of Antwerp.

DNB, ii. 233–5. HPT, typescript. *Al. Oxon.* i. 106. Clark, *Register*, i. 116, 181, 242; ii. 141; iii. 67. LPL, Reg. Doc. Com., f. 46; Whitgift Reg. i, f. 161. Foster, *Gray's Inn*, p. 96. Marchant, *Church Under Law*, pp. 44, 46, 101, 143, 186–7, 245. York Cathedral Library, Chapter Acts 1565–1634, f. 437ᵛ. Borth. Inst., Index of Tudor Clergy. Tyler, 'Ecclesiastical Commission', pp. 179–80. R. R. Reid, *The King's Council of the North* (London, 1921), p. 496. PRO, C 66/1452, 1645, 1907, 2018; C 181/1, ff. 69, 70, 166; 181/2, ff. 9, 22, 41, 101; 181/3, ff. 23ᵛ, 24ᵛ; DEL 5/3, f. 92; 5/6, *passim*; HCA 24/83, ff. 351, 488; index 16818, p. 45. Usher, *High Commission*, p. 346; *Reconstruction*, ii. 226–7. J. E. Neale, *The Elizabethan House of Commons* (London, 1949), p. 164. Townshend, *Historical Collections*, p. 320. Prothero, *Statutes*, pp. 112–13. Bowyer, *Diary*, pp. 58, 224, 227–8. Roberts, *Yonge Diary*, p. 37. Foster, *Proceedings*, ii. 399. Moir, *Addled Parliament*, p. 187. NRS ii. 279–82, 288–9; iii. 56; iv. 44, 219, 223, 238, 245–9; vi. 391–2, 404. *CJ* i. 172, 204, 208, 229, 236–7, 268, 274, 286, 296, 326, 342–3, 350–1. BM, Harl. MS. 787, ff. 3–4. Coke, *Reports*, xiii. 38. Gleason, *Justices*, p. 231. Rabb, *Enterprise*, p. 245. *VCH Berks.* ii. 268; iii. 543; *Middlesex* iii. 262–3.

BENNET (BENET), SIR THOMAS, b. 1592, 2nd son of Sir John, D.C.L. (q.v.). Matric. All Souls College, Oxford, 1613; B.C.L. 1615; D.C.L. 1624; fellow 1611. Warrant Doc. Com. 1624; full admission 1626; in commons 1627–41. Perhaps adm. Gray's Inn 1617. Active in London courts as advocate 1626–41. Delegates 1628. Comr. Piracy London 1633, 1635, 1638. Master in Chancery 1635–70 (reappointed 1660). Joins other ecclesiastical judges residing at Doc. Com. in legal opinion *c.* 1636. Knighted 1661. Perhaps expelled for not submitting to Parliamentary Visitors at Oxford 1648. Estate in Salthrop, Wilts. d. 27 June 1670. Will: PCC 157 Penn, pr. 8 Nov. 1670. All lands to son Thomas; £2,000 to dau. Mary. m. (1) Charlotte Harrison of London; (2) Thomasine, dau. and heir of George Dethick of Gray's Inn, esq.

DNB ii. 237. *Al. Oxon.* I. 108. Clark, *Register*, ii. 332; iii. 342. LPL, Reg. Doc. Com., ff. 48ᵛ, 108ᵛ; Abbot Reg. ii, f. 207ᵛ. PRO, DEL 8/70, pt. ii, f. 35ᵛ; HCA 24/81, f. 35; 24/101; SP 16/339/63; index 16818, pp. 46–7; C 181/4, f. 139; 181/5, ff. 27, 130ᵛ. *LeNeve's Knights* (Harl. Soc. viii), p. 145. Burrows, *Register of the Visitors*, p. 473. *CSPD 1634–1635*, p. 324.

BINGHAM, WILLIAM, matric. sizar Trinity College, Cambridge, 1553; B.A.
1558; M.A. 1561; fellow 1570; proctor 1570–1; LL.D. 1572. Warrant Doc. Com.
1572; full admission 1573; out of commons 1603–10. Rector of Rettendon,
Essex, 1588–1611. Official to Archdeacon of Essex 1575–85; of St. Albans
1581–2; 1584–6. Commissary for Essex and Herts. 1572–8. Lands and ten. in
Essex and Middx. Sold three mess. to Richard Stanes (q.v.) before death.
Will: London Consistory Court, pr. 8 July 1611. Land to sons Adam and
William and dau. Mary. Books on divinity, canon law, and civil law to Mary;
statutes at large to Adam. m. Dorothy.

> *Al. Cant.* i. 153. LPL, Reg. Doc. Com., ff. 41ᵛ, 103ᵛ; Parker Reg., ii. f. 64. R. Peters,
> *Oculus Episcopi* (Manchester, 1963), pp. 12, 15, 57. Quintrell, 'Government of Essex',
> p. 150. Greater London Record Office, Consistory Court Wills Hamer 1609–21,
> ff. 66ᵛ–69. ERO, Will of Stanes, D/ABW/36/227. J. Anglin, 'The Court of the Arch-
> deacon of Essex 1571–1609' (Univ. of California at Los Angeles, Ph.D. thesis, 1965),
> pp. 36–7.

BIRD (BYRD, BYRDE), WILLIAM, b. 1588, 2nd son of Thomas of Littlebury,
Essex, gent., by Anne, dau. of Thomas Parkin of Littlebury. Nephew of Sir
William Bird (q.v.). Matric. as son of commoner St. Edmund Hall, Oxford,
1608; B.A. 1612; fellow; M.A. 1615; B.C.L. 1617; D.C.L. 1622. Warrant Doc.
Com. 1622; full admission 1627; in commons 1624–39. Res.: London. Perhaps
invested in privateers 1625. d. 28 Nov. 1639; bur. at Littlebury.

> Braybrooke, *Audley End*, p. 292. *Al. Oxon*, i. 127. Clark, *Register*, ii. 300; iii. 302.
> Wood, *Fasti*, i. 407. LPL, Reg. Doc. Com., ff. 49, 108ᵛ; Abbot Reg. i, f. 201. Rabb,
> *Enterprise*, p. 247.

BIRD (BYRD, BYRDE), SIR WILLIAM, b. 1561, 2nd son of William of Walden,
Essex, gent. (d. 1568), by Maria, dau. of John Woodhall of Walden. Matric.
All Souls College, Oxford, 1581; fellow 1578–1604; B.C.L. 1583; D.C.L. 1588.
Dean of All Souls 1593. Acting Vice-Chancellor of Cambridge 1591. Warrant
Doc. Com. 1589; full admission 1590; in commons regularly until 1642.
Delegates 1597–1622. J.P. Essex 1603. Comr. Adm. Middx. etc. 1603–19.
Comr. Piracy London 1603–23. Comr. Pol. & Ass. London 1615. Active as
advocate in London courts. M.P. Oxford University 1608. Judge PCC 1611–22
with J. Bennet (q.v.); 1622–4 alone. Master in Chancery; charged with corruption 1621. Dean of Arches 1617–24. Knighted 1617. Represented civilians at
conference concerning prohibitions and High Commission 1611. Commis-
sioned to investigate abuses in government of Isle of Jersey 1617. Rector of
Ickleton, Cambs., 1615–24; Shalbourne, Wilts., 1621–4. Owned house in
Walthamstowe, Essex. Invested in commerce. d. 1624 without issue. Signed
testament: PCC 81 Bird.

> Braybrooke, *Audley End*, pp. 291–2. *Al. Oxon*. i. 127. ERO, Will of William, sen., pr.
> 9 Sept. 1568, 74 CR6. Clark, *Register*, i. 41, 230; ii. 111; iii. 116, 117. *Catalogue of All
> Souls Archives*, pp. 306, 380. *CSPD 1603–1610*, p. 604; *1623–1625*, p. 84. Rex, *University
> Representation*, pp. 42, 364. LPL, Reg. Doc. Com., ff. 44, 106; Whitgift Reg. i, f. 154ᵛ;

MS. 664, ff. 7–9; Bodl., Tanner MS. 280, f. 119ᵛ. PRO, C 181/1, f. 123; C 181/2, ff. 235, 296–334, *passim*; C 193/13/1, f. 35ᵛ; HCA 1/32/1, ff. 29, 38, 55, 90; HCA 24/70, f. 294; 24/77, f. 130; SP 14/93/129; 14/152/71. *APC 1616–1617*, pp. 187–8; *1618–1619*, pp. 158, 162–3, 187–8, 369. Rabb, *Enterprise*, p. 247. *NRS* vi. 92. S. Bond, *The Chapter Acts of the Dean and Canons of Windsor* (Windsor, 1966), pp. 90, 111, 124.

BLINCOW (BLENCOWE, BLENCOW, BLINCO), Anthony, 2nd son of Anthony of Little Blencow, Cumb. Adm. Dudley Exhibitioner at Oriel College, Oxford, 1560; resided at Queen's College 1560–2; B.A. 1562; Fellow of Oriel College 1563; M.A. 1566; proctor 1571–2; B.C.L. and D.C.L. 1586. Provost of Oriel 1574–1618. Respondent in law disputation for Queen's visit 1592. Procured charter from James I for incorporating Oriel College. Warrant Doc. Com. 1592 but not fully admitted. Preb. of Wells 1566–1617. Official of Archdeacon of Oxford by 1593. Chancellor of Chichester diocese 1590–1607. Chancellor of Oxford diocese *c.* 1606. J.P. Oxford 1604. Lands in Warwick devised to him by will of uncle Thomas Audley, but used to pay uncle's debts d. 15 Jan. 1618. Will: PCC 19 Meade, pr. 28 Feb. 1618. £20 to Queen's College; £60 to nephew George and £40 to each of his remaining nephews; rest of goods and chattels, valued at £1,300 and including 67 books, to Oriel College.

Al. Oxon. i. 138. C. L. Shadwell, *Registrum Orielense* (London, 1893), i. 29. Richards and Shadwell, *The Provosts and Fellows of Oriel College* (Oxford, 1922), p. 72. J. Nicholson and R. Burn, *The History and Antiquities of the Counties of Westmoreland and Cumberland* (London, 1778), ii. 376. Clark, *Register*, i. 99, 118, 230, 246; ii. 39. Boase, *Register*, p. 250. LPL, Whitgift Reg. ii, f. 197ᵛ; Bancroft Reg., ff. 213, 217ᵛ. Bodl., MS. Oxf. Diocs. Papers, 7, 8, 9 *passim*. Gleason, *Justices*, p. 256. *Chichester Chapter Acts*, nos. 901, 906, 961. Bond, *Windsor Acts*, pp. 46, 54, 55, 97. *HMC Dean of Wells* ii. 374.

BOSWELL (BOSVILLE), William, b. 1599, son of William, alderman of the city of Oxford. Scholar at Wadham College, Oxford, 1613; matric. 1614; B.A. 1617; M.A. 1620; fellow 1622–39; Dean 1624; Librarian 1625; B.C.L. and D.C.L. 1630; Sub-Warden 1630. Receives patents as Commissary of Exchequer and Prerogative Court at York 1623 and 1624 but never takes office. Full admission Doc. Com. 1630; in commons 1630–42. High Sheriff Oxon. 1652. Held manor of Stanton Yard, Oxon.; lands in Stanton Harcourt, Sutton, and elsewhere in Oxon.; mess. on All Souls parish, Oxford. d. 1678. Will: Oxford VCC, pr. 22 Apr. 1678. All manors and lands to nephew Thomas Boswell but rents and profits for nine years to five nieces. Inventory of goods and chattels, 16 Apr. 1678, valued at £109. 17s. 6d.

Visitation of Oxfordshire (Harl. Soc. v, 1871), p. 471. *Al. Oxon.* i. 153. Clark, *Register*, ii. 334; iii. 352. Wood, *Fasti*, i. 456. LPL, Reg. Doc. Com., ff. 49ᵛ, 109. Oxford University Archives, Wills Be–Bu; Inventories A–Bo. Marchant, *Church Under Law*, p. 47.

BRENT, Sir Nathaniel, b. 1574, 5th son of Anchor of Little Wolford, Warwicks., yeoman. Matric. Merton College, Oxford, 1590; B.A. 1594; fellow

1594; proctor 1607; M.A. 1599; B.C.L. 1623; D.C.L. 1624. Warden of Merton 1621–45; 1646–51. Warrant Doc. Com. 1624; full admission 1637; in commons 1637–41. Tutors Lord Cromwell and serves Lady Carleton in Venice 1613–14. Applies to be Secretary for Ireland 1617 but unsuccessful. Ambassador at The Hague 1617. Rector of Birmingham, Warwicks., 1616; Long Compton, Warwicks. Commissary to Archbishop of Canterbury 1621–9; Vicar-General 1629–41. Delegates 1625–39. Comr. Piracy London 1633. High Commission 1625, 1626, 1629, 1633. Tours England to report ecclesiastical abuses. Accused of improper allocation of funds as Warden of Merton 1638. Knighted 1639. Disagrees with Laud's policy during visitation of Merton. Testifies *v.* Laud at his trial 1641. Impeachment proceedings brought *v.* him 1641 but serves Parlt. during Civil War. Took Covenant 1643. Censor of books 1643; Member of Admiralty Committee 1644. Discusses treaties with Holland and Denmark 1644. Judge PCC 1644–53. Submits to Parliamentary Visitors at Oxford 1648. Patrimony: £150. Holds mortgage for manors of Clapcot and Rush Court, Berks., as security for £2,000 loan 1635; secures possession by 1650. Leases in Embleton and Ponteland, Northumb.; houses in Fleet Street and Temple Bar, London. Res: Fleet Street 1617; Aldersgate Street. Zealously anti-Catholic. Sent to Venice by Abbot to secure copy of Father Paul, *History of the Council of Trent* (1616); translates same 1620. Edited F. Mason, *Vindiciae Ecclesiae*. d. 1652. Will: PCC 222 Brent, pr. 29 Apr. 1653. Manors to son Basil; £2,500 to dau. Ann; £50 to son Nathaniel and dau. Ann Corbet. m. Martha, dau. and heir of Robert Abbot, Bishop of Salisbury, and niece of George Abbot.

DNB ii. 1170–2. *Al. Oxon.* i. 175. Clark, *Register,* i. 186; ii. 181, 294; iii. 177. Wood, *Athenae,* iii. 333–6. LPL, Reg. Doc. Com., ff. 50, 109ᵛ; Abbot Reg. ii, f. 207ᵛ. J. W. Stoye, *English Travellers Abroad* (London, 1952), p. 140. PRO, C 181/4, f. 138ᵛ; DEL 8/70 i, f. 25ᵛ; ii, ff. 43–8; SP 14/89/35; 14/93/123; 16/80/72; 16/477/62; 21/7, pp. 61, 118, 136; 21/8, pp. 41, 97–8. *CSPD 1637–1638,* p. 343; *1641–1643,* pp. 3–4. Broderick, *Merton,* pp. 68, 75, 88, 167–8. Prynne, *Canterburies Doome,* pp. 59, 62, 71, 89, 409–14, 545. Hill, *Economic Problems,* p. 179. Usher, *High Commission,* p. 346. CUL, MS. Mm I. 49 (Baker 38), p. 326. Notestein, *D'Ewes,* pp. 385–6. *Acts of Interregnum,* i. 186, 456, 487–8, 542, 925, 972, 1090; ii. 149. P. Welsby, *George Abbot* (London, 1962), p. 85. Burrows, *Register of Visitors,* p. 520. *VCH Warwicks* ii. 41; *Berks.* iii. 549. PRO, PROB 11/229/222.

BROWNE (BROWN), JONATHAN, b. 1601. From co. Herts. Matric. as son of commoner Gloucester Hall, Oxford, 1620; B.C.L. 1625; D.C.L. 1630. Listed as member Doc. Com. 1639 but no record of warrant or admission. Cleric known for preaching. Rector of Hertingfordbury, Herts., 1630; St. Faith, London, 1630 at value of £172 p.a. Dean of Hereford 1636–43. Canon of Westminster 1639. Prob. one of chaplains to Charles I; if so, accused of acting in popish manner. Sequestered 1643. Bought house and lands at Amwell, Herts., from father, valued at £11 p.a.; lands at Hertingfordbury from J. Scourfield, valued at £5. 8s. p.a.; copyhold lands in Herts. valued at £2 p.a. d. Dec. 1643. Will: PCC at Oxford 8 Apr. 1645. House and lands at Amwell to godson

Jonathan; rest to dau. Anne, wife of H. Crofte, D.D. m. Anne, Lady Lovelace, widow, 1631.

> *Al. Oxon.* i. 195. Clark, *Register*, ii. 384; iii. 445. Wood, *Fasti*, i. 456. LeNeve, *Fasti*, i. 478. Borth. Inst., R. VII PR. 108. PRO, PROB 10/642. Laud, *Troubles and Tryal*, p. 330. *Walker Revised*, p. 43. R. Newcourt, *Repertorium Ecclesiasticum Parochiale Londinensis* (London, 1708), i. 349.

BROWNE, THOMAS. Matric. pens. Christ's College, Cambridge, 1559; B.A. 1564; M.A. Pembroke 1568; LL.D. 1579. Warrant Doc. Com. 1579; full admission 1599; in commons 1604–6; out of commons 1607–27. d. 1627.

> *Al. Cant.* i. 238. LPL, Reg. Doc. Com. ff. 45, 106ᵛ; Grindal Reg., f. 190.

BROWNE, THOMAS, b. 1601, son of Thomas of Little Walsingham, Norf. prob. commoner. Doubtless related to Philip of Walsingham, mercer. LL.B. Trinity Hall, Cambridge, 1625 (inc. Oxford 1625); LL.D. 1630. Ordained deacon at Norwich 1635; priest 1643. m. dau. of Francis Schuldham of Schould-ham, Norfolk, esq.

> NRO, Archdeacon's transcripts, Little Walsingham, 1600–1; will of Philip, pr. 3 **Aug.** 1626, Consistory Court 175 Mittings; Bishop's Reg. REG/16, f. 125; REG/18, f. 27ᵛ. *Al. Cant.* i. 238. *The Visitation of Norfolk*, ii (Harl. Soc. lxxxvi, 1934), 194.

BUDDEN, JOHN, b. 1563, son of John of Canford, Dorset. Matric. Merton College, Oxford, as son of commoner 1582; B.A. Trinity College 1587; M.A. Gloucester Hall 1589; B.C.L. and D.C.L. Magdalen College 1602; proctor 1598. Warrant Doc. Com. 1605 but not fully admitted. Principal of New Inn Hall 1609–18; Principal of Broadgates Hall 1619–20. Deputy of Gentili (q.v.) as Professor of Civil Law 1605–8; Regius Professor 1608–20. Wrote *Vitae Selectorum Aliquot Vivorum* (1681); *Reverendissimi Patris ac Domini Iohannis Mortoni vita obitusque* (1607). Translated Thomas Smith, *Commonwealth of England*; P. Aerodius, *A Discourse for Parents Honour and Authority* (1614). d. 11 June 1620. Inventory: VCC Oxford, 16 June 1620. Goods valued at £110. 9s.

> *DNB* iii. 221–2. Wood, *Athenae*, ii. 56, 347. Clark, *Register*, i. 32, 106, 120, 183, 185, 229, 233, 248, 289–91; ii. 23; iii. 136. LPL, Bancroft Reg. i, f. 129ᵛ. Oxford Univ. Archives, Administrations A–B; Inventories BR–C. J. R. Etherington, 'The Life of Archbishop Juxon, 1582–1663' (Oxford B.Litt. thesis, 1940), p. 17.

BURMAN, JOHN, prob. related to the Burmans of Norwich, freemen of the city. Matric. pens. Corpus Christi College, Cambridge, 1580; B.A. 1584; M.A. 1587; LL.D. Trinity Hall 1596. Warrant Doc. Com. 1600 but not fully admitted. Occasional advocate in HCA. Judge of Vice-Admiralty Court of Norfolk *c*. 1600. Advocate in Consistory Court, Norwich, 1603. Commissary for Archdeaconry of Norwich 1603–20; Official to Archdeacon of Norwich 1604–23. Comr. Piracy Norfolk 1602–4. Delegates 1606. Meets local resistance in Lynn as Judge of Vice-Admiralty Court *c*. 1600. Accused of exacting heavy fines in same capacity. Prosecutes suit for recovery of £3,814. 4s. from executor of Bishop Jegon's will for dilapidation of episcopal lands. Owned lands in Aylsham, Tuttington, Felmingham, and elsewhere in Norf.; in Stradbroke and elsewhere in Suff. d. 21 Sept. 1623. Will: PCC 127 Swann, pr. 9 Dec. 1623. Lands to son John; £500 each to daus. Elizabeth and Dorothy; rest to wife Dorothy, dau. of Anthony Drury of Besthorpe, Norf.

> Al. Cant. i. 259. P. Millican, ed., The Register of the Free Men of Norwich, 1548–1713 (Norwich, 1934), pp. 42, 76, 117, 156, 209. Blomefield, Norfolk, i. 495; iii. 656, 659; v. 211. Registrum Vagum, i. 28. BM, Lansdowne MS. 142, ff. 137–8. Bodl., Tanner MS. 135, f. 145. PRO, C 142/654/63; C 181/1, ff. 35–7, 142. DEL 5/3, f. 121; HCA 24/70, f. 137; 24/72, f. 110; PROB 11/142/127. CUL, MS. Mm. III. 12, p. 167.

BURTON, THOMAS, b. c. 1538 in Beverly, Yorks. Eton College. Adm. scholar King's College, Cambridge, 1553; matric. pens. 1553; fellow 1556–9; B.A. 1558; LL.B. apparently not at Cambridge 1572; LL.D. 1581. Preb. of Carlisle 1574–9. Chancellor of Carlisle diocese 1576–7. Vicar of St. Michael in Appleby, Westmld., 1576–9; Kirk Merrington, Durham, 1583–1606. Rector of Stanhope, Durham, 1577–1608. Chancellor of Durham diocese 1578–82. J.P. Durham 1604. Visits deaneries of Newcastle and Morpeth 1584. Preb. of York 1587–9. Comr. Eccles. Causes York 1599. d. 1608.

> Al. Cant. i. 268. Cooper, Athenae, ii. 496–7. W. Sterry, The Eton College Register 1441–1698 (Eton, 1943), p. 57. Durham Cathedral Library, Hunter MS. 12/5. PRO, C 66/1452ᵛ. BM, Add. MS. 38,139, f. 120. HMCS ix. 396. Hutchinson, Cumberland, ii. 639; W. F. Hutchinson, The History and Antiquities of the County Palatine of Durham (Newcastle, 1787), ii. 255.

BUTTS, JOHN, b. in Norfolk. Perhaps related to William Buttes of Norfolk, yeoman. Matric. pens. Corpus Christi College, Cambridge, 1583; B.A. 1587; M.A 1591; LL.D. Trinity Hall 1598. Warrant Doc. Com. 1599 but not fully adm. Advocate on HCA 1611. Delegates 1605–15. Estate at Chipstead, Surrey; farm at Stretham, Cambs., at value of more than £40 p.a.; leased 'Sutton Court' from Sir Robert Darsey at £30 p.a.; annuity of £12 from lands of T. Johnson of Essex. Will: PCC 102 Rudd, pr. 27 Nov. 1615. Chipstead to be sold; Stretham to be leased. Proceeds to wife; then half to nephews and half at wife's disposal.

> Al. Cant. i. 276. LPL, Whitgift Reg. iii, f. 111. NRO, will of William, Consistory Court 179 Angell. PRO, DEL 5/3, f. 108; 5/4–5, passim; HCA 24/75, f. 244; PROB 11/126/102.

CAESAR (CESAR, ADELMARE), SIR CHARLES, b. 1589, 3rd and 1st surviving son of Sir Julius, D.C.L. (q.v.), by Dorcas, widow of R. Lusher of Middle Temple. Matric. Magdalen College, Oxford, 1602; B.A. All Souls 1606; M.A. 1608; B.C.L. 1608; choice as fellow urged by King 1605; fellow by 1607 until 1611; studied law in Paris; D.C.L. All Souls 1612. Warrant Doc. Com. 1613; full admission 1623; out of commons 1613–22, 1639–41; in commons 1622–38.

Special admission Inner Temple 1610. Master in Chancery 1615. Comr. Piracy London 1619, 1622; Comr. Adm. Middx. etc. 1625. High Com. 1620, 1625, 1626, 1629, 1633. Master of Faculties. Judge of Audience Court. Master of Rolls 1639 at cost of £15,000. M.P. Weymouth and Melcombe Regis, Dorset, 1614 through influence of Thomas Howard, 3rd Viscount Bindon. Tied to 'official group' by relation to his father as well. Inherited bulk of father's estate. Owned 10 manors in Lincs. estate at Bennington, Herts. Invested in commerce. d. 6 Dec. 1642. m. (1) Anne, dau. of Sir Peter Vanlore of London; (2) Jane, dau. of Sir Edward Barkham, Mayor of London.

DNB iii. 654–5. Al. Oxon. i. 229. Clark, Register, i. 95, 116, 187; ii. 255; iii. 254. LPL, Reg. Doc. Com., ff. 47ᵛ, 108ᵛ; Abbot Reg. i, f. 164. ITL, Admissions to Inner Temple, i. 345. Catalogue of All Souls Archives, pp. 307–8, 380. PRO, C 181/2, f. 334–334ᵛ; 181/3, f. 79ᵛ; 193/13/2, f. 32; C 142/774/20; SP 14/1/48; SP 16/80/72; 16/212, ff. 57–8; 16/477/62; HCA 1/32/1, f. 13. Usher, High Commission, p. 347. Philips, Grandeur of the Law, pp. 136–7. Moir, Addled Parliament, p. 188. Rabb, Enterprise, p. 258. CSPD 1638–1639, p. 623; 1641–1643, pp. 535–6.

CAESAR (CESAR, ADELMARE), Sɪʀ Jᴜʟɪᴜs, b. at Tottenham, Middx., 1558, 1st son of Cesare Adelmare, M.D., an Italian immigrant and son of a civilian. Matric. Magdalen Hall, Oxford, 1575; B.A. 1576; M.A. 1578; D.C.L. Paris 1581 (inc. Oxford 1584). Warrant Doc. Com. 1581; full admission 1586; in commons until 1607; out of commons 1608–36. Adm. Inner Temple 1580 as 'late of Clements Inn'; Bencher 1590; Treasurer 1594. Chancellor to Master of Hospital of St. Catherine 1581. Denied office of deputy to Common Serjeant of city of London because of poor knowledge of common law; adm. to freedom of city and made counsellor of civil law causes 1583. Commissary of Arch-deaconry of Essex and Colchester at instance of Bishop Aylmer 1583. Judge HCA 1584–1606 after compounding w. John Herbert at £1,300. Conducts circuit of local port towns to assert authority of HCA. Master in Chancery extraordinary 1584; ordinary 1588. Master of St. Catherine's Hospital 1596. Comr. to hear French piracy appeals 1599. Knighted 1603. Comr. Adm. 1603–25; Comr. Piracy 1581–1622. J.P. Middx., Herts., Lincs., Surrey, Westminster. Negotiates w. France 1602, 1610. High Com. 1601–33. Chancellor of Ex-chequer 1606. Privy Councillor 1607. Reversion to mastership of Rolls 1610; Master of Rolls 1614–36 at income of £1,600–£2,200. Inquires into administra-tion of Poor Law 1631. M.P. Reigate, Surrey, 1589; Bletchingley, Surrey, 1593; New Windsor, Berks., 1597, 1601 through influence of Lord Admiral Howard; Westminster 1607, Middx. 1614, Malden 1621 through court in-fluence. Defeated at Malden 1625. Challenges Commons' right to debate impositions and opposes Great Contract 1610. Challenges Commons' right to refuse messages from King at any time 1610. Ordered to attend all sessions of Parlt. by Privy Council 1621. Seeks larger subsidy 1621. Wrote The Ancient State, Authority and Proceedings of the Court of Requests (London, 1597); 'De Cancellaria' (BM, Lansdowne MS. 132, ff. 216–80); 'Defensio Realis Presentiae

Corporis Christi et Sacrificii ejusdem in Eucharistia', (LPL, MS. 113, ff. 256-8ᵛ); 'Concerning the Private Counsell of the Most High and Mighty King of Great Britaine' (PRO, SP 16/8/77). Held manor of Market Rasen, East Rasen, Lynwode, Legbourne, Lincs.; 'Challers' and 'Chamberlayns' in Herts.; Bennington and Olivers in Herts. Invested in six trading companies. Res.: Doc. Com., Mitcham, Surrey, and London. d. 18 Apr. 1636; bur. St. Helen's Bishopsgate. Will: PCC 34 Pile, pr. 19 Apr. 1636. Lands already assigned to sons Charles, John, Robert. Books to Charles. m. (1) Dorcas, widow of R. Lusher of Middle Temple; (2) Alice, dau. of C. Green of Manchester 1595; (3) Anne, niece of Sir Francis Bacon.

> L. Hill, 'Caesar'. *DNB* iii. 656-9. *Al. Oxon.* i. 229. Clark, *Register*, i. 378; ii. 60; iii. 51. LPL, Reg. Doc. Com. ff. 43ᵛ, 105; Grindal Reg., f. 235. ITL, Admissions to Inner Temple, i. 181. PRO, C 142/560/159; 193/12/1, f. 1; 193/13/1, ff. 46, 62ᵛ; C 181/2, *passim*, HCA 1/32/1, ff. 13–186, *passim*; SP 16/212, ff. 57–8, 119; SP 103/9, f. 22. Usher, *High Commission*, p. 347. *HMCS* vi. 215; xvii. 261. Hatfield House, Salisbury MS. 195/137. Corp. of London Record Office, 'Book of Remembrances 1579–1592', ff. 231, 241–2, 253ᵛ, 254. BM, Lansdowne MS. 55, f. 215; 157, f. 208; Add. MS. 11,406, ff. 150ᵛ, 290; Add. MS. 12,505, f. 270; Add. MS. 34,324, ff. 61, 290; Add. MS. 38,170, ff. 22, 27. Foster, *Proceedings*, ii. 90–1, 96, 142, 143, 150, 308, 397–8. Gardiner, *1610 Debates*, pp. 175–6. *NRS* ii. 22, 88, 99; iii. 470 n. 3. Willson, *Privy Councillors*, pp. 61, 69–72, 81–3, 99. *CJ* i. 430. Trevor-Roper, *Gentry*, p. 40. Rabb, *Enterprise*, p. 258. *VCH Herts.* iii. 75, 131, 193, 250, 274; *Surrey* iv. 229. Andrews, *Elizabethan Privateering*, pp. 22–31. PRO, PROB 11/170/34.

CAREW, Sɪʀ Mᴀᴛᴛʜᴇᴡ, b. 1531, 2nd son of Sir Wymond of Antony, Cornwall, Treasurer of the First Fruits and Tenths, by Martha Denny. Scholar of Trinity College, Cambridge, 1548; B.A. 1551; fellow 1551; LL.D. Louvain. Warrant Doc. Com. 1573; full admission 1573; out of commons 1603–27. Honorific admission Gray's Inn 1589. Archdeacon of Norfolk 1551 as layman on condition he enter orders three years later; took minor orders 1558; refused diaconate and priesthood. Rector of Sheviock, Cornw., 1565. Travelled w. Earl of Arundel to Italy as interpreter. Master in Chancery 1583. Knighted 1603. J.P. Surrey, Hants. 1604. Lost £8,000–£12,000 by fraud in later life. House, fields, and shops in Chancery Lane, London, valued at £1,600. Res. Doc. Com. d. 2 Aug. 1618; bur. St. Dunstan-in-the-West.

> *DNB* iii. 964-5. *Al. Cant.* i. 291. F. Halliday, *Richard Carew of Antony* (London, 1953), pp. 16, 131, 311. LPL, Reg. Doc. Com., ff. 38, 104; Parker Reg. ii, f. 78. Foster, *Gray's Inn*, p. 75. *Visitation of Cornwall* (Harl. Soc. ix, 1874), p. 33 n. 1. Blomefield, *Norfolk*, iii. 644. Jones, *Chancery*, pp. 106–7. PRO, SP 14/86/95; 14/88/9, 135. Chandler, 'Doctors' Commons', 8–9. BM, MS. Add. 38139, ff. 154, 158ᵛ.

CHAWORTH, Rɪᴄʜᴀʀᴅ, b. 1603, 2nd son John of Wiverton, Annesly, and Crophill-Butler, Notts., esq., sheriff and J.P., by Jane, dau. of D. Vincent of Stoke Dabernon, Surrey. Brother of George, 1st Viscount of Armagh. Matric. Christ Church, Oxford, 1621; B.A. 1622; M.A. 1625; proctor 1632; B.C.L. 1634; D.C.L. 1640. Chancellor of London diocese 1637–63. Chancellor of

Chichester diocese 1640. Knighted 1663. Full admission Doc. Com. 1667. M.P. Midhurst, Surrey, through influence of either Viscount Montague or Bishop of Chichester. Recognized as M.P. 6 Jan.–15 Feb. 1641; election voided in favour of William Cawley. Present at debates on Church government. Conveys request of Charles I for loan from Oxford to Vice-Chancellor 1642. Leased manor in Wilts. from Bishop of Salisbury 1646 at £180. d. 1672. m. Sophia, dau. of Robert, Earl of Lindsey.

> Keeler, *Long Parliament*, pp. 131–2. *Al. Oxon.* i. 265. Oxford Univ. Archives, P.P. 2, f. 21. Clark, *Register*, iii. 265. LPL, Doc. Com. Reg., ff. 52ᵛ, 112ᵛ; MS. 958, app. E. *Chichester Chapter Acts*, no. 1293. *Catalogue of All Souls Archives*, p. 316. *Visitations of Nottinghamshire* (Harl. Soc. iv, 1871), p. 128. BM, MS. Add. 6705, f. 29.

CHILD (CHILDE), Sɪʀ Wɪʟʟɪᴀᴍ, 3rd son of William of Northwick, Worcs., esq., by Katherine, dau. of Thomas Coventry of Croome D'Abitot, Worcs., Judge of Common Pleas. B.C.L. Pembroke College, Oxford, 1632; D.C.L. All Souls College 1638. Warrant Doc. Com. before 1640; no record of full admission but listed as member 1639. Comr. Piracy London 1638. Delegates 1638–9. Master in Chancery 1639–59; 1660–73. Knighted 1661. d. May 1678. Established family in Kinlet, Salop, upon marriage to dau. and heir of Rowland Lacon. Father of Sir Lacon William Child, Master in Chancery.

> *Al. Oxon.* i. 272. *The Visitation of Worcestershire* (Harl. Soc., xc, 1938), p. 20. *Le-Neve's Knights*, pp. 139–40. PRO, SP 16/442/125; DEL 8/70, pt. ii, ff. 38, 43–8; C 181/5, f. 131; index 16818, pp. 46–7. Borth. Inst. R. VIII. PR 108.

CHIPPINGDALE (CHIPPENDALE), Jᴏʜɴ, 1st son of George of Craven, Yorks., prob. commoner, by 2nd wife Mary. Fellow of All Souls College, Oxford, 1565; B.C.L. 1570; D.C.L. 1574. Warrant Doc. Com. 1576; full admission 1576; in commons until 1610; out of commons 1610–27. Preb. of Lincoln 1575–1609. Constable and Porter of Leicester Castle 1586. Official of Archdeacon of Leicester 1589–1614. Commissary to Bishop of Lincoln 1589–1601. Commissary of Peculiar of Groby 1591–1622. Grant of Arms 1594. J.P. Leics. 1598–1626. Delegates 1594–1609. M.P. Leicester borough prob. through influence of Earl of Huntingdon 1588. Of Puritan sympathies in 1580s. Purchased manor of Blakenhall, Staffs., for £800 in 1595. Held leases of Worship's Grange, the Bull's House, and Gosling Close in the city of Leicester. Receives farm of two castle mills. Sub-tenant of Newark Grange estate at rent of £50 p.a.; resists attempts of Leicester Corporation to purchase fee farm for fear of losing lease. d. 1627. m. (1) Elizabeth, dau. of G. Harkes of Oxford; (2) Frances Oliver of Houghton. Father of Tobias, John, William, Henry. Inventory of goods, 24 Jan. 1628, valued at £203. 9s. 6d. Res.: Leicester Castle, Doc. Com., Humberstone.

> HPT, typescript. *Al. Oxon.* i. 273. Clark, *Register*, ii. 228; iii. 23. *Visitations of Leicestershire*, p. 157. LPL, Reg. Doc. Com., ff. 42, 104; Grindal Reg., f. 146. Jones *Chancery*, p. 283. PRO, DEL 5/2, ff. 13, 68, 105; 5/3, ff. 33, 80, 116; 5/4, f. 61. E. 179/146/399, f. 5. *Collections for History of Staffordshire*, xvi. 173; n.s. iv. 50. Gleason,

Justices, p. 253. *VCH Leics*. iv. 64, 99, 395. Leics. Record Office, Probate Rec. Inv. 1627/258. J. Nichols, *The History and Antiquities of the County of Leicester* (London, 1795–1815), iii. 278; iv. 632. *Leicester Borough Records 1509- 1603* (Cambridge, 1905), pp. 197, 296–8, 420, 447; *1603–1688* (Cambridge, 1923), pp. 6, 15, 24–5, 27, 42, 44, 103–5.

CLARKE, RICHARD, b. 1572, 2nd son of John of Ardington, Berks., gent. Matric. as son of commoner, New College, Oxford, 1591; B.C.L. 1598; D.C.L. 1619. Warrant Doc. Com. 1618 but not fully adm. Paid dues at Doc. Com. 1622. Surrogate to judge HCA 1621. Comr. Piracy London 1622. Comr. Adm. Middx. etc. 1623; Comr. Pol. & Ass. London 1621. Patrimony: £6 p.a. Res.: St. Benet, Paul's Wharf, London. bur. 28 May 1623. Will: PCC 123 Swann, pr. 13 Nov. 1623. Divides goods, books, and chattels between two daus.

> *Visitations of Berkshire*, i. 81. Clark, *Register*, i. 188; ii. 187; iii. 212. LPL, Abbot Reg. ii, f. 177. PRO, C 181/3, ff. 28, 79ᵛ; HCA 1/32/1, f. 21; HCA 24/79, f. 84; PROB 11/93/54; PROB 11/142/123. *The Register of St. Bene't and St. Peter Paul's Wharf, IV* (Harl. Soc. Registers, xli, 1912), p. 5.

CLERKE (CLERK, CLARKE, CLARK), WILLIAM. Origins unknown. Scholar of Trinty Hall, Cambridge, 1605; fellow 1609–34; LL.B. 1610; LL.D. 1629. Appointed joint commissary of the Exchequer and Prerogative Court in York 1624 but never assumed post. Full admission Doc. Com. 1629; in commons until 1642. Comr. Piracy London 1633, 1635, 1638; Hants 1635, 1636. Active as advocate in London courts 1635–40. Official of Archdeacon of London by 1639. Joins other ecclesiastical judges residing at Doc. Com. in legal opinion *c*. 1636. Joint Comr. Admiralty 1647–53; joint Comr. PCC during Common-wealth period. Judge in case of Don Pantaleon Sa 1653. Wrote *An Epitome of Certaine Late Aspersions Cast at Civilians* (Dublin, 1631). d. Aug. 1655. Res.: Doc. Com. and perhaps St. Martin Ludgate's, London, in 1638.

> *DNB* iv. 500. *Al. Cant*. i. 348. LPL, Reg. Doc. Com., ff. 49ᵛ, 109. PRO, C 181/4, f. 139; 181/5, ff. 24, 27, 58ᵛ, 130ᵛ; DEL 8/70, pt. ii, ff. 27ᵛ–32; HCA 24/91, nos. 272, 278; SP 16/421/108; SP 16/339/63; *CSPD 1635*, p. 182. W. Hale, *A Series of Precedents and Proceedings* . . . (London, 1847), pp. 262–4. Marchant, *Church Under Law*, p. 48. Haydn, *Book of Dignities*, pp. 421–3.

COLMORE, CLEMENT, b. 1550, 2nd son of William of Birmingham, War-wicks., gent., by Joan, dau. of Henry Hunt of Tamworth, Warwicks. Student at Brasenose College, Oxford, 1565; fellow as founder's kin 1569–80; B.A. 1570; junior bursar 1575–8; M.A. 1573; B.C.L. 1580; D.C.L. 1582. Warrant Doc. Com. 1590 but not fully adm. Chancellor of Durham diocese 1582–1619. Preb. of Lichfield 1588; Durham 1590. Cleric. Rector of Brancepeth, Durham, 1584; Gateshead, Durham, 1588; Middleton, Durham, 1599. Comr. to meet Scots at border 1596. J.P. Durham 1604–18. Comr. Adm. Durham and Northumb. 1604, 1610. Wrote unpublished refutation of Bellarmine and answer to 'the Catholic divine'. Owned mess. and 230 acres land at Willington, Durham; mess. (valued at £400), ten., and land in Pinchingthorpe, Morton and Ingleby, Yorks. Other lands and pastures in Yorks. Moitie of tithes of Bedlington, Northumb. d. 18 June 1619. Will: Borth. Inst., pr. 1 Sept. 1619. Lands divided among sons Richard, Clement, and Matthew. Common law books to son-in-law. Manuscripts and notes to sons Matthew and Richard.

J. Foster, *Pedigrees of Durham* (London, 1887), p. 79. *VCH Warwicks.* vii. 83; *Yorkshire North Riding*, ii. 357. *Brasenose College Register 1509–1909*, i. 36. Clark, *Register*, i. 41; ii. 26 n., 79; iii. 31. *Al. Oxon.* i. 311. LPL, Whitgift Reg. i, f. 169ᵛ. Durham Cathedral Library, Hunter MS. 13, f. 17; MS. 11/12; MS. 22, f. 328ᵛ; Dean and Chapter Treasurer's Book 1609–10, f. 3. Hutchinson, *Durham*, ii. 255. BM, Add. MS. 38,139, f. 120. Bodl., Tanner MS. 75, f. 349. PRO, C 181/2, ff. 42ᵛ, 62, 314ᵛ; C 142/393/159; HCA 1/32/1, ff. 54, 80; WARDS 7/60/210. Borth. Inst., Wills 35/435.

COOKE (COOK), James, b. 1572 in Chale, Isle of Wight. Winchester College. Matric. as son of commoner at New College, Oxford, 1591; fellow 1593–1610; B.C.L. 1597; D.C.L. 1608. A cleric. Rector of Houghton, Hants, 1609–10. Chaplain of Bishop Bilson of Winchester. Wrote *Juridica Trium Quaestionum ad Majestatem pertinentium determinatio . . .* (Oxford, 1608); *Poemata Varia.* d. 2 Oct. 1610.

Wood, *Athenae*, ii. 95–6. Clark, *Register*, i. 185; ii. 183; iii. 207. *Al. Oxon.* i. 320. Kirby, *Winchester Scholars*, p. 152. Bodl., MS. Top. Oxon. e. 105/2, ff. 80ᵛ–81. Winchester Cathedral Library, Index of Hants Clergy, f. 105.

CORBETT (CORBET, CORBITT), Clement, 4th son of Sir Miles of Sprowston, Norf., Kt. and High Sheriff of Norf. 1591 by Catherine, dau. of Sir Christopher Heydon. Uncle of Miles Corbett, the regicide. Matric. pens. Trinity Hall, Cambridge, 1592; fellow 1592; LL.B. 1598; LL.D. 1605. Master of Trinity Hall 1611–26. Vice-Chancellor of Cambridge. Warrant Doc. Com. 1606; full admission 1612; in commons 1612–18, 1621–41; out of commons 1619–20. Professor of Law at Gresham College 1607–13. Chancellor of Chichester diocese 1614. J.P. Norf. 1622–35; Sussex 1626. Registrar of Audience and Consistory Courts at Norwich 1624. Comr. Piracy Norf. 1624. Judge of Admiralty Court of Norf. 1629. Comr. Adm. Norf., Cambs., and Ely 1628. Chancellor of Norwich diocese 1625–52. Master in Chancery extraordinary 1629. Sought uniform and orthodox Church; opposed Puritan lecturing. Petitions *v.* him submitted to Long Parlt. 1641. Arrested in Suffolk 1643. Held Saham-Tony's manor, Norf., during life of wife Elizabeth 1616–34; manor at Belaugh, Norf. Leased house in precincts of Norwich Cathedral. Res.: Norwich, London. d. 8 May 1652. Will: PCC 217 Bowyer, pr. 1652. £200 to each of four daus.; rest to son Samuel. m. Elizabeth Kempe.

DNB iv. 1123–4. Ward, *Gresham Professors*, pp. 26, 238–9. *Al. Cant.* i. 396. LPL. Reg. Doc. Com., ff. 47, 107ᵛ; Bancroft Reg., f. 139ᵛ. Peckham, *Chichester Acts*, nos. 1110, 1112. *CSPD 1603–1610*, p. 592; *1641–1643*, pp. 3–4. *APC 1621–1623*, p. 42. PRO, C 193/12/2, ff. 41ᵛ, 59ᵛ; C 193/13/1, f. 73; C 181/3, f. 115ᵛ; HCA 1/32/1, f. 4; C 216/1, f. 103; SP 16/212, p. 124. J. Williams and B. Cozens-Hardy (ed.), *Extracts from the Earliest Minute Books of the Dean and Chapter of Norwich Cathedral 1566–1649* (Norfolk Record Society, xxiv, 1953), pp. 16, 53, 60–81. Bodl., Tanner MS. 68, ff. 1–11, 39. Blomefield, *Norfolk*, ii. 329; viii. 188. Ketton-Cremer, *Norfolk*, pp. 46, 63, 70–1, 80–1, 182. Notestein, *D'Ewes*, p. 414. A. Corbet, *The Family of Corbet* (London, 1915), ii. 261.

COVERT (COBERT), FRANCIS, b. in England but studied at Leyden and took LL.D. there; inc. Oxford 1596. Warrant Doc. Com. 1599 but not fully admitted. d. at Chaldon, Surrey, 1609.

Clark, *Register*, i. 377. Wood, *Fasti*, i. 273. LPL, Whitgift Reg. iii, f. 111.

COWELL, JOHN, b. 1554 at Swymbridge, Devon. Younger brother of William Cowle of Landkey, Devon, commoner. Eton College. Matric. pens. King's College, Cambridge, 1570; fellow 1573–95; B.A. 1575; M.A. 1578; proctor 1585–6; LL.D. 1588. Persuaded by Richard Bancroft to become a civilian. Regius Professor of Civil Law at Cambridge 1594–1611. Master of Trinity Hall 1598–1611. Warrant Doc. Com. 1589; full admission 1590. Official to Archdeacon of Colchester 1602–9. Comr. Pol. & Ass. 1603, 1605; Comr. Piracy London 1606, 1609; Comr. Adm. Middx., etc., 1610. J.P. City of Cambridge 1606–10. Investigates non-conformity at Cambridge Univ. 1603. High Com. 1605–11. Vicar-General of Archbishop of Canterbury 1608–11. Wrote *Institutiones Juris Anglicani* (1605); *The Interpreter* (1607). Held manor and lands in Parracombe and Combe Martin, Devon; land in Landkey, Devon; house in Cambridge. Res.: Cambridge and London. d. 11 Oct. 1611. Will: PCC 86 Wood, pr. 22 Nov. 1611. Manor to nephew John Allen; land in Landkey to brother Simon; house to Trinity Hall to support logic lecture. Books in civil and canon law to Trinity College Library. £30 toward discharge of debt of friend Dr. Mountlowe (q.v.).

DNB iv. 1300. *Eton Register*, p. 88. LPL, Reg. Doc. Com., ff. 44, 105ᵛ; Whitgift Reg. 1, f. 154; Bancroft Reg., ff. 160ᵛ–161. PRO, C 181/1, ff. 127, 213; C 181/2, ff. 10ᵛ, 14, 68, 101ᵛ; HCA 1/32/1, f. 55. Usher, *High Commission*, p. 348; *Reconstruction*, ii. 211. Cooper, *Annals*, ii. 7–8. Chrimes, 'Cowell'. Simon, 'Dr. Cowell'. *CJ* i. 399. *LJ* iii. 818–20. Foster, *Proceedings*, ii. 33, 38–9, 49–50. Winwood, *Memorials*, iii. 125–31. ERO, D/ACA 27–33, *passim*. Quintrell, 'Government of Essex', pp. 148–9. *NRS* vi. 243. *CSPD 1603–1610*, p. 605; *1638–1639*, p. 55. PROB 11/118/86. Exeter City Library, Abstract of will of William Carole (Cowle).

COXE, WILLIAM. Origins obscure. From Beds. Matric. sizar Queens' College, Cambridge, 1601; B.A. 1605; M.A. 1608; fellow 1610–43; taxor 1619; LL.D. 1636.

Al. Cant. i. 409. *Walker Revised*, p. 39.

CRADDOCK, JOHN, b. 1573. From Romsey, Hants. Perhaps son of Nicholas of Romsey. Winchester College. Matric. New College, Oxford, as son of commoner 1591; B.C.L. 1599; fellow 1593–1600; D.C.L. 1617. Warrant Doc. Com. 1619 but not fully admitted. A cleric. Rector of Bradford Peverell, Dorset, 1602–6; Warnford, Hants, 1607–25; Birdham, Sussex, 1616 (presented by Ld. Chancellor Ellesmere). Preb. of Chichester 1610; canon residentiary 1615. Held three mess. in Romsey, Hants. d. 27 Nov. 1625. Father of Thomas.

Al. Oxon. i. 344. Clark, *Register,* i. 188; ii. 182; iii. 218. LPL, Abbot Reg. i, f. 180ᵛ. Peckham, *Chichester Chapter Acts,* nos. 1066, 1083, 1103–4, 1111, 1123, 1162, 1168, 1176, 1189. HRO, will of Matilda Craddock of Romsey, pr. 25 Jan. 1576, Consistory Court. Winchester Cathedral Library, Index of Hants Clergy, ff. 112ᵛ-113. Kirby, *Winchester Scholars,* p. 151.

CREAKE (CREKE), Thomas, b. 1535, 2nd son of Thomas of Kirtling, Cambs., esq., by Alice, dau. of Richard Dearsely of Kirtling. Matric. sizar Trinity Hall, Cambridge, 1553; LL.B. 1563; LL.D. 1573; fellow 1559–77. Warrant Doc. Com. 1573; full admission 1573; out of commons 1603–16. Delegates 1595–1610. Comdr. Adm. Middx., etc. 1603, 1606. Comr. Piracy London 1603, 1606. Active as advocate in London courts 1603–7. Commissary of the Archdeacon of London. Defends Archbishop of Canterbury against Corpus Christi College 1603. Owned houses in London; houses and lands in Fulham and Chelsea, Middx. Leased parsonage of Rushden, Herts. Res.: Doc. Com. and St. Gregory's parish, London. d. 21 June 1616. Will: PCC 29 Weldon, pr. 17 Apr. 1617. Houses and lands to sons Thomas and William and to brother William; £500 to dau. Ann; common law books to son Thomas; canon law books to brother William. m. Elizabeth, dau. of John Jennings of London.

Al. Cant. i. 416. *Visitation of Cambridge,* p. 57. LPL, Reg. Doc. Com., ff. 41ᵛ, 104; Parker Reg. ii, f. 77ᵛ; MS. 1729, f. 109. *HMCS* xv. 150. PRO, DEL 5/2–4, *passim;* HCA 1/32/1, ff. 61, 90; HCA 24/70–2, *passim;* C 181/1, ff. 122–3; C 181/2, f. 10ᵛ; C 142/660/54; E 179/146/399, f. 5; PROB 11/129/29.

CROMPTON, Sir Thomas, b. 1558, 2nd son of William, citizen and mercer of London. Matric. as son of commoner St. Alban's Hall, Oxford, 1567; B.A. 1579; M.A. 1582; grace for D.C.L. refused because of suspected 'backwardness in religion' 1584; B.C.L. and D.C.L. 1589. Adm. advocate at York 1588. Warrant Doc. Com. 1590; full admission 1605. Honorific admission Lincoln's Inn 1606. Accompanies Cecil to France 1598. Advocate-General for foreign causes 1603; for ecclesiastical causes 1603. Knighted 1603. Attends Hampton Court Conference 1604. Judge HCA 1605–9. Comr. Adm. Middx., etc., 1603, 1606; Dorset 1604; Devon 1609. Comr. Piracy London 1603, 1606; Dorset 1601, 1603, 1605; Devon 1606; Cornwall 1607. J.P. Middx., Staffs. 1609. Chancellor of diocese of London 1605–9. Vicar-General of Archbishop of Canterbury w. Sir Edward Stanhope (q.v.) 1605–9. Master in Chancery 1608. M.P. Shaftesbury, Dorset, by patronage of Earl of Pembroke; Boroughbridge, Yorks., 1597 through Cecil; Whitchurch, Hants, 1601 through episcopacy; Oxford Univ. 1604–9. Defends pluralities 1601. Defends commissaries' courts and narrowly avoids parliamentary censure. Wrote '6 Arguments of Kings Right to Tax Trade' (BM, Cotton MS. Titus F IV, ff. 242–3); 'Notes About the Excommunication of Princes' (ITL, Petyt MS. 538/38, ff. 47–8); 'Certain Necessary Considerations concerning the Ecclesiastical Courts' (BM, Cotton

MS. Cleo. F II, f. 427. Lease of Cresswell, Staffs., which yielded £90 p.a. Estate at Milwich, Staffs. Grant of arms 1595. Had farm of the manor of Newcastle under Lyme 1601-9. Invested in commerce. Will: PCC 28 Dorset, pr. 1 Mar. 1609. Lands to sons John, Richard, and Thomas after death of wife; 1,000 marks for marriage of 1st dau.; 500 marks for marriage of Margaret; £200 to dau. Barbara.

HPT, typescript. Clark, *Register*, i. 35, 38, 45, 116, 120, 157, 181; ii. 78; iii. 78. LPL, Reg. Doc. Com. f. 46; Whitgift Reg. i, f. 161; Bancroft Reg., ff. 126ᵛ, 151ᵛ. *Lincoln's Inn Admissions*, p. 143. BM, Lansdowne MS. 145, ff. 59-60. Bodl., Tanner MS. 427, *passim*. PRO, C 181/1, ff. 98, 114, 122, 217; C 181/2, ff. 10, 23ᵛ, 50, 54, 217; HCA 1/32/1, ff. 59, 61, 66, 90; PROB 11/50/7; 11/113/28. Rex, *University Representation*, pp. 41-3. Barlow, *Sum and Substance*, p. 85. Neale, *Parliaments, 1584-1601*, pp. 406-7. *CJ* i. 172-3, 277, 296, 326, 329. Willson, *Privy Councillors*, p. 107. *HMCS* vii. 477; viii. 16; xii. 492; xvi. 244-5; xviii. 167. Marchant, *Church Under Law*, p. 249. *Visitations of Staffordshire*, p. 104. *VCH Staffs*. viii. 184. Gleason, *Justices*, pp. 254, 257. Rabb, *Enterprise*, p. 274.

DALE, GEORGE, b. 1561. 2nd son of Henry of Yeovilton and Limington, Som., perhaps lesser gent. Matric. as son of commoner Balliol College, Oxford, 1575; B.A. 1577; Fellow of Oriel 1578-88; Dean 1587-8; M.A. 1581; B.C.L. and D.C.L. 1590. Principal of St. Mary's Hall 1587-91. Warrant Doc. Com. 1592; full admission 1595; in commons until 1612; out of commons 1612-18. Judge of VCC Oxford 1594. d. 25 Nov. 1625; bur. at Fifield, Berks., where he lived for many years. m. Mary, dau. of William Leech 1590.

Provosts and Fellows of Oriel, p. 78. *Al. Oxon*. i. 367. Clark, *Register*, i. 116; ii. 65, 158; iii. 60. LPL, Reg. Doc. Com., ff. 44ᵛ, 106; Whitgift Reg. i, f. 191. BM, Lansdowne MS. 984, f. 41. Oxford Univ. Archives, Register of the Vice-Chancellor's Court 1594-1596. Collinson, *Somerset*, iii. 219.

DARRELL (DORRELL), NICHOLAS, b. 1582, 5th son of John of Calehill, Kent, esq., by Anna, dau. of R. Horne, Bishop of Winchester. Winchester College. Matric. as son of gent. New College, Oxford, 1603; fellow 1602-14; B.C.L. 1609; D.C.L. 1615. A cleric. Rector of Ham, Wilts., 1614; Baughurst, Hants, 1614-15; Chilcombe, Hants, 1616-29; East Woodhay, Hants, 1618-29. Preb. of Winchester 1615-29. Chaplain to Bishop Montague of Winchester. Surrogate in Winchester Consistory Court 1627. Trustee of impropriate rectory of Kingsclere, Hants. Will: PCC 101 Ridley, pr. 19 Nov. 1629. Goods, plate, and lands in Kent to pay debts and legacies; £600 to dau. Anne; £500 apiece to daus. Jane and Judith; rectory to son Nicholas, whom he supports at university and Inns of Court. m. (1) Elizabeth, dau. of A. Gifford of Devon; (2) Jane, dau. of E. Boyse of Betteshanger, Kent; (3) Agnes, dau. of T. Cesor.

Visitation of Kent (Harl. Soc. xlii, 1898), p. 187. Clark, *Register*, i. 186-8; ii. 267; iii. 291. *Al. Oxon*. i. 373. Kirby, *Winchester Scholars*, p. 157. Bodl., MS. Top. Oxon. e. 105/2, f. 88. PRO, PROB 11/156/101. HRO, Consistory Court Books 103-5, *passim*. Kent Archives Office, Darrell Papers, U 386, F1; will of John Darrell. Winchester Cathedral Library, Index of Hants Clergy, f. 123; Chapter Book 1622-45, f. 23.

DAYE (DEYE), JOHN. Origins unknown. Matric. pens. Jesus College, Cambridge, 1559; B.A. 1563; fellow 1564–75; M.A. 1566; taxor 1568; LL.D. 1576. Not to be confused w. John Daye, D.C.L. 1579. Warrant Doc. Com. 1579; full admission 1582; in commons until 1612. Commissary for Archdeaconry of Sudbury 1576. Conflicts with Puritans of Bury St. Edmunds 1581. Proctor for clergy of Sudbury in Convocation 1586 despite protests of Puritans. Rector of Gedney, Lincs., 1588. J.P. Ely c. 1604. Copyhold lands in Thetford, Ely. Leased houses and chambers in Barnard's Inn. Will: PCC 74 Fenner, pr. 1612. Lands to wife Alice and then to son Robert. Leases to sons Valentine and Nathaniel.

> Cooper, *Athenae*, ii. 383. LPL, Grindal Reg., f. 190; Reg. Doc. Com., ff. 43, 104ᵛ. *Al. Cant.* ii. 23. BM, Add. MS. 38,139, f. 126ᵛ. PRO, C 181/2, f. 8; E 179/146/399, f. 5; PROB 11/120/74. Gleason, *Justices*, p. 250.

DILLON, WILLIAM, b. 1598, prob. younger brother of John of Culworth, Kt. If so, son of Anthony of Culworth, Northants., gent., by Temperance, dau. of John Danvers of Culworth. Related to H. Barker (q.v.). Matric. New College, Oxford, 1618; fellow 1617–29; B.C.L. 1624; D.C.L. 1630. Chaplain of Baptist Hicks, Viscount Campden. Vicar of Steventon, Berks., 1628–30 by patronage of Bishop Williams of Lincoln. Rector of Easington, Oxon., 1628–30; Farthingstone, Northants., 1630–43; Shenely, Bucks., by presentation of Earl of Shrewsbury. Claims tithes of Tattenhoe, Bucks., c. 1634. Presents 36 articles *v.* Bishop Williams for revealing counsels of state relating to Spanish match and for charging King with injustice and oppression. Claims Williams extorted money from him. Sequestered from Farthingstone 1643; Shenley 1644. d. in gaol.

> *Al. Oxon.* i. 405. Clark, *Register*, ii. 367; iii. 436. Bodl., MS. Top. Oxon. e. 105/2, f. 98; MS. Oxford Diocs. Papers e. 12, p. 58. Rymer, *Foedera*, xix. 56. PRO, Institution Books, ser. A.v. 83 (Berks.); SP 16/375/91–2. W. D. Macray, *Register of the Members of St. Mary Magdalen College*, n.s. iii, 159. G. Lipscomb, *History and Antiquities of Buckinghamshire* (London, 1847), iv. 283, 329. *Walker Revised*, p. 278. CPCC i. 98. Metcalfe, *Visitations of Northamptonshire*, p. 177.

DORISLAUS, ISAAC, b. 1595 in Alkmaar, Holland, 2nd son of Isaac, minister in Hensfrock. LL.D. Leyden; inc. Cambridge 1631. Listed among members of Doc. Com. 1639; full admission 1645. Greville lecturer in History at Cambridge 1627; resigned 1628. Allowed by King to examine state papers for historical writing. Occasional advocate in HCA 1637–8. Judge-Advocate in Bishop's War and in Parliamentary army of Essex. Co-judge of HCA 1648. Prepares charge of treason *v.* Charles I. Envoy at The Hague 1649. Assassinated by Royalists there 12 May 1649. Res.: Doc. Com. after 1648. Administration PCC 25 May 1649.

> *DNB* v. 1147–9. *Al. Cant.* ii. 56. LPL, Reg. Doc. Com., f. 50ᵛ. CUL, MS. Mm. I. 47 (Baker 36), pp. 136–52. Cooper, *Annals*, iii. 201–2, 209. PRO, HCA 24/92, ff. 64, 66; HCA 24/95, f. 63. Green, *Religion*, p. 131. Hill, *Intellectual Origins*, pp. 58–9, 176; *Puritanism and Revolution*, p. 64. BM, Add. MS. 29,960, f. 10. Borth. Inst., R. VII. PR 108. Malden, *Trinity Hall*, p. 148. Grotius, *Briefwisseling*, iv. 325. C. V. Wedgwood, *A Coffin for King Charles* (London, 1964), pp. 116, 128, 156. *Acts of Interregnum*, ii. 575. Haydn, *Dignities*, p. 423. *CSPD 1631–1633*, p. 394; *1649–1650*, pp. 143, 181, 313.

DOWNING, CALIBUTE, b. 1606, 1st son of Calibute of Shenington, Glos. (now in Oxon.), gent. (d. 1644) by Anne, dau. of E. Hoogan of Hackney, Middx. Matric. pens. Emmanuel College, Cambridge, 1623; adm. commoner of Oriel College, Oxford, 1626; B.A. 1626 (inc. Cambridge 1629); M.A. Peterhouse, Cambridge, 1630; LL.D. 1637. A cleric. Curate at Quainton, Bucks., 1627. Rector of Hickford, Bucks., 1632; W. Ildesley, Berks., 1632. Vicar of Hackney through patronage of Lady Mary Vere 1637–43. Chaplain of William, Earl of Salisbury 1632 and later sought to be chaplain of Earl of Strafford. Justifies episcopacy and defends profession of civilians in *A Discourse of the State Ecclesiasticall of this Kingdom in Relation to the Civill* (1633). Changes political and religious views between 1633 and 1640. Defends right of resistance in *A Sermon Preached to the Renowned Company of the Artillery* (1640). Circulates petition *v.* Laudian canons 1640. Chaplain in Essex army 1643. Licenser of books on divinity 1643. Member of Westminster Assembly 1643; left within the year and sided w. Independents. Full list of publications in Wood, *Athenae*, iii. 107–8. d. before Oct. 1644. m. Margaret, dau. of R. Brett, D.D., 1627. Father of Calibute, George, Elizabeth, and Anne.

> *DNB* v. 1303. Wood, *Athenae*, iii. 107–8. *Registrum Orielense*, i. 188. *Al. Cant.* ii.62. Pearl, *London and the Puritan Revolution*, pp. 41–2, 168, 174, 195, 215 n. M. Walzer, *The Revolution of the Saints* (Cambridge, Mass., 1965), pp. 175–6. *VCH Oxon.* ix. 142.

DRURY, JOHN, son of Humphrey of Salop. No relation to William Drury, LL.D. (d. 1575). Student at Exeter College, Oxford, 1572; B.C.L. Lincoln College 1578; D.C.L. 1585. Full admission Doc. Com. 1586; in commons until 1614. Preb. of Chichester 1582. Rector of Pulborough, Sussex, 1589; Witney, Oxon., 1592. Archdeacon of Oxford 1592. High Com. 1601–14. Investigates non-conformity in Sussex at request of Privy Council 1603. Attends Hampton Court Conference 1604. Chancellor of Chichester diocese 1607–14. J.P. Sussex 1609. Purchased house in Chichester at end of life. Res.: Chichester Cathedral Close. d. 9 June 1614. Will: PCC 65 Lawe, pr. 9 June 1614. Legacies exceed £4,200. m. Alice. Father of Henry, Thomas, Francis, William, Jane, and Mary.

> *Al. Oxon.* i. 426. Clark, *Register*, i. 157; ii. 33; iii. 62–3. LPL, Reg. Doc. Com., f. 43ᵛ. *Chichester Chapter Acts*, nos. 842, 1034, 1058, 1071. Usher, *High Commission*, p. 349. Barlow, *Sum and Substance*, p. 85. Babbage, *Puritanism*, pp. 191–3. *HMCS* xv. 262–3. Gleason, *Justices*, p. 259. PRO, PROB 11/123/65; C 181/2, f. 134ᵛ.

DUCK, SIR ARTHUR, b. 1580. 2nd son of Richard of Heavitree, Devon, lesser gent. (d. 1603), by Joan. Matric. as son of commoner Exeter College, Oxford, 1595; B.A. 1599; M.A. Hart Hall 1602; Fellow of All Souls 1604; B.C.L. 1607; Bursar 1608; Sub-Warden 1610; D.C.L. 1612. Warrant Doc. Com. 1614; full admission 1614; in commons until 1642. Mission to Scotland *c.* 1617. Chancellor of Bath and Wells diocese 1616–23. Comr. Pol. & Assur. 1615; Comr. Adm.

Middx., etc., 1623; Dorset 1622. Comr. Piracy London 1622–38. Delegates 1625–36. Master in Chancery extraordinary 1617; ordinary 1645–50. Appointed Chancellor of York w. E. Mainwaring but never assumed duties 1624. King's Advocate in Court of Chivalry 1623–40. Chancellor of London diocese 1627–37. High Com. 1633–41. Master of Requests *c.* 1625. M.P. Minehead, Som. 1624, 1640 (Apr.). Objects to bill *v.* wrongful imprisonment for fear of restraining power of Lord Marshal, Lord Admiral, and High Commissioners 1624. Objects to bill *v.* swearing on grounds it would prejudice the spiritual courts 1624. Defends power of High Com. before Parlt. 1641. Petitions *v.* him submitted to Long Parlt. Sent for as delinquent by Parlt. 1642. Donates £6,000 to cause of Charles I. Compounds for estate at a tenth: £2,000. Negotiates for King on Isle of Wight 1648. Owned lands in N. and S. Cadbury, Som. Patron of South Cadbury rectory 1639. Lease of mess. and house in Wells; sub-lease of manor in Chiswick, Middx. Invested in commerce. d. 12 Dec. 1648. Will: PCC 103 Fairfax, pr. 1 June 1649. Land to wife and daus. Mary and Martha; £600 to relatives and friends. m. Margaret, dau. of Henry Southworth of London and Wells. Wrote *De Usu et Authoritate Juris Civilis* (London, 1653) w. assistance of G. Langbaine; *Vita H. Chichele Archepiscopi Cantuarensis sub Regibus Henric V et VI* (1617).

> Vivian, *Visitations of Devon*, p. 309. *DNB* vii. 87–8. *Al. Oxon.* i. 427. LPL, Reg. Doc. Com., ff. 47ᵛ, 78; Abbot Reg. i, f. 162. *HMC Dean of Wells* ii. 370, 391. *APC 1616–1617*, p. 269. *CSPD 1611–1618*, p. 496; *1623–1625*, p. 145; *1628–1629*, p. 554. PRO, C 181/2, f. 235; 181/3, f. 79ᵛ; 181/4, ff. 37, 138ᵛ; 181/5, ff. 26ᵛ, 130ᵛ; HCA 1/32/1, ff. 21–3; HCA 24/88–101, *passim.* Usher, *High Commission*, p. 349. Marchant, *Church Under Law*, p. 48. PRO, SP 14/154/74; SP 14/166, ff. 25, 227ᵛ; DEL 8/70, *passim*; Institution Books, ser. A. ii. 8 (Som.); PROB 11/208/103. Squibb, *Chivalry*, pp. 48–9, 53, 132, 234. BM, Harl. MS. 1601, f. 10. *CJ* i. 680, 738; ii. 697, 701, 845. Notestein, *D'Ewes*, pp. 173, 435–6, 476. *CPCC* ii. 1496. Leadam, *Select Cases*, pp. cvii, cxxiv, n. Rabb, *Enterprise*, p. 287. *Catalogue of All Souls Archives*, pp. 309–10.

DUN (DUNNE, DONNE, DONES), Sɪʀ Dᴀɴɪᴇʟ, 1st son of John of Reading, Berks. Family originally from Radnorshire. B.C.L. All Souls College, Oxford, 1572; fellow; D.C.L. 1580. Principal of New Inn Hall 1580. Warrant Doc. Com. 1580; full admission 1582; in commons until 1612; out of commons 1612–17. Honorific admission Gray's Inn 1599. Official of Archdeacon of Essex 1585–6. Judge of Audience Court 1598. Chancellor of Rochester diocese 1598–1604. Dean of Arches 1598–1617. Master of Requests 1598–1615. M.P. Taunton, Som., 1601 as episcopal nominee; Oxford Univ. 1604, 1614. Judge of HCA 1609–17. Knighted 1603. Defends King's right to remand prisoners 1607. J.P. Essex 1601, 1609. Comr. to adjust union w. Scotland 1604. High Com. 1601–13. Comr. Piracy and Adm. 1603–14. Comr. Pol. & Ass. 1609–11. Master in Chancery extraordinary. Defends procedures of ecclesiastical courts at Hampton Court Conference. Comr. to censor foreign and popish books 1604. Expert on marriage law. Held manor of Garmish at Theydon Garnon, Essex; mess. on Aldersgate St., London. Grant of Arms 1606. Invested in Virginia Co. and in three other companies. d. 27 Sept. 1617, 'no rich man for all he had three offices'. m. dau. of William Awbrey, D.C.L. (d. 1595).

BM, Harl. MS. 6831, f. 341ᵛ. HPT, typescript. *DNB* v. 1127–8. LPL, Reg. Doc. Com., ff. 42ᵛ, 104ᵛ; Grindal Reg., f. 208; Whitgift Reg. iii, f. 118; MS. 2004, f. 65. Kent Archives Office, Rochester Episcopal Reg. DRc R8, ff. 187ᵛ, 188ᵛ. PRO, DEL 5/2–5, *passim*; C 181/2, *passim*; HCA 1/32/1, *passim*; C 142/371/123; SP 14/93, ff. 124, 129, SP 16/208, pp. 580–604; E 179/146/399, f. 5. BM, Add. MS. 38,139, f. 128; Add. MS. 38,170, f. 358. Barlow, *Sum and Substance*, p. 85. Usher, *High Commission*, p. 349. Wilbraham, *Diary*, pp. 50–1. Parr, *Usher*, p. 65. Haydn, *Dignities*, pp. 420, 423. Rabb, *Enterprise*, p. 284. *VCH Essex* iv. 261, 264, 265, 271. Foster, *Gray's Inn*, p. 97. Rex, *University Representation*, pp. 41, 43, 46, 47, 53. Bowyer, *Diary*, pp. 305–6. Anglin, 'Archdeacon of Essex', p. 36.

EASDALL, WILLIAM. Birth and parentage unknown. LL.B. Trinity Hall, Cambridge, 1614; LL.D. 1620. Warrant Doc. Com. 1623; not fully admitted, but paid dues in 1624 and 1625; listed among members in 1639. Commissary of Exchequer and Prerogative Court of Archbishop of York 1624–32. Chancellor of Durham 1627–32. Chancellor of York w. M. Dodsworth 1624–7; w. E. Mainwaring 1627–37; w. G. Riddell 1637–40. Comr. Gaol delivery Durham 1629. Comr. Eccles. Causes York 1625, 1627. J.P. Yorks. 1629–32. Revives Church courts of northern province and becomes chief executive of Laudian administration there. Administration of goods 2 Feb. 1644.

Al. Cant. ii. 81. LPL, Abbot Reg. ii, f. 204. C 181/4, ff. 6, 7ᵛ–9, 125; C 66/2348ᵛ. Marchant, *Church Under Law*, pp. 43, 48–9, 77, 232–4. Tyler, 'Ecclesiastical Commission', pp. 112, 122. Hutchinson, *Durham*, ii. 255. Borth. Inst., R. VII PR. 108; Administrations, f. 260.

EDEN, SIR THOMAS, 2nd son of Richard of Hanningfield, Essex, gent., by Margaret, dau. of Christopher Peyton of Bury St. Edmunds. Younger brother of Philip of Lincoln's Inn. Matric. Trinity Hall, Cambridge, 1596; fellow 1599; LL.B. 1600; LL.D. 1614. Master of Trinity Hall 1626–43. Professor of Civil Law at Gresham College 1613–40. Warrant Doc. Com. 1614; full admission 1615; in commons until 1642. Commissary for archdeaconry of Sudbury 1621. Official to Archdeacon of Sudbury 1621. J.P. Suffolk *c.* 1609; Ely 1626; City of Cambridge 1615–24. Delegates 1619–21. Master in Chancery 1625–40. Active as advocate in London courts 1626–39. Chancellor of Ely diocese 1630. High Com. 1633. M.P. Cambridge Univ. 1626, 1628, 1640. Defends subscription to Book of Common Prayer for university graduates 1628. Defends marriage licences 1628. Opposes and then supports Laud's projected regulation of Cambridge 1635. Defends Canons of 1640. Petition and articles of impeachment brought *v.* him 1641. Gains confidence of Parliament and takes Covenant 1643. Active in Parlt. concerning Admiralty affairs, maritime law, and international law. Composed notes on *De Regulis Juris* (Bodl. Tanner MS. 422). Lands in Trumpington, Cambs. Lent £500 to King 1640; £1,000 to Parlt. later. Donated £504 to Trinity Hall 1633. Invested in commerce. d. 18 July 1645. Will: PCC

96 Rivers, pr. 21 July 1645. £4,000 apiece to nieces Philippa and Nan Eden; £1,600 in foreign notes to J. Bruce of London; other bequests amounting to more than £550.

DNB vi. 361–2. J. Howard, *The Visitation of Suffolke* (London, 1886), i. 18–19. Keeler, *Long Parliament*, p. 163. Ward, *Gresham Professors*, pp. 240–4. LPL, Reg. Doc. Com., ff. 47ᵛ, 108; Abbot Reg. i, f. 180. PRO DEL 5/6, ff. 52, 78; C 181/2, ff. 232, 334–5; 181/3, ff. 13ᵛ, 122; 181/4, ff. 37, 138ᵛ; 181/5, ff. 26ᵛ, 130ᵛ, 176; C 193/12/2, ff. 18, 55; C 193/13/1, f. 92. HCA 1/32/1, ff. 13, 29; HCA 24/82–101, *passim*; index 16818, p. 46; SP 16/421/108; 16/477/62; 16/313/49; PROB 11/193/96. Rex, *University Representation*, pp. 108, 112–13, 120, 149. CUL, MS. Mm. IV, 57, ff. 302–3. Bodl., Tanner MSS. 135, f. 161; 68, f. 200ᵛ; 65, ff. 4–5; 86, f. 202. Usher, *High Commission*, p. 350. BM, MS. Stowe 366, ff. 97–8. Notestein, *D'Ewes*, pp. 38–9, 54, 125–6, 163, 307, 438 n., 539. *CSPD 1641–1643*, pp. 3–4. *VCH Cambs.* iii. 367, 369–71. *Heraldic Cases, passim*.

EDWARDS, Thomas, b. 1554. From Berks. Matric. as son of commoner All Souls College, Oxford, 1581; fellow 1577; B.C.L. 1584; D.C.L. 1591. Warrant Doc. Com. 1592; full admission 1595; in commons until 1618. Chancellor of London diocese 1611–16. Active as advocate in London courts 1603–19. Delegates 1595–1618. Comr. Piracy London 1603–17. Comr. Adm. Middx., etc., 1603–15. Chancellor of Gloucester w. John Seaman 1608. J.P. Gloucester 1609. Commissary of Bishop of London for Essex and Herts. by 1616. Master in Chancery Extraordinary. Rector of Langenhoe, Essex, 1618. House, lands, and ten. in Fulham, Middx. Will: PCC 40 Parker, pr. 21 Apr. 1619. £500 to wife; £1,000 to son John; £500 to son William; £600 apiece to daus. Frances and Alice; £500 to dau. Elizabeth; £400 to dau. Anne; house to wife; lands and ten. to John Ravis. £315 to friends and the poor. Civil and canon law books to All Souls Library and to Drs. Marten, Bird, and Bennet. Benefactor of the Bodleian Library.

Al. Oxon. ii. 450. Clark, *Register*, i. 230, 242, 317–18; ii. 111, 126. LPL, Reg. Doc. Com., ff. 44ᵛ, 106; Whitgift Reg. i, f. 191; Bancroft Reg., f. 239. PRO C 181/1, ff. 122–3; 181/2, ff. 219ᵛ–220; DEL 5/2–6, *passim*; HCA 1/32/1, ff. 38, 55, 61, 90; HCA 24/70–4, *passim*; PROB 11/133/40. Newcourt, *Repertorium*, ii. 364. Gleason, *Justices*, p. 251. Quintrell, 'Government of Essex', pp. 149–50. BM, Add. MS. 38,170, f. 358. Rudder, *Gloucestershire*, p. 163.

ESTMOND (EASTMOND), John, 2nd son of Thomas of Lodge in Chardstock, Devon. Winchester College. Scholar of New College, Oxford, 1569; fellow 1572–90; B.C.L. 1576; D.C.L. 1589. Proctor in VCC Oxford *c.* 1580. Principal of New Inn Hall 1589. Warrant Doc. Com. 1590 but not fully adm. Rector of Saham-Tony, Norf., 1589. Patrimony: 30-acre tenement until he acquires pension, preferment, or estate of living valued at £20 p.a. d. 17 Oct. 1604.

Al. Oxon. ii. 466. Clark, *Register*, i. 105, 115, 181; iii. 63. Kirby, *Winchester Scholars*, p. 138. Bodl., MS. Top. Oxon. e. 105/2, f. 66. Wood, *Fasti*, i. 249. LPL, Whitgift Reg. i. 161. PRO, PROB 11/110/65.

EXTON, JOHN, b. 1600. Origins unknown. Matric. pens. Christ's College, Cambridge, 1617; B.A. Trinity Hall 1620; M.A. 1623; LL.D. 1634. Warrant Doc. Com. 1636; full admission 1638; in commons 1636, 1640–2; out of commons 1637–9. Active as advocate in London courts 1638–40. Delegates 1638. Comr. Piracy London 1638. Comr. Pol. & Ass. London 1639–40. Judge HCA w. W. Clerke 1651; w. Clerke and Stephens 1651; reappointed 1661. Active in Doc. Com. 1656. Wrote *The Maritime Dicaeologie or Sea Jurisdiction* (1664) in order to maintain the jurisdiction of HCA. d. 1668; bur. St. Benet, Paul's Wharf, London. Will: PCC 154 Hene, pr. 4 Dec. 1668. £20 to each grandchild; two-thirds of remainder of estate to son Thomas, D.C.L.; one-third to son Everard. Res.: Doc. Com.; St. Margaret's, Westminster.

> *Al. Cant.* ii. 113. *DNB* vi. 962. J. Peile, *Register of Christ's College*, i. 316. LPL, Reg. Doc. Com., ff. 50, 79ᵛ; Laud, Reg. i, f. 226ᵛ. PRO, DEL 8/70, ii, f. 37; HCA 24/92–8, *passim*; PROB 11/328/154; SP 16/421/108. Haydn, *Dignities*, pp. 422–3. *Acts of Interregnum*, ii. 510. *Heraldic Cases*, pp. 29, 34, 36, 48.

FARMERY, JOHN, 1st son of William, Rector of Heapham, Lincs., by Cassandra, dau. of John Newland of Hackney, Middx. Matric. pens. St. John's College, Cambridge, 1607; B.A. 1611; LL.D. 1620. Warrant Doc. Com. 1624; full admission 1637; in commons until 1642. Chancellor of Lincoln diocese 1621; bishop tries to remove him 1621; Farmery appeals to King for assistance. Bishop prevents him from reaping financial profits of chancellorship and attempts to remove him again 1635. Assists Laud in enforcing conformity. Chancellor of Lincoln Cathedral challenges his right to visit Chapter House 1635. J.P. Lincs. 1620–32. Delegates 1637–9. M.P. City of Lincoln 1640 (Apr.) through Earl of Rutland. Petitions against him directed to Long Parlt. Begs to compound on articles of Newark. Holds land on Isle of Axholme and at Heapham; house in Lincoln. Will: PCC 29 Essex, pr. 5 Feb. 1648. Lands at Heapham to wife; rest to provide for children. m. Bridget, dau. of W. Naylor of Flamborough, Yorks.

> *Lincolnshire Pedigrees*, i (Harl. Soc. l, 1902), 346. *Al. Cant.* ii. 22. LPL, Reg. Doc. Com. ff. 50, 110; Abbot Reg. i, f. 206; MS. 1030, ff. 41, 73. PRO, DEL 8/70, pt. ii, ff. 31ᵛ–34ᵛ; SP 14/124/97; SP 16/421/108; PROB 11/203/29. *CSPD 1619–1623*, p. 431; *1623–1625*, pp. 150, 295, 347, 436; *1634–1635*, p. 426; *1641–1643*, pp. 423–4. CUL, MS. Mm. I. 49, pp. 327–8. Notestein, *D'Ewes*, p. 38. *CPCC* ii. 1371.

FAVOUR, JOHN, b. 1557 in Southampton. Winchester College. Matric. New College, Oxford, as son of commoner 1576; fellow 1578–94; B.C.L. 1584; D.C.L. 1592. A cleric. Chaplain of Earl of Huntingdon *c.* 1575. Vicar of Halifax, Yorks., 1593–1624 at value of £160 p.a. Of Puritan sympathies. Sub-Dean of Ripon 1607. Master of St. Mary Magdalen Hospital, Ripon, 1618. Preb. of Southwell 1611–23. Preb. of York 1614–17. Precentor of York Cathedral; canon residentiary 1619. Chaplain of Archbishop Tobie Matthew of York, his chief patron. Builds and endows Heath Grammar School. Encourages development of cloth industry in Halifax. Practised medicine. Assists in conversion of recusants 1594. Comr. Eccles. Causes, York, 1575–1617. J.P. West Riding,

Yorks., *c*. 1622. J.P. and Comr. Gaol Delivery Ripon, Southwell, and Cawood. Excommunicated for refusing to wear surplice and read canons 1619. d. 23 Mar. 1624. Wrote *Antiquitie Triumphing Over Noveltie* (1619); 'Sermons Preached at West Riding Exercises' (BM, Add. MSS. 4933A, ff. 60, 76, 88; 4933B, ff. 162ᵛ, 174); Epigrams on the Gunpowder Plot conspirators (Hatfield House, Salisbury MS. 140/104).

> *Al. Oxon.* ii. 487. W. J. Walker, *Chapters on the Early Registers of Halifax Parish Church* (Halifax, 1885), pp. 1–3, 6. J. Watson, *The History and Antiquities of the Parish of Halifax in Yorkshire* (London, 1775), pp. 377–8, 467. Wood, *Athenae*, ii. 353–4. Clark, *Register*, i. 182; ii. 72; iii. 126. York Cathedral Library, Chapter Acts, ff. 519, 756. Borth. Inst., R. VII H.C.A.B. 15; Index of Clergy. PRO, C 66/1907ᵛ; 66/2018; C 181/3, ff. 34–108, *passim*; C 193/13/1, f. 33. Tyler, 'Ecclesiastical Commission', pp. 204, 246. Newton, 'Puritanism', pp. 37–8, 282. Marchant, *Puritans*, pp. 204, 246. *CSPD 1611–1618*, p. 226. W. K. Jordan, *The Charities of Rural England* (London, 1961), pp. 323–6. Bodl., MS. Top. Oxon. e. 105/2, f. 72.

FERRAND (FARRAND, FARRANT), William, prob. son of Richard of St. Michael, Cornhill, London, draper (d. 1560), by Joan. Brother of Edmund of the Inner Temple. Matric. pens. Trinity College, Cambridge, 1559; B.A. 1563; fellow 1563; M.A. 1566; proctor 1578–9; LL.D. 1580. Warrant Doc. Com. 1580; full admission 1582; in commons until 1615. Honorific admission Gray's Inn 1603. Delegates 1597–1614. High Com. 1601–13. Comr. to relieve debtors 1597. Reversion to judgeship of PCC. Commissary for deaneries of Shoreham and Croydon 1603. Comr. Piracy London 1603, 1606, 1614. Comr. Pol. & Ass. 1608. Comr. Adm. Middx. 1603, 1609, 1614. Grant of Arms. Capital mess. and copyhold lands in Mitcham, Surrey; land in Carshalton, Surrey. Will: PCC 68 Rudd, pr. 5 July 1615. Lands and goods to wife and to son Richard. m. Mary, dau. of one Haynes and widow of E. Orwell. Father of Margaret.

> *Al. Cant.* ii. 123. Cooper, *Athenae*, iii. 16. LPL, Reg. Doc. Com., ff. 43, 104ᵛ; Grindal Reg., f. 208; Bancroft Reg., f. 224; Whitgift Reg. iii, f. 279. Foster, *Gray's Inn*, p. 105. PRO, DEL 5/2–4, *passim*; C 181/1, ff. 122–3; 181/2, ff. 10, 70, 213; HCA 1/32/1, ff. 38, 55, 90; SP 14/3/11; PROB 11/43/34; 11/126/68. Usher, *High Commission*, p. 350. *Grantees of Arms*, i. 87. *Visitation of Surrey* (Harl. Soc. xliii, 1899), p. 100. BM, Harl. MS. 1397, f. 44ᵛ.

FLETCHER, Giles, b. at Watford, Herts, younger son of Richard Fletcher, Vicar of Bishop's Stortford, Herts. Brother of Richard, Bishop of London. Eton College. Adm. King's College, Cambridge, 1566; fellow 1568–81; B.A. 1570; M.A. 1573; LL.D. 1581. Lectured in Greek 1572–9. Deputy Public Orator 1577. Commissary to Chancellor of Ely diocese 1580. Chancellor of Chichester diocese 1582–90. Warrant Doc. Com. 1583 but not admitted fully. Relies on patronage of Sir Thomas Randolph and Sir Francis Walsingham. Negotiates w. Hamburg merchants 1577. Mission to Scotland 1586; Russia 1588. Remembrancer of City of London 1587–1605. Temporary and honorific appointment as Master of Requests 1587. Treasurer of St. Paul's 1597–1611. Employed by Merchant Adventurers to meet King of Denmark 1610. M.P.

Winchelsea 1584 through patronage of Lord Cobham, Warden of Cinque Ports. Composed poems and tracts, including poem for 1576 edn. of Foxe's *Acts and Monuments*. Financial difficulties late in life. Pays £1,400 in First Fruits and Tenths for deceased brother. Res.: St. Catherine Coleman, London. d. 16 Feb. 1611. Will: PCC 22 Wood, pr. 27 March 1611. Goods and chattels to wife. m. Johann, dau. of T. Sheafe, yeoman and clothier of Cranbrook, Kent. Father of Phineas and Giles.

> *DNB* vii. 299–301. HPT, typescript. *Eton Register*, p. 125. LPL, Grindal Reg., f. 281. PRO, PROB 11/117/22. Berry, *Works of Fletcher*.

FORTH (FOURTH), Sir Ambrose, b. in London 1545, 4th son of Robert, Clerk of the Privy Seal. Brother of Robert, LL.D. Adm. Scholar and matric. pens. King's College, Cambridge, 1560; B.A. Jesus College 1565; M.A. 1568; fellow 1568–73; LL.D. Trinity College 1581. Master in Chancery in Ireland 1579–1610 at salary of £20 p.a. Judge of Court of Faculties and Prerogative Court in Ireland. Comr. Adm. Waterford, Cork, and Limerick 1604. Knighted 1604. Judge of Admiralty Court in Ireland. Leased manor in Donamore at rent of 36s. 8d. p.a. Owned land in Kildare. d. 13 Jan. 1610.

> *Eton Register*, p. 127. *Al. Cant.* ii. 160. Cooper, *Athenae*, ii. 525–6. *Middlesex Pedigrees* (Harl. Soc., lxv, 1914), p. 141. PRO, HCA 1/32/1, f. 68. *CSP Ireland 1586–1588*, pp. 328–9; *1608–1610*, pp. 338, 424.

GAGER, William, nephew of Sir William Cordell, from whom he expected, but did not receive a large fortune. Westminster School. B.A. Christ Church, Oxford, 1578; M.A. 1580; B.C.L. and D.C.L. 1589. Warrant Doc. Com. 1590 but not fully admitted. Surrogate to R. Swale as Chancellor of Ely diocese 1601; Chancellor 1606. Comr. Gaol delivery Ely before 1622. Wrote Latin plays performed at Cambridge; collection of poems (BM, Add. MS. 22,583). Defends stage rights *v.* attack by Dr. Reynolds 1592–3. Defends legality of beating wives 1608. Res.: Cambridge, Ely, and Chesterton, Cambs. Will: Cambridge VCC, pr. 26 Sept. 1622. Goods to wife Mary.

> *DNB* vii. 797–8. Wood, *Athenae*, ii. 87–9. *Al. Oxon.* ii. 542. Clark, *Register*, i. 181, 230; iii. 70. LPL, Whitgift Reg. i, f. 160ᵛ. PRO C 181/3, f. 68. Cambridge Univ. Arch., Wills 3/135.

GARDINER (GARDNER, GARDENER), Samuel, b. 1591. From Culworth, Northants. Cousin of Hugh Barker (q.v.). Winchester College. Matric. New College, Oxford, as son of commoner 1604; B.C.L. 1619; fellow (founder's kin) 1613–29; D.C.L. 1636. Warrant Doc. Com. 1637 but not fully admitted; listed as member 1639. Surrogate to Official of Archdeacon of Berks. 1636–7. d. 1643 or 1644. Not to be confused w. Samuel Gardiner, M.P. for Evesham, Worcs., 1645–8; 1659.

> *Al. Oxon.* ii. 548. Kirby, *Winchester Scholars*, p. 161. Clark, *Register*, ii. 274; iii. 380. Bodl., MS. Top. Oxon. e. 105/2, ff. 93ᵛ–94. LPL, Laud Reg. i, f. 281ᵛ. Borth. Inst.,

R. VII. PR 108. PRO, DEL 8/61, *passim*; SP 16/442/125; will of Barker, PROB 11/162/102.

GENTILI, ALBERICO, b. 1551 in LaMarca d'Ancona, Italy, 2nd son of Matthew, M.D., D.C.L., Perugia, 1572. Left Italy for religious reasons. Secures patronage of Earl of Leicester. Inc. Oxford 1581. Resides in New Inn Hall and teaches at St. John's College. Travels to Wittenberg 1586; returns through influence of Walsingham. Regius Professor of Civil Law at Oxford 1587. Honorific Admission Gray's Inn 1600. Advocate for Spanish embassy in HCA 1605–8. List of writings in Molen, *Gentili*, pp. 330–1. Accused by anonymous Parliamentarian in 1644 of causing the Civil War. Contributes to growth of international law. d. 19 June 1608; bur. St. Helen's, London. Will: PCC 122 Cope, pr. 12 Dec. 1616. Money to be divided between wife and children, but no sum specified; orders writings in manuscript to be burned.

> Molen, *Gentili*. *DNB* vii. 1003–6. Wood, *Athenae*, ii. 90–3. *Al. Oxon.* ii. 557. Foster, *Gray's Inn*, p. 105. G. del Vecchio, 'The Posthumous Fate of Alberico Gentili', *American Journal of International Law*, 50 (1956), 664–7. Simmonds, 'Gentili at Admiralty Bar', pp. 3–23. Mattingly, *Renaissance Diplomacy*, p. 249. Maitland, *English Law*, pp. 14, 60 n.; *Canon Law*, p. 94. Senior, 'Arches', p. 505; *Doctors' Commons*, p. 93. Fulbecke, *Direction*, pp. 31–2.

GERARD, FRANCIS. Origins unknown. Fellow-commoner at Balliol College, Oxford; B.A. 1619; M.A. 1622; B.C.L. 1625; D.C.L. 1632. d. July 1643.

> *Al. Oxon.* ii. 557. Clark, *Register*, iii. 370. Balliol College, Yearly Lists ii, f. 123.

GIBSON, SIR JOHN, 2nd son of Thomas of Ireby, Lancs., prob. commoner, by dau. of one Redman of Gressingham. Matric. sizar Clare College, Cambridge, 1558; B.A. Trinity College 1561; fellow 1561; M.A. 1564; LL.D. 1571. Warrant Doc. Com. 1572; full admission 1572; in commons until 1605; out of commons 1606–12. Honorific admission Gray's Inn 1574. Preb. of York 1571. Chancellor of York diocese 1572–7; 1589–1604 w. J. Bennet. Commissary of Dean and Chapter of York 1573–1613. Precentor of York 1575–1612. Archdeacon of East Riding as a layman 1578–88. Commissary of Archbishop of Canterbury w. S. Lakes (q.v.) 1582; Commissary of Dean of Shoreham and Croydon 1582. Royal dispensation from keeping residence at York rejected by Dean 1582. Master in Chancery 1578–1611. Judge of PCC 1598–1604. Delegates 1603. Knighted 1603. J.P. North Riding 1609. Grant of arms 1574. Held manor of Welburn, Yorks.; lands in Welburn, Nawton, Kerbie, and Wimbleton, Yorks.; mess. in Crayke, Yorks.; farm in Bransdale, Yorks.; mess. and ten. in York. Lands valued by Gibson's estimate at £390 p.a. Will: York, pr. 6 Mar. 1613. Lands to wife and sons; books of canon and civil law to son John. m. (1) Margaret Woodhall; (2) Margaret, dau. of Richard Masterson of Cheshire, esq.; (3) Anne, dau. of John Allett, Lord Mayor of London. Father of John, Thomas, Edward.

Al. Cant. ii. 211. Glover, *Visitation of Yorkshire*, p. 520. LPL, Reg. Doc. Com., ff. 41, 103ᵛ; Parker Reg. ii, f. 64; Grindal Reg., ff. 252ᵛ, 257ᵛ; Lamb. Chart. Misc. xii, f. 9. Foster, *Gray's Inn*, p. 84. Hutton, *Correspondence*, pp. 18–19, 62–3. PRO, C142/338/57; E 179/146/399, f. 5. DEL 5/3, f. 44. Gleason, *Justices*, p. 231. Marchant, *Church Under Law*, pp. 42–3.*VCH Yorks. North Riding*, i. 511 n., 520; ii. 123–4. Borth. Inst., Wills 32/300.

GOAD (GOADE, GOODE), Thomas, baptized at Windsor, Berks., 18 May 1595, 1st son of brother of Roger Goad, D.D., by Jane G. Brother of George, a master at Eton; cousin of Thomas Goad, D.D., chaplain of Archbishop Abbot. Eton College. Matric. pens. King's College, Cambridge, 1611; B.A. 1613; fellow 1614–34; M.A. 1619; Reader in Logic 1620; proctor 1629; LL.D. 1630. Full admission Doc. Com. 1631. Delegates 1635. Regius Professor of Civil Law at Cambridge 1635–66. Friend of Archbishop Laud. Suffered during Civil War and Interregnum. Houses and ten. in New and Old Windsor valued at £100 p.a.; copyhold lands in Cambs. valued at £600; lands purchased from J. Byng valued at £2,700. bur. at Grantchester, Cambs., 11 June 1666. Will: PCC 117 Mico, pr. 6 July 1666. Lands at Windsor to pay debts; then to wife for life and to dau. Mary. £400 from sale of copyhold lands to Byng; £200 to pay debts. m. Mary, dau. of Edmund Woodhall of Saffron Walden, Essex, and Registrar of PCC. Father of Mary, Grace.

DNB viii. 21. *Al. Cant.* ii. 225. *Eton Register*, p. 141. PRO, DEL 8/70, pt. ii, ff. 21–7ᵛ; PROB 11/321/117. LPL, Reg. Doc. Com., ff. 49ᵛ, 109ᵛ. Lloyd, *Memoires*, p. 594.

GOOCH (GOCHE, GOUGH, GOOGE), Barnaby, 4th son of Barnabe of Alvingham, Lincs., poet and retainer of Cecil. Matric. Magdalene College, Cambridge, 1582; B.A. 1587; M.A. 1590; LL.D. 1604. Commissary for Cambridge Univ. 1615–25; Vice-Chancellor 1611–12. Master of Magdalene College 1604–26. Imprisoned on behalf of Magdalene as result of Aldgate lawsuit 1614–16. Full admission Doc. Com. 1613; in commons 1613–25. Adm. Gray's Inn 1610. Chancellor of Worcester diocese 1610–18; Exeter 1615–24. Delegates 1620–4. Comr. Adm. Devon 1616–20; Dorset 1622; Middx., etc., 1625. Comr. Piracy Devon 1615, 1619. Judge of Vice-Admiralty Court for Devon *c.* 1615. Loses contested election to Parlt. 1614; M.P. Cambridge Univ. 1621, 1624, 1625. Opposes bill to restrict rate of usury to 8 per cent because lower price of land would 'overthrow the gentry' 1621. Criticizes attack against the King's children 1621. Defends Parlt.'s jurisdiction without use of formal oaths. Attacks abuses in granting of prohibitions 1621 and 1624. Criticizes Parlt. for not passing bills 1621; feels time is not ripe for redress of grievances because of poor state of kingdom 1621. Defends Prince Elector's right to declare war *v.* Spain 1624. Held lands in Alvingham, Cockerington, North Somercotes, Grimsby, South Somercotes, and Corringham, Lincs. Res.: Magdalene College; Archdeacon of Cornwall's House in Exeter; Doc. Com. Will: PCC 71 Hele, pr. 6 May 1626. £580 to nephews; £100 to maintain Barnabe at Cambridge; £24 annuity to support two fellows at Magdalene, preferably in civil law and not to be tied to the clergy; lands in Alvingham and Corringham to nephew Barnabe, whom he gave in marriage to Passha Parry, his step-daughter. m. Elizabeth Parry, widow of Bishop Parry of Worcester.

DNB viii. 151-2. *Al. Cant.* ii. 231. Foster, *Gray's Inn*, p. 123. Exeter Cathedral Library, MS. 3553, ff. 53, 80. Cassidy, 'Episcopate of Cotton', pp. 120, 122, 166. Nash, *Worcester*, ii. clxviii; *Lincolnshire Pedigrees*, ii (Harl. Soc. li, 1903), 408-9. PRO, DEL 5/6, ff. 85-147, *passim*; DEL 8/70, pt. i, ff. 1-19ᵛ, *passim*. HCA 1/32/1, ff. 13, 23, 25, 27, 31; C 181/2, ff. 240ᵛ, 383; C 142/422/47; PROB 11/149/71. *NRS* ii. 136, 347-8, 350, 469-70; iii. 186, 330, 351-2; iv. 315, 351; v. 148, 169-70; vi. 140-1, 210-11. Yale University Library, typescript of Jervoise Diary, f. 27; typescript of Braye MS., f. 7. LPL, Reg. Doc. Com., ff. 47ᵛ, 107ᵛ; MS. 642, pp. 112, 123-4. *CJ* i. 583-4, 586, 612, 614, 619, 622, 631. *VCH Cambs.* iii. 454. Moir, *Addled Parliament*, pp. 39-40. Hill, *Society and Puritanism*, p. 384.

GOODWYN, MORGAN, b. 1601, younger son of Francis, D.D., Bishop of Hereford. Matric. Christ Church, Oxford, 1619; B.A. 1621; B.C.L. Pembroke 1627; LL.D. Trinity College, Dublin, 1637 (inc. Oxford 1643). Archdeacon of Salop 1631. Preb. of Hereford 1631. Rector of Llangan, Glam., 1638; English Bicknor, Glos., 1639; Lydney, Glos., 1641. Master of Free School at Newland, Glos., 1639. Among those Royalists who surrendered at Hereford 1643. Cited by Committee for Plundered Ministers on charge of deserting cure 1645. Threatened with life by Cromwell for refusing to leave his position at Newland School 1655. Asks Cromwell for licence to import 300 tons of wine without customs for discovering the secret of 'Nuncius inanimatus'. Spared imprisonment in tower by Cromwell because he was consumptive. d. before 1660. Married w. five children.

Al. Oxon. ii. 585. *Walker Revised*, pp. 173-4. Oxford Univ. Archives, P.P. 2, f. 20ᵛ; MS. Rawlinson A 25, f. 449. *CSPD 1638-1639*, p. 79.

GOODYEARE (GOODERE), SAMUEL, 1st son of Michael of Colchester, Essex, minister. Matric. sizar St. John's College, Cambridge, 1576; B.A. 1581; M.A. 1584; fellow 1585; LL.D. before 1596. Warrant Doc. Com. 1596 but not fully admitted. Chancellor of St. Asaph diocese 1603-5. Dean of St. Asaph at income of £45. 11s. 1d. Patrimony: £3. 6s. 8d. Will: PCC 55 Clarke, pr. 17 May 1625. All lands and goods to brother Michael; £30 to repair organ at St. Asaph; £40 to dau. of sister Sarah.

Al. Cant. iii. 240. ERO, will of Michael, pr. 13 Apr. 1572, 319 CR6. Thomas, *St. Asaph*, p. 239. LPL, Whitgift Reg., f. 143; Bancroft Reg., f. 216ᵛ.

GREENE, WILLIAM. Origins obscure. Matric. sizar Christ's College, Cambridge, 1621; B.A. 1625; M.A. Magdalene College 1628; fellow until 1644; LL.D. 1636. Warrant Doc. Com. 1637 and listed as a member in 1639 but not fully admitted. Comr. Piracy London 1638. Advocate in HCA 1639-40. Refers to himself as Doctor of the Arches 1644. Ejected from fellowship 1644. Town Clerk of Newcastle and Chancellor of York diocese by 1644. d. 1655. Will:

PCC 393 Aylett, pr. 29 Oct. 1655. Requests burial in Penrith, Cumb. Horse and clothes to Thomas Lowther; suit to brother Joshua, Merchant Adventurer of Newcastle. Not to be confused w. W. Greene of Leake parish, Yorks.

Al. Cant. ii. 259. LPL, Laud Reg., f. 281ᵛ. *Walker Revised*, p. 38. PRO, C 181/5, f. 131; HCA 12/97, nos. 9, 11; 24/98, nos. 107, 111, 114; 24/101, no. 270; PROB 11/250/393. E. Mackenzie, *A Descriptive and Historical Account of . . . Newcastle Upon Tyne* (Newcastle, 1827), p. 620.

GRIFFITH, WILLIAM, b. 1597, 1st son of William of Llanfaethlu, Anglesey, gent. (d. 1630), by Ann, dau. of Hugh Prichard; younger brother was George, Bishop of St. Asaph in 1660. Winchester College. Matric. New College, Oxford, 1615; fellow 1619–29, B.C.L. 1623; D.C.L. 1627. Warrant Doc. Com. 1627; full admission 1628. Chancellor of St. Asaph diocese 1627; Bangor diocese w. Hugh Griffith 1629–35 and alone after 1635. J.P. Anglesey and Flints. Delegates 1634, 1637–9. Joins other ecclesiastical judges residing at Doc. Com. in legal opinion *c.* 1636. Recommended for judgeship of Vice-Admiralty Court of Devon 1636 but position given to Joseph Marten. Master in Chancery 1637–41. d. 17 Oct. 1648. Res.: Doc. Com. and Llanfaethlu, where his brother was rector. m. Mary, dau. of Bishop John Owen of St. Asaph 1632. Father of three sons and three daus.; son John inherits estate and becomes High Sheriff of Anglesey in 1690.

Al. Oxon. ii. 613. Clark, *Register*, ii. 344; iii. 424. Kirby, *Winchester Scholars*, p. 164. Bodl., MS. Top. Oxon. e. 105/2, ff. 96ᵛ–97. Wood, *Fasti*, i. 432. BM. Lansdowne MS. 985, f. 68. J. E. Griffith, *Pedigrees of Anglesey and Caernarvonshire Families* (Horncastle, 1914), pp. 26, 136. LPL, Reg. Doc. Com., ff. 49, 108ᵛ; Abbot Reg. ii, f. 222ᵛ. PRO, C 193/13/2; DEL 8/70, pt. ii, *passim*; SP 16/212/137; 16/326/80; 16/339/63; index 16818, p. 46. D. R. Thomas, *A History of the Diocese of St. Asaph* (London, 1874), p. 239.

GWYNN (WYNN), THOMAS, younger son of John ap Rees Wynn of Llanbeulan, Anglesey, gent., by Margaret, dau. of William Woods of Llangwyfan, Anglesey. Elder brother was Rhys Wynn, Serjeant-at-law. B.A. St. Edmund Hall, Oxford, 1594; M.A. All Souls 1599; B.C.L. 1602; fellow 1605; D.C.L. 1608. Warrant Doc. Com. 1608; full admission 1610; in commons 1610–42. Chantor of Salisbury Cathedral 1607. Delegates 1611, 1617–40. Active as advocate in London courts 1614–40. Comr. Piracy London 1617–38; Comr. Ad. Middx., etc., 1619, 1623, 1625. High Com. 1633. Chancellor Llandaff diocese. Joins other ecclesiastical judges residing at Doc. Com. in legal opinion *c.* 1636. Fined by Long Parlt. for sentence as High Comr. 1641. Lease of rectory of Lewknor, Oxon., from All Souls 1617. Conveys mess. in Penhow, Mon., to All Souls 1632. Bestows impropriate rectory of Holyhead, Anglesey, on Jesus College, Oxford. Father of John.

Al. Oxon. ii. 625. Clark, *Register*, i. 106, 185–6; iii. 183; iv. 403. Wood, *Fasti*, i. 321–2. LPL, Reg. Doc. Com., ff. 46ᵛ, 107ᵛ; Bancroft Reg., f. 157. *Catalogue of All Souls Archives*, pp. 127–8. PRO, C 181/2, ff. 296ᵛ, 297, 334; 181/3, f. 79ᵛ; 181/4, ff. 37, 138ᵛ;

181/5, ff. 26ᵛ, 130. DEL 5/4, ff. 144, 149; DEL 8/70, *passim*; HCA 1/32/1, ff. 13, 21, 29; SP 16/339/63; 16/421/108; 16/483/59. *CSPD 1635*, p. 549. Usher, *High Commission*, p. 351. *Heraldic Cases*, *passim*.

HARRIS, Nathaniel, b. 1568, son of Richard, Rector of Hardwick, Bucks., and former fellow of New College, Oxford. Matric. New College 1586 as son of commoner; fellow 1588–1601; B.C.L. 1593; D.C.L. 1612. Rector of Langton, Oxon., 1600–9. Vicar of Inkberrow, Worcs., 1602–12. Preb. of Hereford 1602–25. Rector of Bletchingley, Surrey, 1609–25 through patronage of Nicholas Love, by grant of Lord William Howard of Effingham. Brought before Parlt. 1624 for 'indiscreet carriage about election at Bletchingley' and for 'venting his spleen' in the pulpit. Published letters in the church from his patroness Lady Howard defending the claim of Henry Lovell to have been elected in place of John Hayward. Owned mess. in Oving, Bucks., which yielded £31 p.a.; mess. in North Marston, Bucks.; mess. in 'Hoorne', Essex. d. 15 Apr. 1625; bur. at Bletchingley. Will: PCC 44 Clarke, pr. 11 May 1625. £500 to each of his three daus., Mary, Alice, and Jane; mess. in Oving and Hoorne to son John. Also father of Josiah.

Al. Oxon. ii. 657. Clark, *Register*, i. 187, 273; ii. 155; iii. 179. Wood, *Fasti*, i. 348. PRO, C 142/420/91. Kirby, *Winchester Scholars*, p. 150. Bodl., MS. Top. Oxon. e. 105/2, f. 79. U. Lambert, *Bletchingley: A Parish History* (London, 1921), ii. 390. *CJ* i. 695. *VCH Surrey* iv. 256.

HART, Richard, son of John of St. Gregory's parish, London, proctor in the Court of the Arches (d. 1635). B.A. Trinity College, Oxford, 1620; B.C.L. 1625; D.C.L. St. Alban's Hall 1628. Warrant Doc. Com. 1628; full admission 1629. Confessed to being a popish recusant 1632 and consequently excluded from Doc. Com.; reinstated after agreeing to receive sacrament according to forms of Church of England and declaring that he embraced the established religion 1633. Otherwise in commons 1629–40. Active in London courts as advocate 1634–40. At Fulham sold timber, which did not belong to him, for £86 and then had purchaser imprisoned for non-payment 1640.

Al. Cant. ii. 320. Clark, *Register*, iii. 381. LPL, Reg. Doc. Com., ff. 49ᵛ, 79, 109; Abbot Reg. ii, f. 233ᵛ. *CSPD 1634–1635*, pp. 262, 534, 543; *1635*, p. 193; *1639–1640*, p. 481. PRO, SP 16/421/108. *Heraldic Cases*, p. 44.

HARVEY, Gabriel, b. 1550, 1st son of John of Saffron Walden, Essex, ropemaker and yeoman. Related to Sir Thomas Smith, civilian, and Secretary to Queen Elizabeth. Later accused of attempting to conceal his humble origins. School at Saffron Walden. Matric. pens. Christ's College, Cambridge, 1566; B.A. 1569–70; Fellow of Pembroke 1570; M.A. Pembroke 1573; Fellow of Trinity Hall 1578; LL.B. 1585 (inc. Oxford 1585); D.C.L. Oxford 1585. Elected Master of Trinity Hall 1585, but election blocked by pressure from Court. Friend of Spencer. Wrote poetry and almanacs. List of works in Wood,

Fasti, ii. 231. Studied astrology. Retired to Saffron Walden, where he practised physic. Allegedly pompous and pedantic. d. Feb. 1631. Unmarried.

> *Al. Cant.* ii. 323. Clark, *Register*, i. 349. Curtis, *Oxford and Cambridge*, p. 176. Smith, *Family of Withypoll*, p. 60. T. Nash, *Have With You to Saffron Walden* (London, 1596). A. R. Goddard, 'The Harveys of Saffron Walden', *Essex Review* 7 (1898), 13–24. Braybrooke, *Audley End*, pp. 195, 286–91.

HAWKINS, HENRY, son of John of Essex, gent., by Anne, dau. of William Yelverton of Rougham, Norf. Matric. pens. Peterhouse, Cambridge, 1568; B.A. 1571–2; M.A. 1575; fellow 1575–99; proctor 1583–4; LL.D. 1591. Warrant Doc. Com. 1591 but not fully admitted. Adm. Gray's Inn 1584. Receives pass to go abroad w. Lord Zouch 1586; in Prague 1589. Implicated in Essex rising. Comr. Adm. Middx., etc., 1603. Res.: St. Andrew's, Holborn, London. Donates £100 to Feoffees for purchase of impropriations 1629. Will: PCC 2 St. John, pr. 22 Jan. 1631. £300 to R. Heylin, J. Davenport, W. Gouge, and R. Sibbes for purchase of impropriations; £300 for almshouses on Isle of Ely.

> *Visitation of Norfolk* (Harl. Soc. xxxii, 1891), p. 329. T. A. Walker, *A Biographical Register of Peterhouse Men* (Cambridge, 1927), pp. 267–8. *Al. Cant.* ii. 335. Calder, *Activities of Puritan Faction*, p. 33. LPL, Whitgift Reg. i, f. 178ᵛ. PRO, HCA 1/32/1, f. 90.

HAWLEY, JOHN, b. 1566. 2nd son of Jeremy of Boston, Middx., esq. Matric. Balliol College 1581; Fellow of St. John's 1583; B.C.L. 1588; D.C.L. 1614. Principal of Gloucester Hall 1593–1626. Clerk of the Market 1600. Judge of Oxford VCC *c*. 1600–23. Occasional surrogate of Official to Archdeacon of Berkshire 1600–9. J.P. Oxford *c*. 1622 and City of Oxford 1620. Purchased manor of Northbrook in Kirtlington, Oxon. d. 1626. Will: Oxford VCC, pr. 6 June 1626. Leaves management of his estate to brothers William and Henry and to George Buckeridge. Manor of Northbrook passes to his son, who sold it in 1641.

> *Al. Oxon.* ii. 678. Clark, *Register*, i. 106, 122, 254; ii. 96; iii. 151. PRO, C 181/3, ff. 2ᵛ, 43, 44, 84ᵛ; C 193/13/1, f. 79ᵛ; E 179/238/145. Oxford Univ. Archives, Registers of Chancellor's Court 1600–23, *passim*; Wills G–HA. Bodl., MS. Oxf. Archd. Papers Berks. c 44–52, *passim*. *VCH Oxford* vi. 224.

HAYWARD (HAYWARDE, HAYWOOD), SIR JOHN, b. *c*. 1564 at Felixstowe, Suffolk. B.A. Pembroke College, Cambridge, 1581; M.A. 1584; LL.D. 1591. Warrant Doc. Com. 1595; full admission 1616; out of commons 1616–22; in commons 1623–7. Honorific admission Gray's Inn 1619. Imprisoned by Elizabeth 1601 for advocating rebellion and flattering Essex. Historiographer of projected Chelsea College 1610. Occasional advocate in HCA 1609. Comr. Piracy London 1609, 1614. Comr. Adm. Middx., etc., 1609, 1614. Comr. Pol. & Assur. 1613. Delegates 1613–25. Master in Chancery 1617. Commissary of Shoreham and Croydon peculiar by 1617. Knighted 1619. Not to be confused w. John Hayward, M.P. Bridgnorth, Salop., 1621 and Saltash, Corn., 1626.

High Com. 1626. Brought before House of Commons for proceedings *v.*
Robert Howard as High Comr. 1626. Relies upon patronage of J. Caesar. Full
list of writings in *DNB*. Supports James I's policy of union w. Scotland. Attacks
alleged immemoriality of common law. Purchased houses and lands in Wood
Green, Middx.; owned lands in Felixstowe and house in Great St. Bartholomew, London. Res.: London. Invested in Virginia and Bermuda Companies.
Will: PCC 67 Skynner, pr. 28 June 1627. Lands eventually to pass to grand-
daughter Mary Rowe; £220 to relatives and charities.

> *DNB* ix. 311–13. Wood, *Athenae*, i. 368. *Al. Cant.* ii. 342. *Al. Oxon.* ii. 682. LPL, Reg.
> Doc. Com., ff. 47ᵛ, 108; Whitgift Reg. ii, f. 132; MS. 1729, f. 97. Foster, *Gray's Inn*,
> p. 154. C 181/2, ff. 101ᵛ, 194, 213, 214, 219ᵛ, 220; HCA 1/32/1, ff. 38, 55; HCA 24/73,
> f. 110. DEL 5/5–6, *passim*; DEL 8/70, pt. ii, *passim*; index 16818, p. 46. CUL, White-
> locke Journal, f. 175ᵛ. Usher, *High Commission*, p. 352; *Reconstruction*, i. 128. Bodl.,
> Tanner MS. 283, f. 92ᵛ. Allen, *Political Thought*, pp. 256–62. Dowling, 'Hayward's
> Troubles', Clancy, *Papist Pamphleteers*, pp. 70–1. Rabb, *Enterprise*, p. 311.

HEATH, Thomas, b. 1598, son of a gentleman from London. Matric. St. John's
College, Oxford, 1616; B.A. 1618; Fellow of Merton 1619; M.A. 1623; B.C.L.
1629; D.C.L. 1634. Warrant Doc. Com. 1637; full admission 1637; in commons
1637–42. Delegates 1639. Master in Chancery 1640–5. Chancellor of Peterborough diocese; lost position during Civil War. Fled to Netherlands and there
converted to Roman Catholicism. Subsisted on liberality of English nuns at
Ghent. d. at Ghent 1680.

> *Al. Oxon.* ii. 687. Clark, *Register*, ii. 355; iii. 361. LPL, Reg. Doc. Com., ff. 50, 110;
> Laud Reg. i, f. 236. PRO, DEL 8/70, pt. ii, f. 44ᵛ; index 16818, p. 46.

HELME, Christopher, b. in Wilts. Matric. as son of commoner Hart Hall,
Oxford, 1576; B.A. Merton 1579; fellow 1580; M.A. 1585; B.C.L. and D.C.L.
1594. Warrant Doc. Com. 1595 but not fully admitted. Rector of Bredon,
Worcs., 1607. Archdeacon of Derby 1609. Chancellor of Worcester diocese
1618–28. J.P. Worcs. 1608, 1626. Comr. of Sewers for Avon river 1629. Manor
of Chancely Grendour conveyed to him in 1626. m. Mary Fischer.

> *Al. Oxon.* ii. 691. Clark, *Register*, ii. 71; iii. 80. Gleason, *Justices*, pp. 215–17. PRO, C
> 181/4, f. 18; C 193/13/1, f. 104ᵛ; 193/13/2, f. 62ᵛ. LPL, Whitgift Reg. ii, f. 132. *VCH*
> *Worcs.* iv. 54, 56.

HERBERT, Sir John, b. 1540, 2nd son of Matthew of Swansea, Glam., esq.
B.A. Oxford 1559; M.A. 1561; B.C.L. 1565; D.C.L. 'after twenty years in civil
law' 1587. Honorary member of Doc. Com. 1573. Adm. Gray's Inn 1592.
Diplomatic visits to Denmark 1583, 1600, 1603; Poland 1584, 1585; Branden-
burg 1585; Netherlands 1588; France 1598. Negotiated w. Spain at Boulogne
1600. Master of Requests 1586–1600. Dean of Wells Cathedral 1590. 2nd
Secretary to Elizabeth and James 1600–7. Privy Councillor. Knighted 1602.
Council of North; secretary 1601–4. Council of Marches of Wales 1602–17.
J.P. Glam. 1595; Hants 1604; Montgomery during reign of James. M.P.

Grampound, Corn., 1586 prob. through influence of cousin, Lady Warwick; Gatton, Surrey, 1588 perhaps through Charles Howard, Earl of Nottingham; Christchurch, Hants, 1593 perhaps through Earl of Huntingdon; Bodmin, Corn., 1597 through Cecil; Glamorgan and Wallingford, Berks., 1601; Monmouthshire 1604. Committee for union w. Scotland 1606. Spoke in defence of King's financial needs 1606. High Com. 1604. Comr. Adm. Bristol 1604; Middx. 1606, 1611; Welsh counties 1615. Eclipsed at Court by 1614. Leased manor of Neath or Cadoxton, Glam., 1591 and purchased it 1599. Inherited family property in Cardiff and Swansea on death of brother 1609. Owned land in 15 different parts of Wales. Invested in commerce. Res.: Doc. Com. and Neath Abbey, Glam. d. 1617 after duel w. Sir Lewis Tresham. Will: PCC 117 and 107 Weldon, pr. 12 Dec. 1617. Lands to pay legacies and debts.

> DWB, pp. 353–4. Al. Oxon. ii. 695. HPT, typescript. Clark, Register, i. 122, 230; iii. 146. Boase, Register, p. 236. Foster, Gray's Inn, p. 79. HCMS x. 93, 142; xiii. 361–2. HMC Dean of Wells ii. 316–17, 319. LPL, Reg. Doc. Com., ff. 41ᵛ, 88ᵛ. BM, Add. MS. 38,139, f. 153. P. Williams, The Council of the Marches of Wales under Elizabeth (Cardiff, 1958), p. 141. Willson, Privy Councillors, pp. 58, 60, 69, 82–3, 270. Williams, Parliamentary History of Wales, p. 96. PRO, HCA 1/32/1, ff. 37, 55, 61; C 193/12/2, f. 72ᵛ; C 142/378/132. Willson, Bowyer Diary, p. 67. Rabb, Enterprise, p. 312.

HICKMAN, HENRY, 2nd son of Anthony, citizen of London and of Woodford, Essex, by Rose, dau. of Sir William Locke of London. Parents were Marian exiles. Brother of Anthony, D.C.L. St. Paul's School. Matric. pens. St. John's College, Cambridge, 1565; B.A. 1569; fellow 1571; M.A. 1572; proctor 1583–4; LL.D. 1584. Perhaps author of comedy Hymenaeus 1579. Warrant Doc. Com. 1586; full admission 1595; in commons until 1609; out of commons 1614–15. Chancellor of Peterborough diocese 1587. J.P. Northants. 1604–16. M.P. Northampton Borough 1601. Delegates 1595–1611. Master in Chancery 1602. Comr. for Charitable Uses, Northants., 1603. High Com. 1608, 1611. Held Manor of Bushey Hall, Herts. Grant of arms 1590. Res.: Doc. Com. and Northampton. Invested in commerce. d. 24 June 1618. Will: Peterborough, pr. 4 Sept. 1618. m. Mary, dau. of Richard Wallop of Bugbrook, Northants., and widow of one Eccleston of Eccleston, Lancs. Not to be confused w. son Henry (d. 1622).

> HPT, typescript. Al. Cant. ii. 366. Clark, Register, i. 350. Lincolnshire Pedigrees, ii. 493–4. Metcalfe Visitations of Northamptonshire, p. 48. LPL, Reg. Doc. Com., ff. 45, 106ᵛ; Whitgift Reg. i, f. 128. PRO, DEL 5/2–4, passim; index 16818, p. 45. BM, Add. MS. 38,139, f. 144. Grantees of Arms, i. 123–4. Gleason, Justices, p. 171. Rabb, Enterprise, p. 314. VCH Herts. ii. 183. Usher, High Commission, p. 352. W. T. Mellows, Peterborough Local Administration (Northampton Record Soc. x), p. 207.

HILL, OTWELL (ORTHOWELL). Matric. pens. St. John's College, Cambridge, 1573; B.A. 1577; fellow 1579; M.A. 1580; taxor 1588–9; proctor 1591; LL.D. before 1599. Warrant Doc. Com. 1599 but not fully admitted. Commissary for University of Cambridge 1605. J.P. Hunts. 1609. Com. to exercise jurisdiction of Lincoln diocese 1608; Chancellor 1609–16. High Com. 1611. Involved in proceedings against the Puritan Sir William Armyne 1612. Res.: Cambridge 1599; the Close at Lincoln in later life. d. 1616. Inventory of goods 27 May 1616 at total value of £345. 19s. 4d. m. Joan.

Al. Cant. ii. 372. Tanner, *Cambridge Register*, p. 33. LPL, Whitgift Reg. iii, f. 111; Bancroft Reg., f. 242ᵛ. Usher, *High Commission*, p. 352. CUL, MS. Mm. I. 49 (Baker 38), pp. 309-11. PRO, E 115/218/9. J. Hill, *Tudor and Stuart Lincoln*, pp. 113-14. HRO, Consistory Court Book 89, ff. 76-111. Gleason, *Justices*, p. 253.

HONE, JOHN, 1st son of William of London, gent. Matric. pens. Clare College, Cambridge, 1564; LL.B. 1573; LL.D. 1579. Warrant Doc. Com. 1579; full admission 1589; in commons until 1616. Honorific admission Middle Temple 1605. Delegates 1594-1616. Master in Chancery 1596-1616; charged with corruption in that capacity. Comr. Adm. Middx. 1603, 1606, 1610. Active as advocate in London courts 1603-13. Comr. Piracy London 1606, 1614. Comr. Sewers 1606. Comr. Pol. & Ass. 1609, 1613. Owned and leased houses in London. Res.: St. Bene't, Paul's Wharf, London. Will: PCC 122 Cope, pr. 16 Dec. 1616. £100 and maintenance to nephew John Foster. Refers to loss of £800 to insolvent son-in-law. Had already advanced daughter in marriage above ability. Father of Bartholomew and Julian.

Al. Cant. ii. 401. LPL, Reg. Doc. Com., ff. 43ᵛ, 105ᵛ; Grindal Reg., f. 177ᵛ. PRO, DEL 5/2-5, *passim*, HCA 24/70-6, *passim*; HCA 1/32/1, ff. 55, 61, 90; C 181/2, ff. 10ᵛ, 105, 194, 213, 219ᵛ, 220. BM, Lansdowne MS. 168, f. 152. Jones, *Chancery*, p. 118, n. 3. Haydn, *Dignities*, p. 395. PRO, PROB 11/57/45; 11/128/122. *Middle Temple Admissions*, p. 84.

HOSKINS, JOHN, b. 1579, 6th son of John of Llanwarne in Monnington-on-Wye, Herefs., commoner, by Margery, dau. of Thomas Jones. Matric. New College, Oxford, 1601; fellow 1601-13; B.C.L. 1606; D.C.L. 1613. A cleric. Chaplain to Robert Bennet, Bishop of Hereford. Vicar of Clifford, Herefs. through patronage of Bennet. Preb. of Hereford 1612-31; encounters opposition from Bishop Godwin of Hereford 1624. Perhaps chaplain to James I. Rector of Ledbury, Herefs., 1612-31. Master of St. Oswald Hospital through influence of Dr. Lake, Dean of Worcester, and Thomas Egerton. Contributed poem to *Epithalamia* (Oxford, 1613). Wrote *Sermons Preached at Pauls Crosse and Elsewhere* (Oxford, 1615). d. 30 Aug. 1631. Not to be confused w. his elder brother, John Hoskins, Serjeant-at-law and M.P. m. Frances Bourne, step-daughter of elder brother John.

L. B. Osborn (ed.), *The Life, Letters and Writings of John Hoskyns 1566-1638* (Yale Studies in English lxxxvii, New Haven, Conn., 1938), pp. 16, 72, 78, 193, 222, 249, 250, 254-5, 257. *Al. Oxon.* ii. 750. Wood, *Athenae*, ii. 510, 624. Clark, *Register*, i. 187; ii. 246; iii. 268. *CSPD 1623-1625*, pp. 379, 387. LeNeve, *Fasti*, i. 496, 518-19. A. T. Bannister, *Diocese of Hereford Institutions* (Hereford, 1923), p. 27. Bodl., MS. Top. Oxon. e. 105/2, f. 86.

HOTMAN, JOHANN, b. in France, son of François Hotman, French civilian. LL.D. Univ. of Valence; inc. Oxford 1581. Secretary of Leicester and friend of

Sidney, Bodley, and Camden. Friend of Gentili. Returns to France to teach law at Caen 1583. Returns to England because of French civil wars. Honorific admission Gray's Inn 1588. Accompanies Earl of Leicester to the Netherlands. Returns to France and serves Henry IV. Friend of Grotius. d. 1636. Wrote *The Ambassador* (London, 1603); translated James I's *Basilikon Doron* into French (1603).

> Molen, *Gentili*, pp. 46–7, 209, 278 n. 30, 294. *Al. Oxon.* ii. 751. Clark, *Register*, i. 379. P. J. Block, *Correspondance inédite de . . . François et Jean Hotman* (1913).

HUNT, JOHN. Matric. sizar Trinity College, Cambridge, 1566; B.A. 1571; fellow 1572; M.A. 1574; LL.D. 1581. Warrant Doc. Com. 1581; full admission 1583; in commons until 1608; out of commons 1609–29. J.P. Suffolk 1585; Norfolk 1593–6. Commissary for archdeaconry of Norwich 1586–95. Indicted by grand jury at Norwich for administering *ex officio* oath 1591. Comr. Piracy Norf. 1601, 1604; London 1603. Master in Chancery *c.* 1596–1615. Reports on dispute between Masters in Chancery and Cinque Ports 1601. Counsel for Great Yarmouth in Admiralty Causes 1598. Held manor of Thirmingworth, Norf., and two manors in Briston, Norf. Will: PCC 56 Scroope, pr. 12 June 1630. Thirmingworth to wife and then to grandson John. Provides for grandsons to study at Inns of Court.

> *Al. Cant.* ii. 433. LPL, Reg. Doc. Com., ff. 43ᵛ, 105; Grindal Reg., f. 245ᵛ. PRO, C 181/1, ff. 37, 122–3, 142; index 16818, p. 45. BM, Harl. MS. 474, f. 35ᵛ; MS. 6822, f. 293ᵛ. Blomefield, *Norfolk*, iii. 656. Palmer, *Great Yarmouth*, ii. 360–1. A. H. Smith, 'The Gentry of Norfolk', pp. 17–18. Levy, *Fifth Amendment*, p. 222. Jones, *Chancery*, pp. 365, 477–8. PRO, PROB 11/157/56.

HUSSEY (HUSSE, HUSEE), SIR JAMES, b. 1563, 3rd son of Thomas of Edmondsham, Dorset, esq. Winchester College. Matric. New College, Oxford, 1583; B.A. 1586; M.A. 1589; B.C.L. 1593; fellow 1584–8; D.C.L. 1601. Registrar of Oxford 1589–1610. Principal of Magdalen Hall 1602–5. Warrant Doc. Com. 1601; full admission 1604; in commons 1604–10, 1613–25; out of commons 1611–12. Chancellor of Bristol diocese 1603–25. J.P. Dorset 1604; City of Oxford 1608; Oxford 1609. Delegates 1597–1625. Master in Chancery extraordinary. Commissary of Archbishop of Canterbury 1617–21. Judge of Vice-Admiralty Court in Dorset *c.* 1611. Knighted 1619. Held manor of Hemsworth in Dorset; mess. and lands in Hemsworth, Shapwick, Cranborne, and Blandford St. Mary, Dorset; house in Farringdon Ward, London. Res.: Oxford, London, Dorset. d. at Oxford of the plague 11 July 1625. Will: PCC 20 Hele, pr. 6 Feb. 1626. £10 to Doc. Com.; £7 to poor; £5 to R. Swayne; rest to son James. m. Catherine. Father of James, George.

> *Al. Oxon.* ii. 776. *Visitation of Dorset* (Harl. Soc. xx, 1885), pp. 59–60. Clark, *Register*, i. 116, 120, 183, 184, 249; ii. 124; iii. 133. Wood, *Fasti*, i. 286. Kirby, *Winchester Scholars*, p. 147. LPL, Reg. Doc. Com., ff. 45ᵛ, 107; Whitgift Reg. iii, f. 137ᵛ; MS. 2014, f. 148ᵛ. Bodl., MS. Top. Oxon. e. 105/2, ff. 75ᵛ–76. PRO, C 142/487/42; C 216/1, no. 39; C 181/2, f. 71; HCA 1/32/1, f. 51; DEL 5/2–6, *passim*; DEL 8/70, i, ff. 19–25ᵛ;

PROB 11/148/20. Gleason, *Justices*, p. 249. BM, Add. MS. 38,170, f. 358; Lansdowne MSS. 984, f. 44; 81, f. 81ᵛ; J. Hutchins, *The History and Antiquities of the County of Dorset* (Westminster, 1861), i, p. xxiv. *NRS* vi. 92.

HUSSEY (HUSSE, HUSEE), SAMSON (SAMPSON), b. 1565, 4th son of Thomas of Edmondsham, Dorset, esq. Winchester College. Matric. Hart Hall, Oxford, 1584; B.C.L. New College 1592; fellow 1586–1600; D.C.L. 1602. Warrant Doc. Com. 1605; full admission 1609; in commons 1610–13, 1616–17; out of commons 1614–15, 1618–25. Delegates 1597. M.P. Wareham, Dorset, through influence of Rogers family by virtue of a common connection with the family of Sampson Strode, who was perhaps his godfather. Invested in commerce. d. 1625.

HPT, typescript. *Visitation of Dorset*, pp. 59–60. Bodl., MS. Top. Oxon. e. 105/2, ff. 77ᵛ–78; Clark, *Register*, i. 184; ii. 133; iii. 174. *Al. Oxon.* ii. 777. LPL, Reg. Doc. Com., ff. 46ᵛ, 107; Bancroft Reg., f. 129. PRO, DEL 5/2, f. 107. Rabb, *Enterprise*, p. 321.

HYDE, ALEXANDER, b. 1598, 4th son of Sir Lawrence, Kt., of Salisbury, by Barbara Castilion. Cousin of Edward Hyde, 1st Earl of Clarendon. Winchester College. Matric. New College, Oxford, 1615; fellow 1617–35; B.C.L. 1623; D.C.L. 1632. Cleric. Rector of Little Langford and Wylye, Wilts., 1634. Subdean of Salisbury Cathedral 1637. Preb. of Salisbury 1639. Royalist during Civil War. Sequestered from livings during Commonwealth. Dean of Winchester 1660–5; Bishop of Salisbury 1665 through influence of Clarendon. Inherited land in Swindon, Wilts. Purchased land in Swindon, Brigmerston, Milston, and Durnford, Wilts. Lease of impropriations of Grantham rectory. Marriage portion to dau. Margaret Parker at £1,500. d. 22 Aug. 1667. Will: PCC 161 Carr, pr. 21 Nov. 1667. Lands to only son Robert. Profits of lands at Swindon before Robert's majority and sale of lease of Grantham to daus. Barbara, Ann, and Elizabeth. m. Mary, dau. of Bishop Townson of Salisbury.

Al. Oxon. ii. 780. Clark, *Register*, ii. 344; iii. 424. *DNB* x. 366. Wood, *Athenae*, iv. 832. LeNeve, *Fasti*, ii. 621, 656; iii. 22. PRO, PROB 11/325/161. Bodl., MS. Top. Oxon. e. 105/2, f. 97.

HYDE, THOMAS, b. 1609, younger son of Sir Lawrence of Salisbury, Kt. Brother of Alexander (q.v.). Not to be confused w. Thomas, D.D., Precentor of Salisbury Cathedral 1661–6. Matric. New College, Oxford, 1627; fellow 1629–40 B.A. 1631; M.A. New Inn Hall 1635; B.C.L. and D.C.L. 1640. Proctor in Court of Archdeacon of Berks. 1636–8; in Oxford VCC 1636–9. Chancellor of Salisbury diocese 1640. Petitions Committee on Compounding 1649 that he has been subject to Parliament, that he has three sons in service, and that he has spent £40 in connection with discovery of a delinquent. Bur. 20 Oct. 1661 at Salisbury.

Al. Oxon. ii. 783. Wood, *Fasti*, i. 516. J. Fletcher, *Thomas Bennet, LL.D.* (Dorchester, 1924), p. 27. *CSPD 1640–1641*, p. 6. PRO, DEL 8/61, *passim.*Oxford Univ. Archives, Register of Chancellor's Court 1636–9, *passim.*

INGRAM, Sir William, 1st son of Hugh of London, citizen and member of Tallowchandler Co. (d. 1612). Matric. pens. Trinity College, Cambridge, 1582; B.A. 1586; M.A. Magdalene 1589; LL.D. 1604. Knighted 1617. Member and Deputy Secretary of King's Council of the North 1613–23. Judge of Exchequer and Prerogative Court in York Archdiocese *c*. 1609–23. Comr. Eccles. Causes, York, 1612–21. J.P. Yorks. West Riding 1611, 1622, 1635. Warden of Archbishop of York's old palace 1616. Owned mess. and land in Thorpe Underwoods, Yorks., and land in Skelton, Yorks. Leased manors of Rainton and Baldersby, Yorks. Res.: York. d. 24 July 1623. Will: York, pr. 27 Oct. 1625. Dwelling house, £100, and annuity of £30 to wife; lands in Thorpe Underwoods to wife and then to sons Hugh and William; leases to William; £600 to Hugh; lands in Skelton and £500 to son Arthur. Brother Arthur indebted to him for £1,100 in 1623. m. Catherine, dau. of J. Edmonds of Cambridge. Friend of John Favour. Not to be confused w. William Ingram of Earlscourte, Bucks., adm. to Inner Temple 1583.

Visitation of Yorkshire (Surtees Soc. xxxvi, 1859), p. 146. *Al. Cant.* ii. 449. Upton, *Sir Arthur Ingram*, pp. 1, 149, 162, 177. LPL, Bancroft Reg., f. 121. York Cathedral Library, Chapter Acts 1565–1634, ff. 437–8, 561. PRO, C 193/13/1, ff. 33, 36; C 193/13/2, f. 21ᵛ; C 181/2, ff. 156, 189ᵛ, 203ᵛ; C 142/674/77; C 66/1907ᵛ; will of Hugh, PROB 11/123/22. Borth. Inst., Wills 39/500ᵛ. Marchant, *Church Under Law*, pp. 46–7. ITL, Admissions to Inner Temple, i. 201.

JAMES, Francis, b. 1559, younger son of John of Little Onn, Staffs., commoner. Brother of William, Bishop of Durham. Matric. All Souls College, Oxford, 1581; fellow; B.C.L. 1583; D.C.L. 1588. Warrant Doc. Com. 1589; full admission 1590; in commons until 1615. Honorific admission Gray's Inn 1606. Government agent abroad 1590. In service of Walsingham 1591. Judge of Court of Audience 1590. Chancellor of Bath and Wells diocese 1599; Bristol diocese 1587–1603. J.P. Somerset 1607–17; quorum. Comr. Adm. Dorset 1603, 1611; Bristol 1604; Middx. 1609. Judge of Vice-Admiralty Court of Bristol 1604. Comr. Piracy London 1609. High Com. 1601–13. Delegates 1614. M.P. Dorchester, Dorset, 1593 through episcopal influence; Corfe Castle, Dorset, 1597 through Cecil; Minehead, Som., 1601 through George Luttrell; Wareham, Dorset, prob. through Thomas Howard. Brought bill *v*. drunkards 1601. Defends pluralities 1601. Speaks in favour of High Com. 1610. Purchased manor of Minchin Barrow 1592; manor of Barrow Gurney 1603; manors of Kingston Seymour and Hornblotton, all in Somerset. Invested in commerce. d. 28 Mar. 1616. Will: PCC 43 Cope, pr. 14 May 1616. £400 to each of his five daus. £200 to the poor. Civil law books to son-in-law Henry Billingsley. Father of Francis, William, Edward, and John.

HPT, typescript. *Al. Oxon.* ii. 799. LPL, Reg. Doc. Com., ff. 44, 106; Whitgift Reg. i, f. 154ᵛ; Abbot Reg. i, f. 228ᵛ. Foster, *Gray's Inn*, p. 113. *HMC Dean of Wells*, ii. 332, 339, 359. P. Hembry, *The Bishops of Bath and Wells* (London, 1967), pp. 195–6. Clark, *Register*, i. 392; ii. 111; iii. 116. PRO, C 181/2, f. 101ᵛ; C 142/356/110; DEL 5/4, f. 39; HCA 1/32/1, ff. 51, 55, 66, 69, 88; PROB 11/127/43. Usher, *High Commission*,

p. 353. Bowyer, *Diary*, pp. 125–6. Townshend, *Historical Collections*, p. 193. *CJ* i. 172, 204, 236, 268, 291, 300, 312, 326, 350, 351, 374, 375, 430. *HMCS* xii. 508. Rabb, *Enterprise*, p. 322. Venn, *Matriculations*, p. 381. Collinson, *Somerset*, ii. 309, 311. Gleason, *Justices*, pp. 193–4. Hutchins, *Dorset*, ii, p. xxiv. E. Bates, *Quarter Session Records for the County of Somerset*, i (Somerset Record Soc. xxiii), p. xxiv.

JARVIS (JERVIS, JARVICE, GERVAIS), John, b. 1603, 1st son of Arthur of the Pipe Office and Essex, esq. Perhaps related to James Jarvis or Gervis, D.C.L., Warden of Merton College. Matric. Brasenose College, Oxford, 1622; B.A. 1622; M.A. All Souls 1625; suspended from fellowship at All Souls for taking a degree out of his faculty 1626; reinstated in fellowship 1626; resigns fellowship 1631; D.C.L. 1632. Rector of North Fambridge, Essex, 1631, valued at £60 p.a. and of Greenstead-by-Colchester, Essex, 1638, valued at £80 p.a. Charged in 1644 with neglecting cure on Sundays, frequenting alehouses, and reading his sermons out of books. Sequestered 1646. Claimed 'the King was in the right way and the Parliament in the wrong'.

Al. Oxon. ii. 803. Clark, *Register*, ii. 404; iii. 406. *Brasenose Register*, i. 143. *Catalogue of All Souls Archives*, pp. 313, 381. *Visitation of Essex* (Harl. Soc. xiii), p. 376. *Walker Revised*, p. 156. *CSPD 1637–1638*, p. 189.

JESSOP (JESOP, JESOPE), Bartholomew, 4th son of Walter of Chilcombe, Dorset, gent. Chorister Magdalen College, Oxford, 1575–81; B.A. 1582; B.C.L. 1588; deputy registrar 1590; D.C.L. 1599. Warrant Doc. Com. 1599; full admission 1601; in commons until 1620. Active as advocate in London courts 1605–11. Delegates 1602–18. Chancellor of Salisbury diocese 1615–20. Received lease of lands in Whitechurch, Dorset, as legacy from kinsman. Res.: London; occasionally in Salisbury and in Gillingham, Dorset. d. 21 July 1620. Will: PCC 74 Soame, pr. 25 July 1620. £12 to poor; £15 to friends and relatives; goods and chattels to brother John. Unmarried.

Clark, *Register*, i. 184, 249; iii. 95. Wood, *Fasti*, i. 282. LPL, Reg. Doc. Com., ff. 45ᵛ, 106ᵛ; Whitgift Reg. iii, f. 111ᵛ. PRO, HCA 24/71, *passim*; DEL 5/3–6, *passim*; PROB 11/136/74. Fletcher, *Bennet*, p. 27.

JONES, Gilbert, b. 1593, son of an esquire from Worcs. Not to be confused w. Gilbert Jones, son of Gilbert of 'Poole', Montgomery, esq., of Gray's Inn. Matric. Oriel College, Oxford, 1612; B.A. 1615; M.A. 1617; B.C.L. All Souls College 1623; D.C.L. 1628. Chancellor of Bristol diocese 1625–69. Comr. Adm. Dorset 1628. Comr. Piracy Dorchester and Weymouth 1631; Dorset 1639, 1641. Judge of Vice-Admiralty Court of Somerset and Bristol 1636. M.P. Wareham, Dorset, in Short Parlt. 1640, perhaps through influence of Theophilus Howard, Earl of Suffolk. Compounds on Oxford articles for delinquency at fine of £43. 5s.

Clark, *Register*, ii. 328; iii. 328, 424. *Al. Oxon.* ii. 820. PRO, C 181/4, f. 104; 181/5, ff. 152ᵛ, 226ᵛ; HCA 1/32/1, f. 3. *CSPD 1635–1636*, p. 374. Hutchins, *Dorset*, i, p. xxiv. *CPCC* i. 260; iii. 2087. Foster, *Gray's Inn*, pp. 145, 235.

JUXON, WILLIAM, b. 1582, 2nd son of Richard, Receiver-General of the Bishop of Chichester, gentleman and citizen of London. Merchant Taylors' School. Fellow of St. John's College, Oxford, 1598; B.C.L. 1603; D.C.L. 1622. President of St. John's 1621. Vice-Chancellor of Oxford 1621–8. Honorary admission Doc. Com. 1634. Honorific admission Gray's Inn 1636. Registrar of Chichester diocese 1602. Ordained c. 1609. Vicar of St. Giles, Oxford, 1609–15. Rector of Somerton, Oxon., 1615. Preb. of Chichester 1622–33. Dean of Worcester 1627 at income of £133. 6s. 8d. Steward of Chichester Cathedral 1630. Bishop of Hereford 1633; of London 1633. Chaplain to Charles I. Clerk of His Majesty's Closet 1632. Privy Councillor. Lord Treasurer 1635. First Comr. of the Admiralty 1635–8. J.P. Kent, Norfolk, Northants., Somerset, Worcs. 1636. High Com. 1629, 1633. Ally of Laud. Fined for sentence as High Comr. 1641. Accompanies Charles I to the scaffold 1649. Archbishop of Canterbury 1660. d. 1663. Will: PCC 89 Juxon, pr. 4 July 1663. £600 to poor; £1,000 to sister Anne Swayne; £500 apiece to nephews Richard and Lawrence Swayne and nieces Elizabeth Merloff and Frances Fischer; £2,000 to cousins, £7,000 to St. John's College; £2,000 for repair of St. Paul's; £1,200 to servants.

> *DNB* x. 1121–4. J. R. M. Etherington, 'The Life of Archbishop Juxon 1582–1663' (Oxford B.Litt. thesis, 1940). Curtis, *Oxford and Cambridge*, pp. 224–5. *Al. Oxon.* ii. 836. Wood, *Athenae*, iv. 818–20. Clark, *Register*, ii. 257; iii. 244. *Chichester Chapter Acts*, nos. 995, 1170, 1202, 1222, 1251. Foster, *Gray's Inn*, p. 211. Usher, *High Commission*, p. 353. Lloyd, *Memoires*, pp. 595–8. Gleason, *Justices*, pp. 156, 179, 198, 217, 236. Mallett, *Oxford*, ii. 183. BM, Add. MS. 17,685. LPL, MS. 958, p. ii. PRO, SP 16/483/59; PROB 11/311/89.

KING, ROBERT, b. 1600 in Kent, prob. son of Robert of Goudhurst, Kent, yeoman, by Elizabeth. Matric. pens. Christ's College, Cambridge, 1617; B.A. 1621; M.A. 1624; fellow 1625–36; junior proctor 1629–30; LL.D. 1636. Commissary of Cambridge 1638. Elected Master of Trinity Hall 1645 but appointment overruled by House of Commons because of his royalist sympathies. Master of Trinity Hall 1660–76. Warrant Doc. Com. 1637; full admission 1641. Proctor in Consistory Court of Ely 1628. Active as advocate in London courts 1638–40. Comr. Piracy London 1638. Official to Archdeacon of Suffolk 1641–4?; 1660–2. Commissary for Suffolk archdeaconry 1642–5. Official of Archdeacon of Sudbury 1645–74. Commissary for Sudbury archdeaconry 1645. Chancellor of Ely diocese 1660–76. Purchased house and land in Great Thurlow, Suff. Leased estate of Great Bradley, Suff. from St. John's College, Cambridge. d. 5 Nov. 1676. Will: PCC 141 Bence, pr. 13 Nov. 1676. Lands at Great Thurlow to grandson Henry; lease of Great Bradley to wife and then to grandson Robert. m. Frances, dau. of J. Wareyn of Great Thurlow.

> *Al. Cant.* iii. 20. *DNB* xi. 155. Peile, *Christ's College*, i. 318. Kent Archives Office, will of Robert King, PRC 32, f. 97. LPL, Reg. Doc. Com., ff. 50, 110; Laud Reg., i, f. 281ᵛ. Blomefield, *Norfolk*, iii. 657–8, 661. Malden, *Trinity Hall*, pp. 145–6. *CJ* iv. 335. *LJ* vii. 678; viii. 236. PRO, C 181/5, f. 131; HCA 24/98, no. 18; 24/101, loose paper; SP 16/421/108; PROB 11/352/141.

LAKES, Stephen, b. 1537, 3rd son of James of Smarden, Kent, gent., by Catherine, dau. of S. Bishop of Wrotham, Kent. Eton College. Adm. scholar and matric. pens. King's College, Cambridge, 1565; fellow 1568–79; B.A. 1570; M.A. 1573; LL.D. 1579. Warrant Doc. Com. 1581 but not fully admitted. Punished for wearing indecent apparel and for presenting articles *v.* Dr. Roger Goad. Provost of King's College 1576. Commissary of Archbishop of Canterbury 1582. Preb. of Canterbury 1583–9. Reports to Whitgift on activities of Puritans 1584. Accused of unfair prosecution of J. Elvin, Puritan Minister of Westwell, Kent, 1590. High Com. 1600. Referred to as Master in Chancery, but there is no record of his appointment. Wrote Latin verse. Owned 11 mess. in Smarden, Dover, and Gravesend, Kent. Held leases in Thornham, Kent. Res.: St. Dunstan-in-the-West, London. bur. 2 May 1617. Will: PCC 59 Weldon, pr. 12 June 1617. Lands and leases to son Thomas; £500 to dau. Elizabeth. m. Elizabeth, dau. of P. Chapman of Witcham, Cambs., esq.

> Cooper, *Athenae*, ii. 325. *Al. Cant.* iii. 35. LPL, Grindal Reg., ff. 228, 252ᵛ; MS. 2014, ff. 81, 148ᵛ. *Eton Register*, p. 203. Strype, *Whitgift*, i. 276–80; *Annals*, ii, pt. 2, pp. 38–41. *Visitation of London* ii (Harl. Soc. xvii, 1870), 41.

LAMBE (LAMB, LAMME), Sir John, b. *c.* 1566, 1st son of John of Northampton, perhaps gent., by Elizabeth, dau. of W. Aylett of Rivenhall, Essex. Cousin of Robert Aylett, LL.D. (q.v.). Matric. sizar St. John's College, Cambridge, 1583; B.A. 1587; M.A. 1590; LL.D. 1616. No record of admission to Doc. Com., but in commons 1622–42. Schoolmaster *c.* 1590. Clerk to proctor in Peterborough Consistory Court 1592. Purchased registrarship of Ely 1600. Co-registrar of Peterborough 1602. Proctor in Arches 1602. Chancellor of Peterborough diocese w. H. Hickman 1615; alone 1616. Commissary for peculiars of Dean and Chapter of Lincoln 1617. Commissary for archdeaconry of Leics. 1623. Commissary for archdeaconry of Buckingham. Surrogate to C. Wyvell as Chancellor of Lincoln diocese. Registrar of Ely 1630. J.P. Northants. 1626. Knighted 1621. Master in Chancery 1622. High Com. 1629–41. Dean of Arches 1633–47. Comr. Piracy London 1633. Ally of Laud; defends Laud's right to visit Lincoln diocese. Criticizes Bishop Williams of Lincoln for not proceeding *v.* Puritans 1626. Accused by Northampton residents of corruption and vexation in Parlt. of 1621 and 1624; saved by adjournment 1621 and by Bishop Williams of Lincoln 1624. Defends Cowell's *Interpreter* 1638. Chancellor and Keeper of Seal to Queen Henrietta Marie 1640 at fee of £54 p.a. plus profits of office. Unsuccessful candidate for Univ. of Cambridge seat in Short Parlt. 1640. 'Banned and cursed to pit of hell' by Puritans of Beaconsfield, Bucks. Fined for sentence as High Comr. 1641. Object of abuse in Puritan literature 1640–1. Lent £3,000 to King for Scottish war. Estate valued at £5,000 after death. Held advowson to vicarage of St. Giles, Northants. Begs to compound on Oxford Articles 1646; composition fines set at £628 after death. Res.: Tower Close, Northampton, and Doc. Com. d. 14 Dec. 1646.

Administration: PCC 1647. m. Anne, dau. of Sir Thomas Crompton (q.v.). Father of Susan, wife of John Hill.

> *DNB* xi. 443–4. Slatter, 'Study of Lambe'. *Al. Cant.* iii. 36. Coote, *Civilians*, pp. 66–7. Lloyd, *Memoires*, p. 593. Serjeantson, *St. Giles*, pp. 64, 163–4. PRO, C 216/1, no. 84; C 181/4, f. 138ᵛ; SP 14/11/10–11; 14/74/85; 16/442/37; 16/442/122; 16/483/59; 16/484/56; *CSPD 1603–1610*, p. 640; *1611–1618*, pp. 272, 274, 306, 413, 458, 519, 580; *1625–1626*, pp. 17, 148; *1635*, pp. 40, 110; *1640*, p. 59; *1641–1643*, pp. 423–4, 551–2. Rushworth, *Historical Collections*, i. 420–1; ii. 819. *NRS* iv. 346–7; vi. 471–3; vii. 606–9. BM, Add. MS. 18597, f. 190. J. Bridges, *The History and Antiquities of Northamptonshire* (Oxford, 1791), i. 431. Usher, *High Commission*, p. 353.

LEGGE, Thomas, b. 1535, son of Stephen of Norwich, prob. freeman of the city. Matric. pens. Christ's College, Cambridge, 1552. B.A. Trinity College 1557; M.A. 1560; Fellow of Trinity 1560–8; of Jesus College 1568–73; tutor at Jesus; LL.D. Caius College 1575. Regius Professor of Civil Law 1570–4. Master of Gonville and Caius College 1573; quarrels with fellows. Vice-Chancellor of Cambridge 1587–8, 1592–3. Warrant Doc. Com. 1580; full admission 1590; in commons until 1608. Master in Chancery 1595–1607. Comr. Adm. Middx. 1603. J.P. Cambs. 1597. Sent to the Fleet 1581 for contempt of Queen's letter. Articles brought *v.* him for recusancy, favouring papists at Cambridge, and extorting college funds. Hostile to Puritanism. Freeman of Norwich 1600. Donates copyhold lands in Cambs. to Gonville and Caius College. d. 12 July 1607. Will: PCC 81 Huddleston, pr. 27 Oct. 1607. £100 from sale of land to Gonville and Caius. Not certain whether he would die in Cambridge or London. Wrote tragedies: *Destruction of Jerusalem* and *Life of King Richard III*.

> Cooper, *Athenae*, ii. 454–7. *Al. Cant.* iii. 71. LPL, Reg. Doc. Com., ff. 43ᵛ, 105ᵛ; Grindal Reg., f. 200ᵛ. *Freemen of Norwich*, p. 208. J. R. Tanner, *The Historical Register of the University of Cambridge to 1910* (Cambridge, 1917), p. 81. Haydn, *Dignities*, p. 395. Heywood and Wright, *Transactions*, i. 314–41. Nicolas, *Hatton*, p. 261. *VCH Cambs.* iii. 360–2. PRO, PROB 11/110/81.

LEVET (LEVETT, LEVITT), John, 3rd son of Thomas of Melton, Yorks., gent., by Elizabeth Mirfield of Thurcroft, Yorks. Eldest brother Thomas was High Sheriff of Yorks. in 1639. Conisborough and Houghton Schools. Adm. pens. Christ's College, Cambridge, 1623; LL.B. 1623; LL.D. 1633. Succeeds Easdall (q.v.) as Judge of Exchequer and Prerogative Court of York 1632; leaves routine duties as judge to Dr. Phineas Hodson. Listed as member of Doc. Com. in 1639 but no record of admission. Res.: primarily in London. m. Mary, dau. of Emmanuel Mote of Melton, Yorks.

> *Al. Cant.* iii. 78. Peile, *Christ's College*, i. 350. Marchant, *Church Under Law*, pp. 48, 101. Borth. In t., R. VII PR 108. *CPCC* iii. 2129.

LEWIN, Sir Justinian, b. 1613, son of William of Smithfield, London, gent., by Sarah. Grandson of William Lewin, D.C.L. Matric. Pembroke College, Oxford, 1631; B.C.L. 1632; D.C.L. 1637. Warrant Doc. Com. 1637; full admission 1647. Honorific admission Gray's Inn 1641. Commissary for Norfolk archdeaconry 1633; Official of Archdeacon of Norfolk 1639. Judge-Martial of Army under the Earl of Arundel in the Scottish expedition 1639. Deplored 'the ungodly rebellious courses' of the Scots. Master in Chancery 1641–51; 1660–72. Royalist during Civil War. Cited as delinquent in paying parliamentary taxes 1642. Promotes interest of Charles II in Norfolk. Imprisoned 1655. Commissary for Norwich archdeaconry 1660. Knighted 1661. Res.: Heigham, outside walls of Norwich. d. 1 Jan. 1673. m. dau. of Rhees Wynn, serjeant-at-law, and niece of Thomas Gwynne (q.v.).

> DNB xi. 1048. Al. Oxon. iii. 905. R. Waters, Genealogical Memoirs of the Extinct Family of Chester of Chicherley (London, 1887), ii. 411. LPL, Reg. Doc. Com., ff. 50ᵛ, 110; Laud Reg. i, f. 283. Borth. Inst., R. VII. PR 108. CJ ii. 896. Blomefield, Norfolk, iii. 656–7, 660. Norwich Chapter Books, p. 177. Foster, Gray's Inn, p. 234. PRO, index 16818, pp. 46–7. Ketton-Cremer, Norfolk, pp. 158, 345. Wood, Fasti, i. 322 n. Oxford Univ. Archives, P.P. 2, f. 269ᵛ.

LEWIN, WILLIAM, b. 1601, 1st son of Gilbert of Ringstead, Norf., gent. Hardingham School. Matric. pens. Caius College, Cambridge, 1616; B.A. 1619; M.A. 1622; fellow 1623–33; LL.D. 1632. Adm. Gray's Inn 1620. Full admission Doc. Com. 1632. Official of the Archdeacon of Surrey by 1625. Active as advocate in London courts 1634–9. J.P. Norf. 1635. Joins other ecclesiastical judges residing at Doc. Com. in legal opinion c. 1636. Parliamentarians call for his arrest for discouraging payment of parliamentary taxes 1642. Joins Royalist forces. Advocate-General to Prince Rupert's forces. Compounds on Oxford Articles 1648; fine at a tenth, £19. Leased manor and rectory of Ludham, Norf., from the Bishop of Norwich until it was sequestered. Condemned by court martial for machinations against the Commonwealth 1650. Administration: PCC 1667.

> Al. Cant. iii. 80. LPL, Reg. Doc. Com., ff. 49ᵛ, 109ᵛ; MS. 1729, f. 96. Foster, Gray's Inn, p. 157. PRO, C 193/13/2, f. 50ᵛ; SP 16/339/63; HCA 24/95, f. 81; 24/98, nos. 55, 134. Ketton-Cremer, Norfolk, p. 150. CPCC ii. 1615; iii. 1630. Reports of Heraldic Cases, pp. 29, 33. Bodl., Tanner MS. 63, f. 151. CSPD 1634–1635, p. 327; 1635–1636, pp. 88, 98, 473. Visitation of Norfolk . . . 1664, i (Harl. Soc. lxxxv, 1933), 38.

LITTLETON, JAMES, b. 1596, 2nd son of Sir Edward of Pillaton Hall, Staffs., and Henley, Salop, Bt. Eldest brother was Sir Edward, Solicitor-General. Matric. Christ Church, Oxford, 1612; B.A. Broadgates Hall 1618; Fellow of All Souls; M.A. 1621; B.C.L. 1625; D.C.L. 1635. Warrant Doc. Com. before 1640; referred to as member 1639 but no record of full admission. Honorific admission Inner Temple 1639. Master of Temple Church 1639. Associate of the Bar and Assistant of the Bench with all privileges of an absolute bencher 1639 through influence of brother Edward. Chancellor of Worcester diocese 1628. Assists inhabitants of Worcester during plague 1637–8. J.P. Worcs. Delegates 1639. Master in Chancery 1639–45. d. 1645.

> Al. Oxon. iii. 920. Borth. Inst., R. VII. PR 108. ITL, Admissions to Inner Temple, i. 470. F. Inderwick, A Calendar of the Inner Temple Records (London, 1898), ii. 250–1,

254. *Students Admitted to the Inner Temple*, p. 300. Prest, 'Inns of Court', p. 85. T. R. Nash, *Collections for the History of Worcestershire* (London, 1781), ii. clxviii. Wood, *Athenae*, iii. 651. Gleason, *Justices*, p. 218. PRO, DEL 8/70, pt. 2, ff. 43–8; SP 16/442/125; index 16818, pp. 46–7.

LITTLETON, Sir Walter, 3rd son of Sir Edward of Pillaton Hall, Staffs., and Henley, Salop, Bt. Brother of James (q.v.). Matric. pens. St. John's College, Cambridge, 1624; B.A. Lincoln College, Oxford, 1626; M.A. Cambridge 1630; LL.D. 1639. Warrant Doc. Com. 1640 but not fully admitted. Compounded for delinquency for living in the King's quarters in the Close at Lichfield, his only residence for 7 years, 1646. Claims that he never took up arms against Parlt. and that he sent them intelligence. Fined £300 and then pardoned 1649. Chancellor of Lichfield diocese 1661–70. Knighted 1662. Master in Chancery 1660–70. d. 1670. Will: PCC 6 Duke, pr. 16 Jan. 1671. Leases, tithes, and personal estate to wife; lease of Rugeley rectory in Staffs., held from the Dean and Chapter of Lichfield, and tithes from other rectories eventually to pass to son Walter; £200 to son Fisher. m. Priscilla, dau. of L. Pemberton of Rushden.

Al. Cant. iii. 92. *Staffordshire Pedigrees* (Harl. Soc. lxiii, 1912), p. 158. PRO, SP 16/442/125; PROB 11/335/6. Shaw, *Staffordshire*, i. 300. *LeNeve's Knights*, p. 153. Haydn, *Dignities*, p. 396. CPCC ii. 1464.

LLOYD, David, b. 1597, son of David of Llanidloes, Montgomery, gent. Nephew of Oliver Lloyd, sen., D.C.L. (q.v.) and brother of Oliver, jr., D.C.L. (q.v.). Matric. Hart Hall, Oxford, 1612; B.A. 1615; Fellow of All Souls College 1618; B.C.L. 1622; D.C.L. 1628. Chaplain to 6th Earl of Derby 1639. Preb. of Chester 1639–42. Rector of Trefdraeth, Anglesey, 1641–2; Llangynhafal, Denbighs. 1642; Winwick, Lancs. Vicar of Llanfair-Dyffryn-Clwyd, Denbighs., 1642. Warden of Ruthin, Denbighs., 1642. Deprived of benefices during Civil War; reinstated 1660. Dean of St. Asaph 1660. Leased rectory of Cheltington, Bucks. Heavily in debt at end of life. Composed *The Legend of Captaine Jones*. d. 7 Sept. 1663.

DWB, p. 576. *DNB* xi. 1294–5. Al. Oxon. iii, 922. Al. Cant. iii. 93. Clark, *Register*, ii. 327; iii. 336. Wood, *Athenae*, iii. 652; *Fasti*, i. 442. Lloyd, *Memoires*, p. 613.

LLOYD, John, younger son of David of Carnarvons., prob. lesser gent. Brother of Hugh Lloyd, D.C.L. Family described as 'not ignoble'. B.A. Oxford 1542; Fellow of All Souls; B.C.L. 1554; D.C.L. 1565. Fellow of Jesus College 1571. Warrant Doc. Com. 1566; full admission 1566; in commons until 1606; out of commons 1607–8. Deprived as Rector of All Hallows Church in Stratford-on-Avon for contumacy 1559. Dean of St. Asaph 1559. Active as advocate in London courts. Delegates 1595–1607. Comr. to exercise jurisdiction of Chester diocese 1605. High Com. 1605. Chancellor of Bangor diocese 1607. Co-author of memorandum on oaths in ecclesiastical courts c. 1590. J.P. Flints. 1604. d. 20 Feb. 1608. Will: PCC 31 Windebanke, pr. 31 May 1608. Frees David Yale (q.v.) of £300 debt and bequeaths to him money owed by other debtors. m. Elizabeth, dau. of one Pigot of Doddershall, Bucks. Father of Frances, wife of David Yale, and Mary.

> *Al. Oxon.* iii. 925. PRO, will of Hugh Lloyd, PROB 11/98/86; C 66/1645ᵛ; DEL 5/2–3, *passim.* New College, Oxford, brass of H. Lloyd in antechapel. *Visitation of Shropshire* ii (Harl. Soc. xxix, 1889), 329. LPL, Parker Reg. i, f. 257; Bancroft Reg., ff. 212ᵛ, 217; Reg. Doc. Com., ff. 39ᵛ, 103; MS. 2004, f. 65. BM, Lansdowne MS. 980, f. 262; Add. MS. 38,139, f. 172. Usher, *High Commission,* p. 354.

LLOYD, OLIVER, b. 1571, younger son of the house of Berth Lloyd (Bertlloys) in Montgomerys. Matric. St. Mary's Hall, Oxford, 1589; B.C.L. All Souls College 1597; fellow; D.C.L. 1602. Studied 'divers languages'. Warrant Doc. Com. 1602; full admission 1609; in commons until 1625. Chancellor of Hereford diocese *c.* 1602; removed 1609; reappointed 1615. 2nd reversion to judgeship of PCC. Dean of Risborough, Bucks., 1605. Preb. of Windsor 1615–17 by mandate of King dated 1604. Rector of Clynnog, Carnarvons., 1615. Dean of Hereford 1617 at income of £36. 8s. 2d. Occasional service as advocate in Admiralty and Delegates Courts 1605–21. Comr. Adm. Middx. 1614. Held land in Llandinam, Llanwynog, and Trefeglwys, Montgomerys. Will: PCC 128 Clark, pr. 23 Nov. 1625. £350 to St. John's College, Oxford, to support one fellow at £20 p.a. Annuity of £20 to nephew Oliver (q.v.). Lands to nephews James, Richard, John, and Edward.

> BM, Add. MS. 6044, f. 16; *Al. Oxon.* iii. 927. Clark, *Register,* i. 184; ii. 168; iii. 207. *DWB,* p. 587. LPL, Reg. Doc. Com., ff. 46ᵛ, 107ᵛ; Bancroft Reg., ff. 128ᵛ, 215. Bond, *Acts,* pp. 91, 97. Hatfield House, Salisbury MS. 195/22ᵛ. PRO, DEL 5/4, ff. 15, 90; DEL 5/5, f. 122; DEL 5/6, ff. 14, 78, 122; HCA 24/71–7, *passim;* HCA 1/32/1, f. 38; PROB 11/147/128; SP 14/3/11.

LLOYD, OLIVER, younger son of David of Montgomerys., gent. Nephew of Oliver Lloyd (q.v.) and brother of David (q.v.). B.A. St. Edmund Hall, Oxford, 1621; Fellow of All Souls College 1624–48; 1660–2; B.C.L. 1627; D.C.L. 1635. Warrant Doc. Com. 1637; listed as member in 1639 but not fully admitted. Ejected from fellowship at All Souls after long absence 1651; reinstated 1660. Legacy of £20 p.a. from uncle Oliver 1625. d. 17 March 1662. Res.: near Doc. Com. 1662.

> *Al. Oxon.* iii. 927. Clark, *Register,* iii. 399. Wood, *Athenae,* iii. 653. LPL, Laud Reg. i, f. 281ᵛ. Borth. Inst., R. VII. PR 108. *Walker Revised,* p. 23. PRO, PROB 11/147/128.

LLOYD, THOMAS, b. 1607, son of Thomas of Bristol, Glos. Matric. St. John's College, Oxford, as son of a commoner 1623; fellow before 1631; B.C.L. 1630; D.C.L. 1639. Deacon by 1631; priest by 1632. Rector of Rollright, Oxon., 1635; perhaps also of Great Whitcombe, Glos., 1639. Composed two poems for preface to *Amorum Troii et Cressidea* (Oxford, 1635).

> *Al. Oxon.* iii. 930. *Al. Cant.* iii. 96. Bodl., MS. Oxf. Diocs. Papers e. 13, pp. 105, 164; Oxford Univ. Arch., P.P. 2, f. 107. PRO, Institution Books, ser. A, v. 5 (Glos.).

LYNNE, MARMADUKE, 5th son of John of Bassingbourn, Cambs., esq., by Mary, dau. of John Sewster, Attorney of the Court of Wards. Matric. pens. Trinity Hall, Cambridge, 1589; scholar 1590; fellow 1596–1609; LL.B. c. 1612; LL.D. 1617. Proctor in Norwich Consistory Court 1603. Adm. advocate at York Consistory Court 1607. Warrant Doc. Com. 1617; full admission 1628; in commons until 1640. Chancellor of Salisbury diocese 1621–40. J.P. Wilts. 1635. Involved in prosecution of Recorder of Sarum in Star Chamber 1633. Joins other ecclesiastical judges residing at Doc. Com. in legal opinion c. 1636. Comr. Piracy Hants 1635, 1636. Held lands and leases at Royston, Herts.; used rents and profits for maintenance. Will: PCC 118 Coventry, pr. 1 Sept. 1640. Books to eldest son John; provides for education of younger son Thomas. Brother John was citizen and alderman of Exeter.

> Al. Cant. iii. 122. Visitation of Cambridge, p. 102. LPL, Reg. Doc. Com., ff. 49, 108ᵛ; Abbot Reg. ii, f. 177. Fletcher, Bennet, p. 27. Marchant, Church Under Law, pp. 46, 250. PRO, C 193/13/2, f. 73ᵛ; C 181/5, ff. 24, 58; SP 16/233/88 III; SP 16/339/63; PROB 11/184/118. Registrum Vagum i. 28.

MAINWARING (MANWARINGE, MANWAIRING, MANWAYRNGE, MANWARYNG), EDMUND, b. 1579, 2nd son of Sir Randall of Over Peover, Cheshire, Kt., by Margaret, dau. of Sir Edward Fitton of Gawsworth. Younger brother Philip was Secretary of State for Ireland 1638. Matric. Brasenose College, Oxford, 1594; B.A. 1598; M.A. All Souls College 1602; B.C.L. 1605; nominated as Dean 1606; fellow until 1610, created D.C.L. 1629. Advocate at York Consistory Court 1612–34. Commissary of Consistory Court at Richmond through influence of Bishop of Chester 1612–34. Official of Archdeacon of York 1613–38. Commissary of Peculiar of Dean and Chapter of York 1624–37. Chancellor of York diocese w. W. Easdall (q.v.). Comr. Eccles. Causes, York 1612–20. Council of the North 1629–41; Deputy Secretary 1629; Secretary 1630. J.P. Yorks. 1632; Cheshire 1635. Royalist during Civil War. Estate in Chester sequestered for his delinquency. m. Jane, dau. of Michael York. Father of Sir William, Lieutenant-Colonel who defended Chester v. Parliamentary forces 1643.

> Al. Oxon. iii. 959. Clark, Register, ii. 208; iii. 211. J. Croston, County Families of Lancashire and Cheshire (London, 1887), p. 379. Visitation of Cheshire (Harl. Soc. lix, 1909), pp. 157–8. Marchant, Church Under Law, pp. 46–7, 113, 250. Borth Inst., R. VII. H.C.A.B. 16. PRO, C 181/4, f. 175; C 193/13/2, f. 9ᵛ; SP 16/212, p. 39. Reid, Council of the North, p. 498. G. L. Fenwick, A History of the Ancient City of Chester (Chester, 1896), p. 203. Catalogue of All Souls Archives, pp. 308, 380.

MANNING (MAUNINGE), HENRY, b. 1562, only son of Henry of Kent, esq. and Marshal of the Household of Henry VII, Edward VI, Mary, and Elizabeth, by Catherine, dau. and coheir of Erasmus Kerkener. Matric. All Souls College, Oxford, 1581; fellow; B.C.L. 1583; D.C.L. 1589. Warrant Doc. Com. 1590; full admission 1595; in commons 1603–7, 1610–12; out of commons 1608–9, 1613–14. Chancellor of Exeter diocese; presided over Consistory Court

at Exeter regularly 1607–10; intermittently 1610–14. Held lands and ten. in
Pagham, Sussex; leased rectory of Pagham. Will: PCC 99 Lawe, pr. 9 Oct.
1614. Lands to be sold to pay debts and legacies; £200 to eldest son Henry and
eldest dau. Catherine; £100 to each younger son and dau. m. Josoca, dau. of
James Day of Berks.

Al. Oxon. iii. 966. Clark, *Register*, i. 181; ii. 111; iii. 116. Venn, *Matriculations*, p. 445.
LPL, Reg. Doc. Com., ff. 44ᵛ, 106; Whitgift Reg. i, f. 161. Cassidy, 'Episcopate of
Cotton', pp. 117–18, 124. Exeter Cathedral Library, MS. 3553, f. 1ᵛ. PRO, PROB
11/124/99.

MARTEN, Sɪʀ Hᴇɴʀʏ, b. 1559 in parish of St. Michael Bassishaw, London, 1st
son of Anthony, citizen and grocer of London and of Berks., gent. Winchester
College. Matric. New College, Oxford, as son of commoner 1581; fellow
1582–95; B.C.L. 1587; D.C.L. 1592. Warrant Doc. Com. 1595; full admission
1596; in commons 1596–1612, 1615–41; out of commons 1613–14. Nominated
but not selected as law lecturer at Gresham College 1597. Honorific admission
Lincoln's Inn 1623. Official of Archdeacon of Berks. *c.* 1593–1630. J.P. Berks.
Active as advocate in London courts by 1596. King's Advocate 1608–9. Mission
to Palatinate 1613. Conflicts w. Spanish Ambassador 1615. Negotiates between
English and Dutch East India Companies 1619. Chancellor of London diocese
1616–27. Judge of HCA 1617–41. High Com. 1620–41. Judge of PCC 1624–41.
Dean of Arches 1624–33. Argues before Privy Council against prohibitions
1608, 1632. Defends Puritans of St. Gregory's Parish, London, in dispute over
communion table. M.P. St. Germans, Corn., through patronage of John Eliot
1625, 1626; Oxford Univ. 1628; St. Ives, Corn., through court influence 1640
(Apr.). Opposes irregular power of foreign ambassadors, the prevalence of
popish books in the kingdom, and the statutory deprivation of ministers in
Parlt. of 1625. Criticized in Parlt. of 1626 for advising stay of the ship *St. Peter*.
Opponent of the Duke of Buckingham by 1625 but advises moderation in
remonstrance to King *v.* Buckingham 1628. Chosen by Commons to speak
against the Lords' amendment to the Petition of Right. Delivers opinion on
election of Bishop Montague 1629. Rebuked and fined by Parlt. for illegal
proceedings and sentences as High Comr. Estate at Hinton Waldrist, Berks.,
granted by Charles I 1627. Manor House of Longworth attached to Hinton
Waldrist at value of £9,500. Purchased manors of Petwick (1600), Barcote
(1618), Smewyns (1622), Eaton Hastings (1628), Beckett and Stalpits (1633),
Bouton (1635), Shrivenham Salop (1635), and Canon Hill (by 1637), all in
Berks. Believed to be the wealthiest member of Doc. Com. 1639. Lent £3,000
to the King. Res.: Doc. Com. and Aldersgate Street, London. d. Sept. 1641.
Will: PCC 124 Evelyn, pr. 15 Oct. 1641. £2,000 for almshouses in Longworth
and Shrivenham, Berks.; £500 to granddau. Mary Edmond; £100 to granddau.
Margaret Marten; £350 to redeem English captives from slavery in Turkey;
£200 to servant. Land to son Henry, the regicide. m. Elizabeth.

DNB xii. 1146–8. *Al. Oxon.* iii. 977. Fuller, *Worthies*, ii. 370–1. *Visitations of Berkshire*,

i. 43–4. Ward, *Gresham Professors*, p. 58. LPL, Reg. Doc. Com., ff. 45, 106ᵛ; Whitgift
Reg. ii, f. 132. Bodl., MS. Oxf. Archd. Papers Berks. cc. 34–70, *passim*; MS. Top.
Oxon. e. 105/2, f. 75; Tanner MS. 280, f. 121. PRO, C 193/13/1, f. 7ᵛ; C 193/13/2,
f. 4ᵛ; SP 14/93/123; SP 16/148/6; 16/477/62; 16/483/59; 16/499/42; 16/212, p. 8. Aylmer,
King's Servants, p. 353. Usher, *High Commission*, p. 354. Forster, *Eliot*, i. 336, 447,
508–9; ii. 104 n. Rex, *University Representation*, pp. 115–16, 118–19. Rushworth,
Historical Collections, i. 521, 579, 617. Gardiner, *Commons Debates 1625*, pp. 29, 30,
55, 120, 143–5. *CJ* i. 903, 930. ITL, Petyt MS. 537/23, ff. 209ᵛ–211, 279ᵛ, 297, 327ᵛ,
330, 346, 356–7. W. D. Courtney, *The Parliamentary Representation of Cornwall to 1832*
(London, 1889), pp. 64, 284. Gardiner, *History of England*, vi. 282–3; vii. 310–12.
Trevor-Roper, *Laud*, pp. 45, 151–2. Laud, *Troubles and Tryal*, p. 327. CUL, Whitelocke Journal, ff. 63ᵛ, 87, 237. Gleason, *Justices*, p. 24. *VCH Berks.* iii. 107, 175; iv.
457, 464, 467, 511, 530, 533, 535, 538, 542. C. Roberts, *The Growth of Responsible
Government in Stuart England* (Cambridge, 1966), p. 51.

MARTIN, JOSEPH, b. 1598 in St. Petrock's parish, Exeter, Devon, 2nd son of
William of Exeter, merchant, by Margerie Achim. Matric. Wadham College,
Oxford, 1621 as son of an esquire; B.A. 1625; M.A. 1627; B.C.L. and D.C.L.
1633. Warrant Doc. Com. 1634; full admission 1634; in commons until 1642.
Active as advocate in London courts 1637–40. Judge of Vice-Admiralty Court
of Devon 1636. Comr. Piracy Devon 1637, 1638; London 1638. Official of
Archdeacon of Totnes. Compounds on Exeter Articles for delinquency as
Judge of Vice-Admiralty Court, adhering to forces of the King, and taking
a protestation against Parlt. 1646. Fine at a tenth, £121. Surgeon of Exeter by
1646. Chancellor of Exeter diocese 1660–3. Res.: Doc. Com. and Exeter. d.
17 Mar. 1676. Will: PCC 78 Hale, pr. 4 July 1678. Civil law, canon law, and
common law books to be sold to satisfy debts. Books and goods to son Richard
and dau. Mary.

    Al. Oxon. iii. 979. R. B. Gardiner, *The Registers of Wadham College, Oxford* (London,
1889), i. 60. Clark, *Register*, ii. 399; iii. 438. LPL, Reg. Doc. Com., ff. 50, 109ᵛ; Laud
Reg., i, f. 202ᵛ. PRO, C 181/5, ff. 84, 131–3; HCA 24/92–101, *passim*; SP 16/421/108;
16/326/80. *CSPD 1636–1637*, pp. 21–2. *CPCC* ii. 1387. PRO, PROB 11/98/84 (will
of William); PROB 11/352/78; PC 2/43, p. 263.

MASON, ROBERT, b. 1590, son of George of New Windsor, gent., by Barbara,
dau. of John Parkins of Flints. Not to be confused w. namesake, the Recorder
of London (d. 1635) or Sir Robert Mason of Winchester (d. 1669). Scholar of
St. John's College, Cambridge, 1606; B.A. 1610; fellow 1610–32; M.A. 1613;
senior proctor 1619–20; LL.D. 1628 by royal letters. Full admission Doc. Com.
1629; in commons until 1642. Secretary to Duke of Buckingham during
expedition to Isle of Rhe 1628; active in election of Duke as Chancellor of
Cambridge; received £500 by the Duke's will. Chancellor of Winchester
diocese 1628–62. Commissary for archdeaconry of Surrey 1629. Official of
Archdeacons of Surrey and of Winchester 1630. Joins other ecclesiastical judges
residing at Doc. Com. in legal opinion *c.* 1636. Judge of Vice-Admiralty Court
of Hants and the Isle of Wight 1637; seeks recompense for expenses as judge
1637–8. Comr. Piracy Hants 1635, 1636; London 1635, 1638. Delegates 1633–9

Master of Requests *c.* 1635. Advocate in HCA 1638. Chancellor of Rochester diocese 1661–2 w. E. Alderne (q.v.). Purchased manor of Itchell in Crondall, Hants, 1629. Res.: Doc. Com., Hants, and Greenwich. m. Judith, dau. of Sir Charles Buckle 1633.

> DNB xii. 1321. *Al. Cant.* iii. 57. *Visitation of London 1633–1635,* ii (Harl. Soc. xvii, 1883), p. 85. LPL, Reg. Doc. Com., ff. 49, 109. PRO, C 181/5, ff. 24, 27, 58, 130ᵛ; HCA 24/95, f. 111; DEL 8/70, pt. 2, ff. 13–48, *passim;* SP 16/339/63. Leadam, *Select Cases in Requests,* p. cvii. Senior, *Naval History in the Law Courts* (London, 1927), pp. 20–1. *Wills from Doctors' Commons* (Camden Soc. lxxxiii, 1863), p. 91. *CSPD 1636–1637,* pp. 279, 507. Winchester Cathedral Library, Index of Hants Clergy, f. 320ᵛ; Baigent Papers. HRO, Consistory Court Book 108, *passim;* Register of Bishop Neile 1627–31, ff. 19ᵛ, 198, 198ᵛ. Kent Archives Office, Rochester Episcopal Register 1638–1678, DRc R9, f. 113–113ᵛ. *VCH Hants* iv. 8.

MASTER (MASTERS), ROBERT, b. *c.* 1565, 3rd son of Richard of London and Cirencester, Glos., M.D., by Elizabeth, dau. of John Fulnetby of Fulnetby, Lincs. Matric. Trinity College, Oxford, as son of an esquire 1579; B.C.L. All Souls 1590; Dean of Law 1591; D.C.L. 1594. Principal St. Alban's Hall 1599–1603. Warrant Doc. Com. 1596; full admission 1598; in commons until 1614; out of commons 1615–25. Judge of Oxford VCC 1594–1600. Surrogate to Daniel Dun (q.v.) as Chancellor of Rochester diocese before 1604; Chancellor 1604–14. Official of Archdeacon of Rochester. Comr. Piracy London 1609. Comr. Adm. Middx. 1610. Chancellor of Lichfield diocese 1613–25. J.P. Staffs. 1621. Master in Chancery extraordinary 1622. Patrimony: £10 annuity and use of family house in London rent free. Purchased mess., cottage, gardens in Alrewas, Staffs. M.P. Cricklade, Wilts., 1601 through promotion by fellow M.P. Gifford or by Cecil. d. 1625. m. Catherine, dau. of Thomas Pagitt of Northants. and the Middle Temple.

> HPT, typescript. *Al. Oxon.* iii. 986. DNB xiii. 22. Clark, *Register,* i. 233, 317–20; ii. 86; iii. 163. *Visitation of Gloucester* (Harl. Soc. xxi, 1885), p. 111. LPL, Reg. Doc. Com., ff. 45, 106ᵛ; Whitgift Reg. ii, f. 143; Bancroft Reg., f. 217. PRO C 181/2, f. 101ᵛ; C 181/3, f. 52; C 216/1, no. 87; HCA 1/32/1, f. 55; will of Richard, PROB 11/72/34. *The Visitation of Kent* (Harl. Soc. xlii, 1898), pp. 10–11. *Catalogue of All Souls Archives,* p. 306. Shaw, *Staffordshire,* i. 300. Kent Archives Office, DRb/Pa 22, *passim;* DRb/Pwr 20, *passim.* Oxford Univ. Archives, Registers of Chancellor's Court 1594–1600.

MASTERS (MASTER), JAMES, b. 1607, 2nd son of Edward of Ospringe, Kent, esq., later kt. Winchester College. Matric. New College, Oxford, 1627; fellow 1627–63; B.C.L. 1633; D.C.L. 1638. Surrogate of Official of Archdeacon of Berks. 1636–8. Full admission Doc. Com. 1648. Inherited some land as second son. Owned mess., lands, and ten. in Kent. d. 1663. Will: PCC 18 Bruce, pr. 22 Feb. 1664. Lands to wife Mary and remainder to brother Robert and nephew Edward according to indenture of 1654. Civil law and canon law books to nephew Edward of New College. Friend of Dr. Mills, D.C.L.

> *Al. Oxon.* iii. 986. Bodl., MS. Top. Oxon. e. 105/2, f. 103. Kirby, *Winchester Scholars,* p. 167. LPL, Reg. Doc. Com., ff. 50ᵛ, 110ᵛ. PRO, DEL 8/61, *passim;* PRO 11/313/18.

MERRICK (MEYRICK), EDMUND, 6th son of Meyrick ap Llewelyn of Bodorgan, Anglesey, Captain of the Guards to Henry VIII (d. 1537), by Margaret, dau. of Rowland ap Howel, Rector of Aberffraw, Anglesey. Brother Rowland, LL.B., was Bishop of Bangor. B.A. Oxford 1545; B.C.L. 1558; D.C.L. 1567. Archdeacon of Bangor 1559. Chancellor of St. Asaph diocese 1570–6. Rector of Corwen, Merioneth. Preb. of Lichfield. d. 1606. Will: PCC 49 Stafforde, pr. 4 June 1606. Profits arising from archdeaconry toward preferment of his daus. Elizabeth and Grace; rest to his son George. Held land of the Bishop of Bangor in Merioneth. Of Ucheldre, Montgomery. m. Elizabeth, dau. of William ap Gruffydd ap Thomas ap Robin of Cochwillan.

Griffith, *Pedigrees*, pp. 126, 308. *Al. Oxon*. iii. 1006. Boase, *Register*, p. 227. Clark, *Register*, i. 117. Thomas, *St. Asaph*, p. 239.

MERRICK (MEYRICK), WILLIAM, prob. 2nd son of Owen ap Hugh ap Meyrick of Bodeon, Anglesey, esq., by Elizabeth, dau. of Robert Gruffydd. Uncle of Sir William Merrick (q.v.). Possibly 2nd son of Richard of Bodorgan by Jane, dau. of John Wynn ap Rhys of Anglesey, and nephew of Edmund Merrick (q.v.). Scholar of New College, Oxford, 1565; fellow 1566–82; B.C.L. 1574; D.C.L. 1582. Practised in Oxford VCC 1582. A cleric. Preb. and Precentor of Bangor Cathedral 1582. Rector of Trefdraeth and Llanfechell, Anglesey, 1581. Chancellor of Bangor diocese 1582. d. 1605.

Gentleman's Magazine xcv, pt. 1 (1825), 405–6. Griffith, *Pedigrees*, pp. 58, 126. *DNB* xiii. 319. *Al. Oxon*. iii. 1007. Clark, *Register*, i. 41, 105; iii. 22. Wood, *Athenae*, ii. 843–4; *Fasti*, i. 221. A. Pryce, *The Diocese of Bangor in the Sixteenth Century* (Bangor, 1923), pp. 24, 25, 32.

MERRICK (MERICK, MEROCKE, MERICKE, MERYCK), SIR WILLIAM, 1st son of Maurice Owen or Merrick of Hart Hall, Oxford, and Bodeon, Anglesey, gent. (d. 1640), by Jane, dau. of Lewis Evans. Maurice was half-brother of Bishop John Merrick of Sodor and Man (d. 1599) and brother of William Owen or Merrick, LL.D. (q.v.). Referred to as of West Meon, Hants, during years at Winchester College. Matric. New College, Oxford, 1614; fellow 1616–26; B.C.L. 1621; D.C.L. 1627. Warrant Doc. Com. 1627; full admission 1628; in commons until 1642. Honorific admission Lincoln's Inn 1640 at request of Charles Jones. Perhaps Chancellor of Winchester diocese 1632 w. Robert Mason (q.v.); active in visitation of 1633 as commissary of Bishop. Delegates 1628–39. Active as advocate in London courts 1634–40. Comr. Piracy London 1629, 1633, 1635, 1638; Hants 1635, 1636. Comr. Pol. & Ass. London 1629, 1634–7. Judge of PCC 1641–4. Fled to Oxford to join Royalists 1643. Allegedly fled to Continent w. Charles II. Reinstated as judge of PCC 1660. Knighted 1661. Res.: St. Peter's, Paul's Wharf, London 1638. d. 1668. Will: PCC 20 Coke, pr. 12 Feb. 1669. Gowns to Dr. Sweit and Dr. Lewin; £50 to Dr. Read; £100 to Lady Parry, dau. of Dr. Sweit; £91 to servants and poor; rest to brother Benjamin.

DNB xiii. 323. *Gentleman's Magazine* xcv, pt. 1 (1825), 404–7. *Al. Oxon.* iii. 1007. Clark, *Register*, ii. 334; iii. 403. Wood, *Fasti*, i. 432. Bodl., MS. Top. Oxon. e. 105/2, f. 96. LPL, Reg. Doc. Com., ff. 49, 108ᵛ; Abbot Reg. ii, f. 222ᵛ. *Lincoln's Inn Admission Register*, i. 242. PRO, C 181/4, ff. 7, 37, 139, 157ᵛ; 181/5, ff. 9, 24, 27, 58ᵛ, 59ᵛ, 98ᵛ, 130ᵛ; DEL 8/70, pt. 1, ff. 41ᵛ–45; pt. 2, *passim*; PROB 11/190/102; 11/329/20. *Heraldic Cases*, pp. 23, 46. Winchester Cathedral Library, Index of Hants Clergy, f. 326ᵛ; Baigent Papers. *Acts of the Interregnum*, i. 564–5. Dale, *Inhabitants of London*, p. 179. *CSPD 1634–1635*, pp. 318, 539, 550; *1635–1636*, p. 112; *1640*, pp. 387, 400.

MITCHELL (MITCHILL), ROBERT, b. 1581. From Devon. Matric. as son of a gent. Exeter College, Oxford, 1597; B.C.L. 1619; D.C.L. 1625. Registrar in the Exeter Consistory Court *c.* 1626. Accused of corruption in that capacity.

> *Al. Oxon.* iii. 1008. Clark, *Register*, ii. 223; iii. 380. Wood, *Fasti*, i. 416. PRO, SP 16/530/131.

MORICE, EVAN. From Cardiganshire. Matric. as son of commoner Jesus College, Oxford, 1578; Fellow of All Souls; B.C.L. 1584; dispensed from taking doctorate 1591; D.C.L. 1592. Warrant Doc. Com. 1599 but not fully admitted. Chancellor of Exeter diocese 1592–1605. d. 1605. Father of William.

> *Al. Oxon.* iii. 1034. Clark, *Register*, i. 119, 183; ii. 84; iii. 126. Cassidy, 'Episcopate of Cotton', pp. 113–15, 165. *Catalogue of All Souls Archives*, p. 305. LPL, Whitgift Reg. iii, f. 111.

MORRISSON, THOMAS, b. 1566 at Newton, Lincs., perhaps son of Henry of World Newton. Matric. pens. King's College, Cambridge, 1586; fellow 1589–1612; B.A. 1591; M.A. 1594; proctor 1601–2; LL.D. 1606. Regius Professor of Civil Law 1611. J.P. Hunts. Commissary of Archdeaconry of Huntingdon. Friend of Bishop Williams of Lincoln. Res.: Buckden, Hunts.

> *Al. Cant.* iii. 216. *Eton Register*, p. 238. CUL, MS. Mm. 1. 49 (Baker 38), p. 311. PRO, E 403/2693, f. 43; C 193/13/1, f. 49; SP 16/212, p. 60. Lloyd, *Memoires*, p. 594. *CSPD 1639–1640*, p. 365. LPL, MS. 1030, f. 41.

MOSTON (MOSTYN), HENRY, 5th son of Peter of Talacre, Flints., esq., whose family gave armed support to the Tudors. Matric. Jesus College, Cambridge, 1567; B.A. 1572; fellow 1573–83; M.A. 1574; LL.D. 1589. Warrant Doc. Com. 1590; full admission 1599; out of commons until 1617. Chancellor of Bangor diocese 1586. Vicar of Whitford, Flints., 1586–91. Rector of Yseifiog, Flints., 1587; Aber, Carnarvons., 1592–1600 through patronage of W. Thomas and the Queen (1593); Llanllechid, Carnarvons., 1600. Preb. of Bangor 1600. J.P. Flints. 1604. Farm in Anglesey. Will: PCC 55 Weldon, pr. 23 June 1617. Farm in Anglesey to dau. Mary. Lands and mess. to son and heir Samuel. Refers to himself as of 'Pickton', Flints. m. Ellen, dau. of Edward ap Hugh Gwynn of Bodewyrd, Anglesey.

> *DWB*, pp. 673–5. *Al. Cant.* iii. 221. LPL, Reg. Doc. Com., ff. 45, 106ᵛ; Whitgift Reg. ii, f. 161. D. L. Mostyn and T. A. Glenn, *History of the Family of Mostyn* (London, 1925), pp. 79, 191–4. Pryce, *Bangor*, pp. 28, 29, 31. PRO, PROB 11/129/55. BM, Add. MS. 38,139, f. 171ᵛ.

MOTTERSHED (MOTTERSHEAD, MOLTERSHED), Edward, b. 1601, son of Thomas, Registrar of the High Commission, of London, gent. Winchester College. Matric. New College, Oxford, 1618; B.C.L. 1626; fellow 1620–34; D.C.L. 1632. Adm. advocate at York through influence of his father and of W. Easdall (q.v.); practised as advocate until death. Full admission Doc. Com. 1634; out of commons until 1640. Official of East Riding archdeaconry 1632; raises fees because he does not have additional ecclesiastical preferments. Official of Archdeacon of Nottingham 1635. Enforces Archbishop Neile's Laudian policies. Judge of Admiralty Court of York 1633. Comr. Piracy Kingston-on-Hull 1637. King's Advocate in the North 1635. Commissary of the Peculiar of the Dean and Chapter of York 1637. Advocate in High Commission proceedings at Durham 1637. Proctor in Convocation to the Short Parlt. but more moderate opponent elected for the Long Parlt. Did not trust the local clergy. Refused to delegate authority to subordinates.

Al. Oxon. iii. 1042. Clark, *Register*, ii. 371; iii. 445. Kirby, *Winchester Scholars*, p. 166. Bodl., MS. Top. Oxon. e. 105/2, ff. 99ᵛ–100. Marchant, *Church Under Law*, pp. 143, 196–7, 202, 250; *Puritans*, p. 53. LPL, Reg. Doc. Com., ff. 49ᵛ, 109ᵛ. PRO, C 181/5, f. 80. *CSPD 1634–1635*, p. 233. *The Acts of the High Commission within the diocese of Durham* (Surtees Soc. xxxiv, 1858), p. 181.

MOUNTLOWE (MONTLOWE, MOUTLOWE, MONTLOE), Henry, b. 1555, prob. 2nd son of John Mucklow or Mowtloew of Winchcomb, Glos., by Joan, dau. of Arthur Sandford of Stowe. Matric. King's College, Cambridge, 1571; fellow 1574–95; B.A. 1576; M.A. 1579; scrutator 1585; proctor 1590, 1594; LL.D. 1594. Public Orator of the University 1589–94. 1st Professor of Civil Law at Gresham College 1596–1607. Moderator in civil law when King visited Cambridge 1614. Warrant Doc. Com. 1596; full admission 1607; out of commons until 1634. Nominated by Queen to mastership of Clare College, but not elected 1599. M.P. Cambridge Univ. 1604. Dispensed to become Prebendary of York but never installed. Poet. In debt 1611. bur. 17 Oct. 1634. Will: Cambridge VCC, pr. 9 Oct. 1634. £50 to dau. of son-in-law Benjamin Hinton. Leases, goods, books to Richard Love, D.D. m. Margaret, widow of Richard Love, apothecary of Cambridge.

Ward, *Gresham Professors*, pp. 237–8. *Al. Cant.* iii. 225. *Eton Register*, p. 240. LPL, Reg. Doc. Com., ff. 46ᵛ, 107; Whitgift Reg. ii, f. 146. Rex, *University Representation*, pp. 42–3. *HMCS* ix. 421. Cooper, *Annals*, iii. 39–40. *The Visitation of Gloucester* (Harl. Soc. xxi), p. 221. Cambridge Univ. Archives, Wills, 3/209. PRO, PROB 11/118/86.

NEVILL, Nicholas, b. 1558 at Ingrave, Essex. Matric. pens. Peterhouse, Cambridge, 1580; B.A. 1584; LL.D. Clare College 1592. A cleric. Rector of Great Tey, Essex. Res.: hamlet of Chapel in Great Tey. d. 1632. Will: London Consistory Court, pr. 18 May 1632. Bedding to eldest son William; beaker to son Edward; rest of money and goods to wife. Perhaps m. Mary Darcy.

Al. Cant. iii. 244. Newcourt, *Repertorium*, ii. 572. *Visitation of Essex*, i. 187. Greater London Record Office, DL/C/343, f. 132; DL/C/362, ff. 144ᵛ–145.

NEVILL (NEVILE), WILLIAM, b. 1596, 3rd son of Sir Henry of Mayfield, Sussex, and Billingbear, Berks., by Anne, dau. of Sir Henry Killigrew of Cornwall. Not to be confused w. William Nevill of Cambridge, B.A. 1616. Matric. Merton College, Oxford, 1609; B.A. 1614; M.A. 1618; B.C.L. 1626; D.C.L. 1633. Warrant Doc. Com. 1634; full admission 1634; in commons 1635–9. Chancellor of Chichester diocese 1627. Commissary for Lewes archdeaconry 1627. Commissary to Dean of Chichester 1627. Proctor in Convocation 1628. J.P. Sussex 1635. Comr. Piracy Hants 1635, 1636; Sussex 1637. Judge of Vice-Admiralty Court of Sussex 1637. Delegates 1639. Advocate in HCA 1639. d. 1640. Will: PCC 32 Coventry, pr. 5 Mar. 1640. Goods and chattels to wife Katherine.

> Visitations of Berkshire i. 250. Al. Oxon. iii. 1058. Clark, Register, ii. 308; iii. 325. LPL, Reg. Doc. Com., ff. 49ᵛ, 109ᵛ; Laud Reg. i, f. 202ᵛ. Chichester Chapter Acts, nos. 1193, 1196, 1200. PRO, C 193/13/2, f. 87; DEL 8/70, pt. 2, ff. 43–8; C 181/5, ff. 24, 58ᵛ, 68ᵛ; HCA 24/97, no. 147; PROB 11/182/32.

NEWCOMB (NEWCOMEN), ROBERT, only son of Thomas of Ingoldmells, Lincs., lesser gent. or yeoman (d. 1598). Matric. sizar Clare College, Cambridge, 1577; B.A. 1581; M.A. 1584; LL.D. 1592. Warrant Doc. Com. 1599. Commissary for Cambridge 1610. J.P. City of Cambridge 1619. Opposes nonconformity at Cambridge 1619. Commissary for archdeaconry of Sudbury 1603–14. bur. St. Botolph's, Cambridge, 21 Feb. 1621. Will: PCC 34 Dale, pr. 3 May 1621. £1,000 to dau. Jane; £800 to wife; £500 and house to son Thomas.

> Lincolnshire Pedigrees, ii. 713. Al. Cant. iii. 247. Fuller, History of Cambridge, pp. 162–3. HMCS xi. 119. PRO, C 181/2, f. 345ᵛ; C 181/3, f. 13ᵛ; PROB 11/137/34. Lincolnshire Archives Office, will of Thomas, 1598. 144. LPL, Whitgift Reg. iii, f. 111.

NEWMAN, SIR GEORGE, b. 1562, son of Richard. Matric. Trinity Hall, Cambridge, 1581; LL.B. 1584; LL.D. 1589. Warrant Doc. Com. 1598; full admission 1604; in commons until 1627. Commissary of Archbishop of Canterbury by 1587. Clerk of Faculties by 1618. Judge of the Admiralty Court of Cinque Ports 1602–27. Comr. Piracy Cinque Ports 1613. Refutes claims of Cinque Ports to be independent of HCA 1616. Master in Chancery extraordinary 1603. High Com. 1605, 1608, 1613. Delegates 1611–22. Knighted 1616. Judge of Court of Audience 1617. Surrogate of Daniel Dun as Dean of Arches 1613–17 at income of £40 p.a. J.P. Kent 1604. M.P. Dover, Kent, 1601; Canterbury, 1614, 1621 through influence of Archbishop. Bequeathed coach and four geldings by Archbishop Bancroft 1610. Held land in Eastry, Woodnesborough, and Thanet, Kent. Held lease of Cranbrook parsonage. Res.: Canterbury and Doc. Com. Will: PCC 65 Skynner, pr. 22 June 1627. Had disposed of most of estate beforehand. £10 to Doc. Com. m. (1) Elizabeth, dau. of P. Wycliffe of Yorks.; (2) Mary Gough; (3) Sybill, dau. of G. Wenland of Allens Moore, Herefs. Father of Richard, George, James, Mary, and Margaret.

> HPT, typescript. Al. Cant. iii. 250. LPL, Reg. Doc. Com., ff. 46, 107; Whitgift Reg. iii, f. 90ᵛ; MS. 2014, f. 148ᵛ; Lam. Chart. Misc. XII, p. 29. BM, Lansdowne MS. 156,

f. 326; Add. MS. 38,139, f. 136ᵛ. Cotton MS. Cleo. F II, ff. 169–70. Usher, *High Commission*, p. 355. *CSPD 1611–1618*, p. 489; *1623–1625*, pp. 162, 194, 200, 222, 493. *APC 1625–1626*, p. 95. Moir, *Addled Parliament*, p. 187. PRO, C 142/770/74; C 181/2, f. 185; DEL 5/4, f. 116; DEL 8/70, pt. 1, ff. 9ᵛ–12ᵛ; SP 14/86/83; PROB 11/152/65.

NICHOLAS, MATTHEW, b. 1594, 2nd son of John of Winterbourne Earls, Wilts., gent. (d. 1644), by Susan, dau. of W. Hunton of Knoyle, Wilts. Younger brother of Sir Edward, Secretary of State to Charles I and Charles II. Winchester College. Matric. New College, Oxford, 1614; fellow 1615–20; B.C.L. 1620; D.C.L. 1627. Warrant Doc. Com. 1640 but not fully admitted. Rector of West Dean, Wilts., 1621 at value of £32 p.a. Rector of Broughton, Hants, 1629–30. Master of St. Nicholas Hospital in Harnham, Wilts., through influence of Earl of Pembroke. Vicar of prebandal rectory of Wherwell, Hants, 1637–62. Canon residentiary at Salisbury. Appointed Vicar of Berkeley, Glos., by Dean and Chapter of Bristol but exchanges living for vicarage of Olveston, Glos., 1639. Dean of Bristol 1639 through influence of the King. Preb. of Bristol 1639. Preb. of Westminster 1642. Sides w. Royalists. Deserts West Dean to live at Salisbury and then at Bristol. Sequestered Olveston 1643; West Dean before 1645; St. Nicholas before 1646. Dean and Preb. of St. Paul's 1660. Purchased estate at Laverstock, Wilts., 1637. Leased manor and rectory at Winterbourne Earls from Dean and Chapter of Salisbury. Fails to compound on Oxford Articles before 1649 on grounds that estate was valued at less than £200. Fine at a tenth, £15. 6s. in 1649. d. 15 Aug. 1661. Will: PCC 22 Laud, pr. 6 Feb. 1662. £800 to sons. Had already settled marriage portions on daus. Father of George, Edward, John, Elizabeth, and Susan. m. Elizabeth, dau. of William Fookes.

> *DNB* xiv. 426. *Al. Oxon.* iii. 1067. Kirby, *Winchester Scholars*, p. 163. Bodl., MS. Top. Oxon. e. 105/2, f. 96. Hoare, *The Modern History of South Wiltshire*, v (London, 1837), 214. *Walker Revised*, p. 378. Wood, *Fasti*, i. 431. LeNeve, *Fasti*, i. 223; ii. 315. *VCH Wilts.* iii. 351–2. *CSPD 1637*, pp. 25, 112; *1637–1638*, p. 524; *1639*, pp. 356, 502. PRO, SP 16/442/125; PROB 11/307/22; Institution Books, ser. A, v. 37, 42 (Glos.) Winchester Cathedral Library, Index of Hants Clergy, f. 353. HRO, Register of Bishop Neile, ff. 15, 23ᵛ–24.

NICOLSON (NICHOLSON), JOHN, b. 1606, son of Thomas, Rector of Stapleford Tawney, Essex, cleric. Matric. Magdalen Hall, Oxford, 1621; demy of Magdalen College 1622–38; B.A. 1625; M.A. 1627; fellow 1628–38; leave to study medicine 1629; proctor 1638; B.C.L. and D.C.L. 1639. In custody of Parlt. 1647 for withholding tithes from Rector of Stapleford Tawney and paying tithes to brother Richard, sequestered rector. Chancellor of Gloucester diocese 1669–77. Held farm at Stapleford Tawney valued at £30 p.a.; two farms at Stanford Rivers, Essex, valued at £58 p.a.; other real estate valued at £22 p.a. Owed £20 by two annuities, £218 in legacies, and £1,248. 9s. 8d. in other debts upon the estate in 1651. d. 1677. Father of John, barrister of Inner Temple.

Al. Oxon. iii. 1071. Clark, *Register*, ii. 390; iii. 438. Wood, *Fasti*, i. 509. *Register of Magdalen College*, n.s. iii. 168–9. Newcourt, *Repertorium*, ii. 556. Rudder, *Gloucestershire*, p. 164. *CPCC* i. 396. PRO, SP 23/254/24 I. *Walker Revised*, p. 160.

NORTON, JOHN, b. 1612, son of John of Colchester, Essex, esq. School at Colchester. Matric. pens. Sidney Sussex College, Cambridge, 1627. Attended University of Leyden in the Netherlands. LL.B. Trinity Hall 1633; LL.D. 1639. Warrant Doc. Com. 1640, but not fully admitted.

Al. Cant. iii. 268. PRO, SP 16/442/125.

PARKINS (PERKINS), SIR CHRISTOPHER, b. *c.* 1543. From Ufton Court, Berks., 'of no great matter by birth'. Winchester College. B.A. Oxford 1565. Joined Society of Jesus in Rome 1566. Studied in Rome, Venice, Cologne and other parts of Germany. LL.D. from a Continental university. Met W. Cecil in Italy 1585. Entered service of F. Walsingham while abroad. Renounces Catholicism 1589. Unofficial agent of Queen at Elbing *c.* 1589. Missions to Poland and Prussia 1590, Denmark 1591, and Germany 1593. Seeks admission to regular service of Queen 1592, 1594, 1595 but hampered by earlier religious convictions. Dean of Carlisle 1595 at income of £120. 7s. 6d. Honorific admission Gray's Inn 1597. Master of Requests extraordinary 1598; ordinary 1617. Missions to Denmark 1598, 1600. Latin Secretary to Queen 1601. Knighted 1603. Censor of unauthorized or imported books 1604. Honorary admission Doc. Com. 1604, but not a practising advocate. High Com. 1605–22. Comr. Adm. Middx. 1606. J.P. Surrey 1609. Assists Bancroft in drawing up oath of allegiance. M.P. Ripon, Yorks., 1597, 1601, made available to Cecil by Archbishop of Canterbury; Morpeth, Northumb., 1604 through clerical patronage or influence of Cecil. Bought manor of Padding Bray, Surrey, 1618. Owned dwelling house at Cannon Rowe. Value of manor and house at 300 marks. Invests in Virginia Co. Res.: Harrow, London, and Westminster. Will: PCC 84 Savile, pr. 2 Sept. 1622. £50 to St. Peter's, Westminster; £25 to Oxford Univ.; £10 to Doctors' Commons; £10 to Gray's Inn; £10 to Company. £1,000 from Merchant Adventurers to four friends. One-third of rents to wife; two-thirds to servant out of revenge to wife and Duke of Buckingham. m. Anne, dau. of A. Beaumont of Glenmore, Leics., widowed sister of Countess of Buckingham in order to rise higher in King's service 1617; alienates Buckingham by refusing to assume wife's debts.

DNB xv. 889–90. HPT, typescript. *Al. Oxon.* iii. 1117. *HMCS* iii. 411; iv. 239, 576; v. 369; vii. 516; ix. 76, 110, 376, 411; xix. 450. *CSPD 1581–1590*, p. 664; *1591–1594*, p. 232; *1598–1601*, pp. 54–5. *VCH Surrey* iii. 133. Rex, *University Representation*, p. 41. Strype, *Whitgift*, ii. 503–4. LPL, Reg. Doc. Com., f. 46; MS. 958, p. 97. Usher, *High Commission*, p. 356. PRO, HCA 1/32/1, f. 61; index 6800, f. 404; PROB 11/140/84. Gleason, *Justices*, p. 258. Rabb, *Enterprise*, p. 353. *CJ* i. 257, 274, 277, 291, 296, 300, 303, 326, 329, 351, 374, 445.

PARRY, SIR GEORGE, b. *c.* 1601, 3rd son of Henry, D.D., Bishop of Worcester (d. 1617). Special admission to Inner Temple 1616. Matric. Merton College,

Oxford, 1617; B.A. 1619; Fellow of Magdalene College, Cambridge, 1619; LL.D. 1628. Warrant Doc. Com. 1628; full admission 1628; in commons until 1642. Chancellor of Exeter diocese 1624–53, perhaps until 1660. Denies charges that he took excessive fees and abused power of excommunication at Exeter *c.* 1630. Delegates 1631–9. Active as advocate in London courts 1635–9. Joins other ecclesiastical judges residing at Doc. Com. in legal opinion *c.* 1636. Comr. Piracy Devon 1637–9. Judge-Marshal of Devon Muster 1639; reported defaulter from muster 1639 but case dismissed by Privy Council. M.P. St. Mawes, Cornw., to Short and Long Parlts. 1640 through episcopal influence. Defends Canons of 1640. Commons objects to his taking oath to support Canons. Votes *v.* attainder of Strafford. Disabled 1644. Comr. to raise militia in Devon for King. Knighted 1644. Surrogate to Judge of HCA in the West 1645. Surrogate to judge of PCC 1652. Patrimony: £30 p.a. and £300 at 24 years. Purchased land called Larkbear near Exeter 1642, valued at £50 p.a. Held four manors in Cornwall. Planned to provide portions of £1,000 and £500 for daus. in 1642. Compounds for estate 1646–9 at a tenth: £200. Res.: the Close, Exeter, and Doc. Com. d. in Ireland 1670. Administration to son Suetonius, 16 Nov. 1670. m. (1) Dorothy, dau. of Sir Ralph Honey and widow of Sir Nicholas Smith of Larkbear, Devon, before 1638; (2) Mary before 1642. Four daus.

Keeler, *Long Parliament*, pp. 297–8. *Al. Cant.* iii. 314. *Al. Oxon.* iii. 1120. LPL, Reg. Doc. Com., ff. 49, 109; Abbot Reg. ii, f. 233ᵛ. ITL, Admissions to Inner Temple i. 374. PRO, C 181/5, ff. 84, 132ᵛ; DEL 8/70, pt. 2, *passim*; HCA 24/92, ff. 159, 161; 24/97, f. 144. SP 16/178/27; 16/421/108; 16/530/131; SP 23/208/60–1. *CSPD 1634–1635*, p. 545; *1635–1636*, p. 57; *1638–1639*, pp. 256, 316, 365, 496; *1639*, p. 69. Notestein, *D'Ewes*, pp. 163, 307. Brunton and Pennington, *Long Parliament*, p. 239.

PEIRCE (PIERCE), Sɪʀ Eᴅᴍᴜɴᴅ. From Bucks. Adm. Corpus Christi College, Cambridge, 1629; matric. sizar Trinity Hall 1633; LL.B. 1635; LL.D. 1639. Warrant Doc. Com. 1640; full admission 1661. Commissary for archdeaconry of Suffolk 1637–42. Judge of Vice-Admiralty Court of Suffolk 1637–*c.* 1640. Comr. Piracy Suffolk 1640. Legal action brought *v.* him for presenting one Bedwall for not receiving communion 1639. Petition submitted to Long Parlt. against him for forcing men to take the oath, extorting fees, and abusing power of excommunication. Left London to follow King to York 1642. Captured by Parliamentarians in Kent 1642 and imprisoned for several weeks. Officer of R. Life Guards. Colonel of the Regiment of the Horse of Greenwich 1643–8. Judge-Marshal and Advocate-General of royal armies. Master of Requests 1644–9. Knighted 1645. Fought in several battles. Imprisoned 1645 and 1655. Compounds on Oxford Articles; fine at a tenth, £82. Grant of arms 1661. Master in Chancery 1660–7. J.P. Kent 1660–7. M.P. Maidstone 1661–7 through influence of father-in-law James Franklin, Recorder of Maidstone. Author of nine royalist and anti-Puritan tracts shortly before Restoration, including *Englands Monarchy Asserted* and *The English Episcopacy and Liturgy Asserted*. Res.: London; Colchester in 1655; Greenwich, Kent, after 1660.

d. Sept. 1667. Not to be confused w. Edmund Peirce of Wilcott, Salop, adm. Inner Temple 1660.

HPT, typescript. Venn, *Matriculations*, p. 525. *Al. Cant.* iii. 328. LPL, Abbot Reg. ii, f. 238; Reg. Doc. Com., ff. 51ᵛ, 111. PRO, SP 16/442/125; index 16818, p. 47; C 181/5, f. 176. Blomefield, *Norfolk*, iii. 658. *Notes and Queries*, 10th ser. viii. 490. *CSPD 1637*, p. 142; *1638–1639*, p. 226; *1639–1640*, p. 221; *1655*, p. 367. CPCC ii. 1566. Notestein, *D'Ewes*, p. 414. *Grantees of Arms*, i. 195. D. Wing, *Short-title Catalogue* (New York, 1951), iii. 26. ITL, Admissions to Inner Temple, ii. 1.

PELHAM, HERBERT, b. *c.* 1597, 4th son of Sir William of Brocklesby, Lincs., Kt. (d. 1629), by Catherine, dau. of Charles, 2nd Lord Willoughby of Parham, Suff. Matric. Magdalen Hall, Oxford, 1619; B.A. 1621; Fellow of Magdalen College 1621; M.A. 1623; proctor 1634; B.C.L. 1635; D.C.L. 1639. Submitted to Visitors of Oxford University 1648; released from submission and appointed one of 20 delegates to administer university affairs. Evades 1 per cent tax levied by Parlt. on ready cash of university doctors, having £800 in his possession 1666. Patrimony: £50 annuity. Res.: Oxford. d. 17 Jan. 1671.

Al. Oxon. iii. 1138. Clark, *Register*, ii. 378; iii. 392. Wood, *Athenae*, i. lxix; iv. 110. *Register of Magdalen College*, n.s. iii. 157–8, 189. *Lincolnshire Pedigrees*, iii. 766. Lincolnshire Archives Office, will of W. Pelham, Consistory Court wills D.70. Burrows, *Register of Visitors*, pp. 28, 83–4, 88, 102 n., 513.

PONDER, JOHN, 1st son of John of Braintree, Essex, gent. Matric. pens. Queens' College, Cambridge, 1577; B.A. 1580; M.A. 1583; LL.D. before 1605. A cleric. Rector of Rollesby, Norf., 1591 through patronage of Sir Dru Drewrie. Rector of Thelnetham, Suff., 1595–1603. Rector of Ashby, Norf., 1603–25, through patronage of Bishop of Norwich. Rector of Thurne, Norf., 1604. Held land in Essex and in Billockby, Norf. Paid £400 for marriage portion of dau. Res.: Ashby. Will: Norwich Consistory Court, Belward 267, pr. 6 Dec. 1625. Lands in Essex to son John of Panfield, Essex; lands in Norf. to son-in-law Thomas Mayhewe. Probate inventory, exec. 6 Dec. 1625. Goods and chattels valued at £835. 2s. 8d., including £314. 10s. in ready cash.

J. J. Muskett, *Suffolk Manorial Families* (Exeter, 1908), i. 39. *Al. Cant.* iii. 377. *Registrum Vagum* i. 191–2; ii. 294–5. NRO, Consistory Court wills 267 Belward; Prob. Inv. 32/210.

POPE, EDMUND. Origins unknown. B.C.L. All Souls College, Oxford, 1595; Dean 1596; D.C.L. 1599. Warrant Doc. Com. 1599; full admission 1601; out of commons until 1622; in commons 1623–30. Commissary of Westminster 1613. Chancellor of Rochester diocese 1614–30. Official to Archdeacon of Rochester. Comr. Adm. Middx., etc., 1603–25. Comr. Piracy London 1614–29. Delegates 1609–30. Comr. Pol. & Ass. 1619–29. High Com. 1625, 1626, 1629. Occasional surrogate for Judge of PCC and Official of Archdeacon of Essex. Brought before Parlt. 1626 for excommunication and imprisonment of Sir Robert Howard, M.P. Res.: St. Botolph's, London, and Doc. Com. d. 1630.

Clark, *Register*, i. 183, 242; iii. 193. LPL, Reg. Doc. Com., ff. 45ᵛ, 107; Whitgift, Reg. iii, f. 111ᵛ; MS. 1729, f. 95. Wood, *Fasti*, i. 282. *Catalogue of All Souls Archives*, pp. 305–6. Kent Archives Office, Drb/Pwr 19, pt. 1, f. 56; 20, f. 385; Drb/Pa, *passim*. Bodl., Tanner MS. 427, f. 226ᵛ. PRO, HCA 1/32/1, ff. 13, 21, 29, 38, 90; HCA 24/73–82, *passim*; DEL 5/4, *passim*; DEL 8/70, *passim*; C 181/2, ff. 143, 219ᵛ, 296ᵛ; 181/3, ff. 61, 79; 181/4, ff. 7, 37. CUL, Whitelocke Journal, f. 176–176ᵛ. Usher, *High Commission*, p. 357. Quintrell, 'Government of Essex', p. 156.

POPE, JOHN, 3rd son of Nicholas of Buckstead, Sussex, esq. (d. 1599), by Mary, dau. of John Gill of Hertford. Matric. Clare College, Cambridge, 1576; B.A. 1580; M.A. 1583; LL.D. 1590. Warrant Doc. Com. 1591; full admission 1618; in commons 1618–20, 1623–30; out of commons 1619–22. Comr. Pol. & Ass. 1602–5. Comr. Piracy London 1603–29; Comr. Adm. Middx. 1619, 1622, 1629. Active as advocate in London courts. Refused to contribute to naval expenditures of Elizabeth. Recommended for judgeship of HCA by Sir Thomas Walsingham 1626. Patrimony: £100. Owned house in London. Will: PCC 58 Scroope, pr. 11 June 1630. £100 to sister Kirby; £60 to eldest grandchild. Had conveyed most of estate at marriage of son Dudley. m. Barbara Onely of Pulborough, Sussex.

> *Visitation of Sussex* (Harl. Soc. liii, 1905), pp. 98–9. *Al. Cant.* iii. 380 LPL, Reg. Doc. Com., ff. 48, 108; Whitgift Reg. i, f. 178ᵛ. PRO, C 181/1, ff. 41, 122–3, 127, 213; 181/2, f. 10; 181/3, f. 97ᵛ; 181/4, f. 37; HCA 1/32/1, ff. 13, 21, 29; SP 16/35/79; E 179/146/399, f. 5; PROB 11/93/15; 11/158/58. BM, MS. Lansdowne 81, f. 81.

PORTER, GEORGE, 3rd son of George of Wery Hall, Cumb., gent., by Anne, dau. of W. Skelton of Armsthwaite, Cumb. Matric. pens. Queens' College, Cambridge, 1593; B.A. 1597; M.A. 1599; fellow 1601–35; LL.D. 1612. Regius Professor of Law on death of T. Morrisson until 1635. bur. St. Botolph's, Cambridge, 1635. Will: Cambridge VCC, pr. 13 Nov. 1635. Six volumes of Bellarmine to eldest brother Joseph. £34 in debts; £20 owed to him. d. without issue.

> *Al. Cant.* iii. 382. J. Foster (ed.), *Pedigrees . . . of Cumberland and Westmoreland* (Carlisle, 1891), p. 108. Cambridge Univ. Arch., wills 3/219.

POWELL, GRIFFITH, b. 1561, 3rd son of John ap Howel ap John of Llansawel, Carmarths., gent., by Anne, dau. of Gruffyd ap Henry. Cousin of Dr. Griffith Lloyd, D.C.L. (d. 1586). Matric. Jesus College, Oxford, 1581; B.A. 1584; M.A. 1589; fellow 1590; B.C.L. 1593; Clerk of the Market 1597; LL.D. 1599. Vice-Principal of Jesus College; acting Principal 1586; Principal 1613–20. Raises money for the college. Author of philosophical works. Dedicates *Analysis Lib. Aristotelis de Sophisticis Elenchis* (1598) to the Earl of Essex. d. 28 June 1620. Will: Oxford VCC, pr. 15 June 1621. Entire estate, valued at £648. 17s. 4d., to Jesus College, of which £200 was for purchase of lands to sustain one fellow. Inventory of goods taken 10 Feb. 1621.

> *DNB* xvi. 243. Wood, *Athenae*, ii. 283. Clark, *Register*, i. 116, 120, 183–4, 254, 189–90, ii. 106; iii. 121. *Al. Oxon.* iii. 1191. Mallett, *History of Oxford*, ii. 197–9. E. G. Hardy,

Jesus College (London, 1899), pp. 22, 27, 33–5, 71. Oxford Univ. Archives, Wills O–P; Inventories P.

PRYTHERGE (PRETHERCH, PRYTHERD, PRICHARD, PRITHERCH), WILLIAM. Prob. from Anglesey. Prob. related to, but not to be confused w. William Prycherch or Prichard, 2nd son of Richard ap Rhydderch of Llanidan, Anglesey (B.C.L. 1561; perhaps D.C.L. 1582; d. 1596). B.C.L. Jesus College, Oxford, 1567 'after fifteen years in law'; D.C.L. 1582. Warrant Doc. Com. 1600; full admission 1601; in commons 1601–7, 1610–11; out of commons 1608–9, 1612–27. Rector of Maidwell St. Mary 1579 and Ashby Castle, Northants., 1586. Official of Archdeacon of Norfolk 1585–1613. Commissary for Norfolk archdeaconry 1585–7. J.P. Northants. 1604, 1608. Comr. for Charitable Uses Northants. 1603. d. 1627.

> Griffiths, *Pedigrees*, p. 115. *Al. Oxon.* iii. 1201, 1211. Clark, *Register*, i. 119; iii. 99. Boase, *Register*, pp. 215, 268. LPL, Reg. Doc. Com., ff. 45ᵛ, 107; Whitgift Reg. iii, f. 115ᵛ. Blomefield, *Norfolk*, iii. 657. Gleason, *Justices*, pp. 170–1. *Peterborough Administration*, p. 207. BM, Add. MS. 38,139, f. 144. *CSPD 1603–1610*, p. 520.

RAXTER (RACKSTER, RACHSTON, RACSTER, RADCLIFFE), JOHN, b. 1602, son of a cleric from Worcs. Matric. Oriel College, Oxford, 1619; B.A. 1623; M.A. 1629, inc. Cambridge 1634; LL.D. King's College, Cambridge, 1638. Warrant Doc. Com. 1640 but not fully admitted. Res.: London and Worcs.

> *Al. Oxon.* iii. 1227. *Al. Cant.* iii. 413. Clark, *Register*, ii. 378; iii. 419. PRO, SP 16/442/125. *CSPD 1639*, p. 438.

READ (READE), THOMAS, b. 1606, 2nd son of Robert of Linkenholt, Hants, gent. (d. 1621), by Mildred, sister of Francis Windebank, Secretary of State to Charles I. Not to be confused w. Thomas Read or Rhaedus, a Scot, named Latin Secretary 1620 (d. 1624). Winchester College. Scholar New College, Oxford, 1624; fellow 1627–45 by order of the King; B.C.L. 1631; D.C.L. 1638. Warrant Doc. Com. 1640; full admission 1661. Claimed to be more indebted to Windebank than to a parent 1639. Trains as Royalist at Oxford 1642. Delegated to maintain King's troops at Oxford. Serves w. Sir John Bryon's troops. Escapes from Chipping Norton to Worcester. Seeks residence in Maryland 1643. Principal of Magdalen Hall 1643–6 by appointment of King. Ordered before Parlt. 1648. Flees to Paris. Enters Douai College; professes Catholic faith 1648. Entered Carthusian monastery for short time but not ordained a priest. Surrogate to Judge of PCC 1661–9. Wrote *An Answer to Two Letters by Mr. T. B. giving an account of the Church Catholic* (Paris, 1654). Res.: Oxford before 1643; Doc. Com. after 1661. d. March 1669. Will: PCC 76 Coke, pr. 5 June 1669. Few pieces of gold and silver to brother Robert in Paris.

> *DNB* xvi. 796–7. Wood, *Athenae*, iii. 390, 831–2. J. Gillow, *Bibliographical Index of the English Catholics* v. 399. *Al. Oxon.* iii. 1241. LPL, Reg. Doc. Com., ff. 51, 111. PRO, SP 16/442/125; PROB 11/330/76. *CSPD 1639*, p. 396; *1639–40*, pp. 364–5; *1641–1643*, p. 268.

REDMAN (REDMAYNE), Robert, b. 1551. From the same family as Bishop Redman of Lancs. Matric. St. John's College, Cambridge, 1571; B.A. 1576; fellow 1577; M.A. 1579; LL.D. 1586. Commissary for archdeaconry of Suffolk 1586–9. Chancellor of Norwich diocese 1589–1625. J.P. Norf. 1590–1625. Comr. Adm. Norf. 1624. Comr. Piracy Norf. 1602, 1604, 1624. Comr. Sewers 1604. Appeals to common law judges to assist him in prosecution of non-conformists. Defends use of *ex officio* oath. Conflicts w. subordinate officials and w. Bishop Jegon over extent of his jurisdiction. Held land in Hunstanton, Little Ringstead, Sedgeford, and Catton, Norf.; leased rectory of Potter Higham. Res.: house leased by Dean and Chapter of Norwich in the Close. d. 5 Aug. 1625. Will: Norwich Consistory Court 131 Mittings. Lands and lease to wife Dorothy and then to dau. Frances, wife of J. Burrell of Londonthorpe, Lincs.

Al. Cant. iii. 436. Blomefield, *Norfolk*, ii. 634, 658; x. 310. *Registrum Vagum* i. 32–4, 103–4, 123, 151–2; ii. 271, 342. *Norwich Chapter Books*, pp. 36, 38. A. H. Smith, 'The Elizabethan Gentry of Norfolk' (Univ. of London, Ph.D. thesis, 1959), pp. 16–17. PRO, C 181/1, ff. 11, 35–7, 142; 181/3, f. 115ᵛ; C 193/13/1, f. 73; HCA 1/32/1, f. 17; E 179/153/583, f. 2ᵛ. Gleason, *Justices*, p. 151.

RIDDELL, George, b. 1609, 4th son of Sir Thomas of Gateshead and New-castle upon Tyne, Northumb., Kt. (d. 1650), by Elizabeth, dau. of Sir John Conyers of Sockburn, Durham. Matric. Queen's College, Oxford, 1628; B.A. 1628; B.C.L. 1630; D.C.L. 1635. Adm. advocate at York 1636 and practised until Civil War. Joint patent w. W. Easdall of chancellorship of York 1637. Counsel on High Commission at Durham 1639–40; criticized for high fees. Judge-Advocate in army of William, Marquis of Newcastle. Died in siege of Hull, Sept. 1643.

J. Foster (ed.), *Pedigrees . . . of Northumberland* (Newcastle upon Tyne, 1891), p. 101. *Al. Oxon.* iii. 1256. Marchant, *Church Under Law*, p. 251. *High Commission Within Durham*, p. 189 n.

RIDLEY, Sir Thomas, b. before 1549, 2nd son of Thomas of Bouldon, Salop, and of Ely, yeoman, by Alice, dau. of William Day of Worfield, Salop. Matric. pens. King's College, Cambridge, 1566; fellow 1569–79; B.A. 1571; M.A. 1574; LL.D. 1583. Warrant Doc. Com. 1585; full admission 1590; in commons until 1619; out of commons 1620–8. Honorific admission Gray's Inn 1690. Headmaster of Eton. Official of Archdeacon of Surrey 1594. Chancellor of Winchester diocese 1596–1627. J.P. Hants 1596; Surrey 1596. Comr. Adm. Dorset 1603, 1605; Middx. 1606; Hants 1607. Comr. Piracy London 1606; Dorset 1601, 1603; Hants 1603. Delegates 1595–1618. Master in Chancery extraordinary 1598; ordinary 1609–20. High Com. 1611–29. Vicar-General to Archbishop of Canterbury 1608–29. Wrote verse for dedication of 1576 edn. of Foxe, *Acts and Monuments*. Assisted Bancroft with Canons of 1604. Wrote *A View of the Civile and Ecclesiastical Law* (1607), which W. Prynne considered to be a popish book. M.P. Chipping Wycombe, Bucks., 1586 through influence of Bishop Day of Winchester; Lymington, Hants, 1601 through influence of Earl of Nottingham, possibly at instance of Cecil. Knighted 1619. Patrimony: 1 close and 2 closes on mother's death. Joint lessee of manor of Ockholt in Berks. Leased manor of Poyle in Stanwell, Middlesex, 1591. Purchased manors of Greane (Barnt Green) in Worcs. 1590 and Babridge in Hants 1610. Grant of arms 1581. Res.: Winchester early in career; London in St. Benet, Paul's Wharf. d. 22 Jan. 1629. Will: PCC 19 Ridley, pr. 26 Feb. 1629. Had already devised most of estate to daus. Anne and Elizabeth. Manor of Babridge and lease of Poyle to wife Margaret. m. (1) Alice, dau. of Bishop Day 1596; (2) Margaret, dau. of Sir William Boleyn.

> *DNB* xvi. 1176. HPT, typescript. *Al. Cant.* iii. 458. *Eton Register*, pp. 280–1. *Visitation of Shropshire*, ii. 419–20. LPL, Reg. Doc. Com., ff. 44, 106; Whitgift Reg. i, f. 113. PRO, C 216/1, nos. 40, 73. C 181/1, ff. 18, 114, 124; 181/2, f. 10ᵛ; C 193/13/1, f. 96; SP 16/80/72; PROB 11/155/19. *VCH Berks.* iii. 104; *Worcs.* iii. 254; *Middlesex* iii. 39; *Hants* iii. 334. *HMCS* xii. 676–7. Usher, *Reconstruction*, i. 335; ii. 211. Hill, *Economic Problems*, pp. 84–5, 91, 97–8. *Grantees of Arms*, i. 214. Gleason, *Justices*, pp. 257, 259. Prynne, *Canterburies Doome*, pp. 186, 218. HRO, Consistory Court Books 100–5, *passim*. Winchester Cathedral Library, Index of Hants Clergy, f. 408ᵛ.

ROANE (ROAN), WILLIAM, b. 1608, son of Anthony of Wellingborough, Northants., prob. gent. Adm. Scholar Trinity Hall, Cambridge, 1626; fellow 1629–43; LL.B. 1630; LL.D. 1637. Warrant Doc. Com. before 1640; listed as member of Doc. Com. 1639 but no record of full admission. Practised in Arches 1639. Commissary of Official of Archdeacon of Buckingham 1637. Deprives Henry Earl of Huntingdon of seats in Church of Longborough, Leics., during visitation. Petition to King 1639 complained that Roan removed seats that were reserved for the 'better sort of inhabitants' from the church of All Saints in Huntingdon. Pledged administrative subservience to Lambe 1640. Accused of harassment, extortion, and illegal excommunication 1642. Accused of exacting more than requisite funds for war *v*. Scots. Puritan pamphlet *A Letter from Roan in France* (1641) accuses him of corruption and lack of proficiency, and alleges that he fled to France. Res.: Trinity Hall and London.

> *Al. Cant.* iii. 464. Borth. Inst., R. VII. PR 108. PRO, SP 16/421/108; 16/442/125. *CSPD 1634–1635*, p. 523; *1637–1638*, pp. 48, 577; *1638–1639*, p. 620; *1640–1641*, pp. 6, 35; *1641–1643*, pp. 423–4.

ROGERS, JOHN, b. in Wittenberg, Germany *c*. 1540, 2nd son of John, Divinity Lecturer and Preb. of St. Paul's Cathedral and martyr. Naturalized 1552. Matric. pens. St. John's College, Cambridge, 1558. B.A. Trinity College 1563; fellow 1563; M.A. 1567; LL.D. Magdalene College 1574. Full admission Doc. Com. 1574; out of commons 1603–6. Chancellor of Cathedral of Wells 1596–1602. Diplomatic service in Denmark, Poland, and Netherlands. m. Mary, dau. of W. Leete of Everden, Cambs. Not to be confused w. John of Bryanston, Dorset, M.P. Wareham 1584, 1586, 1589.

> *Al. Cant.* iii. 479. Cooper, *Athenae*, ii. 385. *HMC Dean of Wells*, ii. 406. *DNB* xvi. 129. LeNeve, *Fasti*, i. 178. LPL, Reg. Doc. Com., ff. 42, 104.

RYVES (RIVES), GEORGE, b. 1600, prob. 1st son of Henry of Damery Court, Dorset, esq. Cousin of Thomas Ryves (q.v.). Matric. Wadham College, Oxford, 1617 as from Hants; B.C.L. Hart Hall 1627; D.C.L. 1634. Not to be confused w. son and heir of John of Randleston, Dorset (b. 1589; matric. Hart Hall 1605; adm. Middle Temple 1609).

> *Register of Wadham College*, p. 39. *Al. Oxon.* iii. 1295. Clark, *Register*, ii. 286, 363; iii. 445. *Visitation of Dorset*, pp. 80–1. Hutchins, *Dorset*, iv. 97.

RYVES (RIVES, REEVES), SIR THOMAS, 8th and 5th surviving son of John of Damery Court, Dorset, esq., by Elizabeth, dau. of Sir John Marvin of Fonthill, Wilts. Winchester College. B.C.L. New College, Oxford, 1605; fellow; D.C.L. 1610. Warrant Doc. Com. 1610; full admission 1611; in commons 1611–12, 1621–2, 1625–42; out of commons 1613–20, 1623–4. Judge of Prerogative Court and Court of Faculties in Ireland 1615–25. Conflicts w. Archbishop Usher and the Bishop of Neath over extent of jurisdiction. Master of Chancery in Ireland. Advocate-General for James I 1620 and for Charles I. Active as advocate in London courts 1620–41. Delegates 1622–41. Mission to Cologne 1623. Comr. Adm. Dorset 1628. Comr. Piracy Cinque Ports 1630, 1638; Dorchester 1631; Dorset 1639. Judge of Admiralty Court of Dover 1635–7; Judge of Admiralty Court of Cinque Ports 1637. Delivers opinion on King's right to translate bishops 1626. Called before Parlt. 1629 for role in confirmation of Montague as bishop. Master of Requests extraordinary 1626. Dean of Shoreham and Croydon 1633. Royalist during Civil War. Assists King in negotiations on Isle of Wight. Defends rights of Irish clergy in *Poore Vicars Plea* (1620). Also wrote *Regiminis Anglicani Hibernia defensio adversus Analecten* (1624); *Imperatoris Justiniani defensio contra Alemannum* (1626); *Historia Navalis Antiqua* (1633); *Historia Navalis Media* (1640). Patrimony: £100. Owned 430 acres of land near Wainfleet, Lincs.; other lands in Lincs. Res.: London after 1620 in house near Doc. Com. d. 2 Jan. 1652; bur. St. Clement Danes. Will: PCC 12 Bowyer, pr. 5 Jan. 1652. All lands and goods to wife Elizabeth.

> *Visitation of Dorset*, p. 80. Clark, *Register*, i. 120, 186, 380; iii. 260. Wood, *Athenae*, iii. 304–6. Lloyd, *Memoires*, p. 592. *CSP Ireland 1611–1614*, pp. 295, 354–5; *1615–1625*, pp. 105–6, 173–4. LPL, Reg. Doc. Com., ff. 47, 107ᵛ; Bancroft Reg., f. 175; Abbot Reg. iii, f. 203. PRO, E 403/2455, f. 25. C 181/4, ff. 48ᵛ, 104; 181/5, ff. 131ᵛ, 152; DEL 8/70, *passim*; HCA 1/32/1, f. 3; HCA 24/79–98, *passim*; SP 14/214, pp. 240, 265; SP 16/339/63; 16/421/108. Bodl., MS. Top. Oxon. e.105/2, f. 84. *CSPD 1623–1625*, pp. 5, 16; *1636–1637*, p. 281; *1637*, p. 315. *APC 1615–1616*, p. 47. Parr, *Usher*, pp. 63–4. Fuller, *Church History*, vi. 57–8. Notestein and Relf, *1629 Debates*, p. 123. R. Lovell, *Publican Becoming a Penitent* (London, 1625), dedication. *Heraldic Cases, passim*. PRO, PROB 11/70/22; 11/220/12.

SAMMES (SAMES, SAMS), WILLIAM. Parentage unknown, but prob. nephew of Thomas of Great Totham, Essex. Related to Robert Aylett and John Lambe (q.v.) through cousin Edward. Matric. pens. Corpus Christi College, Cambridge, 1582; B.A. 1586; M.A. 1589; LL.D. Trinity Hall 1595. Warrant

Doc. Com. 1599; full admission 1601; in commons 1601–10, 1616–33; out of commons 1611–15, 1634–42. Active as advocate in London courts 1604–41. Surrogate of Sir Henry Marten as Judge of HCA. Vice-Admiral of Essex 1609–17. Comr. Adm. Middx. 1619, 1623, 1625. Comr. Piracy London 1617–38. High Com. 1626, 1629, 1633. Fined and criticized by Long Parlt. for activities as High Comr. Sides w. Parlt. and replaces R. Zouch as Judge of HCA 1641. Held copyhold lands and tenements in Benwick, Cambs. Invested in drainage schemes. Res.: London. Will: PCC 163 Twisse, pr. 3 Nov. 1646. £20 apiece to Sir Miles Sandys, Thomas Wyan, and M. Cottle; £150 to niece. Lands to wife.

> *Al. Cant.* iv. 10. LPL, Reg. Doc. Com., f. 45ᵛ; Whitgift Reg. iii, f. 111. R. Marsden, 'The Vice-Admirals of the Coast', *EHR* 23 (1908), 742–3. PRO, C 181/2, ff. 296ᵛ, 334; 181/3, f. 79; 181/4, ff. 37, 138ᵛ; 181/5, ff. 26ᵛ, 130; HCA 1/32/1, ff. 13, 21, 29. Usher, *High Commission*, p. 358. G. Mercator, *Atlas* (Amsterdam, 1636), p. 65. Notestein, *D'Ewes*, p. 476. *Visitation of Essex* i. 482–3. Dale, *Inhabitants of London*, p. 179. *CSPD 1641–1643*, pp. 92, 516, 535–6.

SAVAGE, Repent, b. in Brentwood, Essex. Perhaps related to the Savages of Corringham, Essex. Matric. pens. Christ's College, Cambridge, 1581; B.A. 1585; LL.B. by 1599; LL.D. Pembroke College 1607. Ordained deacon 1599. Rector of Corringham, Essex, 1599–1619 at income of £22. 10s. p.a. Official of Archdeacon of Essex 1597–1620. Litigants complained that he was too young to be a judge 1606. d. 1620. m. Mercy Chace.

> *Al. Cant.* iv. 21. Peile, *Christ's College*, i. 164. Quintrell, 'Government of Essex', pp. 150, 156. Anglin, 'Archdeacon of Essex', pp. 36, 38. ERO, D/AEA 24, f. 33.

SCUDAMORE (SCIDMER), Rowland, b. 1610, younger son of William of Ballingham, Herefs., esq. Not to be confused w. Rowland, son of George of Treworgan. Matric. Brasenose College, Oxford, 1631; grace for B.A. 1633; B.C.L. 1635; D.C.L. 1640. Rector of Ross, Herefs., through patronage of Bishop of Hereford 1642–5. Rector of Preston-on-Wye, Herefs., 1643–5. Preb. of Hereford 1643–5. Killed during siege of Hereford Aug. 1645.

> *Al. Oxon.* iv. 1328. *Brasenose Register* i. 161. LeNeve, *Fasti*, i. 521. *Walker Revised*, p. 8. J. H. Matthews, *Collections Towards the History . . . of Hereford: Hundred of Wormelow* (Hereford, 1912), i. 67. *A Letter Sent . . . from Sir Barnabas Scudamore* (Oxford, 1645), p. 3.

SEAMAN, John, b. 1564, 1st son of John of Chelmsford and later of Panfield Priory, Essex, woollendraper and later gent. (d. 1604). Matric. pens. Queens' College, Cambridge, 1579; B.A. 1583; fellow 1583–94; M.A. 1586; taxor 1588; LL.D. before 1596. Warrant Doc. Com. 1596 but not fully admitted. Comr. Piracy Cornwall 1601. Chancellor of Gloucester diocese 1600–23; w. Dr. Thomas Edwards (q.v.) 1608. J.P. Gloucester. Succeeds father at Panfield Priory 1604. d. 1623.

> *Al. Cant.* iv. 37. Morant, *Essex*, ii. 408. PRO, C 181/1, f. 5; 181/2, f. 232; C 193/13/1, f. 42ᵛ. LPL, Whitgift Reg. ii, f. 143; Bancroft Reg., f. 239. Rudder *Gloucestershire*, p. 163.

SHEPPARD, ALEXANDER. B.C.L. and D.C.L. Oxford 1609. Referred to as going to London after receipt of degree.

Clark, *Register*, i. 119; iii. 291. *Al. Oxon.* iv. 1344.

SKINNER, WILLIAM, b. 1593, 3rd son of Edward of Ledbury, Herefs., the 5th son of a gent. Matric. Brasenose College, Oxford, as son of commoner; B.A. 1612; B.C.L. All Souls 1617; D.C.L. 1625. Chancellor of Hereford diocese after 1625. J.P. Herefs. 1635. Rector Beckenham, Essex, 1628. Preb. of Hereford. Sequestered before May 1644. Assessed at £250 by Com. for Advance of Money 1643. Sequestration of estate discharged 1649. Res.: Broad Cabbach Lane, Hereford. d. 1647. m. Mary, dau. of E. Style of Kent. Father of Elizabeth and Mary.

BM, Harl. MS. 1450, ff. 39ᵛ-40. Clark, *Register*, ii. 308; iii. 314. *Walker Revised*, pp. 8, 225. *Calendar of Committee for the Advance of Money*, i. 275. *Al. Oxon.* iv. 1362. PRO, C 193/13/2, f. 30ᵛ.

SMITH, SIMON, younger son of Thomas of Credenhill, Herefs. (d. 1575), esq., by Elizabeth, dau. of Thomas Welsh. Matric. pens. Christ's College, Cambridge, 1560; B.A. 1565; M.A. 1568; LL.D. Trinity Hall 1578. Full admission Doc. Com. 1582; in commons until 1606. Preb. of Hereford 1561-1606. Chancellor of St. David's diocese 1605-6. Comr. Piracy Cornwall 1601. Rector of Credenhill and of Kenchester, Herefs. Refused to contribute money to Elizabeth's navy. Patrimony: £40 and one-eighth of lands. Res.: London at Doc. Com. and in St. Faith's parish. Will: PCC 86 Stafford, pr. 10 Nov. 1606. Books in divinity and ecclesiastical attire to Roger Brenton; £76 to relatives. Lease of chambers at Doc. Com. to W. Creake.

F. Weaver (ed.), *The Visitation of Herefordshire, 1569* (Exeter, 1886), p. 96. *Al. Cant.* iv. 109. LPL, Reg. Doc. Com., ff. 43, 104ᵛ; Bancroft Reg., f. 184ᵛ. Cooper, *Athenae*, ii. 441. LeNeve, *Fasti*, i. 510. PRO, C 181/1, f. 5; E 179/146/399, f. 5; PROB 11/57/44; 11/108/86. BM, Lansdowne MS. 81, f. 81ᵛ.

SMITH, WILLIAM. Prob. from Worlaby, Lincs. Fellow of New College, Oxford, 1558-71; matric. 1565; B.C.L. 1565; D.C.L. 1574. Full admission Doc. Com. 1577; out of commons until 1627. Preb. of Lincoln 1581-1614. Prob. travelled to Florence. Confronts difficulties finding employment 1600. Of Brickhill, Bucks. Father of Mary, sister-in-law of Hugh Barker (q.v.). d. 1627.

Clark, *Register*, i. 104; ii. 58; iii. 23. Boase, *Register*, p. 258. *Al. Oxon.* iv. 1384. LeNeve, *Fasti*, ii. 120. *HMCS* x. 77, 381-2. LPL, Reg. Doc. Com., ff. 42ᵛ, 104. Metcalfe, *Visitation of Northamptonshire*, p. 164.

SMITHSON, JOHN, b. in London 1579. Eton College. Adm. Scholar King's College, Cambridge, 1597; matric. pens. *c.* 1597; fellow 1600-31; B.A. 1602; M.A. 1605; taxor 1614; proctor 1617-18; commissary 1625; Vice-Provost 1626-30; LL. D. 1630. 'Of Trinity Hall' 1633. Owned ten. in Cambridge and London. bur. St. Antholin's, London, 11 Dec. 1635. Will: Cambridge VCC, pr.

10 Dec. 1635. £40 to niece Jane; London property to brother Arthur; Cambridge property and possessions to Francis Brasbone. £50 to relatives, friends, and servants.

> *Eton Register*, pp. 313–14. *Al. Cant.* iv. 116. *The Parish Register of St. Antholin* (Harl. Soc. Registers viii), p. 69. Cambridge Univ. Arch., Wills 3/220.

SPICER, WILLIAM, b. 1582, 1st son of William of Exeter, Devon, merchant and gent. Winchester College. Matric. New College, Oxford, 1602; adm. as fellow commoner to Caius College, Cambridge, 1604; LL.B. 1615; LL.D. University of Leyden 1616. Perhaps adm. Middle Temple 1607. Inherited his father's lands and ten. in Exeter. No record of legal activity.

> *Al. Cant.* iv. 135. *Al. Oxon.* iv. 1399. Clark, *Register*, i. 349, 377. PRO, will of William sen., PROB 11/104/62.

STANES (STANE, STAENS), RICHARD, b. 1558, 1st son of Richard of High Ongar, Essex, gent. (d. 1600). Matric. pens. Jesus College, Cambridge, 1578; B.A. Corpus Christi College 1582; M.A. 1585; LL.D. 1611. Proctor in courts of the Archdeacons of Essex and of Middx. before doctorate. Official of Archdeacon of Middx. by 1609. Held manor of Folyot's or Fobot's Hall in High Ongar, Essex, jointly w. father 1562–1600; alone after 1600; valued at £1,127. Leased manor of Fyfield, Essex. Purchased three mess. from Dr. William Bingham (q.v.). Res.: Halstead, Essex. d. 1614. Will: ERO, D/ABW/36/227, pr. 1614. Manor and lands to wife and then to son William; £200 apiece to daus. Bridget and Anne.

> *Al. Cant.* iv. 143. Morant, *Essex*, i, pt. 2, 130. Quintrell, 'Government of Essex', pp. 150–1. PRO, C 142/266/87. ERO, D/AEA, f. 99; D/DHW Z9. *VCH Essex* iv. 179.

STANHOPE, SIR EDWARD, b. *c.* 1546 in Kingston-on-Hull, Yorks., 4th son of Sir Michael of Shelford, Notts. Not to be confused w. his brother Edward. Elder brother John became 1st Baron Stanhope. Scholar Trinity College, Cambridge, 1560; B.A. 1563; fellow 1564; M.A. 1566; LL.D. 1575. Warrant Doc. Com. 1575, full admission 1576; in commons until 1608. Preb. of York 1572–91 at instance of Cecil; St. Paul's 1591–1608. Master in Chancery 1591–1608. Chancellor of London diocese 1578–1608. Vicar-General of Archbishop of Canterbury 1583–1608. High Com. 1584–1605. Rector of Terrington, Norf., 1589. Com. touching Jesuits 1593. Comr. to try R. Lopez and others for treason 1594. Comr. to try W. Ralegh for treason. Comr. Piracy London 1601, 1603. Comr. Adm. Middx. 1603. Knighted 1603. Censor of popish and foreign books 1604. M.P. Marlborough, Wilts., 1584, 1586 through influence of Earl of Hertford, his cousin. Included on committees for Mary, Queen of Scots, Nov. 1586 and ecclesiastical discipline May 1587. Narrowly avoids political disfavour by testifying to legitimacy of Thomas Seymour 1592 and by support of Essex 1599. Implacable opponent of Puritanism; attacked in *The Marprelate Tracts*. Engaged in money-lending. Granted manor of Hucknall Torkard, Notts., from

Elizabeth 1600. Held manors of Edlington, Stanton, Wyvell, Maltby, and Grimston in Yorks.; manor of Gonsell in Lincs.; leases of Weston and Ascon in Derbyshire; farm of Calcutt in Warwicks.; land on Isle of Axholme, Lincs.; ten. in High Holborn, London; mess. in Kirklington, Notts. Estate valued at £40,000. d. March 1608. Will: PCC 22 Windebanke, pr. 25 March 1608. Dispenses with £2,000 in addition to lands and profits therefrom. £700 and books on divinity, canon law, civil law, common law, and statute law to Trinity College. Estate divided among three brothers.

DNB xviii. 894–5. Cooper, *Athenae*, ii. 470. HPT, typescript. *Al. Cant.* iv. 146. Clark, *Register*, i. 349. LPL, Reg. Doc. Com., ff. 42, 104; Parker Reg. ii, f. 113. PRO, C 142/300/173; 142/310/53; C 181/1, ff. 122–3; HCA 1/32/1, f. 90; E 179/146/399, f. 5. Usher, *High Commission*, p. 358. Trevor-Roper, *The Gentry*, p. 11. *Marprelate Tracts*, pp. 32, 46–7, 51. Wilbraham, *Diary*, pp. 99–100. *HMCS* ix. 107. *APC 1596–1597*, pp. 425–6. Stoughton, *An Assertion*, p. 370. Strype, *Whitgift*, ii. 504. BM, Lansdowne MSS. 16, f. 84; 39, f. 156; 58, f. 96; 81, f. 81.

STEDE (STEED, STEAD), WILLIAM, b. 1594, 2nd son of Sir William of Harrietsham, Kent (d. 1621), by Cicilia, dau. of J. Culpepper. Matric. sizar University College, Cambridge, 1606. B.A. 1610; B.C.L. All Souls 1615; fellow; D.C.L. 1622. Warrant Doc. Com. 1621; full admission 1622; in commons until 1642. Judge of ecclesiastical court at Canterbury by 1634. Joins ecclesiastical judges residing at Doc. Com. in legal opinion *c.* 1636. Sends money and arms to King's forces in Kent; joins them at Maidstone; provides sanctuary for King's servants and horses at Harrietsham. Estate at Harrietsham avoids sequestration by act of pardon 1649. Lease of New Land from All Souls w. William, sen. 1619; renewed to him alone 1625, 1640. Inherited father's estate on death of nephew Cromer 1646. m. Hester, dau. of Sir Edwin Sandys 1632. d. after 1671.

Visitation of Kent, pp. 71–2. *LeNeve's Knights* (Harl. Soc. viii), p. 443. Clark, *Register*, i. 189; ii. 289; iii. 290. *Al. Oxon.* iv. 1415. LPL, Reg. Doc. Com., ff. 48ᵛ, 108; Abbot Reg. ii, f. 196. *CPCC* iv. 2614. *CSPD 1634–1635*, p. 244. PRO, SP 16/339/63. *Catalogue of All Souls Archives*, pp. 146–7. R. H. Goodsall, *Stede Hill: Annals of a Kentish Home* (London, 1949), pp. 50–75.

STEWARD (STYWARD), NICHOLAS, 6th son of Symeon of Lakenheath, Suff., esq. Matric. pens. Trinity College, Cambridge, 1560; LL.B. Trinity Hall 1568; LL.D. 1574. Warrant Doc. Com. 1573; full admission 1573; in commons until 1632. Delegates 1595–1629. Active as advocate in London courts. Co-author of memorandum on oaths in ecclesiastical courts *c.* 1590. Comr. to relieve debtors 1597. Comr. Adm. Middx. 1603–25. Counsellor for Queen's Causes 1599. J.P. Hants *c.* 1622. High Com. 1625, 1626, 1629. Reversion to office of Chamberlain of the Exchequer 1628. Defends Archbishop of Canterbury *v.* Corpus Christi College 1603. Attends Hampton Court conference 1604. Delivers opinion on election of Bishop Montague 1629. M.P. Cambridge Univ. 1604. Rector impropriate of Henham, Essex. Patrimony: £100.

Purchased manor of Hartley Mauditt, Hants, 1614. Leased two manors of Leckhampton and Ratherly and lands from son-in-law R. Norwood for 100 years. Res.: Doc. Com. Will: PCC 52 Russell, pr. 6 and 26 June 1633. £500 apiece to granddaughters Dorothy, Elizabeth, and Anne; 2,000 marks to grandson Richard; 100 marks to each grandchild; £40 to each great-grandchild. Leases to dau. Elizabeth. Estate passes to grandson Nicholas, heir.

> *Visitations of Hertfordshire* (Harl. Soc. xxii, 1886), p. 94. *Al. Cant.* iv. 161. LPL, Reg. Doc. Com., ff. 41ᵛ, 103ᵛ; MS. 2014, f. 65; Parker Reg. ii, f. 77ᵛ. DEL 5/2–6, *passim*; DEL 8/70, pt. 1, *passim*. C 193/13/1, f. 88ᵛ; C 142/725/60; 142/499/18; 142/150/188; HCA 1/32/1, ff. 13, 29, 38, 55, 90; HCA 24/68–80, *passim*; SP 39/26/1. Bodl., Tanner MS. 427, *passim*. Rex, *University Representation*, pp. 41–2, 47–8. Usher, *High Commission*, p. 358. *HMCS* xv. 150. *APC 1597*, pp. 143–4. Notestein and Relf, *Commons Debates 1629*, p. 257. *VCH Hants* ii. 509. Gleason, *Justices*, p. 257. PRO, PROB 11/50/10; 11/163/52.

STEWARD (STEUART, STEWART), RICHARD, b. 1595, 3rd son of Nicholas of Pattishall, Northants., esq. Matric. Magdalen Hall, Oxford, 1609; B.A. 1612; fellow 1613–26; M.A. All Souls 1615; B.C.L. 1617; proctor 1622; D.C.L. 1624. A cleric. Rector of Harrietsham, Kent, 1626; Mildenhall, Norf., 1630; Alon Barnes, Wilts., 1630. Vicar of Aldbourne, Wilts., 1630. Preb. of Worcester 1629–38; Salisbury 1629; Westminster 1638. Warden of St. Mary's Hospital 1634. Dean of Chichester 1634. Archdeacon of Chichester 1635. Nominated Dean of St. Paul's 1641. Dean of Chapel Royal 1643. Chaplain and Clerk of Closet to Charles I 1633. Provost of Eton 1639 by royal nomination. Nominated Dean of Westminster 1645. Defends episcopacy *v.* Presbyterian criticism. List of religious writings in *DNB*. Receives £100 annuity from Royal Exchequer 1635. Deprived of preferments during Civil War. d. in Paris 14 Nov. 1651.

> *The Visitation of the County of Northampton . . . 1681* (Harl. Soc. lxxxvii, 1935), pp. 209–10; Clark, *Register*, i. 62; ii. 307, 405; iii. 311. *Al. Oxon.* iv. 1423. *DNB* xviii. 1145–7. *Chichester Chapter Acts*, nos. 1254, 1264, 1281. *Catalogue of All Souls Archives*, p. 381. *CSPD 1629–1631*, p. 503. *Walker Revised*, p. 10.

SUTCLIFFE (SOUTCLIFFE), Matthew, 2nd son of John of Halifax, Yorks., and of Grimsby, Lincs., yeoman or lesser gent., by Margaret, dau. of one Holdsworth of Astley, Yorks. Adm. Peterhouse, Cambridge, 1565; Scholar Trinity College, Cambridge, 1568; B.A. 1571; minor fellow 1572; M.A. 1574; major fellow 1574; Lector in Mathematics 1579; LL.D. 1580. Full admission Doc. Com. 1582; out of commons 1603, 1605, 1614–29; in commons 1604, 1606–13. Chancellor of Exeter diocese 1582–92. A cleric. Archdeacon of Taunton 1588. Preb. of Exeter 1588–1629; Wells 1588. Dean of Exeter 1588–1629 at income of £158. 16s. p.a. Conflicts w. Chapter at Exeter. Vicar of West Abington and of Harberton, Devon, 1590. Rector of Newton Ferrers, Devon, 1591; Lezant, Corn., 1594. Captain of the Horse for the clergy of Devon 1598. High Com. 1610–11. Provost of projected Chelsea College *c.* 1610. Donated £1,000 and annuity of £300 to the College. Comr. Adm. and Piracy Devon 1615. Assisted Captain John Smith in landing schemes 1584. Member of Council for New England 1620. Opposed Spanish marriage project 1621 on religious grounds and imprisoned by James. Wrote against Puritans, Catholics, and Arminians. List of works in *DNB*. Patrimony: ten. and lands in Yorks. Owned farms in Staverton, Harberton, Churchtown, and Stoke Rivers, Devon. Lands in West Worlington, Chawleigh, and elsewhere in Devon costing £3,000. Owned 'Barton Demesnes' and manor of Efford. Invested in Virginia Co. 1609 and in New England ventures 1607. Res.: London by 1581; the Close at Exeter. Will: PCC 94 Ridley, pr. 24 Nov. 1629. Barton and Efford to wife and then to grandson Matthew Halse; all other land for benefit of Chelsea College. Lent £460. 13*s*. 4*d*. to Thomas Clifford. m. Anne, dau. of John Bradley of Louth, Lincs., esq.

Familiae Minorum Gentium ii. 541. *DNB* xix. 175–7. *Al. Cant.* iv. 186. Fuller, *Church History*, v. 387–8, 390, 394–6. *HMC Dean of Wells*, ii. 316. LeNeve, *Fasti*, i. 47, 86. LPL, Reg. Doc. Com., ff. 43, 104ᵛ. *HMCS* xiv. 54. Usher, *High Commission*, p. 358. Winwood, *Memorials*, iii. 160–1. Camden, *Annales Jac. I*, p. 73. Yonge, *Diary*, p. 41. PRO, SP 14/54/91; HCA 1/32/1, f. 33; C 181/2, f. 240. Trevor-Roper, *Laud*, p. 75. Cassidy, 'Episcopate of Cotton', pp. 36–7, 113. Rabb, *Enterprise*, p. 385. *Notes and Queries* iv. 152, 239. *Devon and Cornwall Notes and Queries*, xv. 218.

SWALE (SWAYLE), SIR RICHARD, b. 1545, son of Thomas of Askham Richard, Yorks., gent., from minor branch of ancient Yorks. family at West Grinton. Matric. sizar Jesus College, Cambridge, 1566; B.A. 1569; fellow 1571; M.A. 1572; Fellow of Caius College 1577; tutor; LL.D. 1587. President of Caius 1582. Warrant Doc. Com. 1587; full admission 1590; in commons until 1607. Rector of Elm, Cambs., and Emneth, Norf., on presentation of Queen 1591–1606. Preb. of York but not resident there 1589–1608. Chancellor of Ely diocese 1588–1606. Auditor in Court of Audience 1598–1608. High Com. 1601–8. Mission to Denmark 1600. Knighted 1603. J.P. Oxon. 1604. Attends Hampton Court conference 1604. Comr. for suppressing popish books 1604. Comr. Piracy London 1601, 1603. Comr. Adm. Middx. 1603. Suspected of abetting Catholicism at Caius 1581; articles presented *v.* him. M.P. Higham Ferrers, Northants., 1589 through influence of Sir Christopher Hatton. Referred to as 'creature' of Hatton. Held manors of Askham Richard, Angram, and Copmanthorpe, Yorks. Held land and parsonage in Marston, Yorks. Held two closes in Rufforth, Yorks. Leased house in Rodrith, Surrey. Res.: Rodrith and London. Invested in commerce. Will: PCC 49 Windebanke, pr. 4 July 1608. Copmanthorpe and Angram manors, lands, and lease of house to wife. m. Susanna Rolfe of Herts.

P. Harrison, *The History of Yorkshire* (London, 1855), p. 236. *DNB* xix. 194–5. *Al. Cant.* iv. 189. Cooper, *Athenae* ii. 492. HPT, typescript. LPL, Reg. Doc. Com., ff. 44, 105; Whitgift Reg. i, f. 136ᵛ; Lam. Chart. Misc. xii, f. 9. PRO, C 142/302/115; HCA 1/32/1, f. 90; C 181/2, f. 296ᵛ; C 66/1452ᵛ; PROB 11/111/49. Usher, *High Commission*, p. 358. Heywood and Wright, *Transactions*, i. 331–3. *HMCS* x. 129. *APC 1591–1592*, pp. 144–5; *1592–1593*, p. 208; *1599–1600*, pp. 227–8. *CSPD 1603–1610*, p. 216. Wilbraham, *Diary*, p. 51. Barlow, *Sum and Substance*, p. 85. BM, Cotton MS. Cleo. F II, f. 120ᵛ. Rabb. *Enterprise*, p. 386. Jones, *Chancery*, p. 42.

SWALMAN (SWALLMAN), GEOFFREY. Matric. pens. Corpus Christi College, Cambridge, 1593. B.A. 1597; M.A. Sidney Sussex College 1600; fellow;
LL.D. 1613. Warrant Doc. Com. but not fully admitted. Official of Archdeacon
of Middx. Res.: near Doc. Com. and at an inn in Stebbing, Essex.

> Al. Cant. iv. 189. Quintrell, 'Government of Essex', p. 151. LPL, Abbot. Reg. i, f. 180.
> CSPD 1631–1633, p. 410.

SWEIT (SWETT, SWEAT), SIR GILES, b. 1586. From Oxon. Matric. as son
of commoner St. John's College, Oxford, 1602; B.A. Oriel 1605; M.A. 1611;
B.C.L. and D.C.L. St. Mary's Hall 1632. Principal St. Alban's Hall 1641–64.
Regius Professor of Civil Law 1661–72. Full admission Doc. Com. 1633; in
commons until 1642. Proctor in Oxford VCC 1615–23; Commissary 1641.
Official of Dorchester Peculiar, Oxon. by 1625. Official of Archdeacon of
Oxford 1632–70. Official of Peculiar of King's Sutton 1626. Allegedly assisted
Sir Thomas Sackville in vexation of R. Knollys, Vicar of Bibury, Glos., 1640.
Active as advocate in London courts 1634–41. Delegates 1639. Com. to exercise
jurisdiction of deanery of Risborough 1633. Assisted King's forces during Civil
War. Compounds for estate on Oxford Articles; fine at a tenth: £66. Dean of
the Arches 1660–72. Knighted 1664. Preb. of Salisbury 1661. Purchased land
in Middx. valued at £16 p.a. Held lease of land in Barbican, Middx.; ten. in
the Strand, London. d. 13 Sept. 1672. Will: PCC 126 Eure, pr. 15 Oct. 1672.
£610 to dau. Mary; £90 to friends; £100 and Barbican lease to grandson.
Res.: London and Oxford. Father of Mary, wife of George Parry (q.v.).

> Al. Oxon. iv. 1446. Clark, Register, i. 94; ii. 262; iii. 252. LPL, Reg. Doc. Com.,
> ff. 49ᵛ, 109ᵛ; Laud Reg. i, f. 192ᵛ. PRO, DEL 8/70, pt. 2, ff. 43–8; SP 16/421/108; PROB
> 11/340/126. Bodl., MSS. Archd. Papers Oxon. b. 67, f. 124; b. 71, f. 181; b. 55, f. 103.
> Queen's College Deeds 2. P. 4. LeNeve, Fasti, ii. 657. LeNeve's Knights, pp. 181, 256.
> CSPD 1634–1635, p. 333; 1640, pp. 325–6, 387, 391. CPCC ii. 1567.

TALBOT, CLERE, 3rd son of Thomas, D.C.L. (q.v.) of Gunvill's Hall, Norf.,
by Anne Herne. Scholar at Trinity Hall, Cambridge, 1608; LL.B. 1614; LL.D.
1619. Warrant Doc. Com. 1620; full admission 1623; in commons until 1641.
Commissary for archdeaconry of Norwich 1620. Official of Archdeacon of
Norf. 1628. Comr. Adm. Norf., Cambs., Ely 1628. J.P. Norf. 1635. Delegates
1621–39. Master in Chancery extraordinary 1628. Comr. Piracy London 1633,
1635, 1638. Active as advocate in London courts 1635–40. Judge of Vice-
Admiralty Court of Lincoln 1634. Delivers opinion on election of Bishop
Montague; joins other ecclesiastical judges residing at Doc. Com. in legal
opinion c. 1636. Patrimony: lands in Wymondham, Norf. Leased manor of
Rookheeles and Gransvilles from the Bishop of Norwich. Held mess. in the
Close, Norwich. Will: 253 Alchin, pr. 18 May 1654. Land to children; coach
and horses to wife. m. (1) Margaret by 1626; (2) Anne, dau. of William
Harborne. Father of Thomas, William, Clere, Margaret.

> Al. Cant. iv. 196. LPL, Reg. Doc. Com., ff. 48ᵛ, 108ᵛ. Abbot. Reg. ii, f. 190. Visitation
> of Norfolk . . . 1664, ii (Norfolk Record Soc. v, 1934), 214. Blomefield, Norfolk, iii.

656, 659. PRO, C 181/4, f. 139; 181/5, ff. 27, 130ᵛ; C 216/1, no. 101; C 193/13/2, f. 50ᵛ; DEL 5/6, *passim*; DEL 8/70, *passim*; HCA 24/94, f. 186; 24/95, ff. 68, 90; 24/98, no. 88A; 24/101, no. 46; SP 16/339/63; 16/421/108. *Norwich Chapter Book*, p. 77. Notestein and Relf, *Commons Debates 1629*, pp. 134–5. *CSPD 1634–1635*, p. 297; *1635*, p. 191. Marchant, *Church Under Law*, p. 54.

TALBOT, THOMAS, 1st son of Thomas of Wymondham and Gunvill's Hall, Norf., esq., originally a merchant from Lancs., by Katherine, dau. of Thomas Hast of Wymondham. Adm. Scholar Trinity Hall, Cambridge, 1577; LL.B. 1581; LL.D. 1588. Warrant Doc. Com. 1590; full admission 1608; in commons 1611–27. Delegates 1597. Judge of Vice-Admiralty Court of Norf. 1589. J.P. Norf. 1600. Advocate in Norwich Consistory Court 1603. Official of Archdeacon of Norf. 1619–28. Comr. Piracy Norf. 1604, 1624; London 1602–22. Comr. Adm. Norf. and Cambs. 1624; Middx. 1614, 1619, 1622, 1625. Active as advocate in London courts 1604–28. High Com. 1626. Defends King's rights to wreck of the sea 1608. Inherited manor of Gunvill's Hall. Held manor of Noothes, land in Wymondham, and land in Wigmore Close, all in Norf. Will: PCC 15 Barrington, pr. 16 Feb. 1628. Gunvill's manor to son Thomas; Noothe manor to son Henry; lands in Wymondham to son Clere; land in Wigmore Close to son Peter. m. Anne, dau. of W. Herne of Tibbenham, Norf., esq.

Visitation of Norfolk ii (Norfolk Record Soc. v), 213–14. Blomefield, *Norfolk*, ii. 503; iii. 660. *Al. Cant.* iv. 198. *Registrum Vagum*, i. 28. LPL, Reg. Doc. Com., ff. 46ᵛ, 107; Whitgift Reg. i, f. 161. PRO, C 181/1, f. 142; 181/2, ff. 10ᵛ, 220, 334ᵛ; 181/3, f. 79; DEL 5/2–6, *passim*; HCA 1/32/1, ff. 13, 17, 21, 29, 38. PROB 11/153/15. Usher, *High Commission*, p. 358. BM, Lansdowne MS. 132, ff. 3–5; MS. 142, ff. 137ᵛ–138; MS. 145, ff. 334–5. *APC 1588–1589*, p. 78.

TEMPLE, THOMAS, b. 1603, 3rd son of Sir Thomas of Barton, Warwicks., and Stowe, Bucks., Bt., by Hester, dau. of Miles Sandys of Latimer, Bucks. Matric. Hart Hall, Oxford, 1620; B.C.L. St. Edmund Hall 1624; D.C.L. 1633. Student at Lincoln's Inn 1622. Not to be confused w. 2nd son of Sir John Temple of the Inner Temple 1631. Rector of Bourton on the Water, Glos., 1630 at income of £30 p.a. Accused of committing adultery in Church w. Mary Toms 1635. Prevents reading of prayers in adjacent chapel of Clapton and threatens to pull down chapel. Inhabitants of Clapton protest to Laud *v.* Temple 1636. Presbyterians C. Flower and S. Ford attempt to substitute Temple for William Lloyd as Rector of Bradfield, Berks. Candidate for Clerk of Convocation from Gloucester 1640. Perhaps petition to compound 1645. m. sister of Sir William Andrewes, against whom Temple brought suit in Privy Council 1634.

Al. Oxon. iv. 1465. Clark, *Register*, ii. 384. Wood, *Athenae*, iv. 715; *Fasti*, i. 469. *Visitation of . . . Buckingham . . . 1634* (Harl. Soc. lviii, 1909), p. 115. *Lincoln's Inn Admissions*, p. 189. *CSPD 1635*, p. 491; *1635–1636*, p. 248; *1639–1640*, p. 583. PRO, PC 2/44, pp. 282–3.

TOOKER (TUCKER), CHARLES, b. 1598, 2nd son of Charles of Abingdon, Berks., and of Lincoln's Inn, esq. (d. 1626), by Anne Horton of London. Matric.

Balliol College, Oxford, 1615; B.A. 1618; M.A. 1621; B.C.L. 1624; D.C.L. 1627. Warrant Doc. Com. 1628; full admission 1628; in commons until 1642. Official of Archdeacon of Berks. 1630–44. Archdeacon attempts to deprive him of office for not providing proper substitute while in London 1639. Delegates 1632–3. Active as advocate in London courts 1637–40. Joins ecclesiastical judges residing at Doc. Com. in legal opinion *c.* 1636. Inherits manor of Caldecott in Sutton Courtenay, Berks., and advowson of Vange in Essex. Res.: Doc. Com. and Sutton Courtenay. d. 1660 at Abingdon. Bequeaths manor of Caldecott to son Charles.

> *Al. Oxon.* iv. 1495. Clark, *Register*, ii. 338; iii. 35. *Visitations of Berkshire* i, 135, 294. LPL, Reg. Doc. Com., ff. 49, 109; Abbot. Reg. ii, f. 232ᵛ. PRO, DEL 8/61, *passim*; DEL 8/70, pt. 2, ff. 10–27; HCA 24/98, no. 80a; SP 16/339/63; 16/421/108; will of Charles, sen., PROB 11/151/6. Marchant, *Church Under Law*, p. 113. Squibb, *Court of Chivalry*, p. 67. *Heraldic Cases, passim. VCH Berks.* iv. 375. Bodl., MSS. Oxford Archd. Papers, Berks. cc. 70–80, *passim*.

TREVOR (TREVER), RICHARD, prob. 2nd son of Edward of Denbighs., esq. Brother of John of Trevalun. Denbighs. (d. 1574), and uncle of Sir Richard (d. 1638). Matric. sizar Queens' College, Cambridge, 1577; B.A. 1581; M.A. 1584; LL.D. Trinity Hall 1591. Warrant Doc. Com. 1595; full admission 1598; in commons until 1608, 1613–14; out of commons 1609–11. Rector of Llantyr-noke 1584–1600. Judge of Vice-Admiralty Court of Cornwall 1601. Comr. Piracy Corn. 1601, 1605–6. Comr. Piracy London 1603, 1606, 1609. Surrogate of Daniel Dun (q.v.) as Chancellor of Rochester 1598–9 and as Official Principal of Arches 1609. Co-judge of HCA w. Dun 1608–14. Comr. Adm. Middx. and all other counties 1606–12. Delegates 1613. Chancellor of Llandaff diocese w. one Griffin 1610; sold share in office for £350. Converted publicly to Catholic-ism before death 1614. Assessed for London subsidy 1600 at lower figure than any member of Doc. Com. Died in 'poor estate'. m. (1) Winifred, dau. of Daniel Dun; (2) Mistress Lassells.

> *DWB*, p. 980. *Al. Cant.* iv. 264. LPL, Reg. Doc. Com., ff. 45, 106ᵛ; Whitgift Reg. i, f. 132. McClure, *Chamberlain Letters*, i. 544–5. Pryce, *Bangor*, p. 25. PRO, C 181/1, ff. 5, 123; 181/2, ff. 10ᵛ, 101, 138ᵛ–200, *passim*; HCA 1/32/1, ff. 45–61, *passim*; DEL 5/4, f. 150; E 179/146/399, f. 5. BM, MS. Stowe 558, f. 3. Foster, *London Marriage Licences*, p. 1358. Kent Archives Office, DRb/Pa 17, *passim*. Croke, *Reports . . . James I*, p. 269. Brownlow, *Reports*, ii. 11–12.

TUER, JOHN, b. 1567. Matric. as son of commoner Christ Church, Oxford, 1584; B.A. 1587; M.A. 1590; LL.D. by 1609. Warrant Doc. Com. 1609 but not fully admitted. Vicar of Elsenham, Essex, 1592–1621 at income of £11. 10s. p.a. Official of Archdeacon of Colchester *c.* 1609–1617; surrogate 1617–21. Will: London Consistory Court 91 Bellamy, pr. 18 Dec. 1621. Refers to books at Doctors' Commons. 40s. to godson; goods to niece and nephew.

> *Al. Oxon.* iv. 1516. *Al. Cant.* iv. 271. Newcourt, *Repertorium*, ii. 246. Greater London Record Office, DL/c/361. LPL, Bancroft Reg., f. 157. Quintrell, 'Government of Essex', p. 149.

TURNER, Sir William, b. 1604, son of a cleric from Burrington, Somerset. Matric. Wadham College 1620; B.A. 1625; M.A. 1627; Sub-Dean 1626–7; Dean 1629–31; B.C.L. and D.C.L. 1636. Warrant Doc. Com. 1637; full admission 1641; in commons 1642. Did not practise as advocate. Comr. for settling militia in Surrey 1660. Appointment as judge of HCA by Parlt. 1653 returned to committee. Sat as judge in trial of Don Pantaleon Sa 1653. Judge of HCA and PCC 1659. M.P. Bodmin, Corn., Jan.–Apr. 1659 as a 'stranger'; Harwich, Essex, in place of Sir Henry Wright 1664 but apparently never sat. Knighted 1664. Advocate to James, Duke of York. Estate in Richmond, Surrey, valued at more than £200 p.a. Lease of land from Brasenose College valued at less than £200 p.a. Inherited land in Smalbridge, Axminster, Devon, which together with leases in Westwater and lands in Axminster were valued at £100 p.a. Purchased manor of Butcombie, Somerset. Lands in Somerset, lease from Brasenose, and personal estate valued at £2,000. Res.: Richmond, Surrey, and London. d. 1670. Will: PCC 142 Penn, pr. 18 Oct. 1670. Annuity of £200 to wife; £1,000 apiece to daus. Mary and Jane and son John; £500 to dau. Frances. Rest to son William. Lands in Devon to maintain William in study of law. Father also of Bryan.

Al. Oxon. iv. 1522. Wood, Fasti, i. 492. Wadham College Register, i. 57. Clark, Register, ii. 385; iii. 431. LPL, Reg. Doc. Com., ff. 50ᵛ, 110; Laud Reg. i, f. 281ᵛ; MS. 958, p. 112. Borth. Inst., R. VII. PR 108. PRO, PROB 11/334/142. Acts of Interregnum, ii. 1444. Courtney, Representation, p. 234. CSPD 1653–1654, p. 43. LeNeve's Knights, p. 180.

TWYSDEN, Charles, b. 1576 at Hythe, Kent, 3rd surviving son of Roger of Wye, Chelmington, and E. Peckham, Kent, esq. Matric. St. Mary's Hall, Oxford, 1591; B.C.L. All Souls 1600; Dean 1602; fellow 1602–6; D.C.L. 1618. Principal of New Inn Hall 1618–21. Warrant Doc. Com. 1618; full admission 1619. Advocate in Consistory Court at Coventry 1619. Chancellor of Lichfield Cathedral 1621. Chancellor of Lichfield diocese 1625–40. J.P. Staffs. 1635. Comr. Adm. Middx. 1625. Patrimony: Lands called King's Wood near Colchester, Essex, and £1,000. Purchased lands in Staffs. for £400. Owned house in the Close at Lichfield. Lost house and goods during siege of Lichfield 1643. Will: PCC 14 Fines, pr. 3 Feb. 1647. Lands to nephew John. m. Anne, widow of Robert Master, LL.D. (q.v.).

Twisden, Family of Twysden, pp. 130–1 and pedigree 4. LPL, Reg. Doc. Com., ff. 48, 108; Abbot Reg. i, f. 217ᵛ. Clark, Register, i. 188, 290, 293; ii. 186; iii. 224. Al. Oxon. iv. 1526. Shaw, Staffordshire, i. 248. PRO, C 193/13/2, f. 62; HCA 24/79, f. 135; HCA 1/32/1, f. 13; PROB 11/103/46; 11/199/14. Catalogue of All Souls Archives, pp. 307, 380.

VAUGHAN, Sir William, b. 1586, 2nd son of Walter of Golden Grove, Carmarths., esq. Younger brother John later became Earl of Carbery. Matric. Jesus College, Oxford, 1592; B.A. 1595; M.A. 1597; B.C.L. 1600; LL.D. University of Vienna; incorporated at Oxford 1605. Reports from Pisa to Privy

Council concerning Jesuits 1602. Comr. Piracy Carmarths. J.P. Carmarths. Sheriff Carmarths. 1616. At Oxford 1621. Undertaker for Plantation of New-foundland. Travels to New World 1622; returns by 1630. d. at home in Torcoed, Carmarths. m. (1) Elizabeth, dau. of David ap Robert of Llangyn-deryn, Carmarths.; (2) Anne, dau. of John Christmas of Colchester. Father of Francis, Edward, and five daus. Literary works listed in *DNB*.

> *DNB* xx. 183–5. *Al. Oxon.* iv. 1539. PRO, C 181/2, f. 273; C 193/13/1, f. 112. Hardy,
> *Jesus College*, pp. 45–6. HMCS xii. 211–13. Oxford Univ. Archives, Inventories P.

WALKER, SIR WALTER, b. 1600 at Barton under Needwood, Staffs. Matric. Oriel College, Oxford, as son of a commoner 1615; LL.B. Christ's College, Cambridge, 1628; LL.D. by royal letters 1640. Adm. Inner Temple 1642. Seeks admission to the Bar 1642. Full admission Doc. Com. 1657. Commissary for archdeaconry of Leicester 1630; appointment contested by John Lambe (q.v.), the incumbent, who lost case but continued in possession 1632 by securing order in Chancery. Lambe prevented further legal action by royal injunction; Lords voted Walker £1,250 damages for loss of eight years' profits. Commissary for Bedford archdeaconry 1632. Advocate to Queen Catherine. Advocate of the Parliamentary Fleet 1644. Justifies restraint of trade against ports hostile to Parlt. 1644. Comr. for establishing a court martial within London 1646. Judge of HCA 1659–60. Advocate-General 1659–60. Comr. of militia for Herts. 1660. Knighted 1660. Joint Lord of Stretham manor, Isle of Ely, 1657 w. J. Hampson, esq. Held manor of Bushey Hall, Herts.; manor of Caldecote, Cambs. Lent Sir Henry Poole £4,335 16s. d. 1674. Will: PCC 52 Bunce, pr. 14 Apr. 1674. Manors and lands to wife; £3,880 to relatives and friends. Res.: London; Bushey Hall after 1665. m. Mary, dau. of George Lynn of Southwick, Nor-thants.

> *Al. Cant.* iv. 319. Peile, *Christ's College*, i. 363. *Al. Oxon.* iv. 1558. ITL, Admissions to
> Inner Temple, i. 481. *Inner Temple Records*, ii. 268. LPL, Reg. Doc. Com., ff. 51, 111ᵛ.
> *LJ* iv. 183. PRO, SP 16/503/41; PROB 11/344/52. *CSPD 1639–1640*, p. 140; *1640–1641*,
> pp. 550–1, 581, 586, 591; *1644*, p. 203; *1658–1659*, p. 57; *1659–1660*, p. 459. *Acts of the
> Interregnum*, i. 842; ii. 149, 1432. CPCC ii. 1050. *VCH Cambs.* iv. 154. BM, Add.
> MSS. 5,847, f. 7; 5,820, f. 76.

WESTON, JOHN, b. 1552, only son of Robert, D.C.L., Chancellor of Ireland (d. 1573). B.A. Christ Church, Oxford, 1572; M.A. 1575; B.C.L. 1590; D.C.L. 1591. Warrant Doc. Com. 1599 but not fully admitted. Perhaps Rector of Snetterton, Norf., 1578–82. Preb. of Oxford 1591. Inherits leases to two houses and leases of two prebends 1573. Held leases of land in Oxon. from Christ Church, Oxford; house in London. Will: Oxford VCC, pr. 14 July 1632. One lease to wife; 2 leases to dau. Anne, wife of W. Piers, Bishop of Peterborough. £300 to dau. Dorothy; dau. Elizabeth already received portion. Father of John.

> Clark, *Register*, i. 115, 120, 230; iii. 14. *Al. Oxon.* iv. 1604. Wood, *Fasti*, i. 252.
> LeNeve, *Fasti*, ii. 527. LPL, Whitgift Reg. iii, f. 111. PRO, will of Robert, PROB
> 11/55/25. Oxford Univ. Archives, Wills W–Z.

WHETCROFT (WHEATCROFT), HENRY, son of William of Ipswich, Suff., gent. Matric. pens. Clare College, Cambridge, 1567; Fellow of Trinity Hall 1574–92; LL.B. 1576; LL.D. 1586. Warrant Doc. Com. 1587; full admission 1590; out of commons until 1616. Translated French and Dutch diplomatic documents and speech of French King to House of Lords 1599. Owned mess., ten., and land in Wherstead, Suff.; mess. in Ipswich. Had lease to build at Doc. Com. but project never undertaken. Will: PCC 76 Cope, pr. 1 July 1616. £500 to dau. Barbara; 400 marks to son Robert; 300 marks apiece to sons Anthony and Glenham. Lands to sons Henry and Philip. m. Elizabeth, sister of Sir Henry Glenham and widow of one Jennings.

Al. Cant. iv. 379. Cooper, *Athenae*, ii. 286–7. Metcalfe, *The Visitation of Suffolke* (Exeter, 1882), p. 140. LPL, Reg. Doc. Com., ff. 44, 105ᵛ; Whitgift Reg. i, f. 133. PRO, C 142/656/32; PROB 11/128/76.

WILKINSON, WILLIAM. Matric. pens. St. John's College, Cambridge, 1570; B.A. 1575; M.A. 1578; LL.D. 1589. Warrant Doc. Com. 1590; not fully admitted. Chancellor of Salisbury diocese 1591–1613. Official of Archdeacon of Wilts. through influence of Cecil. J.P. Wilts. 1608–13. Preb. of York 1587–1613; listed as not residing at York 1594. Dispensed to hold prebend at Salisbury but never installed. Conflicts w. Bishop Cotton over extent of jurisdiction as chancellor 1600. Owned land in Wellow, Wilts. Leased house from Vicars Choral of Sarum Cathedral. d. Oct. 1613. Will: PCC 110 Capell, pr. 13 Nov. 1613. Land to wife Mary and then to nephew William, £150 to nephews and niece.

Al. Cant. iv. 412. Clark, *Register*, i. 349. LPL, Whitgift Reg. i, f. 160ᵛ; Lamb. Chart. Misc. XII, f. 9. LeNeve, *Fasti*, iii. 188. HMCS x. 160–1; xi. 437. Gleason, *Justices*, p. 260. A. Wall, 'The Wiltshire Commission of the Peace 1590–1620: A Study of its Social Structure' (Univ. of Melbourne, M.A. thesis, 1966), pp. 120, 133, 192.

WISEMAN (WYSEMAN), SIR ROBERT, b. 1613, 7th and 5th surviving son of Sir Thomas of Rivenhall, Essex (d. 1654). Matric. pens. Trinity Hall, Cambridge, 1628; LL.B. 1634; fellow 1631–53; LL.D. 1639. Warrant Doc. Com. 1640; full admission 1663. Fails to secure chancellorship of Salisbury 1640. Comr. Pol. & Ass. London 1645. Dean of Arches 1672–84. Commissary of Peculiar of Monks Risborough 1681. King's Advocate General. Estate valued at £20,000 at death. Res.: Doc. Com. and Little Chelsea, Middx. d. 17 Aug. 1684. Will: PCC 106 Hare, pr. 28 Aug. 1684. £505 to relatives; copyhold land in Essex and £400 to servant. Commonplace books of civil and common law to Dr. Richard Lloyd. m. (1) dau. of one Paynter of Kent; (2) Elizabeth, dau. of Lord North. Wrote *The Law of Lawes* (1656).

Al. Cant. iv. 442. *LeNeve's Knights*, pp. 138–9. LPL, Reg. Doc. Com., ff. 51ᵛ, 111ᵛ. PRO, C 181/5, f. 251ᵛ; PROB 11/377/106; SP 16/442/125. *CSPD 1640–1641*, p. 6. *Gentleman's Magazine*, lxiii, pt. 1, 106–7. Veall, *Law Reform*, pp. 109–10. Bodl., MS. Oxford Archd. Papers, Berks., c. 201, f. 8.

WITHYPOLL (WITHIPOLL), Peter, b. 1549, 8th son of Edmund of Ipswich, Suff., merchant and later gent. (d. 1582), by Elizabeth, dau. of Thomas Hind of London. Matric. sizar Magdalene College, Cambridge, 1564; Fellow of Trinity Hall 1572–83; LL.B. 1573; LL.D. in 1590s. Warrant Doc. Com. 1599 but not fully admitted. Friend of Gabriel Harvey (q.v.) at Trinity Hall. Commissary for archdeaconry of Norwich 1580–6; lost office when Bishop Scrambler claimed that his predecessor had given Withypoll too much authority. Advocate in Norwich Consistory Court 1603. Comr. Piracy Norf. 1604. Claims money by his father's will in suit in Arches 1606. Res.: Stowmarket, Suff., 1583. d. 1613. m. Thomassin, dau. of Thomas Cobb, 1583.

> Smith, *Family of Withypoll*, pp. 45–62. Strype, *Annals*, iii, pt. 1, pp. 480–1. *Registrum Vagum*, i. 28. LPL, Whitgift Reg. iii, f. 111. PRO, C 181/1, f. 142.

WOOD, Basil, 2nd surviving son of Alexander of Shineton, Salop, esq., by Elizabeth, dau. of Thomas Jennings. B.A. All Souls College, Oxford, 1602; fellow 1605–13; B.C.L. 1608; Dean 1610; Bursar 1612; D.C.L. 1612. Warrant Doc. Com. 1612; full admission 1614; in commons until 1642. Chancellor of St. Asaph diocese 1605; Rochester 1630–44. Delegates 1614–39. Active as advocate in London courts 1618–41. Joins ecclesiastical judges residing at Doc. Com. in legal opinion *c*. 1636. Comr. Piracy London 1617–38. Comr. Adm. Middx. 1623, 1625; Comr. Pol. & Ass. 1618–19; 1634–7. High Com. 1633. Fined and criticized by Long Parlt. for activities as High Comr. Patrimony: £10. Res.: Doc. Com. d. 1644 at Lincoln College, Oxford. Father of Thomas and Basil.

> *Visitation of Shropshire*, ii, 510. *Al. Oxon.* iv. 1669. Clark, *Register*, i. 187, 265; iii. 239. *Catalogue of All Souls Archives*, pp. 310–11, 380. LPL, Reg. Doc. Com., ff. 47ᵛ, 79, 107ᵛ; Abbot Reg. i, f. 162ᵛ. Thomas, *St. Asaph*, p. 239. Kent Archives Office, Rochester Episcopal Registers v, ff. 207ᵛ, 222. Usher, *High Commission*, p. 360. PRO, C 181/2, f. 297, 334ᵛ; 181/3, f. 79; 181/4, ff. 37, 138ᵛ, 157ᵛ; 181/5, ff. 9, 26ᵛ, 59ᵛ, 98ᵛ, 130ᵛ; HCA 1/32/1, ff. 13, 21; HCA 24/78–101, *passim*; SP 16/339/63; 16/483/59; PROB 11/124/66. Notestein, *D'Ewes*, p. 476.

WOOD (WODE, WEALD), William, b. 1558, son of Hugh of Talyllyn Anglesey, by Jane, dau. of Hugh Prees. Fellow of All Souls College, Oxford, 1577; B.C.L. 1583; D.C.L. 1587. Warrant Doc. Com. 1589; full admission 1590; in commons until 1604. Chancellor of Worcester diocese 1598. J.P. Worcester 1604. Owned mess. and land in Llandaff. Will: PCC 30 Hayes, pr. 9 May 1605. Provides for wife's children; £100 in tithes to wife; £100 to sons Jervace and Hugh; lands and meadows to Jervace; £200 apiece to daus. Jane and Mary. m. (1) Susan, dau. of Antony Caranuso of Seville; (2) widow of Marmaduke Matthews. Father also of William and Owen.

> Griffiths, *Pedigrees*, p. 132. Clark, *Register*, i. 157; iii. 116. LPL, Reg. Doc. Com., ff. 44, 105ᵛ; Whitgift Reg. i, f. 154ᵛ; Bancroft Reg., f. 186. BM, Add. MS. 38,139, f. 163ᵛ. Nash, *Worcester*, ii. clxvii. HMCS xvi. 440. PRO, PROB 11/105/30.

WOODHOUSE (WOODHOWSE), HENRY, 2nd son of Sir Henry of Breckles, Norf., by Ann, dau. of Sir Nicholas Bacon, Lord Keeper. B.A. Trinity Hall 1584; fellow 1584–90; B.C.L. Oxford 1587; LL.D. Cambridge by 1596. Adm. Gray's Inn 1590. Warrant Doc. Com. 1596 but not fully admitted. A cleric. Rector of Smallburgh, Norf., 1602. Advocate in Norwich Consistory Court 1603. m. Mary Chamberlayne, dau. of Edward Chamberlayne of Barnham Broom, Norf.

Visitation of Norfolk (Harl. Soc. xxxii, 1891), pp. 71, 321. Al. Cant. iv. 458. Al. Oxon. iv. 1666. LPL, Whitgift Reg. ii, f. 143. Registrum Vagum, i. 28. Clark, Register, i. 368; ii. 159. Foster, Gray's Inn, p. 78.

WORLICH (WOLRICH, WOOLRICH, WOOLRIDGE, WORLIDGE), TOBIAS, son and heir of Thomas of Cooling, Kent., esq.; nephew of William Wickham, Bishop of Winchester. Matric. sizar King's College, Cambridge, 1628; B.A. 1628; M.A. Trinity Hall 1631; fellow 1633–40; LL.D. 1639. Adm. advocate at York 1637. Warrant Doc. Com. 1640; full admission 1647. Occasional surrogate in Ely Consistory Court while fellow at Trinity Hall. Sinecure registrarship of Exchequer Court at York 1637. Official of Archdeacon of York 1638. Commissary of Peculiar of Dean and Chapter of York 1641. Master in Chancery 1660. Knighted 1661. Of Bishopsbourne and Cooling, Kent. d. 1664. m. Jane, dau. of Sir Robert Hatton of Hatton House, Holborn, and Bishopsbourne.

Al. Cant. iv. 449. Marchant, Church Under Law, pp. 11, 251. PRO, SP 16/442/125; index 16818, p. 47. LPL, Reg. Doc. Com., ff. 50ᵛ, 110. LeNeve's Knights, p. 142.

WORSLEY, JOHN. Origins unknown. B.C.L. Pembroke College, Oxford, 1629; D.C.L. Christ Church 1637. Surrogate of Official of Archdeacon of Berks. 1637. Warrant Doc. Com. before 1640 but not fully admitted.

Al. Oxon. iv. 1681. PRO, DEL 8/61, passim; SP 16/442/125.

WYVELL (WYVILL, WYFIELD), CHRISTOPHER, 1st son of Sampson or Walworth, Durham, gent., by Faith, dau. of N. Girlington of Hackforth. Grandson of Sir Marmaduke Wyvill of Burton Constable, Yorks., whose arms he displayed. LL.B. Trinity Hall, Cambridge, 1589; LL.D. 1615. Warrant Doc. Com. 1615 but not fully admitted. Chancellor of Lincoln diocese w. O. Hill (q.v.) 1609–16; alone 1616–21. Conflicts w. commissaries of archdeaconries over extent of their jurisdiction. Granted Regius Professorship of Law at Cambridge w. T. Morrisson 1611 but never assumed post. Retires to Saffron Walden, Essex, c. 1621. J.P. Borough of Walden 1624. d. 1632. Will: ERO, 265 CW11. Goods and money to wife; 3 volumes of canon course to E. Tillingham; other books, including statutes at large to Capt. Mordant. m. Margery, dau. of W. Brockett of Herts. and widow of S. Cage of Saffron Walden.

Surtees, Durham, iii. 263. Al. Cant. iv. 485. Clark, Register, i. 349. PRO, C 181/3, f. 121ᵛ; SP 14/93/116; 14/74/85. CSPD 1611–1618, p. 36. CUL, MS. Mm. I. 49 (Baker

38), p. 311. LPL, Abbot Reg. i, f. 183ᵛ. Durham University, Durham Probate Records: Reg. iii, ff. 81ᵛ-85.

YALE (YEALE), Davɪᴅ, illegitimate son of John Wyn or Yale of Plas yn Yale, Denbighs., esq.; nephew of Thomas Yale, LL.D. Matric. sizar Queen's College, Oxford, 1555; B.A. 1564; M.A. 1567; fellow 1565-81; proctor 1575-6; LL.D. 1579. Warrant Doc. Com. 1579; full admission 1582; in commons 1604-5, 1607-8; out of commons 1603, 1606, 1609-27. Adm. minor orders 1556. Chancellor of Bangor diocese 1562-70; Chester 1587-1608. Rector of Llandelgla, Denbighs., 1564; Llantyrnoke 1583. Preb. of St. Asaph 1578-1613; Chester 1582-1608. Comr. Eccles. Causes York 1599, 1627. J.P. Denbighs. by 1604. Lands in Denbighs. and Derbys. valued at £500. Res.: Chester. Will: Chester, pr. 13 June 1626. Lands, leases, and goods for benefit of children and nephews. Inventory of goods and chattels at £692. m. Frances, dau. of John Lloyd, D.C.L. (q.v.).

DWB, p. 1110. Al. Cant. iv. 486. LPL, Grindal Reg., f. 185; Reg. Doc. Com., ff. 43, 104ᵛ; Visitation of Shropshire, ii. 330. LeNeve, Fasti, i. 85; iii. 269-70. Pryce, Bangor, p. 25. HMCS ix. 396. PRO, C 193/13/1, f. 115; C 66/1452. Cheshire County Record Office, WS 1626. BM, Add. MS. 38,170, f. 325; MS. 38,139, f. 170ᵛ. Rymer, Foedora, xviii. 258.

ZOUCH (ZOUCHE, SOUCH), b. 1590, son of Francis of Ansty, Wilts., gent., the cadet of an ancient family. Winchester College. Matric. New College, Oxford, 1607; fellow 1609-22; B.C.L. 1614; D.C.L. 1619. Warrant Doc. Com. 1618; full admission 1618; in commons until 1642. Principal of St. Alban's Hall, Oxford, 1625-41. Regius Professor of Civil Law 1620-61. Preb. of Salisbury. Chancellor of diocese of Oxford. Advocate for Admiralty Causes 1628. Comr. Adm. Middx. 1623, 1625. Comr. Piracy London 1633, 1635, 1638; Hants 1635-6; Dorset 1641. Delegates 1626-34. Active as advocate in London courts 1622-41. Judge of HCA 1641-3?; 1660-2. M.P. Hythe 1621, 1624 through patronage of cousin, Edward Lord Zouch, Warden of Cinque Ports. Defends right of Commons to punish offence done to King by Sir Robert Floyd 1621. Seeks proviso for Cinque Courts in bill on penal statutes 1624. Royalist during Civil War. Compounds for estate 1646 at a tenth: £333. Acquiesced in Cromwell's rule and included on commission to try Don Pantaleon Sa 1653. Wrote Elementa Jurisprudentiae (1629) and other legal writings listed in Wood, Athenae, iii. 511-12. Invested in commerce. d. 1 Mar. 1662 at London. Will: PCC 56 Laud, pr. 25 Apr. 1662. Estate to be divided into three parts for wife Sara, son Richard, and dau. Anne.

DNB xxi. 1332-5. Wood, Athenae, iii. 510-14. Al. Oxon. iv. 1706. Lloyd, Memoires, p. 545. LPL, Reg. Doc. Com., ff. 48, 108; Abbot Reg. ii, f. 177. PRO, C 181/4, f. 139; 181/5, ff. 24, 27, 58, 130ᵛ, 126; HCA 1/32/1, ff. 13, 21. NRS iii. 192-3. CPCC ii. 513. Walker Revised, p. 15. Bodl., MS. Top. Oxon. e. 105/2, f. 90. Holdsworth, History of Law, v. 17. LJ vi. 22. PRO, SP 14/165/48; 14/165/70; 16/117, f. 77; PROB 11/308/56. Rabb, Enterprise, p. 410.

SELECT BIBLIOGRAPHY

The footnotes contain a complete record of all the sources used in this work. This bibliography lists only the important manuscripts and published works. Most genealogical sources and county histories are not included.

I. MANUSCRIPTS

(1) Public Record Office, London

    C 66. Patent Rolls.

    C 142. *Inquisitiones post mortem.*

    C 181/1–5. Entry Books of Commissions.

    C 193/13. Crown Office Books, Commissioners of the Peace.

    C 216/1. Admission Rolls of Chancery Officers.

    DEL 5/2–6. Court of Delegates, sentences.

    DEL 8/70. Court of Delegates Repertory Book.

    DEL 8/61. Act book of the Court of the Archdeacon of Berkshire 1636–1639.

    E 179. Subsidy Rolls.

    E 403. Index of Registrations of Appointments.

    HCA 1/32/1. Commissions of Oyer and Terminer for Admiralty Criminal Causes.

    HCA 24/70–101. Admiralty Court Libels, Sentences, Decrees 1603–1641.

    PC 2. Registers of the Privy Council.

    PRO 30/26/8. Treasurer's Book of Doctors' Commons.

    PROB 11. Registers of Prerogative Court of Canterbury Wills.

    REQ. 1. Court of Requests, Order and Decree Books.

    SP 14. State Papers, James I.

    SP 16. State Papers, Charles I.

    SP 21. State Papers, Committee for Both Kingdoms.

    SP 23. State Papers, Committee for Compounding with Delinquents.

    WARDS 7/60. *Inquisitiones post mortem.*

    Index 16818. Index of Chancery Officers.

    Institution Books, ser. A. 1556–1660.

(2) Lambeth Palace Library, London

    Register of Doctors' Commons.

    Parker Register.

    Grindal Register.

    Whitgift Register.

    Bancroft Register.

Abbot Register.
Laud Register.
MS. 958. Andrew C. Ducarel, 'Summary Account of the Society of Doctors' Commons'.
MS. 1351. Extracts from the Registers of the Archbishops of Canterbury relating to Croydon, Surrey, and Doctors' Commons.
MS. 1729. Formulary Book compiled by a Welsh civilian.
MSS. 2004, 2014. Fairhurst Papers.
MSS. 113; 642; 664; 943; 1030.
Lambeth Chart. Miscellany VI, XII.

(3) British Museum, London
Additional MSS. 4933; 6209; 11,406; 12,496; 12,505; 13,170; 17,685; 29,960; 34,324; 38,139.
Cotton MSS. F I; F II. Collections Relating to Prohibitions.
Harleian MSS. 358; 474; 1450; 1601; 2078; 5058; 6822.
Lansdowne MSS. 55; 81; 129; 142; 145; 146; 157; 160; 161; 170; 980; 984.
Sloane MS. 171.
Stowe MS. 366. William Borlase, 'Some Notes Taken in the Sessions of Parliament (1628)'.

(4) Bodleian Library, Oxford
Ashmole MS. 857.
Barlow MS. 9.
Rawlinson MS. Statutes 62.
Tanner MS. 427. Causes in the Court of the Arches 1596–1602.
Tanner MSS. 51; 63; 65; 68; 71; 75; 134; 135; 280; 422; 427.
MS. Top Oxon. e. 105/2. List of fellows of New College.
MSS. Oxford Arch. Papers. Berks. Act books of the Court of the Archdeacon of Berkshire.

(5) Cambridge University Library, Cambridge
MSS. Dd. II. 44; Gg. II. 31; Ll. IV. 11; Mm. I. 46, 47; Mm. III. 12; Mm. VI. 57, 58.
Bulstrode Whitelocke's Journal of the Parliament of 1626.

(6) Oxford University Archives, Oxford
P.P. 2. Register or Book of Matriculations.
Registers of the Chancellor's Court.
Wills.
Inventories.

(7) Cambridge University Archives, Cambridge
Wills.

(8) Inner Temple Library, London
    Admissions to the Inner Temple, 3 vols., typescript.
    Petyt MS. 537/23. Proceedings in Parliament 1628.
    Petyt MS. 518. Arguments on the ecclesiastical question of Prohibitions.
    temp. James I.
    Petyt MSS. 538/38; 538/55.

(9) Durham Cathedral Library
    Dean and Chapter Treasurer's Book 1609–1617.
    Hunter MSS. 11/12; 12/1; 12/5; 12/188; 13; 22.

(10) Winchester Cathedral Library
    Alphabetical Index of Hants Clergy (Beneficed), typescript.
    Francis J. Baigent Papers.

(11) Exeter Cathedral Library
    MS. 3553. Chapter Book.
    MS. 7155/1. Cause papers concerning the case of Robert Withers.

(12) York Cathedral Library
    Chapter Acts.

(13) Borthwick Institute of Historical Research, York
    Wills.
    Index of Tudor Clergy.
    R. VIII. PR 108. Members of Doctors' Commons in 1639.
    R. VII. H.C.A.B. 15, 16. List of Commissioners for Ecclesiastical Causes
    in York.

(14) Institute of Historical Research, London
    History of Parliament Trust, biographies of M.P.s during reign of Eliza-
    beth, typescript.

(15) Corporation of London Record Office
    Book of Remembrances 1579–1602.

(16) Greater London Record Office
    Vicar General's Books.
    Wills.

(17) Cheshire Record Office, Chester
    Will and Inventory of David Yale, WS 1626.

(18) Essex Record Office, Chelmsford
    Wills.
    Act Books of the courts of the Archdeacons of Colchester, Essex, and
    Middlesex.

(19) Hampshire Record Office, Winchester
　　Act books of the Consistory Court of Winchester.
　　Register of Bishop Neile of Winchester 1627–31.
　　Wills.

(20) Kent Archives Office, Maidstone
　　Rochester Episcopal Registers, vols. v, vi.
　　Act books of the Rochester Consistory Court.
　　Darrell Papers. U 386 F I.

(21) Leicestershire Record Office
　　Inventory of John Chippingdale. Probate Rec. Inv. 1627/258.

(22) Norfolk and Norwich Record Office, Norwich
　　Wills.
　　Norwich Consistory Court, Deposition and Act Book 49.
　　Inventory of John Ponder, Prob. Inv. 32/210.
　　Archdeacon's Transcripts, parish of Walsingham 1600–1.

(23) Hatfield House, Hertfordshire
　　Salisbury MS. 195.

(24) All Souls College Library, Oxford
　　MS. CXXXIX. Extracts from the Register of Doctors' Commons.

II. PUBLISHED PRIMARY SOURCES

A. STATUTES AND OFFICIAL PAPERS

Acts of the Privy Council of England, London, 1890–.
Calendar of the Proceedings of the Committee for Compounding 1643–1660, 5 vols., London, 1889.
Calendar of State Papers, Domestic Series.
Calendar of State Papers Relating to Ireland.
Firth, C. H., and Rait, R. S., *Acts and Ordinances of the Interregnum 1642–1660*, 3 vols., London, 1911.
Historical Manuscripts Commission, *Calendar of the Manuscripts of . . . the Marquis of Salisbury Preserved at Hatfield House*, 19 vols., London, 1883–.
Rymer, Thomas, *Foedera*, London, 1704–35.
Statutes of the Realm, vols. i–v, London, 1810–28.

B. LAW REPORTS AND CASES

Brownlow, R., and Goldesborough, J., *Reports of Diverse Choice Cases in Law*, London, 1651.
Coke, Sir Edward, *The Reports of Sir Edward Coke*, London, 1658.
Croke, Sir George, *The Reports of Sir George Croke*, London, 1657.

Howell, T. B., *State Trials*, vols. ii and iii, London, 1809.

Leadam, I. S., *Select Cases in the Court of Requests A.D. 1497–1569*, Publications of the Selden Society, xii, 1898.

Marsden, R. G., *Select Pleas in the Court of Admiralty*, 2 vols., Publications of the Selden Society vi, xi, 1892, 1897.

Moore, Francis, *Cases Collect and Report*, London, 1663.

[Rothery], *Return of All Appeals in Causes of Doctrine or Discipline Made to the High Court of Delegates*, London, 1868.

Squibb, G. D., *Reports of Heraldic Cases in the Court of Chivalry, 1623–1732*. Harl. Soc. cvii. 1956.

C. ECCLESIASTICAL RECORDS

Barton, T. (trans.), *The Registrum Vagum of Anthony Harison*, 2 vols., Norfolk Record Society, xxxii, xxxiii, 1963.

Bond, S., *The Chapter Acts of the Dean and Canons of Windsor*, Windsor, 1966.

Cardwell, Edward (ed.), *Documentary Annals of the Reformed Church of England*, 2 vols., London, 1844.

Cardwell, Edward, *Synodalia: A Collection of Articles of Religion, Canons, and Proceedings of Convocations in the Province of Canterbury from the Year 1547 to the Year 1717*, Oxford, 2 vols., 1842.

Historical Manuscripts Commission, *Calendar of the Manuscripts of the Dean and Chapter of Wells*, 2 vols., London, 1907, 1914.

Peckham, W. D., *The Acts of the Dean and Chapter of the Cathedral Church of Chichester, 1545–1642*, Sussex Record Society, lviii, 1959.

Williams, J. F., and Cozens-Hardy, B., *Extracts From the Earliest Minute Books of the Dean and Chapter of Norwich Cathedral, 1566–1649*, Norfolk Record Society, xxiv, 1953.

D. ACADEMIC RECORDS

Boase, C. W., *Register of the University of Oxford*, vol. i, Oxford, 1885.

Clark, A., *Register of the University of Oxford*, vol. ii, 4 pts., Oxford Historical Society, x, xi, xii, xiv, 1887–9.

Foster, Joseph, *The Register of Admissions to Gray's Inn 1521–1889*, London, 1889.

Griffiths, John, *The Statutes of the University of Oxford Codified in the Year 1636*, Oxford, 1888.

Heywood, J., and Wright, T., *Cambridge University Transactions During the Puritan Controversies of the Sixteenth and Seventeenth Centuries*, 2 vols., London, 1854.

The Historical Register of the University of Oxford, Oxford, 1900.

Macgeagh, H. F. (ed.), *Register of Admissions to the Honourable Society of The Middle Temple*, vol. i, London, 1949.

Martin, C. T., *Catalogue of the Archives in the Muniment Rooms of All Souls' College*, London, 1877.

The Records of the Honourable Society of Lincoln's Inn, vol. i: *Admissions from 1420 to 1799*, London, 1896.

Students Admitted to the Inner Temple 1547–1660, London, 1887.

Tanner, J. R., *The Historical Register of the University of Cambridge to 1910*, Cambridge, 1917.

Venn, John, and J. A., *The Book of Matriculations and Degrees, 1544–1659*, Cambridge, 1913.

E. PARLIAMENTARY PROCEEDINGS

Cobbett, William, *The Parliamentary History of England from the Normans . . . to the Year 1802*, vol. i, London, 1806.

Foster, E. R., *Proceedings in Parliament, 1610*, 2 vols., New Haven, Conn., 1966.

Gardiner, S. R., *Debates in the House of Commons in 1625*, Camden Society, n.s. vi, 1873.

—— *Parliamentary Debates in 1610*, Camden Soc. cxxxi, 1862.

Journals of the House of Commons, vols. i–v.

Notestein, Relf, and Simpson, *Commons Debates 1621*, 7 vols., New Haven, Conn., 1935.

Notestein, W., and Relf, F., *Commons Debates for 1629*, Minneapolis, Minn., 1921.

Notestein, W., *The Journal of Sir Simonds D'Ewes*, New Haven, Conn., 1923.

Townshend, Heywood, *Historical Collections or An Exact Account of the Proceedings of the Four Last Parliaments of Queen Elizabeth*, London, 1680.

Willson, D. H., *The Parliamentary Diary of Robert Bowyer 1606–1607*, Minneapolis, Minn., 1931.

F. LETTERS AND JOURNALS

Cabala Sive Scrinia Sacra: Mysteries of State and Government in Letters of Illustrious Persons, London, 1691.

Camden, William, *Gulielmi Camdeni Annales Ab Anno 1603 ad Annum 1623*, London, 1691.

D'Ewes, Simonds, *The Autobiography and Correspondence of Sir Simonds D'Ewes*, ed. J. O. Halliwell, 2 vols., London, 1845.

Hutton, Matthew, *The Correspondence of Dr. Matthew Hutton, Archbishop of York*, Surtees Society, xvii, 1843.

McClure, N. E., *The Letters of John Chamberlain*, Philadelphia, Pa., 1939.

Parr, Richard, *The Life of the Most Reverend Father in God, James Usher . . . With A Collection of Three Hundred Letters*, London, 1686.

Roberts, G., *Diary of Walter Yonge, Esq.*, Camden Soc. xli, 1848.

Wilbraham, Roger, *The Journal of Sir Roger Wilbraham For the Years 1593–1616*, The Camden Miscellany, x, 1902.

Winwood, Sir Ralph, *Memorials of Affairs of State in the Reigns of Q. Elizabeth and K. James I*, 3 vols., London, 1725.

G. TRACTS AND TREATISES

Anonymous, *The Downfall of the Pretended Divine Authority of the Hierarchy into the Sea of Rome*, London, 1641.

——, *Englands Monarch or A Conviction and Refutation By the Common Law of those False Principles and Insinuating Flatteries of Albericus*, London, 1644.

——, *The Last Will and Testament of the Doctors Commons*, London, 1641.

——, *A Letter From Rhoan in France Written by Doctor Roane one of the Doctors of the late sicke Commons to his Fellow Doctor of the Civil Law*, London, 1641.

——, *A Looking-Glasse for all Proud, Ambitious, Covetous and Corrupt Lawyers*, London, 1646.

——, *The Organs Echo To the Tune of the Cathedral Service*, London, 1641.

——, *The Pimpes Prerogative*, London, 1641.

——, *The Proctor and the Parator their mourning: or the Lamentation of the Doctors Commons for their Downfall*, London, 1641.

——, *Saint Pauls Potion Prescribed by Doctor Commons*, London, 1641.

——, *The Sisters of the Scabards Holiday*, London, 1641.

——, *The Spiritual Courts Epitomized, In A Dialogue Betwixt Two Proctors*, London, 1641.

——, *A True Description or Rather A Parallel Betweene Cardinal Wolsey, Archbishop of York and William Laud, Archbishop of Canterbury*, London, 1641.

Barlow, William, *The Summe and Substance of the Conference*, London, 1604.

Bodin, Jean, *Les Six Livres de la République*, Paris, 1576.

Buc, George, *The Third University of England*, London, 1615.

[Carew, George], 'A Treatise of the Masters of the Chauncerie', in *A Collection of Tracts Relative to the Law of England*, ed. F. Hargrave, London, 1787, pp. 293–319.

Clerk, William, *An Epitome of Certain Late Aspersions Cast At Civilians*, Dublin, 1631.

Clerke, Francis, *The Practice of the High Court of Admiralty*, pt. 2 of John Hall, *The Practice and Jurisdiction of the Court of Admiralty*, Baltimore, Md., 1809.

[Cocke, Charles G.], *Englands Compleat Law-Judge and Lawyer*, London, 1655.

Coke, Sir Edward, *The Fourth Part of the Institutes of the Laws of England*, London, 1644.

Consett, Henry, *The Practice of the Spiritual or Ecclesiastical Courts*, London, 1685.

Cooke, James, *Juridica Trium Quaestionum ad Majestatem pertinentum determinatio*, Oxford, 1608.

Cooper, Thomas, *An Admonition to the People of England*, London, 1589.

Cosin, Richard, *An Apologie For Sundrie Proceedings by Jurisdiction Ecclesiasticall*, London, 1593.

Cowell, John, *The Interpreter: Or Booke Containing the Signification of Words*, Cambridge, 1607.

——, *The Institutes of the Lawes of England*, trans., London, 1651.

Downing, Calibute, *A Discourse of the State Ecclesiasticall of this Kingdome in Relation to the Civill*, Oxford, 1633.

——, *A Sermon Preached to the Renowned Company of the Artillery, 1 September 1640*, London, 1641.

Duck, Arthur, *De Usu et Authoritate Juris Civilis Romanorum in Dominiis Principum Christianorum*, London, 1679.

Favour, John, *Antiquitie Triumphing Over Noveltie*, London, 1619.

Fletcher, Giles, *The English Works of Giles Fletcher, The Elder*, ed. L. E. Berry, Madison, Wis., 1964.

Fulbeck, William, *A Direction or Preparative to the Study of the Lawe*, London, 1600.

——, *A Parallele or Conference of the Civill Law, The Canon Law and the Common Law of England*, London, 1602.

Gentili, Alberico, *De Jure Belli Libri Tres*, 2 vols., Oxford, 1933.

——, *Regales Disputationes Tres*, London, 1605.

Hayward, John, *Annals of the First Four Years of the Reign of Queen Elizabeth*, ed. John Bruce, Camden Society, vii, 1840.

——, *An Answer to the First Part of A Certain Conference Concerning Succession*, London, 1603.

——, *The First Part of the Life and Raigne of King Henrie The IIII*, London, 1599.

——, *The Lives of the III Normans, Kings of England*, London, 1613.

——, *A Treatise of Union of the Two Realmes of England and Scotland*, London, 1604.

——, *A Reporte of a Discourse Concerning Supreme Power in Affairs of Religion*, London, 1606.

Hoskins, John, *Sermons Preached at Pauls Crosse and Elsewhere*, London, 1615.

Laud, William, *The History of the Troubles and Tryal of the Most Reverend Father in God, and Blessed Martyr, William Laud*, London, 1695.

McIlwain, C. H. (ed.), *The Political Works of James I*, Cambridge, Mass., 1918.

Ogg, David (ed.), *Ioannis Seldeni Ad Fletam Dissertatio*, Cambridge, 1925.

[Parker, Henry], *Reformation in Courts and Cases Testamentary*, London, 1650.

Pierce, William (ed.), *The Marprelate Tracts, 1588, 1589*, London, 1911.

Prynne, William, *Canterburies Doome*, London, 1644.

——, *Hidden Works of Darkness Brought to Public Light*, London, 1645.

Ridley, Thomas, *A View of the Civile and Ecclesiastical Law*, 2nd edn., London, 1634.

Ruggles, George, *Ignoramus, A Comedy*, trans. R. Codrington, London, 1662.

Ryves, Thomas, *The Poore Vicars Plea*, London, 1620.

Smith, Thomas, *The Commonwealth of England and Maner of Government Thereof*, London, 1589.

Starkey, Thomas, *A Dialogue Between Reginald Pole and Thomas Lupset*, ed. K. Burton, London, 1948.

Stoughton, William, *An Assertion for True and Christian Church-Policie*, London, 1604.

Sutcliffe, Matthew, *An Answere to a Certaine Libel Supplicatorie*, London, 1592.
——, *The Examination of M. Thomas Cartwrights Late Apologie*, London, 1596.
——, *A Ful and Round Answer to N.D. alias Robert Parsons*, London, 1604.
Wilson, Thomas, *The State of England Anno Dom. 1600*, ed. F. J. Fisher, Camden Society, 3rd ser., lii, 1936.
Wiseman, Robert, *The Law of Lawes or the Excellency of the Civil Law Above All Other Humane Laws*, London, 1656.
Zouch, Richard, *Descriptio Juris et Judicii Temporalis Secundum Consuetudines Feudales et Normannicas*, Oxford, 1636.
——, *Elementa Jurisprudentiae*, Oxford, 1636.

H. MISCELLANEOUS

Marsden, R. G., *Documents Relating to the Law and Custom of the Sea*, vol. i: 1205–1648. Publications of the Navy Record Society, vol. xlix, 1915.
Prothero, G. W., *Select Statutes and Other Constitutional Documents*, 2nd edn., London, 1898.

III. SECONDARY SOURCES

A. BIOGRAPHICAL AND GENERAL

Aylmer, G. E., *The King's Servants: The Civil Service of Charles I, 1625–1642*, London, 1961.
Babbage, S. B., *Puritanism and Richard Bancroft*, London, 1962.
Bell, H. E., *Maitland: A Critical Examination and Assessment*, Cambridge, Mass., 1965.
Blomefield, F., *An Essay Towards a Topographical History of the County of Norfolk*, 11 vols., London, 1806.
Brunton, D., and Pennington, D., *Members of the Long Parliament*, Cambridge, Mass., 1954.
Bryneston, W. E., 'Roman Law and Legislation in the Middle Ages', *Speculum*, 41 (1966), 420–37.
Burn, Richard, *Ecclesiastical Law*, 4 vols., 6th edn., London, 1797.
Burrows, M., *The Worthies of All Souls*, London, 1874.
Calder, I., *Activities of the Puritan Faction of the Church of England 1625–33*, London, 1957.
Carlyle, A. J., *A History of Medieval Political Theory in the West*, 6 vols., Edinburgh, 1903–36.
Chandler, P. W., 'Doctors' Commons', *London Topographical Record*, 15 (1931), 4–20.
Charlton, K., *Education in Renaissance England*, London, 1965.
Chrimes, S. B., 'The Constitutional Ideas of Dr John Cowell', *EHR* 44 (Oct. 1949), 461–87.
Collinson, P., *The Elizabethan Puritan Movement*, London, 1967.

Cooper, C. H., *The Annals of Cambridge*, 4 vols., Cambridge, 1842–52.
—— and Cooper, T., *Athenae Cantabrigiensis 1586–1609*, 3 vols., Cambridge, 1858–1913.
Coote, Charles, *Sketches of the Lives and Characters of Eminent English Civilians*, London, 1804.
Cowie, L. W., 'Doctors' Commons', *History Today*, 20 (June 1970), 419–26.
Curtis, Mark, *Oxford and Cambridge in Transition 1558–1642*, Oxford, 1959.
Dawson, J. P., *A History of Lay Judges*, Cambridge, Mass., 1960.
Dewar, Mary, *Sir Thomas Smith: A Tudor Intellectual in Office*, London, 1964.
Dowling, M., 'Sir John Hayward's Troubles Over His Life of Henry IV', *The Library*, 4th ser. 11 (1931), 212–24.
Dunham, W. H., 'Regal Power and the Rule of Law: A Tudor Paradox', *The Journal of British Studies*, 3 (1964), 24–56.
Eusden, J. D., *Puritans, Lawyers and Politics in Early Seventeenth Century England*, New Haven, Conn., 1958.
Forster, John, *Sir John Eliot*, 2 vols., London, 1864.
Foster, Joseph, *Alumni Oxoniensis: The Members of the University of Oxford, 1500–1714*, 4 vols., Oxford, 1891–2.
Fuller, Thomas, *The Church History of Britain*, 6 vols., Oxford, 1845.
——, *The History of the Worthies of England*, 3 vols., 2nd edn., London, 1840.
——, *The History of the University of Cambridge Since The Conquest*, London, 1655.
Gardiner, S. R., *History of England From the Accession of James I to the Outbreak of the Civil War, 1603–1642*, vols. vi and vii, London, 1884.
Gleason, J. H., *The Justices of the Peace in England 1558 to 1640*, Oxford, 1969.
Green, V. H., *Religion at Oxford and Cambridge*, London, 1964.
Hall, Basil, 'John Calvin, the Jurisconsults and the Jus Civile', *Studies in Church History*, iii, Leiden, 1966, 202–16.
Harding, Alan, *A Social History of English Law*, London, 1966.
Hexter, J. H., *More's Utopia: The Biography of An Idea*, Princeton, N.J., 1952.
Hill, Christopher, *Economic Problems of the Church*, Oxford, 1956.
——, *Intellectual Origins of the English Revolution*, Oxford, 1965.
——, *Puritanism and Revolution*, London, 1958.
——, *Society and Puritanism in Pre-Revolutionary England*, London, 1964.
Holdsworth, William, *A History of English Law*, vols. i, iv, vi, London, 1922.
Humberstone, T. L., *University Representation*, London, 1951.
Ives, E. W., 'The Common Lawyers in Pre-Reformation England', *Transactions of the Royal Historical Society*, 5th ser., 18 (1968), 145–73.
Jones, W. J., *The Elizabethan Court of Chancery*, Oxford, 1967.
Judson, M. A., *The Crisis of the Constitution*, New Brunswick, N.J., 1949.
Keeler, M. F., *The Long Parliament, 1640–1641: A Biographical Study of its Members*, Philadelphia, Pa., 1954.
Lawson, F. H., *The Oxford Law School 1850–1965*, Oxford, 1968.
LeNeve, John, *Fasti Ecclesiae Anglicanae*, London, 1716.

Levy, Leonard, *Origins of the Fifth Amendment*, New York, 1958.

Lewis, E., 'King Above Law? "Quod Principi Placuit" in Bracton', *Speculum*, 39 (Apr. 1964), 240–69.

Lloyd, David, *Memoires of the Lives, Actions, Sufferings, Deaths, etc. of those . . . Excellent Personages that Suffered . . . for the Protestant Religion and . . . Allegiance to their Sovereign*, London, 1668.

Lucas, Paul, 'Blackstone and the Reform of the Legal Profession', *EHR* 77 (July 1962), 456–89.

Maitland, F. W., *English Law and the Renaissance* (The Rede Lecture for 1901), Cambridge, 1901.

——, *Roman Canon Law in the Church of England*, London, 1898.

Malden, H. E., *Trinity Hall*, London, 1902.

Marchant, R. A., *The Church Under The Law: Justice, Administration and Discipline in the Diocese of York 1560–1640*, Cambridge, 1969.

——, *The Puritans and the Church Courts in the Diocese of York 1560–1642*, London, 1960.

Martines, L., *Lawyers and Statecraft in Renaissance Florence*, Princeton, N.J., 1968.

Moir, T. L., *The Addled Parliament of 1614*, Oxford, 1958.

Molen, Gezinga van der, *Alberico Gentili and the Development of International Law*, Amsterdam, 1938.

Morant, P., *The History and Antiquities of the County of Essex*, 2 vols., London, 1768.

Mostyn, D. L., and Glenn, T. A., *History of the Family of Mostyn*, London, 1925.

Mullinger, J. B., *The University of Cambridge From the Royal Injunctions of 1535 to the Accession of Charles I*, Cambridge, 1884.

Neale, J. E., *Elizabeth I and Her Parliaments, 1584–1601*, London, 1958.

Newcourt, Richard, *Repertorium Ecclesiasticum Parochiale Londinense*, 2 vols., London, 1708–10.

Nys, Ernest, *Le Droit romain, le droit des gens, et le college des docteurs en droit civil*, Brussels, 1910.

Ogilvie, C., *The King's Government and the Common Law 1471–1641*, Oxford, 1958.

Padelford, F. M., 'Robert Aylett', *The Huntington Library Bulletin*, 10 (Oct. 1936), 1–48.

Peile, John, *Biographical Register of Christ's College 1505–1905*, 2 vols., Cambridge, 1910–13.

Pocock, J. G. A., *The Ancient Constitution and the Feudal Law*, Cambridge, 1957.

Rabb, T., *Enterprise and Empire*, Cambridge, Mass., 1967.

Relf, F. H., *The Petition of Right*, Minneapolis, Minn., 1917.

Rex, M. B., *University Representation in England, 1604–1690*, New York, 1954.

Ritchie, C., *The Ecclesiastical Courts of York*, Arbroath, 1956.

Schulz, Fritz, 'Bracton on Kingship', *EHR* 60 (1945), 136–76.

Senior, W., 'The Advocates of the Court of Arches', *Law Quarterly Review*, 39 (Oct. 1923), 493–506.

——, *Doctors' Commons and the Old Court of Admiralty*, London, 1922.

——, 'Early Writers on Maritime Law', *Law Quarterly Review*, 37 (July 1921), 323–36.

Simon, Sir Jocelyn, 'Dr. Cowell', *Cambridge Law Journal*, 26 (Nov. 1968), 262–70.

Simpson, A., *The Wealth of the Gentry, 1540–1640*, Chicago, Ill., 1961.

Smith, G. C. Moore, *The Family of Withypoll*, Walthamstow Antiquarian Society Pub., lxxxiv, 1936.

Smith, Lacy Baldwin, *Tudor Prelates and Politics 1536–1558*, Princeton, N.J., 1953.

Squibb, G. D., *The High Court of Chivalry*, Oxford, 1959.

Sterry, W., *The Eton College Register*, Eton, 1943.

Stone, Lawrence, 'The Educational Revolution in England, 1540–1640', *Past and Present*, 28 (July 1964), 41–80.

Strachey, G. Lytton, *Elizabeth and Essex: A Tragic History*, New York, 1928.

Strype, John, *Annals of the Reformation and Establishment of Religion*, Oxford, 1824.

——, *The Life and Acts of John Whitgift, D.D.*, 3 vols., Oxford, 1822.

Tierney, B., 'Bracton on Government', *Speculum*, 38 (Apr. 1963), 295–317.

Trevor-Roper, H. R., *Archbishop Laud, 1573–1645*, 2nd edn., London, 1962.

——, *The Gentry 1540–1640*, London, 1953.

Twisden, John R., *The Family of Twysden and Twisden*, London, 1939.

Upton, Anthony, *Sir Arthur Ingram c. 1565–1642: A Study of the Origins of An English Landed Family*, London, 1961.

Usher, R. G., *The Reconstruction of the English Church*, 2 vols., New York, 1910.

——, *The Rise and Fall of the High Commission*, Oxford, 1913.

Vaisey, H. B., *The Canon Law of the Church of England*, London, 1947.

Veall, Donald, *The Popular Movement for Law Reform*, Oxford, 1970.

Venn, John and J. A., *Alumni Cantabrigiensis*, Cambridge, 1922.

Walker, T. A., *A Biographical Register of Peterhouse Men*, Cambridge, 1927.

Ward, John, *The Lives of the Gresham Professors*, London, 1740.

Williams, W. R. J., *The Parliamentary History of the Principality of Wales*, Brecknock, 1895.

Willson, D. Harris, *King James VI and I*, New York, 1956.

——, *The Privy Councillors in the House of Commons, 1604–1629*, Minneapolis, Minn., 1940.

Wood, Anthony, *Athenae Oxoniensis*, 4 vols., 2nd edn., London, 1813–20.

——, *Fasti Oxoniensis*, 2 vols., 2nd edn., London, 1813–20.

——, *The History and Antiquities of the University of Oxford*, 2 vols., ed. J. Gutch, Oxford, 1792–6.

Wormuth, Francis, *The Royal Prerogative, 1603–1649*, Ithaca, N.Y., 1939.

B. UNPUBLISHED THESES

Anglin, J. P., 'The Court of the Archdeacon of Essex 1571–1609: an institutional and social study', University of California, Los Angeles, Ph.D., 1965.

Cassidy, I., 'The Episcopate of William Cotton, Bishop of Exeter 1598–1621', Oxford, B.Litt., 1963.

Duncan, G. I. O., 'The High Court of Delegates', Cambridge, Ph.D., 1964.

Etherington, J. R., 'The Life of Archbishop Juxon, 1582–1663', Oxford, B.Litt, 1940.

Hill, Lamar, 'The Public Career of Sir Julius Caesar, 1584–1614', London, Ph.D., 1968.

Newton, J. A., 'Puritanism in the Diocese of York (excluding Nottinghamshire) 1603–1640', London, Ph.D., 1955.

Prest, W. R., 'Some Aspects of the Inns of Court, 1590–1640', Oxford, D.Phil., 1965.

Quintrell, B. W., 'The Government of the County of Essex 1603–1642', London, Ph.D., 1965.

Slatter, M. D., 'A Biographical Study of Sir John Lambe c. 1566–1646', Oxford, B.Litt., 1952.

Smith, A. H., 'The Elizabethan Gentry of Norfolk: Office Holding and Faction', London, Ph.D., 1959.

Tyler, P., 'The Ecclesiastical Commission for the Province of York 1561–1641', Oxford, D.Phil., 1967.

INDEX

With the exception of individual civil lawyers, names and places which appear only in the Biographical Dictionary are not included